D0119165

DISCOVERING FRENCH

BLEU

Jean-Paul Valette
Rebecca M. Valette

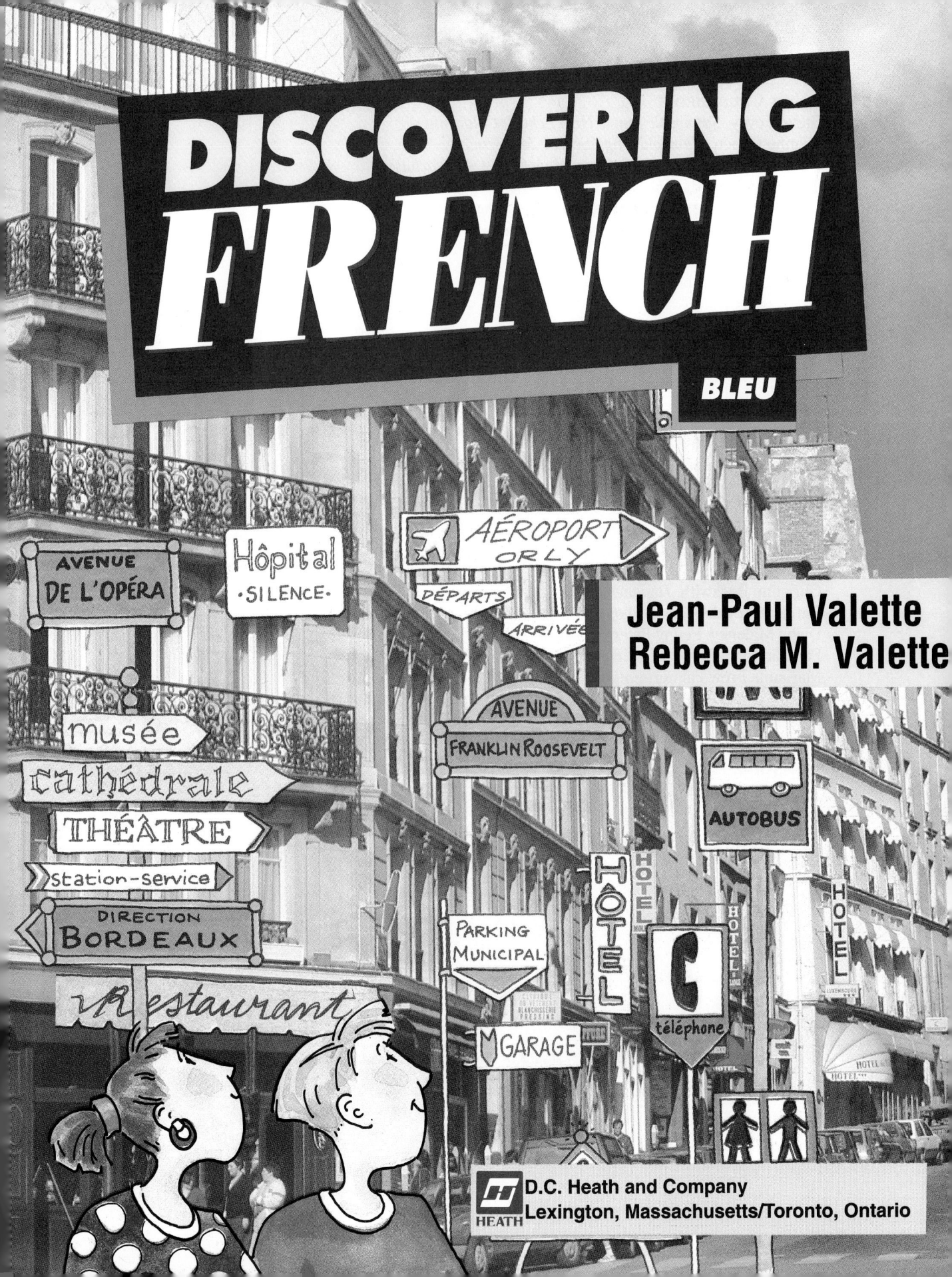

D.C. Heath and Company
Lexington, Massachusetts/Toronto, Ontario

Teacher Consultants
Steve Covey, *Sunnyvale Junior High School, California*
Dianne Hopen, *Humboldt High School, Minnesota*
Patricia McCann, *Lincoln-Sudbury High School, Massachusetts*
T. Jeffrey Richards, *Theodore Roosevelt High School, South Dakota*
Frank Strell, *La Salle-Peru Township High School, Illinois*
Susan Wildman, *Western Albemarle High School, Virginia*

Director, Modern Languages
Roger D. Coulombe

Managing Editor
Gail G. Smith

Project Editors
Valentia B. Dermer
Gloria A. Ryan

National Modern Language Coordinator
Teresa Carrera-Hanley

D.C. Heath Consultant
Karen Ralston

Design and Production
Victor Curran, *Design Section Manager*
Christine Beckwith, *Designer*
Caroline Bowden, Irene Elios, Tama Hochbaum,
Diana Maloney, Penny Peters, *Design Staff*
Pamela Wing, *Production Coordinator*
Marianna Frew Palmer, *Editorial Services*
Design Five, *Design Concept and Cover Design*
Linda Finigan, *Photo Research*
Studio Goodwin-Sturges, *Art Coordination*

Illustrations
Yves Calarnou
Jean-Pierre Foissy
Elizabeth Schlossberg

Copyright © 1993 by D. C. Heath and Company

All rights reserved. No part of this publication may be reproduced or transmitted in any form by any means, electronic or mechanical, including photocopy, recording, or any information storage or retrieval system, without permission in writing from the publisher.

Published simultaneously in Canada

Printed in the United States of America

International Standard Book Number: 0-669-23919-4

1 2 3 4 5 6 7 8 9 0

Lycée Jean-Baptiste Corot

MERCI

Special thanks to the students and staff of
•Collège Eugène Delacroix, *Paris*
•Lycée Jean-Baptiste Corot, *Savigny-sur-Orge*
for their cooperation and assistance.

Collège Eugène Delacroix

Contents

CULTURAL PHOTO ESSAY: Parlons français! 1

NIVEAU A Faisons connaissance! 10

UNITÉ 1 Bonjour! 12

Introduction culturelle: Salutations
Thème: Getting acquainted

LEÇON 1 La rentrée 14

Notes culturelles: 1. La rentrée
2. Les prénoms français
Petit commentaire: Astérix
Pour communiquer: Bonjour! Je m'appelle ..., Comment t'appelles-tu?
L'alphabet
Les signes orthographiques
Les nombres de 0 à 10

LEÇON 2 Tu es français? 18

Note culturelle: Fort-de-France et la Martinique
Pour communiquer: Tu es de ...? Je suis de ...; Les nationalités
Petit commentaire: Statue of Liberty et la Tour Eiffel
Français, française
Les nombres de 10 à 20
Prononciation: Les lettres muettes

LEÇON 3 Salut! Ça va? 22

Note culturelle: Bonjour ou Salut?
Pour communiquer: Bonjour! Comment vas-tu?
Les nombres de 20 à 60
Prononciation: Les consonnes finales

LEÇON 4 LE FRANÇAIS PRATIQUE L'heure 26

Pour communiquer A: Les heures
Pour communiquer B: Les quarts d'heure, les minutes

À VOTRE TOUR: Communication et révision 30

ENTRACTE 1 Lecture et culture 32

UNITÉ 2

Les copains et la famille

34

Introduction culturelle: L'amitié
Thème: Talking about people

LEÇON 5 **Copain ou copine?** **36**

Note culturelle: Amis et copains
Pour communiquer: Qui est-ce; les personnes
Petit commentaire: Cycling
Un garçon, une fille
Les nombres de 60 à 79
Prononciation: La liaison

LEÇON 6 **Une coïncidence** **40**

Note culturelle: Montréal et la province de Québec
Pour communiquer: Tu connais ...? Comment s'appelle ...?
Petit commentaire: The French and the U.S.
Le garçon, la fille
Les nombres de 80 à 100
Prononciation: La voyelle nasale/ɛ̃/

LEÇON 7 **Les photos d'Isabelle** **44**

Note culturelle: La famille française
Pour communiquer: La famille
Petit commentaire: Pets
Mon cousin, ma cousine
Pour communiquer: Quel âge as-tu?
Prononciation: Les voyelles nasales/ɑ̃/et/ɔ̃/

LEÇON 8 LE FRANÇAIS PRATIQUE **Le jour et la date** **48**

Pour communiquer A: Jours de la semaine
Pour communiquer B: Mois de l'année
La date

À VOTRE TOUR: Communication et révision **52**

ENTRACTE 2 **Lecture et culture** **54**

UNITÉ

3 Bon appétit 56

Introduction culturelle: Bon appétit!
Thème: Having a snack in France

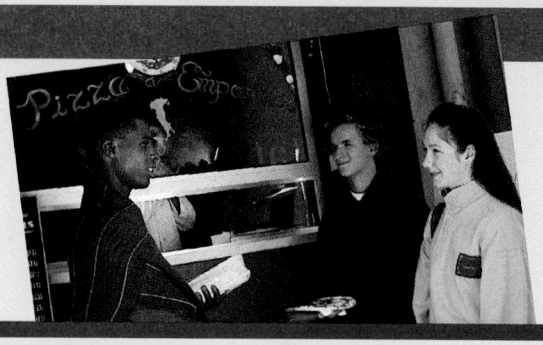

LEÇON 9 **Tu as faim?** **58**

Note culturelle: Les jeunes et la nourriture
Pour communiquer: Tu as faim? Tu veux ...?; les nourritures
Petit commentaire: Sandwiches
Un sandwich, une pizza
Prononciation: L'intonation

LEÇON 10 **Au café** **62**

Note culturelle: Le café
Pour communiquer: Tu as soif? S'il vous plaît ...; les boissons
Petit commentaire: Favorite beverages
Prononciation: L'accent final

LEÇON 11 **Ça fait combien?** **66**

Pour communiquer: C'est combien? Il/elle coûte ...; Prête-moi . . .
Note culturelle: L'argent français
Petit commentaire: Restaurants
Prononciation: La consonne «r»

LEÇON 12 LE FRANÇAIS PRATIQUE **Le temps** **70**

Pour communiquer: Le temps; les saisons

À VOTRE TOUR: Communication et révision **72**

ENTRACTE 3 **Lecture et culture** **74**

CULTURAL PHOTO ESSAY: À l'école en France 76

NIVEAU B La vie de tous les jours 84

UNITÉ 4 Qu'est-ce qu'on fait? 86

Thème: Daily activities

LEÇON 13 LE FRANÇAIS PRATIQUE Mes activités 88

Accent sur... Les activités de la semaine
A. Préférences B. Souhaits
C. Invitations

À VOTRE TOUR: Communication/révision

LEÇON 14 Qui est là? 96

Note culturelle: Le mercredi après-midi
A. Le verbe **être** et les pronoms sujets
Vocabulaire: **Où?** B. Les questions à réponse affirmative ou négative
Expressions pour la conversation: How to answer a yes/no question
C. La négation Vocabulaire: Mots utiles (**à, de,** etc.)
Prononciation: La voyelle /**a**/

À VOTRE TOUR: Communication/révision

LEÇON 15 Une boum 96

Note culturelle: Une boum
A. Les verbes en **-er**: le singulier
Vocabulaire: Les verbes en **-er**
B. Les verbes en **-er**: le pluriel
C. Le présent des verbes en **-er**: affirmative, négative Vocabulaire: Mots utiles (**bien, mal,** etc.)
Expressions pour la conversation: How to express approval or regret
D. La construction: verbe + infinitif
Prononciation: Les voyelles /**i**/ et /**u**/

À VOTRE TOUR: Communication/révision

LEÇON 16 Une interview 118

Note culturelles 1: Le Sénégal
2: l'Unesco
A. Les questions d'information
Vocabulaire: Expressions interrogatives Expressions pour la conversation: How to express surprise or mild doubt B. Les expressions interrogatives avec **qui**
C. **Qu'est-ce que** D. Le verbe **faire** Vocabulaire: Expressions avec **faire** E. L'interrogation avec inversion
Prononciation: La voyelle /**y**/

À VOTRE TOUR: Communication/révision

ENTRACTE 4 Lecture et culture 128

UNITÉ 5

Le monde personnel et familier

134

Thème: People and possessions

LEÇON 17 LE FRANÇAIS PRATIQUE **Les personnes et les objets** **136**

Accent sur... les Français
A. La description des personnes
B. Les objets C. Les possessions personnelles D. Ma chambre

À VOTRE TOUR: Communication/révision

LEÇON 18 **Vive la différence!** **148**

Note culturelle: Montpellier et Strasbourg
A. Le verbe **avoir** B. Les noms et les articles: masculin et féminin
C. Les noms et les articles: le pluriel D. L'article indéfini dans les phrases négatives Expressions pour la conversation: How to contradict a negative statement or question
E. L'usage de l'article défini dans le sens général F. L'usage de l'article défini avec les jours de la semaine
Prononciation: Les articles **«le»** et **«les»**

À VOTRE TOUR: Communication/révision

LEÇON 19 **Le copain de Mireille** **160**

Note culturelle: L'amitié
A. Les adjectifs: masculin et féminin Vocabulaire: La description B. Les adjectifs: le pluriel Vocabulaire: Les adjectifs de nationalité Expression pour la conversation: To introduce a conclusion C. La place des adjectifs
Prononciation: Les consonnes finales

À VOTRE TOUR: Communication/révision

LEÇON 20 **La voiture de Roger** **170**

Note culturelle: Les Français et l'auto
A. Les couleurs Vocabulaire: Les couleurs B. La place des adjectifs avant le nom Vocabulaire: Les adjectifs qui précèdent le nom
Expression pour la conversation: How to get someone's attention C. **Il est** ou **c'est?** D. Les expressions impersonnelles avec **c'est**
Vocabulaire: Opinions
Prononciation: Les lettres **«ch»**

À VOTRE TOUR: Communication/révision

ENTRACTE 5 **Lecture et culture** **180**

UNITÉ

6 En ville 186

Thème: Visiting a French city

LEÇON 21 LE FRANÇAIS PRATIQUE **La ville et la maison** **188**

Accent sur ... Les villes françaises
A. Où habites-tu? B. Ma ville
C. Pour demander un renseignement
D. Ma maison

À VOTRE TOUR: Communication/révision

LEÇON 22 **Weekend à Paris** **198**

Note culturelle: À Paris
A. Le verbe **aller** B. La préposition **à**; **à** + l'article défini Vocabulaire: En ville C. La préposition **chez**
D. La construction: **aller** + l'infinitif
Prononciation: Les semi-voyelles /**w**/ et /**j**/

À VOTRE TOUR: Communication/révision

LEÇON 23 **Au café de l'Univers** **210**

Note culturelle: Au café
A. Le verbe **venir** B. La preposition **de**; **de** + l'article défini Vocabulaire: Les sports, les jeux et la musique
C. Les pronoms accentués
Expression pour la conversation: How to contradict someone Expression pour la conversation: How to express surprise D. La construction: nom + **de** + nom
Prononciation: Les voyelles /**ø**/ et /**œ**/

À VOTRE TOUR: Communication/révision

LEÇON 24 **Mes voisins** **220**

Notes culturelles: 1. Versailles 2: La vie en appartement
A. La possession avec **de**
Vocabulaire: La famille
B. Les adjectifs possessifs: **mon, ton, son** Expression pour la conversation: How to question a statement or express a doubt C. Les adjectifs possessifs: **notre, votre, leur** D. Les nombres ordinaux
Prononciation: Les voyelles /**o**/ et /**ɔ**/

À VOTRE TOUR: Communication/révision

ENTRACTE 6 **Lecture et culture** **230**

CULTURAL PHOTO ESSAY: À Paris 236

UNITÉ 7

Le shopping 244

Thème: Buying clothes

LEÇON 25 LE FRANÇAIS PRATIQUE **L'achat des vêtements** **246**

Accent sur... L'élégance française
A. Les vêtements B. D'autres vêtements et accessoires C. Dans un magasin Vocabulaire: Les nombres de 100 à 1000

À VOTRE TOUR: Communication/révision

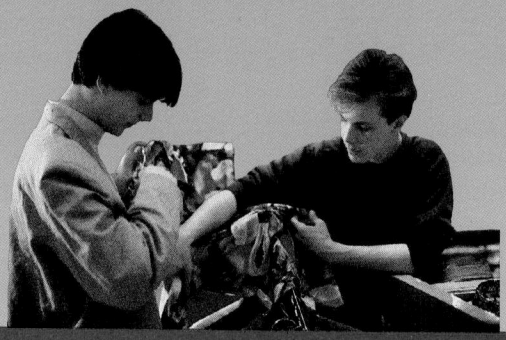

LEÇON 26 **Rien n'est parfait!** **256**

Note culturelle: Le grand magasin
A. Les verbes **acheter** et **préférer**
Vocabulaire: Verbes comme **acheter** et **préférer** B. L'adjectif démonstratif **ce** Expression pour la conversation: How to emphasize a question or remark C. L'adjectif interrogatif **quel** D. Le verbe **mettre**
Prononciation: Les lettres «**e**» et «**è**»

À VOTRE TOUR: Communication/révision

LEÇON 27 **Un choix difficile** **266**

Note culturelle: Le choix de vêtements
A. Les verbes réguliers en **-ir**
Vocabulaire: Verbes réguliers en **-ir**
B. Les adjectifs **beau, nouveau** et **vieux** C. La comparaison avec les adjectifs Expression pour la conversation: How to introduce a personal opinion Prononciation: Les lettres «**ill**»

À VOTRE TOUR: Communication/révision

LEÇON 28 **Alice a un job** **274**

Note culturelle: L'argent des jeunes
Vocabulaire: **L'argent**
A. Le pronom **on** Expression pour la conversation: to indicate approval
B. Les verbes réguliers en **-re**
Vocabulaire: Verbes réguliers en **-re**
C. L'impératif Prononciation: Les lettres «**an**» et «**en**»

À VOTRE TOUR: Communication/révision

ENTRACTE 7 **Lecture et culture** **286**

NIVEAU C

Le monde des jeunes 292

UNITÉ 8

Le temps libre 294

Thème: Leisure time activities

LEÇON 29 — LE FRANÇAIS PRATIQUE — Le weekend et les vacances 296

Accent sur ... Les loisirs
A. Le weekend B. Les vacances
Note culturelle: Le calendrier des fêtes françaises

À VOTRE TOUR: Communication/révision

LEÇON 30 — Vive le weekend! 306

Note culturelle: Le weekend
A. Les expressions avec **avoir**
Vocabulaire: Expressions avec **avoir**
B. Le passé composé des verbes en **-er** Expressions pour la conversation: How to indicate the order in which actions take place
C. Le passé composé: forme négative D. Les questions au passé composé Prononciation: Les lettres **«ain»** et **«in»**

À VOTRE TOUR: Communication/révision

LEÇON 31 — L'alibi 318

Note culturelle: Les jeunes Français et la télé
A. Le verbe **voir** B. Le passé composé des verbes réguliers en **-ir** et **-re** C. Le passé composé des verbes **être, avoir, faire, mettre** et **voir** Vocabulaire: **Quand?**
Prononciation: les lettres **«gn»**

À VOTRE TOUR: Communication/révision

LEÇON 32 — Qui a de la chance? 328

Note culturelle: Les jeunes Français et la musique
A. Le passé composé avec **être**
Vocabulaire: Quelques verbes conjugués avec **être**
B. La construction négative **ne...jamais** C. Les expressions **quelqu'un, quelque chose** et leurs contraires
Prononciation: les lettres **«qu»**

À VOTRE TOUR: Communication/révision

ENTRACTE 8 Lecture et culture 338

UNITÉ

9 Les repas

344

Thème: Foods and meals

LEÇON 33 LE FRANÇAIS PRATIQUE **Les repas et la nourriture** **346**

Accent sur ... Les repas français
A. Les repas et la table
B. La nourriture et les boissons
C. Les fruits et les légumes
Note culturelle: Le marché

À VOTRE TOUR: Communication/révision

LEÇON 34 **À la cantine** **358**

Note culturelle: À la cantine
A. Le verbe **vouloir** B. Le verbe **prendre** Vocabulaire: Verbes comme **prendre** C. L'article partitif: **du, de la** D. L'article partitif dans les phrases négatives E. Le verbe **boire**
Prononciation: les lettres **«ou»** et **«u»**

À VOTRE TOUR: Communication/révision

LEÇON 35 **Un client difficile** **370**

Note culturelle: Les restaurants français et la cuisine française
A. Les pronoms compléments **me, te, nous, vous** Vocabulaire: Services personnels B. Les pronoms compléments à l'impératif
C. Les verbes **pouvoir** et **devoir**
Prononciation: les lettres **«s»** et **«ss»**

À VOTRE TOUR: Communication/révision

LEÇON 36 **Pique-nique** **380**

Note culturelle: Un pique-nique français
A. Le verbe **connaître**
B. Les pronoms compléments **le, la, les** C. La place des pronoms à l'impératif D. Les pronoms compléments **lui, leur** Vocabulaire: Verbes suivis d'un complément indirect E. Les verbes **dire** et **écrire** Prononciation: Les lettres **«on»**

À VOTRE TOUR: Communication/révision

ENTRACTE 9 **Lecture et culture** **392**

Reference Section **R1**

Appendix 1 Maps **R2**
Appendix 2 Sound/Spelling Correspondences **R5**
Appendix 3 Numbers **R7**
Appendix 4 Verbs **R8**
French-English/English-French Vocabulary **R13**
Index **R49**
Photo Credits **R51**

DISCOVERING
FRENCH
BLEU

Parlons français!

Chers amis,

Welcome to DISCOVERING FRENCH and congratulations on your choice of French as a foreign language!

There are many reasons why people decide to learn French. Some people choose French because they plan to visit Canada or Europe or French-speaking Africa. Others want to learn to read articles or books written in French. Still others study French because in their work, they will come into contact with French speakers or because their own family is of French or French-American heritage. And there are many people who learn French for pleasure: They want to enjoy French films and French music, and they like French poetry and French art.

There is another reason for studying French that you have perhaps not thought about. As you learn another language, you develop a better understanding of your own language and how it works. You also develop a better appreciation of your own country and culture as you expand your world view and discover the various French-speaking areas of the globe. You will discover cultural similarities and differences, and you will realize how much French civilization has contributed to our life in the United States.

And, of course, everyone will agree that studying a foreign language also helps us get to know and communicate with people from other cultures. By speaking French, you will be in touch with the many millions of people who use that language in their daily lives. These French speakers ***(les francophones)*** *represent a wide variety of ethnic and cultural backgrounds. As you will see, they live not only in France and other parts of Europe but also in Africa, in North and South America, in Asia . . . in fact, on all continents!*

On the pages of this book and in the accompanying video, you will meet many young people who speak French. Listen carefully to what they say and how they express themselves. They will help you understand not only their language but also the way they live.

Bonne chance!

Jean-Paul Valette Rebecca M. Valette

Bienvenue!

Je m'appelle Jean-Paul.

Je m'appelle Nathalie.

Je m'appelle François.

Bonjour!

Je m'appelle David.

Je m'appelle Marc.

Salut!

Je m'appelle Dominique.

Bonjour, les francophones!

The people portrayed on these pages represent many different backgrounds. Some live in France, some in the United States. They are from Europe, Africa, Asia, and North America. They do, however, have one thing in common. They all speak French. Let's meet them.

1
Sophie Lafont, 14, is from Toulouse, a city in southern France. She is a student at the Lycée Saint-Exupéry. (A **lycée** is the equivalent of an American high school.)

2
Philippe Martin, 15, lives in Paris and goes to the Collège Eugène Delacroix.

3
Stéphanie Malle, 14, also lives in Paris and attends the Collège Eugène Delacroix. Her family is from Martinique, a French island in the Caribbean.

4
Ahmed Belkacem, 14, lives in Lyon, France, and goes to the Lycée Jean Moulin. His parents are from Algeria and speak French and Arabic. Ahmed, who was born in France, speaks only French.

5
Fredy Vansattel, 20, lives near Lausanne, a city in French-speaking Switzerland. He is a student at the well-known École Hôtelière. In addition to French, Fredy also speaks English and German.

6
Prak Maph, 15, left Cambodia with his family when he was four. He lives in Paris and goes to the Lycée Claude Monet. Maph speaks French as well as Khmer, the national language of Cambodia.

7

Amélan Konan, 13, lives in Abidjan, the capital of the Ivory Coast, a country of West Africa. Amélan goes to the Collège Moderne Voltaire, where many of the teachers are from France. Amélan is fluent in both French and Baoulé, the tribal language that she speaks with her relatives.

8

Pauline Lévêque, 14, is from Quebec City in the province of Quebec, in Canada. Pauline goes to the École Louis-Jolliet. She speaks both French and English, but she prefers to speak French with her friends and family.

9

Moustapha Badid is a French athlete of North African origin who lives in Paris. At age 23, he won the wheelchair title at the Boston Marathon and established a world record in the event. In that same year, he also won an Olympic gold medal. He speaks French, Arabic, and some English.

10

Dr. Michèle Klopner, a clinical psychologist, grew up in Haiti, where her family resides. She came to the United States to study at the University of Michigan and Rutgers University. Dr. Klopner speaks French, Haitian Creole, and English. She uses all these languages in her work at the Cambridge Hospital in Cambridge, Massachusetts.

11

Marie-Christine Mouis was born in Canada of a French father and a Canadian mother. At the age of 16, Marie-Christine joined the Paris Opera Ballet, becoming the youngest dancer in the world's oldest ballet company. She was the principal ballerina of the Boston Ballet for ten years.

12

Dr. Larry Phan was born in Vietnam. At the age of ten, he went to France, where he received his high school education. In 1976, he came to the United States to pursue a medical career. He attended the University of California and Tufts School of Dental Medicine. Dr. Phan is on the staff of the Children's Hospital in Boston.

ACTIVITÉS CULTURELLES

1. On a world map or globe, locate the cities and countries of origin for each of the people pictured.
2. Do you know any people in your community who have French names or people who speak French? Where are their families originally from?

Bonjour, le monde français!

In today's world, French is an international language spoken daily by more than 100 million people. French is understood by another 100 million in many countries and regions of the globe.

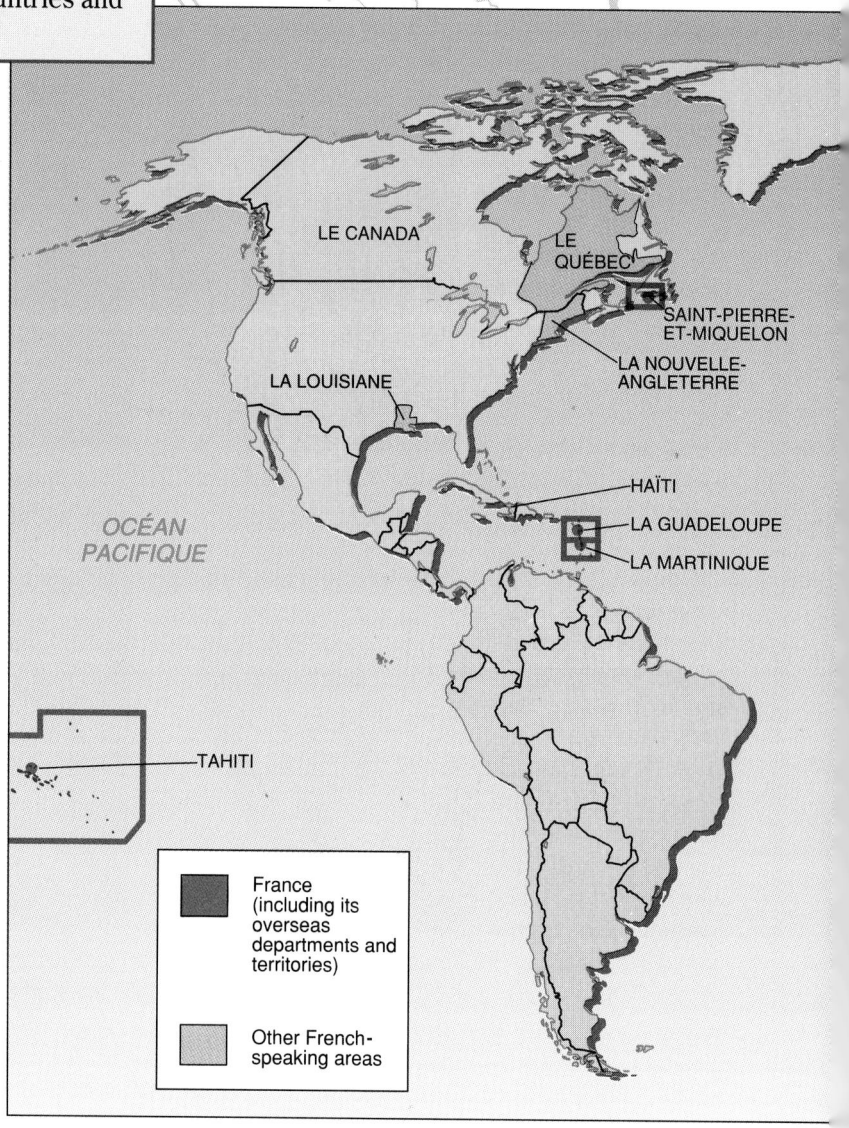

IN NORTH AMERICA

■ In Canada, about one third of the population speaks French. These French speakers live mainly in the province of Quebec **(le Québec)**. They are descendants of French settlers who came to Canada in the 17th and 18th centuries.

■ In the United States, French is understood and spoken in many families whose French and French-Canadian ancestors came to Louisiana **(la Louisiane)** and New England **(la Nouvelle-Angleterre)** at various times in our history.

■ In the Caribbean, French and Creole are spoken in the Republic of Haiti **(Haïti)**. French is also spoken on the islands of Martinique **(la Martinique)** and Guadeloupe **(la Guadeloupe)**; the inhabitants of these two islands are French citizens.

IN OTHER PARTS OF THE WORLD

■ French is spoken as far away as Tahiti **(Tahiti)** and New Caledonia **(la Nouvelle-Calédonie)**, two French territories in the South Pacific.

■ In the Middle East, French is still taught and spoken in Lebanon **(le Liban)**.

■ French is also used and understood by many Vietnamese and Cambodian families who have left their countries **(le Viêt-nam, le Cambodge)** to settle in other parts of the world.

IN EUROPE

French is not only spoken in France **(la France)** but also in parts of Belgium **(la Belgique)**, Switzerland **(la Suisse)**, and Luxembourg **(le Luxembourg)**.

IN AFRICA

French is an important language in countries which have strong commercial and cultural ties to France.

■ In Western and Central Africa, about 20 countries have adopted French as their official language. These countries include Senegal **(le Sénégal)**, the Ivory Coast **(la Côte d'Ivoire)**, and Zaire **(le Zaïre)**. French is also spoken on the large island of Madagascar **(Madagascar)**.

■ In North Africa, French is understood and spoken by many people of Algeria **(l'Algérie)**, Morocco **(le Maroc)**, and Tunisia **(la Tunisie)**. More than two million people from these countries have emigrated to France and have become French citizens.

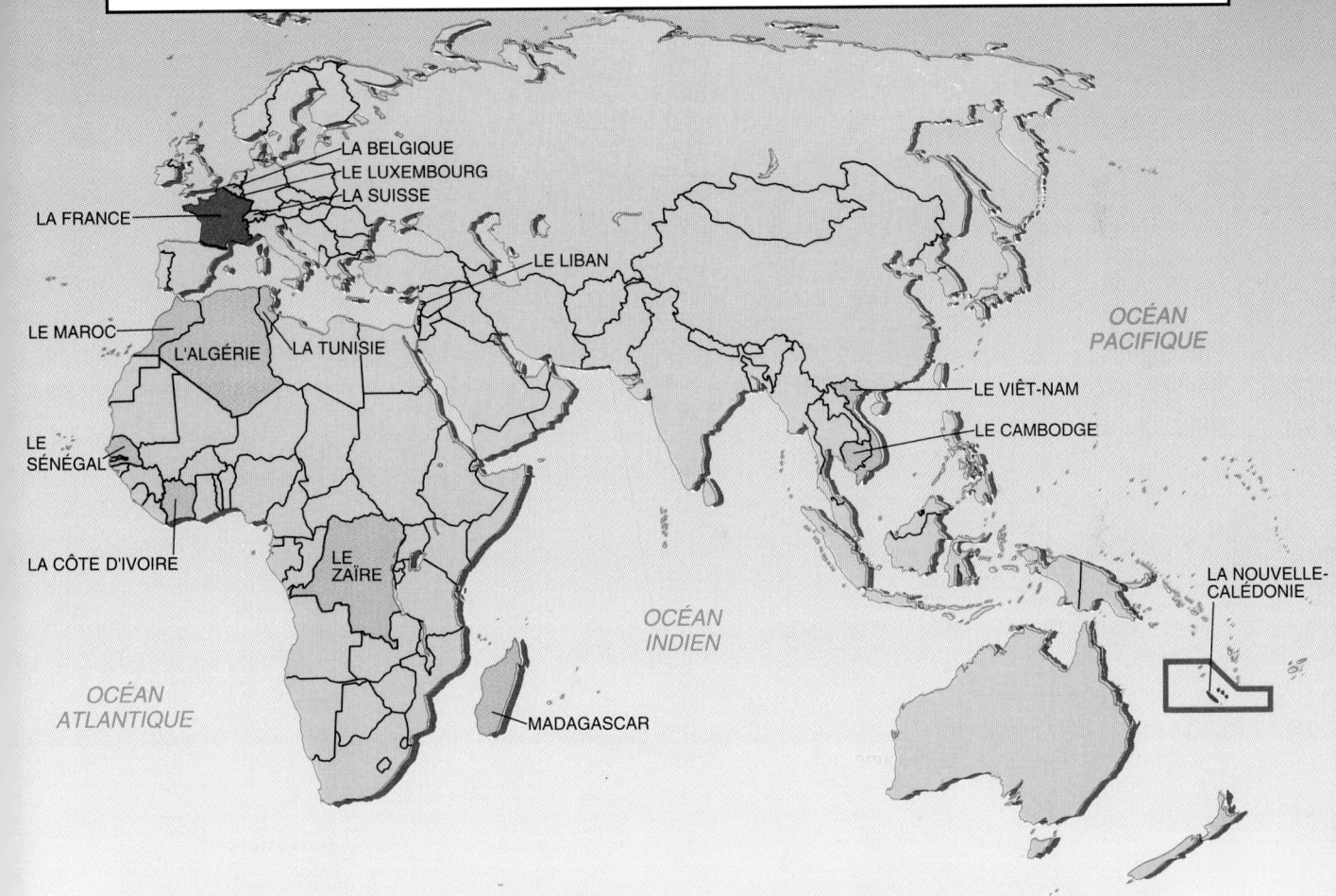

ACTIVITÉS CULTURELLES

1. Name at least six African countries where French is spoken. Find out the capital of each country. (Source: atlas, encyclopedia)
2. Collect clippings from newspapers and magazines in which a French-speaking country is mentioned. Try to find one clipping for each of the areas on the map.

NOTE: You may also wish to refer to the reference map of the French-speaking world on pages R2–R3.

Bonjour, la France!

Château d'Azay-le-Rideau, Touraine

Les Pyrénées

Eguisheim, Alsace

Les Alpes, Chamonix

Menton, Côte d'Azur

Before starting your study of French, you may be interested in learning a few facts about France.

- In area, France is the largest country in Western Europe.
- Economically, France is one of the most developed countries of the world with a sophisticated high-tech industry.
- France is the only European country with a space exploration program. French communication satellites provide 400 million Europeans with direct TV transmission.
- France is a country with a strong cultural tradition. French philosophers, writers, and artists have influenced our ways of thinking and looking at the world.
- France has a long history reaching back through Roman times into distant prehistory.
- Geographically, France is a very diversified country with the highest mountains in Europe **(les Alpes et les Pyrénées)** and an extensive coastline along the Atlantic **(l'océan Atlantique)** and the Mediterranean **(la Méditerranée)**.
- France consists of many different regions which have maintained their traditions, their culture, and—in some cases—their own language. Some of the traditional provinces are Normandy and Brittany **(la Normandie et la Bretagne)** in the west, Alsace **(l'Alsace)** in the east, Touraine **(la Touraine)** in the center, and Provence **(la Provence)** in the south.

ACTIVITÉS CULTURELLES

1. Find the countries which have a common border with France. What are their capitals? (Source: atlas, encyclopedia)
2. Imagine that you are spending a year in France. Where would you go if you wanted to ski in the winter? Which provinces would you want to visit in the summer if you wanted to swim in the Atlantic? in the Mediterranean? Are there any particular parts of France you would like to explore?

NOTE: You may also wish to refer to the reference map of France on page R4.

Bonjour! Je m'appelle ...

Here is a list of some traditional French names. As you begin your study of the French language, you may want to "adopt" a French name from the list.

Alain
Albert
André
Antoine
Bernard
Bertrand
Charles
Christophe
Daniel
David
Denis
Dominique
Édouard
Éric
Étienne
François
Frédéric
Geoffroy
Georges
Grégoire
Guillaume
Henri
Jacques
Jean
Jean-Claude
Jean-François
Jean-Louis
Jean-Paul
Jérôme
Joseph
Julien
Laurent
Marc
Mathieu
Michel
Nicolas
Olivier
Patrick
Paul
Philippe
Pierre
Raoul
Raymond
Richard
Robert
Roger
Samuel
Simon
Thomas

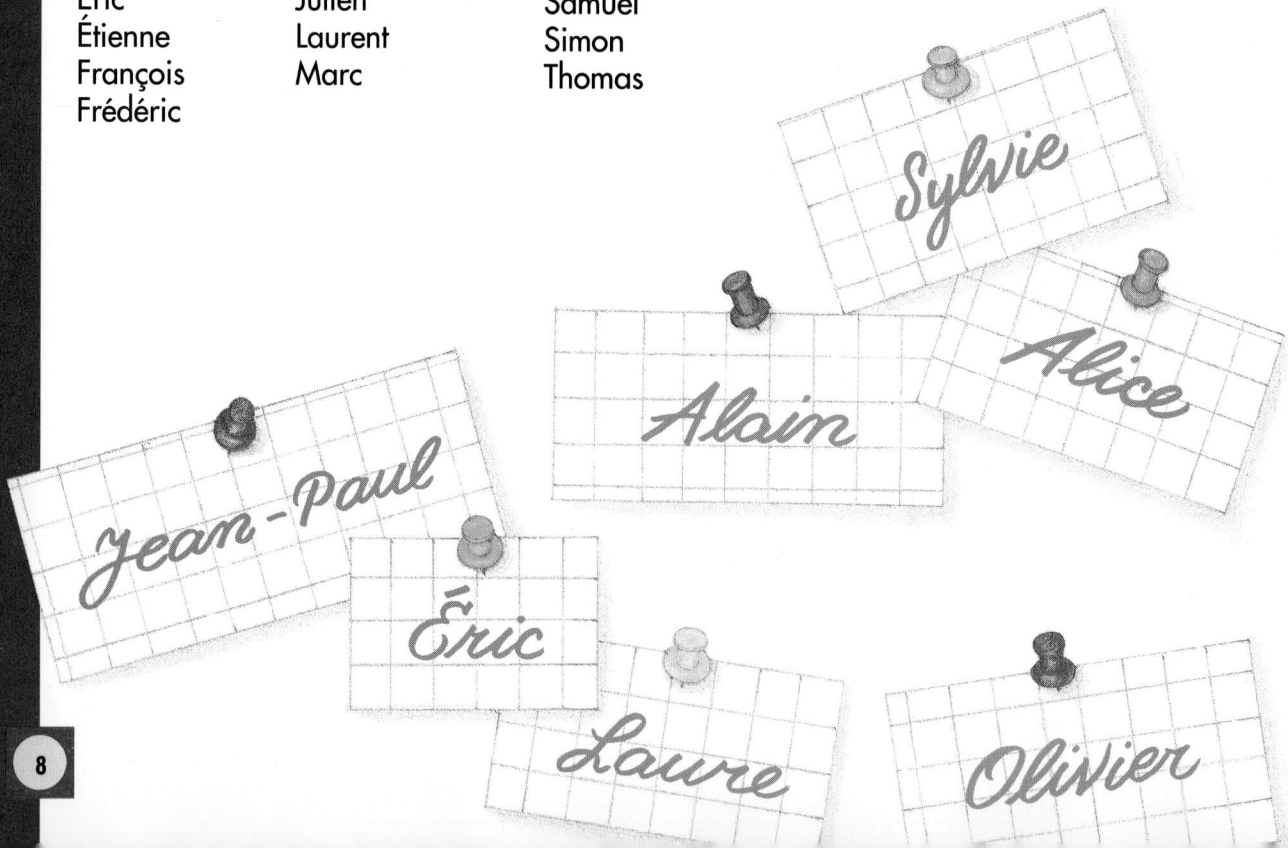

Alice
Andrée
Anne
Anne-Marie
Barbara
Béatrice
Brigitte
Caroline
Catherine
Cécile
Charlotte
Christine
Claire
Corinne
Delphine
Denise
Diane
Dominique
Éléonore
Élisabeth
Émilie
Florence
Françoise
Hélène
Isabelle
Jeanne
Judith
Juliette
Karine
Laure
Lise
Louise
Lucie
Marguerite
Marie
Marie-Christine
Marthe
Michèle
Monique
Nathalie
Nicole
Patricia
Pauline
Rachel
Renée
Rose
Sophie
Stéphanie
Suzanne
Sylvie
Thérèse
Véronique
Virginie

Jean?
Henri?
Jacques?
Sébastien?
Jean-Paul?
Lucien?
Guillaume?
Philippe?
Charles?
Gérard?
Pierre?
Jean-Pierre?
André?
Georges?
François?
Michel?
Paul?
Marc?
Luc?

NIVEAU A

Faisons

Bonjour et bienvenue!

Hello and welcome, as you begin your study of French. The title of the first part of your French program is **Faisons connaissance!** *Let's get acquainted!*

What are some of the kinds of things you would like to learn to say in French? Well, when you meet new French friends, you will want to tell them about yourself: your name, your hometown, your family, your friends. And you will want to find out some of the same information about them.

So, as you begin your study of French, here are some of the things that you will be learning:

- how to greet people
- how to introduce yourself and say where you are from
- how to talk about yourself, your family, and your friends
- how to give your age and ask your friends how old they are

You will also learn expressions that will be useful when you travel to a French-speaking country, for example:

- how to count to 100
- how to ask about the weather
- how to tell time
- how to give the date
- how to order something to eat or drink in a café, and how to ask for the check

And now . . . **En avant!** *Let's begin!*

Jean-Paul Valette Rebecca M. Valette

connaissance!
Salut, les amis!
Bonjour, ça va?
Salut!

UNITÉ

1 Bonjour!

INTRODUCTION *culturelle*

Salutations *(Greetings)*

How do you greet people in the United States? You may nod or smile. With adults, you may shake hands when you are introduced for the first time.

In France, people shake hands with friends and acquaintances each time they see one another, and not only to say hello but also when they say good-bye. Among teenagers, boys shake hands with boys. Girls kiss each other on the cheeks two or three times. (This is called **une bise**). Boys and girls who are close friends also greet each other with **une bise.**

LEÇON 1 La rentrée

LEÇON 2 Tu es français?

LEÇON 3 Salut! Ça va?

LEÇON 4 Le français pratique: L'heure

THÈME ET OBJECTIFS

Getting acquainted

In this unit, you will be meeting French people.

You will learn . . .

- to say hello and good-bye
- to introduce yourself and say where you are from

You will also learn . . .

- to count to 60
- to tell time

LEÇON 1

La rentrée

This is the first day of school. Students are greeting their friends and meeting new classmates.

«
—Bonjour! Je m'appelle Philippe.
—Et moi, je m'appelle Stéphanie.
»

«
—Je m'appelle Marc. Et toi?
—Moi, je m'appelle Isabelle.
»

«
—Comment t'appelles-tu?
—Je m'appelle Nathalie.
—Bonjour.
—Bonjour.
»

POUR *COMMUNIQUER*

How to say hello:

Bonjour!	*Hello!*	—**Bonjour,** Nathalie! —**Bonjour,** Jean-Paul!

How to ask a classmate's name:

Comment t'appelles-tu?	*What's your name?*	—**Comment t'appelles-tu?**
Je m'appelle . . .	*My name is . . .*	—**Je m'appelle** Stéphanie.

OTHER EXPRESSIONS

moi	*me*	**Moi,** je m'appelle Marc.
et toi?	*and you?*	**Et toi,** comment t'appelles-tu?

NOTES CULTURELLES

1 La rentrée *(Back to school)*

French and American students have about the same number of days of summer vacation. In France, summer vacation usually begins at the end of June and classes resume in early September. The first day back to school in fall is called **la rentrée.**

2 Les prénoms français *(French first names)*

Many traditional French names have corresponding equivalents in English.

For boys:	For girls:
Jean *(John)*	**Marie** *(Mary)*
Pierre *(Peter)*	**Monique** *(Monica)*
Marc *(Mark)*	**Cécile** *(Cecilia)*
Philippe *(Philip)*	**Alice**
Nicolas *(Nicholas)*	**Caroline**

Often the names **Jean** and **Marie** are combined in double names such as **Jean-Paul** and **Marie-Christine.** In recent years, names of foreign origin, like **Dimitri** and **Karine,** have become quite popular.

Petit commentaire

Astérix le Gaulois *is one of the best-loved cartoon characters in France. Small in size but extremely clever and courageous, he represents the "little man" defending his country Gaul (the ancient name of France) against the invading Roman legions led by Julius Caesar.*

1 Bonjour!

Say hello to the student nearest to you.

▶ **Bonjour!**

2 Je m'appelle . . .

Introduce yourself to your classmates.

▶ **Je m'appelle (Paul).**

▶ **Je m'appelle (Denise).**

3 Et toi?

Ask a classmate his or her name.

▶ **—Comment t'appelles-tu?**
—Je m'appelle (Christine).

4 Bonjour, les amis! *(Hello everyone!)*

Say hello to the following students.

▶ **Bonjour, Marc!**

▶

Marc

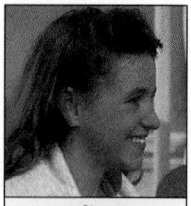
Juliette

Jean-Paul

Isabelle

Philippe

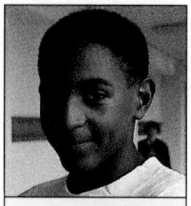
François

Stéphanie

Nathalie

L'alphabet

A	B	C	D	E	F	G	H	I	J	K	L
a	bé	cé	dé	e	effe	gé	hache	i	ji	ka	elle

Les signes orthographiques *(Spelling marks)*

French uses accents and spelling marks that do not exist in English. These marks are part of the spelling and cannot be left out.

In French, there are four accents that may appear on vowels.

´	**l'accent aigu** *(acute accent)*	C**é**cile, St**é**phanie
`	**l'accent grave** *(grave accent)*	Mich**è**le, Hél**è**ne
^	**l'accent circonflexe** *(circumflex)*	Jér**ô**me
¨	**le tréma** *(diaeresis)*	No**ë**l, Jo**ë**lle

There is only one spelling mark used with a consonant. It occurs under the letter "**c**".

¸	**la cédille** *(cedilla)*	Fran**ç**ois

5 La rentrée

It is the first day of class. The following students are introducing themselves. Act out the dialogues with your classmates.

▶ Hélène et Philippe

1. Stéphanie et Marc
2. Cécile et Frédéric
3. Michèle et François
4. Béatrice et Joël
5. Céline et Jérôme

Les nombres de 0 à 10

0 zéro	**1** un	**2** deux	**3** trois
4 quatre	**5** cinq	**6** six	**7** sept
8 huit	**9** neuf	**10** dix	

6 Numéros de téléphone

Imagine you are visiting a family in Quebec. Give them your American phone number in French.

▶ 617-963-4028 **six, un, sept — neuf, six, trois — quatre, zéro, deux, huit**

M	N	O	P	Q	R	S	T	U	V	W	X	Y	Z
emme	enne	o	pé	ku	erre	esse	té	u	vé	double vé	ixe	i grec	zède

LEÇON 2

Tu es français?

It is the opening day of school and several of the students meet in the cafeteria (**la cantine**) at lunchtime. Marc discovers that not everyone is French.

MARC: Tu es français?
JEAN-PAUL: Oui, je suis français.

MARC: Et toi, Patrick, tu es français aussi?
PATRICK: Non! Je suis américain. Je suis de Boston.

MARC: Et toi, Stéphanie, tu es française ou américaine?
STÉPHANIE: Je suis française.
MARC: Tu es de Paris?
STÉPHANIE: Non, je suis de Fort-de-France.
MARC: Tu as de la chance!

MARC: Are you French?
JEAN-PAUL: Yes, I'm French.

MARC: And you, Patrick, are you French too?
PATRICK: No! I'm American. I'm from Boston.

MARC: And you, Stéphanie, are you French or American?
STÉPHANIE: I'm French.
MARC: Are you from Paris?
STÉPHANIE: No, I'm from Fort-de-France.
MARC: You're lucky!

POUR COMMUNIQUER

How to talk about where people are from:

Tu es de . . . ?	*Are you from . . . ?*	—**Tu es de** Denver?
Je suis de . . .	*I'm from . . .*	—Non, **je suis de** Dallas.

How to talk about one's nationality:

Tu es . . . ?	*Are you . . . ?*	—Pierre, **tu es** français?
Je suis . . .	*I am . . .*	—Oui, **je suis** français.

Les nationalités

	français	**française**
	anglais	**anglaise**
	américain	**américaine**
	canadien	**canadienne**

OTHER EXPRESSIONS

oui	*yes*	Tu es français? **Oui,** je suis français.
non	*no*	Tu es canadien? **Non,** je suis américain.
et	*and*	Je suis de Paris. **Et** toi?
ou	*or*	Tu es français **ou** canadien?
aussi	*also, too*	Moi **aussi,** je suis française.

NOTE CULTURELLE

Fort-de-France et la Martinique

Fort-de-France is the capital of Martinique, a small French island in the Caribbean. Because Martinique is part of the French national territory, its inhabitants are French citizens. Most of them are of African origin. They speak French as well as a dialect called **créole.**

Martinique is also known as the Island of the Flowers **(l'Île aux Fleurs)** because of its warm tropical climate and magnificent vegetation. In the winter months, it attracts thousands of European and American tourists.

Petit commentaire

*The Statue of Liberty (**la statue de la Liberté**) was a gift to the United States from the French people on the occasion of the 100th anniversary of the American Revolution. The Eiffel Tower (**la tour Eiffel**) was built to celebrate the 100th anniversary of the French Revolution.*

français, française

Names of nationalities may have two different forms, depending on whom they refer to:

	MASCULINE	FEMININE
Je suis ... **Tu es ...?**	français américain	française américaine

➡ Note that in written French the feminine forms always end in **-e.**

1 Et toi?

Give your name, your nationality, and your city of origin.

Bonjour!
Je m'appelle Bob Jones.
Je suis américain.
Je suis de Providence.

Bonjour!
Je m'appelle Linda Carlson.
Je suis américaine.
Je suis de Boston.

2 Français ou française?

You meet the following young people. Ask them if they are French. A classmate will answer you, as in the model. (Be sure to use **français** with boys and **française** with girls.)

▶ **— Sophie, tu es française?**
— Oui, je suis française. Je suis de Strasbourg.

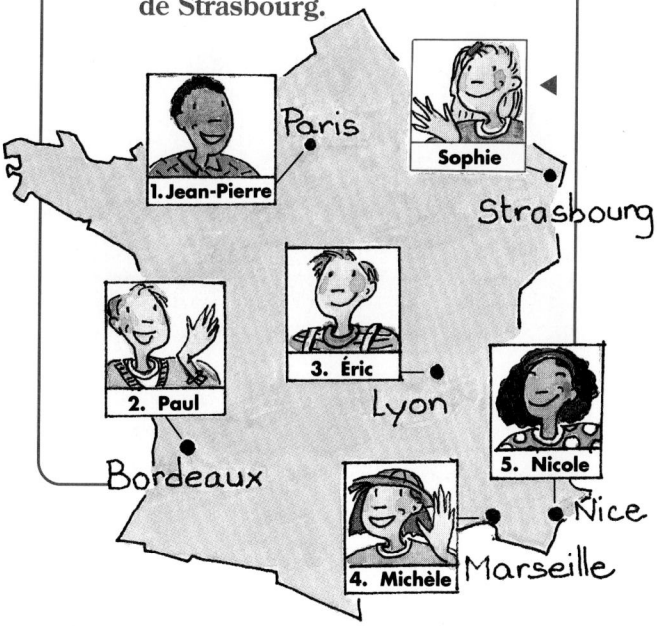

3 Quelle nationalité? *(Which nationality?)*

Greet the following young people and find out each one's nationality. A classmate will answer you, according to the model.

▶ —Bonjour, Marc. Tu es canadien?
—Oui, je suis canadien. Je suis de Montréal.

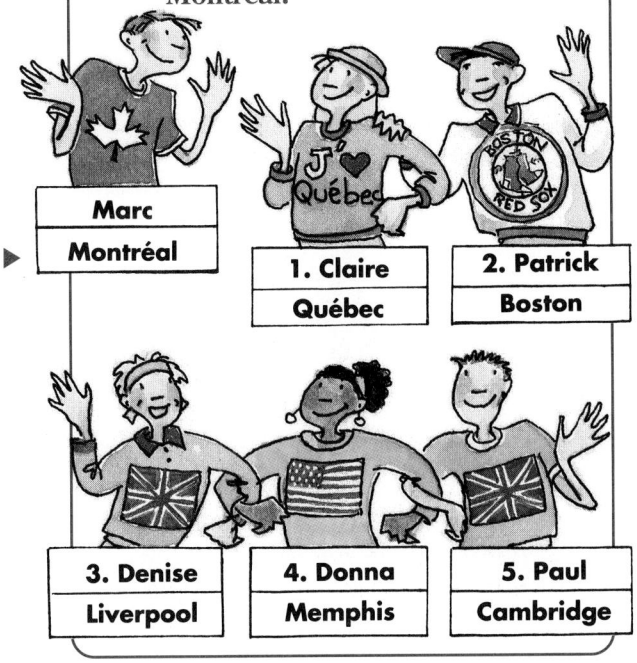

Les nombres de 10 à 20

10 dix	**11** onze	**12** douze
13 treize	**14** quatorze	**15** quinze
16 seize	**17** dix-sept	**18** dix-huit
19 dix-neuf	**20** vingt	

4 La fusée Ariane

(The Ariane rocket)

Give the countdown for the lift-off of the French rocket Ariane, from 20 to 0.

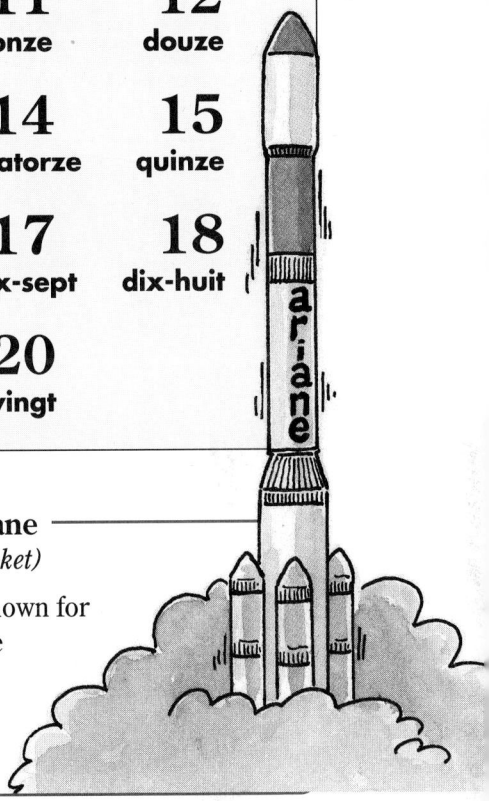

Prononciation

Les lettres muettes *(Silent letters)*

In French, the last letter of a word is often not pronounced.

Paris

- Final "**e**" is always silent.
  Répétez: **Sophie Philippe Stéphanie anglaise française onze douze treize quatorze quinze seize**
- Final "**s**" is almost always silent.
  Répétez: **Paris Nicolas Jacques anglais français trois**
- The letter "**h**" is always silent.
  Répétez: **Hélène Henri Thomas Nathalie Catherine**

LEÇON 3

Salut! Ça va?

On the way to school, François meets his friends.

François also meets his teachers.

Monsieur Masson

Madame Chollet

Mademoiselle Lacour

After class, François says good-bye to his teacher and his friends.

POUR COMMUNIQUER

How to greet a friend or classmate:

Salut! *Hi!*

How to greet a teacher or another adult:

Bonjour! *Hello!* **Bonjour, monsieur.**
Bonjour, madame.
Bonjour, mademoiselle.

How to say good-bye:

Au revoir! *Good-bye!* **Au revoir, Philippe.**
Au revoir, monsieur.

➡ In written French, the following abbreviations are commonly used:

M. Masson	Monsieur Masson
Mme Chollet	Madame Chollet
Mlle Lacour	Mademoiselle Lacour

➡ Young people often use **Salut!** to say good-bye to each other.

NOTE CULTURELLE

Bonjour ou Salut?

French young people may greet one another with **Bonjour,** but they often prefer the less formal **Salut.** When they meet their teachers, however, they always use **Bonjour.** French young people are generally much more formal with adults than with their friends. This is especially true in their relationships with teachers, whom they treat with great respect.

Have you noticed that in France adults are addressed as **monsieur, madame,** or **mademoiselle?** The last name is almost never used in greeting people.

1 Bonjour ou salut?

You are enrolled in a French school. Greet your friends and teachers.

▶ Salut, Sophie!

▶ Bonjour, mademoiselle!

Sophie

Mademoiselle Pinot

1. Anne

2. Monsieur Masson

3. Nathalie

4. Marc

5. Madame Albert

6. Mademoiselle Boucher

POUR *COMMUNIQUER*

How to ask people how they feel:

—Ça va? *How are you? How are things going? How's everything?*
—Ça va! *(I'm) fine. (I'm) okay. Everything's all right.*

Ça va . . . **très bien**

bien

comme ci, comme ça

mal

très mal

How to express one's feelings of frustration and appreciation:

Zut! *Darn!* **Zut!** Ça va mal! **Merci!** *Thanks!* Ça va, **merci.**

➡ **Ça va?** *(How are you?)* is an informal greeting that corresponds to the following expressions:

Comment vas-tu? (when addressing a friend)
Bonjour, Paul. Comment vas-tu?
Comment allez-vous? (when addressing an adult)
Bonjour, madame. Comment allez-vous?

2 Dialogue

Exchange greetings with your classmates and ask how they are doing.

▶ —Salut, (Thomas)! Ça va?
—Ça va! Et toi?
—Ça va bien. Merci.

3 Situations

Sometimes we feel good and sometimes we don't. How would you respond in the following situations?

▶ You have the flu.
—**Ça va?**
—**Ça va mal!**

1. You just received an "A" in French.
2. You lost your wallet.
3. Your uncle gave you five dollars.
4. Your grandparents sent you a check for 100 dollars.
5. You bent the front wheel of your bicycle.
6. Your parents bought you a new bicycle.
7. Your little brother broke your walkman.
8. It's your birthday.
9. You have a headache.
10. You just had an argument with your best friend.
11. Your favorite baseball team has just lost a game.
12. Your French teacher has just canceled a quiz.

Les nombres de 20 à 60

20 vingt	**30 trente**	**40 quarante**
vingt et un	**trente et un**	**quarante et un**
vingt-deux	**trente-deux**	**quarante-deux**
vingt-trois	**trente-trois**	**quarante-trois**
. . .	. . .	. . .
vingt-neuf	**trente-neuf**	**quarante-neuf**

50 cinquante	**60 soixante**
cinquante et un	
cinquante-deux	
cinquante-trois	
. . .	
cinquante-neuf	

➡ Note the use of **et** in numbers with **un:** **vingt et un.**

5 Loto

Read out loud the numbers on the French Loto tickets.

4 Ça va?

How would the following people answer the question **Ça va?**

Prononciation

Les consonnes finales
(Final consonants)

1 2 3
un deux trois

In French, the last consonant of a word is often not pronounced.

- Remember: Final "**s**" is usually silent.
  Répétez: **trois français anglais**
- Most other final consonants are usually silent.
  Répétez: **Richard Albert Robert salut américain canadien bien deux**

EXCEPTION: The following final consonants are usually pronounced: "**c,**" "**f,**" "**l,**" and sometimes "**r.**"
Répétez: **Éric Daniel Lebeuf Pascal Victor**

However, the ending **-er** is usually pronounced /e/.
Répétez: **Roger Olivier**

▶ ▶

LE FRANÇAIS PRATIQUE

LEÇON 4

L'heure

A. Un rendez-vous

Jean-Paul and Stéphanie are sitting in a café. Stéphanie seems to be in a hurry to leave.

STÉPHANIE: Quelle heure est-il?
JEAN-PAUL: Il est trois heures.
STÉPHANIE: Trois heures?
JEAN-PAUL: Oui, trois heures.
STÉPHANIE: Oh là là. J'ai un rendez-vous avec David dans vingt minutes. Au revoir, Jean-Paul.
JEAN-PAUL: Au revoir, Stéphanie. À bientôt!

STÉPHANIE: What time is it?
JEAN-PAUL: It's three o'clock.
STÉPHANIE: Three o'clock?
JEAN-PAUL: Yes, three o'clock.
STÉPHANIE: Uh, oh! I have a date with David in twenty minutes. Good-bye, Jean-Paul.
JEAN-PAUL: Good-bye, Stéphanie. See you soon!

POUR COMMUNIQUER

How to talk about the time:

Quelle heure est-il? *What time is it?*
Il est . . . *It's . . .*

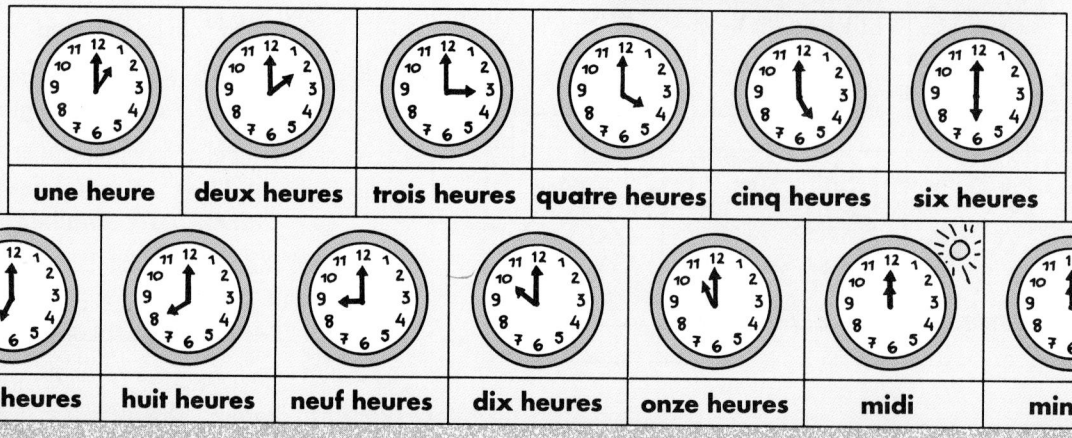

1 Quelle heure est-il?

Ask your classmates what time it is.

2 L'heure d'été *(Daylight saving time)*

Philippe forgot to set his watch ahead for daylight saving time, so he is an hour off. Isabelle gives him the correct time.

▶ PHILIPPE: **Il est sept heures.**
ISABELLE: **Mais non, il est huit heures!**

➡ Although <u>o'clock</u> may be left out in English, the expression **heure(s)** must be used in French when giving the time.

It's ten. (It's ten o'clock.) **Il est dix heures.**

➡ To distinguish between A.M. and P.M., the French use the following expressions:

du matin	*in the morning*	Il est dix heures **du matin.**
de l'après-midi	*in the afternoon*	Il est deux heures **de l'après-midi.**
du soir	*in the evening*	Il est huit heures **du soir.**

NOTE DE PRONONCIATION: In telling time, the NUMBER and the word **heure(s)** are linked together. Remember, in French the letter "**h**" is always silent.

une heure · **deux heures** (z) · **trois heures** (z) · **quatre heures** · **cinq heures** (k) · **six heures** (z)

sept heures (t) · **huit heures** (t) · **neuf heures** (v) · **dix heures** (z) · **onze heures**

B. À quelle heure est le film?

Stéphanie and David have decided to go to a movie.

STÉPHANIE: Quelle heure est-il?
DAVID: Il est trois heures et demie.
STÉPHANIE: Et à quelle heure est le film?
DAVID: À quatre heures et quart.
STÉPHANIE: Ça va. Nous avons le temps.

STÉPHANIE: What time is it?
DAVID: It's three-thirty (half past three).
STÉPHANIE: And at what time is the movie?
DAVID: At four-fifteen (quarter past four).
STÉPHANIE: That's okay. We have time.

POUR *COMMUNIQUER*

How to ask at what time something is scheduled:

À quelle heure est . . .? — *At what time is . . . ?*
—À quelle heure est le concert? — *At what time is the concert?*
—Le concert est à huit heures. — *The concert is at eight.*

How to say that you have an appointment or a date:

J'ai un rendez-vous à . . . — *I have an appointment (a date) at . . .* — **J'ai un rendez-vous à** deux heures.

How to indicate the minutes:

Il est . . .	dix heures dix	six heures vingt-cinq	sept heures trente-cinq	deux heures cinquante-deux

How to indicate the half hour and the quarter hours:

et quart

et demie

moins le quart

Il est une heure **et quart.**

Il est deux heures **et demie.**

Il est trois heures **moins le quart.**

3 L'heure

Give the times according to the clocks.

▶ **Il est une heure et quart.**

4 À quelle heure?

Ask your classmates at what time certain activities are scheduled. They will answer according to the information below.

▶ 8h50 le film

—**À quelle heure est le film?**
—**Le film est à huit heures cinquante.**

1. 7h15 le concert
2. 2h30 le match de football *(soccer)*
3. 3h45 le match de tennis
4. 5h10 le récital
5. 7h45 le dîner

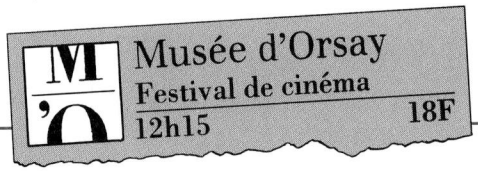

5 Rendez-vous

Isabelle has appointments with various classmates and teachers. Look at her notebook and act out her dialogues with Philippe.

▶ ISABELLE: **J'ai un rendez-vous avec Marc.**
PHILIPPE: **À quelle heure?**
ISABELLE: **À onze heures trente.**

▶

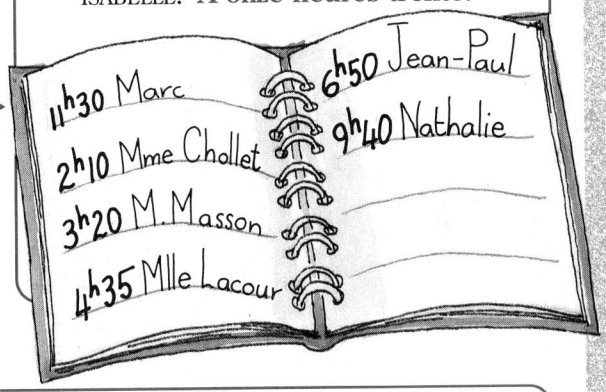

6 À la gare *(At the train station)*

You are at the information desk of a French train station. Travelers ask you the departure times for the following trains. Answer them according to the posted schedule.

▶ le train de Nice

▶

DÉPARTS			
NICE	6 h 10	TOULON	9 h 35
LYON	7 h 15	COLMAR	10 h 40
CANNES	7 h 30	TOULOUSE	10 h 45
TOURS	8 h 12	MARSEILLE	10 h 50
DIJON	8 h 25	BORDEAUX	10 h 55

À votre tour!

1 Nathalie et Marc

It is the first day of school. Nathalie is talking to Marc and you hear parts of their conversation. For each of Nathalie's greetings or questions, select Marc's reply from the suggested responses on the right.

- Bonjour!
- Au revoir!
- Non, je suis canadien.
- Il est deux heures moins le quart.
- Marc Boutin.
- Oui, ça va bien! Merci!

2 Et toi?

You and Nathalie meet at a sidewalk café. Respond to her greetings and questions.

1. Salut! Ça va?
2. Comment t'appelles-tu?
3. Tu es canadien (canadienne)?
4. Quelle heure est-il?
5. Oh là là. J'ai un rendez-vous dans *(in)* dix minutes. Au revoir.

3 Conversation dirigée

Two students, Jean-Pierre and Janet, meet on the Paris-Lyon train. With a partner, compose and act out their dialogue according to the suggested script.

Jean-Pierre			Janet
says hello	→	responds and asks how things are	
says things are fine	→	asks him what his name is	
says his name is Jean-Pierre . . . asks her name	→	says her name is Janet	
asks her if she is English	→	says no and responds that she is American	
asks her if she is from New York	→	replies that she is from San Francisco	

4 Minidialogues

Create original dialogues on the basis of the pictures below.

1. David et Nicole

2. Monsieur Bertin et Mademoiselle Laval

3. Florence et Alain

4. Jean-Pierre et Sylvie

5. Thomas et Nicole

5 En scène

With a classmate, act out the following scene.

CHARACTERS:
You and a French exchange student

SITUATION:
You are at a party and meet a French exchange student who is happy to respond to your greetings and questions.

- Greet the student.
- Ask how things are going.
- Introduce yourself and ask his/her name.
- Ask if he/she is French.
- Ask if he/she is from Paris.
- Say good-bye.

6 Les nombres

1. Select any number between 0 and 15 and give the next five numbers in sequence.
2. Select a number between 1 and 9. Use that number as a starting point and count by tens to 60.

▶ deux
douze, vingt-deux, trente-deux, etc.

Oui, vous parlez *français!*

Yes, you speak French! If you were visiting a French city, you would be able to understand many of the signs around you.

Look at the words on the following signs and compare them to their English equivalents. Which ones are spelled exactly the same? Which ones are spelled a little differently? What are the differences?

La présence FRANÇAISE *en Amérique*

Between 1600 and 1750, the French explored large parts of Canada and the United States, which they called **La Nouvelle France** *(New France)*. Today many American towns have French names, as you will see on the map below.

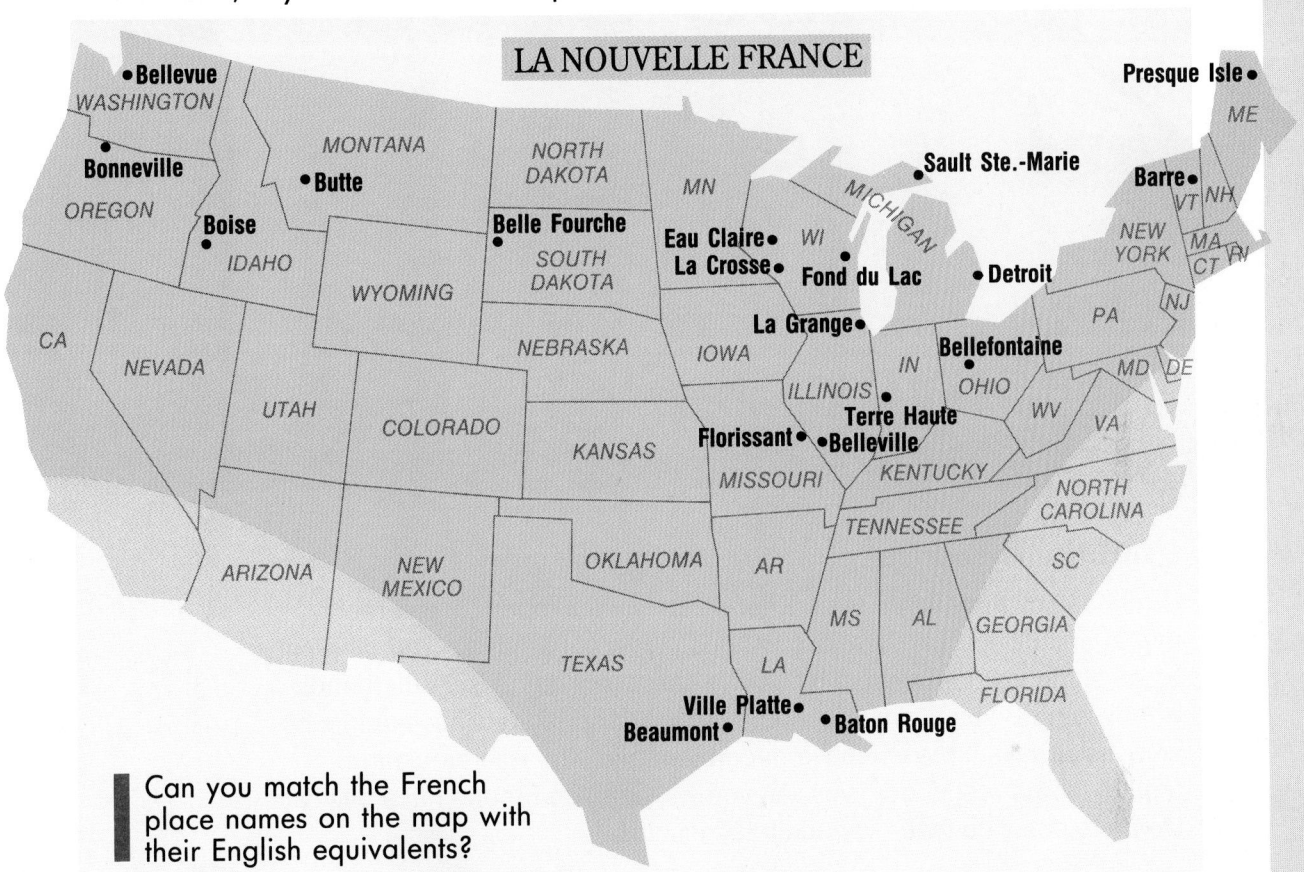

Can you match the French place names on the map with their English equivalents?

Almost an Island
The Barn
Barred
Beautiful City
Beautiful Fork
Beautiful Fountain
Beautiful Mountain
Beautiful View
Bottom of the Lake
Clear Water
Flat City
Flowering (place)
Good City
High Land
Small Hill
Red Pole
Saint Mary's Waterfall and Rapids
Stick
Strait
Wooded (place)

Un jeu *(game)*

Many American cities were also named after:

- French people (such as King Louis XIV and his patron Saint Louis, General La Fayette, Napoleon, and of course, explorers like Champlain, Jolliet, Marquette, La Salle, Duluth, Dubuque)
- French cities (such as Paris, Montpellier, La Rochelle, Orléans)

In teams of three or four, see how many cities with French names you can locate on a map of the United States.

UNITÉ

2 Les copains et la famille

INTRODUCTION *culturelle*

L'amitié *(Friendship)*

Is friendship important to you? Friendship is very important to French teenagers. Of course, there are various levels of friendship and different types of friends: classmates whom we see every day in school, friends with whom we spend time outside of school, and the few special friends who are always there when we need them and who will remain our friends for the rest of our lives. As you will see, the French have different words to describe these various relationships.

LEÇON 5 Copain ou copine?

LEÇON 6 Une coïncidence

LEÇON 7 Les photos d'Isabelle

LEÇON 8 Le français pratique: Le jour et la date

THÈME ET OBJECTIFS

Talking about people

In this unit, you will be talking about people you know. You will learn . . .

- to identify friends, family, and relatives
- to say how old you are and find out someone's age
- to talk about birthdays and holidays

You will also learn . . .

- to count from 60 to 100
- to give the date and the day of the week

LEÇON 5

Copain ou copine?

In French, there are certain girls' and boys' names that sound the same. Occasionally this can be confusing.

Scène 1. Philippe et Jean-Paul

Philippe is at home with his friend Jean-Paul. He seems to be expecting someone. Who could it be . . . ? The doorbell rings.

PHILIPPE: Tiens! Voilà Dominique!
JEAN-PAUL: Dominique? Qui est-ce? Un copain ou une copine?
PHILIPPE: C'est une copine.

Scène 2. Philippe, Jean-Paul, Dominique

PHILIPPE: Salut, Dominique! Ça va?
DOMINIQUE: Oui, ça va! Et toi?
JEAN-PAUL: *(thinking)* C'est vrai! C'est une copine!

Scene 1. *Philippe and Jean-Paul*

PHILIPPE: Hey! There's Dominique!
JEAN-PAUL: Dominique? Who's that? A boy(friend) or a girl(friend)?
PHILIPPE: A girl(friend).

Scene 2. *Philippe, Jean-Paul, Dominique*

PHILIPPE: Hi, Dominique! How's everything?
DOMINIQUE: Fine! And you?
JEAN-PAUL: (thinking) It's true! She is a girlfriend!

POUR *COMMUNIQUER*

How to introduce or point out someone:

Voici . . .	*This is . . . , Here come(s) . . .*	**Voici** Jean-Paul. **Voici** Nathalie et François.
Voilà . . .	*This (That) is . . . , There's . . .*	**Voilà** Isabelle. **Voilà** Philippe et Dominique.

How to find out who someone is:

Qui est-ce?	*Who's that? Who is it?*	—**Qui est-ce?**
C'est . . .	*It's . . . , That's . . . , He's . . . , She's . . .*	—**C'est** Patrick. **C'est** un copain.

How to get someone's attention or to express surprise:

Tiens!	*Look! Hey!*	**Tiens,** voilà Dominique!

Les personnes

un garçon	*boy*
un ami	*friend (male)*
un copain	*friend (male)*

une fille	*girl*
une amie	*friend (female)*
une copine	*friend (female)*

un monsieur	*gentleman*
un prof	*teacher*

une dame	*lady*
une prof	*teacher*

NOTE CULTURELLE

Amis et copains

French young people, like their American counterparts, enjoy spending time with their friends. They refer to their friends as **un ami** (for a boy) and **une amie** (for a girl) or — more commonly — as **un copain** or **une copine.** Note that the words **copain, copine** can also have special meanings. When a boy talks about **une copine,** he is referring to a friend who is a girl. However, when he says **ma** *(my)* **copine,** he may be referring to his girlfriend. Similarly, a girl would call her boyfriend **mon copain.**

Petit commentaire

Cycling is a popular competitive sport throughout France. The most popular races are the ***Tour de France*** *and the* ***Tour de France féminin,*** *which take place every year in July. French women cyclists have won many world titles.*

un garçon, une fille

In French, all NOUNS are either MASCULINE or FEMININE.
Nouns referring to boys or men are almost always MASCULINE.
They are introduced by **un** *(a, an)*.
Nouns referring to girls or women are almost always FEMININE.
They are introduced by **une** *(a, an)*.

MASCULINE

un garçon *a boy*
un ami *a friend (male)*

FEMININE

une fille *a girl*
une amie *a friend (female)*

1 Copain ou copine?

Say that the following people are your friends. Use **un copain** or **une copine,** as appropriate.

▶ **Christine est une copine.**

▶ **Christine**

1. Alice

2. Marie-Jeanne

3. Éric

4. David

5. Sylvie

2 Les amis

The same young people are visiting your school. Point them out to your classmates, using **un ami** or **une amie,** as appropriate.

▶ **—Tiens, voilà Christine!**
—Qui est-ce?
—C'est une amie.

3 Un ou une?

Identify the people below by completing the sentences with **un** or **une.**

1. Voici . . . fille.
2. Voilà . . . garçon.
3. Voici . . . dame.
4. C'est . . . amie.
5. Olivier est . . . ami.
6. Jean-Paul est . . . copain.
7. Cécile est . . . copine.
8. Voici Mlle Lacour. C'est . . . prof.
9. Voici M. Masson. C'est . . . prof.
10. Voici Mme Chollet. C'est . . . prof.

4 À la fenêtre *(At the window)*

You and a friend are walking down the street and you see the following people at their windows. Identify them in short dialogues.

▶ —Tiens, voilà un monsieur!
—Qui est-ce?
—C'est Monsieur Mercier. ▶

Monsieur Mercier

1. Nicole

2. Mademoiselle Lasalle

3. Éric

4. Madame Albert

5. Monsieur Lavie

6. Alain

Les nombres de 60 à 79

60 soixante

61 soixante et un
62 soixante-deux
63 soixante-trois
64 soixante-quatre
65 soixante-cinq
66 soixante-six
67 soixante-sept
68 soixante-huit
69 soixante-neuf

70 soixante-dix

71 soixante et onze
72 soixante-douze
73 soixante-treize
74 soixante-quatorze
75 soixante-quinze
76 soixante-seize
77 soixante-dix-sept
78 soixante-dix-huit
79 soixante-dix-neuf

➡ Note that in counting from 70 to 79, the French continue adding numbers to 60:
70 = 60 + 10 71 = 60 + 11 72 = 60 + 12, etc.

5 Numéros de téléphone

Read aloud the phone numbers of Jean-Paul's friends in Paris.

▶ Philippe **quarante-deux, soixante et un, dix-neuf, soixante-quinze**

Prononciation

La liaison

un ami

Pronounce the following words:

un ami un Américain un Anglais un artiste

In general, the "**n**" of **un** is silent. However, in the above words, the "**n**" of **un** is pronounced as if it were the *first* letter of the next word. The two words are *linked* together in LIAISON.

Liaison occurs between two words when the second one begins with a VOWEL SOUND, that is, with "**a**", "**e**", "**i**", "**o**", "**u**", and sometimes "**h**" and "**y**".

➡ Although liaison is not marked in written French, it will be indicated in your book by the symbol ‿ where appropriate.

Contrastez et répétez:

LIAISON: **un‿ami un‿Américain un‿Italien un‿artiste**

NO LIAISON: **un copain un Français un Canadien un prof**

LEÇON 6

Une coïncidence

Isabelle is at a party with her new Canadian friend Marc. She wants him to meet some of the other guests.

ISABELLE: *Do you know the girl over there?*
MARC: *No. Who is she?*
ISABELLE: *She's a friend. Her name is Juliette Savard.*

MARC: *Is she French?*
ISABELLE: *No, she's Canadian. She is from Montreal.*
MARC: *Me too!*
ISABELLE: *What a coincidence!*

POUR *COMMUNIQUER*

How to inquire about people:

Tu connais . . . ?	*Do you know . . . ?*	**Tu connais** Jean-Paul?

How to describe people and give their nationalities:

Il est . . .	*He is . . .*	**Il est** canadien.
Elle est . . .	*She is . . .*	**Elle est** canadienne.

How to find out another person's name:

Comment s'appelle . . . ?	*What's the name of . . . ?*	**Comment s'appelle** le garçon? **Comment s'appelle** la fille?
Il s'appelle . . .	*His name is . . .*	**Il s'appelle** Marc.
Elle s'appelle . . .	*Her name is . . .*	**Elle s'appelle** Juliette.

NOTE CULTURELLE

Montréal et la province de Québec

In population, metropolitan Montreal is the second-largest city in Canada. After Paris, it is also the second-largest French-speaking city in the world.

Montreal is located in the province of Quebec, where French is the official language. In fact, French speakers represent over 90% of the population. These people are the descendants of French settlers who came to Canada in the 17th and 18th centuries. If you visit Montreal, you will discover that the people of Quebec **(les Québécois)** are very proud of their heritage and dedicated to maintaining French as their language.

Petit commentaire

French teenagers are very much interested in the United States. They love American music and American movies. Every year, more and more French high school students come to visit our country either through exchange programs or summer homestays.

le garçon, la fille

The French equivalent of *the* has two basic forms: **le** and **la.**

MASCULINE		FEMININE	
le garçon	*the boy*	**la** fille	*the girl*
le copain	*the friend*	**la** copine	*the friend*

NOTE: Both **le** and **la** become **l'** before a vowel sound.

un copain → le copain une copine → la copine
un ami → **l'**ami une amie → **l'**amie

1 Qui est-ce?

Ask who the following people are, using **le, la,** or **l'.**

▶ une prof
Qui est la prof?

1. un monsieur
2. une dame
3. une fille
4. un garçon
5. un prof
6. un ami
7. une amie

2 Tu connais . . . ?

Ask your classmates if they know the following people. They will answer that they do.

▶ une dame / Madame Vallée

1. un prof / Monsieur Simon
2. un garçon / Christophe
3. une fille / Sophie
4. une dame / Mademoiselle Lenoir
5. une prof / Madame Boucher
6. un monsieur / Monsieur Duval

3 Comment s'appelle . . . ?

Ask the names of the following people, using the words **le garçon, la fille.** A classmate will respond.

▶ **—Comment s'appelle la fille?**
—Elle s'appelle Stéphanie.

4 Français, anglais ou américain?

Give the nationalities of the following people.

▶ Jane Fonda?
Elle est américaine.

1. le prince Charles?
2. la princesse Diana?
3. Catherine Deneuve?
4. Vanna White?
5. Pierre Cardin?
6. Bill Cosby?
7. Oprah Winfrey?
8. Tom Cruise?
9. Paul McCartney?

Les nombres de 80 à 100

80 quatre-vingts

81 quatre-vingt-un
82 quatre-vingt-deux
83 quatre-vingt-trois
84 quatre-vingt-quatre
85 quatre-vingt-cinq
86 quatre-vingt-six
87 quatre-vingt-sept
88 quatre-vingt-huit
89 quatre-vingt-neuf

90 quatre-vingt-dix

91 quatre-vingt-onze
92 quatre-vingt-douze
93 quatre-vingt-treize
94 quatre-vingt-quatorze
95 quatre-vingt-quinze
96 quatre-vingt-seize
97 quatre-vingt-dix-sept
98 quatre-vingt-dix-huit
99 quatre-vingt-dix-neuf

100 cent

➡ Note that in counting from 80 to 99, the French add numbers to the base of **quatre-vingts** *(fourscore)*:

80 = 4 × 20 90 = 4 × 20 + 10
85 = 4 × 20 + 5 99 = 4 × 20 + 19

5 Au téléphone

In France, the telephone area code (**l'indicatif**) is always a two-digit number. Your teacher will name a city (**une ville**) from the chart. Give the corresponding area code.

▶ Nice?
C'est le quatre-vingt-treize.

VILLE	INDICATIF
Albi	63
Avignon	90
Cannes	93
Dijon	80
Marseille	91
Montpellier	67
Nancy	83
▶ Nice	93
Nîmes	66
Rennes	99
Saint-Tropez	94
Strasbourg	88
Vichy	70

Prononciation /ɛ̃/

La voyelle nasale /ɛ̃/

cinq

In French, there are three nasal vowel sounds:

/ɛ̃/ **cinq** (5) /ɔ̃/ **onze** (11) /ɑ̃/ **trente** (30)

Practice the sound /ɛ̃/ in the following words. Note that this vowel sound can have several different spellings.

➡ Be sure not to pronounce an "**n**" or "**m**" after the nasal vowel.

Répétez: "**in**" **cinq quinze vingt vingt-cinq quatre-vingt-quinze**
"**ain**" **américain Alain copain**
"**(i)en**" **bien canadien tiens!**
"**un**" **un**

Tiens! Voilà Alain. Il est américain. Et Julien? Il est canadien.

LEÇON 7

Les photos d'Isabelle

Isabelle is showing her family photo album to her friend Jean-Paul.

ISABELLE: Voici ma mère.
JEAN-PAUL: Et le monsieur, c'est ton père?
ISABELLE: Non, c'est mon oncle Thomas.
JEAN-PAUL: Et la fille, c'est ta cousine?
ISABELLE: Oui, c'est ma cousine Béatrice. Elle a seize ans.
JEAN-PAUL: Et le garçon, c'est ton cousin?
ISABELLE: Non, c'est un copain.
JEAN-PAUL: Un copain ou ton copain?
ISABELLE: Dis donc, Jean-Paul, tu es vraiment trop curieux!

ma mère

mon oncle Thomas

ma cousine Béatrice

??

ISABELLE: This is my mother.
JEAN-PAUL: And the man, is he your father?
ISABELLE: No, that's my uncle Thomas.
JEAN-PAUL: And the girl, is she your cousin?
ISABELLE: Yes, that's my cousin Béatrice. She's sixteen.
JEAN-PAUL: And the boy, is he your cousin?
ISABELLE: No, that's a friend.
JEAN-PAUL: A friend or a boyfriend?
ISABELLE: Hey there, Jean-Paul, you are really too curious!

POUR COMMUNIQUER

How to introduce your family:

Voici mon père. *This is my father.*
Et voici ma mère. *And this is my mother.*

La famille *(Family)*

un frère	*brother*	**une soeur**	*sister*
un cousin	*cousin*	**une cousine**	*cousin*
un père	*father*	**une mère**	*mother*
un oncle	*uncle*	**une tante**	*aunt*
un grand-père	*grandfather*	**une grand-mère**	*grandmother*

Les animaux domestiques *(Pets)*

un chat

un chien

NOTE CULTURELLE

La famille française

When you and your friends talk about your families, you usually are referring to your brothers, sisters, and parents. In French, however, **la famille** refers not only to parents and children but also to grandparents, aunts, uncles, cousins, as well as a whole array of more distant relatives related by blood and marriage.

Since the various members of a family often live in the same region, French teenagers see their grandparents and cousins fairly frequently. Even when relatives do not live close by, the family finds many occasions to get together: for weekend visits, during school and summer vacations, on holidays, as well as on special occasions such as weddings and anniversaries.

Petit commentaire

The French people love pets, especially cats and dogs. What is important is the animal's personality and friendliness rather than its pedigree. Some common names given to animals are:

Minou, Pompon, Fifi *(cats)*
Titus, Milou, Médor *(dogs)*

mon cousin, ma cousine

The French equivalents of *my* and *your* have the following forms:

MASCULINE		FEMININE	
mon cousin	*my cousin (male)*	**ma** cousine	*my cousin (female)*
mon frère	*by brother*	**ma** soeur	*my sister*
ton cousin	*your cousin (male)*	**ta** cousine	*your cousin (female)*
ton frère	*your brother*	**ta** soeur	*your sister*

➡ Note that the feminine **ma** becomes **mon** and the feminine **ta** becomes **ton** before a vowel sound. Liaison is required.

une amie → **mon** amie **ton** amie

1 L'album de photos

You are showing a friend your photo album. Identify the following people, using **mon** and **ma,** as appropriate.

▶ cousine Jacqueline **Voici ma cousine Jacqueline.**

1. frère
2. soeur
3. tante Monique
4. oncle Pierre
5. père
6. mère
7. copain Nicolas
8. ami Jérôme
9. copine Pauline
10. amie Florence
11. grand-mère Michèle
12. grand-père Robert
13. chien Toto
14. chat Minou
15. cousine Sophie

2 Comment s'appelle . . . ?

Ask your classmates to name some of their friends, relatives, and pets. They can invent names if they wish.

▶ le copain

1. l'oncle
2. la tante
3. le cousin
4. la cousine
5. la copine
6. le grand-père
7. la grand-mère
8. le chien
9. le chat

POUR COMMUNIQUER

How to find out how old a friend is:

Quel âge as-tu?	*How old are you?*	**—Quel âge as-tu?**
J'ai . . . ans.	*I'm . . . (years old).*	**—J'ai treize ans.**

How to ask about how old others are:

—Quel âge a ton père?	*How old is your father?*
—Il a quarante-deux ans.	*He is 42 (years old).*
—Quel âge a ta mère?	*How old is your mother?*
—Elle a trente-neuf ans.	*She is 39 (years old).*

➡ Although *years old* may be left out in English, the word **ans** must be used in French when talking about someone's age.
Il a vingt ans. *He's twenty. (He's twenty years old.)*

3 Quel âge as-tu?

Ask your classmates how old they are.

▶ **—Quel âge as-tu?**
—J'ai (treize) ans.

4 Joyeux anniversaire!

(Happy birthday!)

Ask your classmates how old the following people are.

▶ 

Stéphanie

▶ **—Quel âge a Stéphanie?**
—Elle a quatorze ans.

1. Éric

2. Mademoiselle Doucette

3. Monsieur Boucher

4. Madame Dupont

5. Monsieur Camus

6. Madame Simon

5 Curiosité

Find out the ages of your classmates' friends and relatives. If they are not sure, they can guess or invent an answer.

▶ la copine **—Quel âge a ta copine?**
—Ma copine a (treize) ans.

1. le père	4. la tante	7. le grand-père
2. la mère	5. le cousin	8. la grand-mère
3. l'oncle	6. la cousine	

Prononciation

Les voyelles nasales /ã/ et /õ/

tante **oncle**

The letters "**an**" and "**en**" usually represent the nasal vowel /ã/. Be sure not to pronounce an "**n**" after the nasal vowel.

Répétez: **ans tante grand-père français anglais quarante cinquante trente comment Henri Laurent**

The letters "**on**" represent the nasal vowel /õ/. Be sure not to pronounce an "**n**" after the nasal vowel.

Répétez: **non mon ton bonjour oncle garçon onze**

Contrastez: **an—on tante—ton onze—ans**
Mon oncle François a trente ans.

LE FRANÇAIS PRATIQUE

LEÇON 8

Le jour et la date

A. Quel jour est-ce?

For many people, the days of the week are not all alike.

Dialogue 1. Vendredi

PHILIPPE: Quel jour est-ce?
STÉPHANIE: C'est vendredi.
PHILIPPE: Super! Demain, c'est samedi!

Dialogue 2. Mercredi

NATHALIE: Ça va?
MARC: Pas très bien.
NATHALIE: Pourquoi?
MARC: Aujourd'hui, c'est mercredi.
NATHALIE: Et alors?
MARC: Demain, c'est jeudi! Le jour de l'examen.
NATHALIE: Zut! C'est vrai! Au revoir, Marc.
MARC: Au revoir, Nathalie. À demain!

Dialogue 1. *Friday*

PHILIPPE: What day is it?
STÉPHANIE: It's Friday.
PHILIPPE: Great! Tomorrow is Saturday!

Dialogue 2. *Wednesday*

NATHALIE: How are things?
MARC: Not very good.
NATHALIE: Why?
MARC: Today is Wednesday.
NATHALIE: So?
MARC: Tomorrow is Thursday! The day of the exam.
NATHALIE: Darn! That's right! Good-bye, Marc.
MARC: Good-bye, Nathalie. See you tomorrow!

POUR *COMMUNIQUER*

How to talk about days of the week:

Quel jour est-ce? *What day is it?*
Aujourd'hui, c'est mercredi. *Today is Wednesday.*
Demain, c'est jeudi. *Tomorrow is Thursday.*

How to tell people when you will see them again:

À samedi! *See you Saturday!*
À demain! *See you tomorrow!*

Les jours de la semaine *(Days of the week)*

lundi	*Monday*	**vendredi**	*Friday*	**aujourd'hui**	*today*
mardi	*Tuesday*	**samedi**	*Saturday*	**demain**	*tomorrow*
mercredi	*Wednesday*	**dimanche**	*Sunday*		
jeudi	*Thursday*				

1 Questions

1. Quel jour est-ce aujourd'hui?
2. Et demain, quel jour est-ce?

2 Un jour de retard *(One day behind)*

Georges has trouble keeping track of the date. He is always one day behind. Monique corrects him.

▶ samedi

1. lundi
2. mardi
3. jeudi
4. vendredi
5. dimanche
6. mercredi

3 Au revoir!

You are on the phone with the following friends. Say good-bye and tell them when you will see them.

▶ Christine / lundi
Au revoir, Christine. À lundi.

1. David / dimanche
2. Roger / samedi
3. Delphine / mercredi
4. Sophie / vendredi
5. Alain / mardi
6. Éric / jeudi

B. Anniversaire

François and Isabelle are on their way to Nathalie's birthday party. As they are talking, François wants to know when Isabelle's birthday is.

FRANÇOIS: C'est quand, ton anniversaire?
ISABELLE: C'est le 18 mars!
FRANÇOIS: Le 18 mars? Pas possible!
ISABELLE: Si! Pourquoi?
FRANÇOIS: C'est aussi mon anniversaire.
ISABELLE: Quelle coïncidence!

FRANÇOIS: When is your birthday?
ISABELLE: It's March 18!
FRANÇOIS: March 18? That's not possible!
ISABELLE: Yes, it is! Why?
FRANÇOIS: It's my birthday too.
ISABELLE: What a coincidence!

POUR *COMMUNIQUER*

How to talk about the date:

Quelle est la date?	*What's the date?*
C'est le 12 (douze) octobre.	*It's October 12.*
C'est le premier juin.	*It's June first.*

How to talk about birthdays:

—C'est quand, ton anniversaire?	*When is your birthday?*
—Mon anniversaire est le 2 (deux) mars.	*My birthday is March 2.*

Les mois de l'année *(Months of the year)*

janvier	**avril**	**juillet**	**octobre**
février	**mai**	**août**	**novembre**
mars	**juin**	**septembre**	**décembre**

La date

To express a date in French, the pattern is:

le	+ NUMBER	+ MONTH
le	11 (onze)	novembre
le	20 (vingt)	mai

EXCEPTION: The first of the month is **le premier.**

➡ In front of numbers, the French use **le** (and never **l'**): **le onze, le huit.**

➡ Note that when dates are abbreviated in French, the day always comes first.

2/8 **le deux** août **1**/11 **le premier** novembre

Les Rolling Stones
à Paris
Au Parc des Princes
le 23 juin

4 Anniversaires

Ask your classmates when their birthdays are.

▶ C'est quand, ton anniversaire?

Mon anniversaire est le 3 février.

5 Quelle est la date?

Ask what the date is.

▶ —Quelle est la date?
—C'est le douze septembre.

6 Dates importantes

Give the following dates in French.

▶ Noël *(Christmas)*: 25/12 **C'est le vingt-cinq décembre.**

1. le Jour de l'An *(New Year's Day)*: 1/1
2. la fête *(holiday)* de Martin Luther King: 15/1
3. la Saint-Valentin: 14/2
4. la Saint-Patrick: 17/3
5. la fête nationale américaine: 4/7
6. la fête nationale française: 14/7
7. la fête de Christophe Colomb: 12/10

À votre tour!

1 Nathalie et Philippe

Nathalie is talking to Philippe and you hear parts of their conversation. For each of Nathalie's questions, select Philippe's response from the suggested answers.

a. Vendredi.
b. Oui, c'est une copine.
c. Quinze ans.
d. Non, c'est ma cousine.
e. Quarante-cinq ans.
f. Elle s'appelle Madame Doucette.
g. Le dix-huit décembre.
h. C'est mon cousin Christophe.

2 Et toi?

You have just met Nathalie at a party. Answer her questions.

1. Quel âge as-tu?
2. Quel âge a ton copain (ta copine)?
3. C'est quand, ton anniversaire?
4. C'est quand, l'anniversaire de ton copain (ta copine)?
5. Comment s'appelle le (la) prof de français?

3 Conversation dirigée

Nathalie and Christophe are in a café. Christophe sees another girl that Nathalie seems to know. He wonders who she is.

Christophe		Nathalie
asks Nathalie if she knows the girl	→ ↙	says she does and that she is a friend
asks Nathalie the name of her friend	→ ↙	says that her name is Michèle Lafontaine
asks if she is Canadian	→ ↙	says yes and adds that she is from Quebec City **(de Québec)**
says what a coincidence **(Quelle coïncidence!)** and adds that he is also from Quebec City		

4 Ma famille *(My family)*

You are showing your friends a picture of your family. Introduce everyone, giving their ages.

▶ **Voici ma soeur. Elle a douze ans.**

12

1

17

2

9

3

15

4

42

5

37

6

59

5 En scène

With a classmate, act out the following scene.

CHARACTERS:
You and a French guest

SITUATION:
You are in France. Your French friends have invited you to a picnic. You meet one of the guests and have a conversation.

- Greet the guest.
- Introduce yourself and ask the guest's name.
- Tell the guest how old you are and ask his / her age.
- Tell the guest the date of your birthday and ask the date of his / her birthday.
- *(The guest waves to a friend.)* Ask the guest the name of his / her friend.
- *(It is the end of the picnic.)* Say good-bye.

6 Le loto

Loto is a French version of Bingo. Read out loud the numbers on your board.

	13	24		42			75	89
8		25	31		53	68		
	16		36		57		79	90

LES BRUITS FRANÇAIS *(French sounds)*

People in various countries can hear the same noises and interpret them differently. Notice how the French express certain common sounds.

What sounds do animals make in France? They make French sounds, of course!

ASTÉRIX *en action*

Astérix and his friends lead an action-packed life. Can you match the sounds with the corresponding cartoon frames?

a CRAAAC!

b POM POM! POM!

c RRROAAOOO! GRRRAOOR!

d GLOU! GLOU! GLOU! GLOU! GLOU!

e TATARARA TATA!

f PAFF!

1 From ASTÉRIX LE GAULOIS

2 From ASTÉRIX GLADIATEUR

3 From ASTÉRIX CHEZ LES BRETONS

4 From ASTÉRIX CHEZ LES BRETONS

5 From ASTÉRIX GLADIATEUR

6 From ASTÉRIX LE GAULOIS

© 1991 LES ÉDITIONS ALBERT RENÉ/GOSCINNY-UDERZO

UNITÉ 3 Bon appétit!

INTRODUCTION cultivelle

Bon appétit!

Where do you go when you want something to eat or drink? Maybe to a fast-food restaurant or an ice cream place?

French teenagers also have a large choice of places to go when they are hungry or thirsty. Some go to a bakery **(une boulangerie)** or a pastry shop **(une pâtisserie)** to buy croissants, éclairs, or other small pastries. Some may buy pizzas, crepes, hot dogs, or ice-cream cones from street vendors. Still others may go to a fast-food restaurant **(un fast-food).** But the favorite place to get something to eat or drink is the café. There are cafés practically everywhere in France. As you will see, the café plays an important role in the social life of all French people.

LEÇON 9 Tu as faim?

LEÇON 10 Au café

LEÇON 11 Ça fait combien?

LEÇON 12 Le français pratique: Le temps

THÈME ET OBJECTIFS

Having a snack in France

When in France, you will often want to buy something to eat or drink. In this unit, you will learn . . .

- to order some common foods and beverages in a café
- to ask about prices and pay the check
- to ask friends to give or lend you something

You will also learn . . .

- to identify French money
- to talk about the weather
- to name the seasons

LEÇON 9

Tu as faim?

Pierre, Philippe, and Nathalie are on their way home from school. They stop by a street vendor who sells sandwiches and pizza. Today it is Pierre's turn to treat his friends.

Scène 1. Pierre et Nathalie

PIERRE: Tu as faim?
NATHALIE: Oui, j'ai faim.
PIERRE: Tu veux un sandwich ou une pizza?
NATHALIE: Donne-moi une pizza, s'il te plaît.
PIERRE: Voilà.
NATHALIE: Merci.

Scène 2. Pierre et Philippe

PIERRE: Et toi, Philippe, tu as faim?
PHILIPPE: Oh là là, oui, j'ai faim.
PIERRE: Qu'est-ce que tu veux? Un sandwich ou une pizza?
PHILIPPE: Je voudrais un sandwich . . . euh . . . et donne-moi aussi une pizza.
PIERRE: C'est vrai! Tu as vraiment faim!

Scene 1. *Pierre and Nathalie*

PIERRE: *Are you hungry?*
NATHALIE: *Yes, I'm hungry.*
PIERRE: *Do you want a sandwich or a pizza?*
NATHALIE: *Give me a pizza, please.*
PIERRE: *Here you are.*
NATHALIE: *Thanks.*

Scene 2. *Pierre and Philippe*

PIERRE: *And you, Philippe, are you hungry?*
PHILIPPE: *Oh yes, I'm hungry.*
PIERRE: *What do you want? A sandwich or a pizza?*
PHILIPPE: *I would like a sandwich . . . er . . . and give me a pizza too.*
PIERRE: *It's true! You are really hungry!*

POUR COMMUNIQUER

How to say that you are hungry:

J'ai faim.	*I'm hungry.*
Tu as faim?	*Are you hungry?*

How to offer a friend something:

Tu veux . . . ?	*Do you want . . .?*	**Tu veux** un sandwich?
Qu'est-ce que tu veux?	*What do you want?*	**Qu'est-ce que tu veux?** Un sandwich ou une pizza?

How to ask a friend for something:

Je voudrais . . .	*I would like . . .*	**Je voudrais** un sandwich.
Donne-moi . . .	*Give me . . .*	**Donne-moi** une pizza.
S'il te plaît . . .	*Please . . .*	**S'il te plaît,** François, donne-moi une pizza.

Les nourritures *(Foods)*

un croissant

un sandwich

un steak

un steak-frites

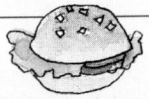
un hamburger

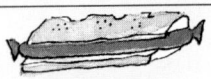
un hot dog

une salade

une pizza

une omelette

une crêpe

une glace

NOTE CULTURELLE

Les jeunes et la nourriture

In general, French teenagers eat their main meals at home with their families. On weekends or after school, however, when they are with friends, they often stop at a fast-food restaurant or a café for something to eat.

At fast-food restaurants, French teenagers order pretty much the same types of foods as Americans: hamburgers, hot dogs, and pizza.

At a café, teenagers may order a croissant, a sandwich, or a dish of ice cream. Some favorite sandwiches are ham **(un sandwich au jambon),** Swiss cheese **(un sandwich au fromage),** or salami **(un sandwich au saucisson).** And, of course, they are made with French bread, which has a crunchy crust. Another traditional quick café meal is a small steak with French fries **(un steak-frites).**

Petit commentaire

In France, sandwiches are traditionally very simple: a piece of French bread with a slice of ham or cheese. Usually sandwiches are not made with mayonnaise or lettuce.

un sandwich, une pizza

You may have noted that the names of some foods are masculine and others are feminine. In French, ALL NOUNS, whether they designate people or things, are either MASCULINE or FEMININE.

MASCULINE NOUNS	FEMININE NOUNS
un sandwich **le** sandwich **un** croissant **le** croissant	**une** pizza **la** pizza **une** salade **la** salade

1 Au choix *(Your choice)*

Offer your classmates a choice between the following items. They will decide which one they would like.

▶ une pizza ou un sandwich?

1. un hamburger ou un steak?
2. un hot dog ou un sandwich?
3. une salade ou une omelette?
4. un steak-frites ou une pizza?
5. une crêpe ou un croissant?
6. une glace à la vanille ou une glace au chocolat?

2 Au café

You are in a French café. Ask for the following dishes.

▶ 

▶ **Je voudrais un croissant.**

1 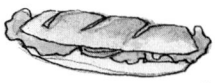
2 
3 
4 
5 
6 

3 Tu as faim?

You have invited French friends to your home. Ask if they are hungry and offer them the following foods.

▶ — Tu as faim?
— Oui, j'ai faim.
— Tu veux un hamburger?
— Oui, merci.

4 Qu'est-ce que tu veux?

Say which foods you would like to have in the following circumstances.

▶ You are very hungry.

1. You are at an Italian restaurant.
2. You are on a diet.
3. You are a vegetarian.
4. You are having breakfast.
5. You would like a dessert.
6. You want to eat something light for supper.

Prononciation

L'intonation

When you speak, your voice rises and falls. This is called INTONATION. In French, as in English, your voice goes down at the end of a statement. However, in French, your voice rises after each group of words in the middle of a sentence. (This is the opposite of English, where your voice drops a little when you pause in the middle of a sentence.)

Voici un steak . . . et une salade.

Répétez: **Je voudrais une pizza.**

Je voudrais une pizza et un sandwich.

Je voudrais une pizza, un sandwich et un hamburger.

Voici un steak.

Voici un steak et une salade.

Voici un steak, une salade et une glace.

LEÇON 10

Au café

This afternoon Jean-Paul and Isabelle went shopping. They are now tired and thirsty. Jean-Paul invites Isabelle to a café.

Scène 1. Jean-Paul, Isabelle

JEAN-PAUL: Tu as soif?
ISABELLE: Oui, j'ai soif.
JEAN-PAUL: On va dans un café? Je t'invite.
ISABELLE: D'accord!

Scène 2. Le garçon, Isabelle, Jean-Paul

LE GARÇON: Vous désirez, mademoiselle?
ISABELLE: Un jus d'orange, s'il vous plaît.
LE GARÇON: Et pour vous, monsieur?
JEAN-PAUL: Donnez-moi une limonade,* s'il vous plaît.

Scène 3. Le garçon, Isabelle, Jean-Paul

LE GARÇON: *(à Isabelle)* La limonade, c'est pour vous, mademoiselle?
JEAN-PAUL: Non, c'est pour moi.
LE GARÇON: Ah, excusez-moi. Voici le jus d'orange, mademoiselle.
ISABELLE: Merci.

Scene 1. *Jean-Paul, Isabelle*

JEAN-PAUL: *Are you thirsty?*
ISABELLE: *Yes, I'm thirsty.*
JEAN-PAUL: *Shall we go to a café? I'm treating (inviting) you.*
ISABELLE: *Okay!*

Scene 2. *The waiter, Isabelle, Jean-Paul*

WAITER: *May I help you, Miss?*
ISABELLE: *An orange juice, please.*
WAITER: *And for you, Sir?*
JEAN-PAUL: *Give me a "limonade," please.*

Scene 3. *The waiter, Isabelle, Jean-Paul*

WAITER: *The "limonade" is for you, Miss?*
JEAN-PAUL: *No, it's for me.*
WAITER: *Oh, excuse me. Here is the orange juice, Miss*
ISABELLE: *Thank you.*

*__Une limonade__ is a popular inexpensive soft drink with a slight lemon flavor.

POUR COMMUNIQUER

How to say that you are thirsty:

J'ai soif.	*I'm thirsty.*
Tu as soif?	*Are you thirsty?*

How to order in a café:

Vous désirez?	*May I help you?*	—**Vous désirez?**
Je voudrais . . .	*I would like . . .*	—**Je voudrais** un Perrier.

How to request something . . .

from a friend:	*from an adult:*	
S'il te plaît, donne-moi . . .	**S'il vous plaît, donnez-moi . . .**	*Please, give me . . .*

➡ Note that French people have two ways of saying *please.* They use
s'il te plaît with friends, and
s'il vous plaît with adults.

As we will see later, young people address their friends as **tu** and adults that they do not know very well as **vous.**

Les boissons *(Beverages)*

un soda

un jus d'orange

un jus de pomme

un jus de tomate

un jus de raisin*

une limonade

un café

un thé

un chocolat

NOTE CULTURELLE

Le café

The café is a favorite gathering place for French young people. They go there not only when they are hungry or thirsty but also to meet their friends. They can sit at a table and talk for hours over a cup of coffee or a glass of juice. French young people also enjoy mineral water and soft drinks, which they order by brand name **(un Coca, un Orangina, un Pepsi, un Schweppes, un Perrier).** In a French café, a 15% service charge is included in the check. However, most people also leave some small change as an added tip.

***Jus de raisin** is a golden-colored juice made from grapes. It is not at all like American grape juice.

Petit commentaire

On the whole, French young people prefer natural beverages, such as flavored mineral water or juices, to carbonated soft drinks. In the larger cities, one can find inviting juice bars that offer a wide selection of freshly blended fruit drinks.

1 Tu as soif?

You have invited a French friend to your house. You offer a choice of beverages and your friend (played by a classmate) responds.

▶ un thé ou un chocolat?
—Tu veux un thé ou un chocolat?
—Donne-moi un chocolat, s'il te plaît.

1. un thé ou un café?
2. une limonade ou un soda?
3. un jus de pomme ou un jus d'orange?
4. un jus de raisin ou un jus de tomate?

2 Au café

You are in a French café. Get the attention of the waiter **(Monsieur)** or the waitress **(Mademoiselle)** and place your order. Act out the dialogue with a classmate.

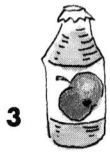

3 Que choisir? *(What to choose?)*

You are in a French café. Decide what beverage you are going to order in each of the following circumstances.

▶ You are very thirsty.
S'il vous plaît, une limonade (un jus de pomme) . . .

1. It is very cold outside.
2. You do not want to spend much money.
3. You like juice but are allergic to citrus fruits.
4. It is breakfast time.
5. You have a sore throat.

4 La faim et la soif *(Hungry and thirsty)*

You are having a meal in a French café. Order the food suggested in the picture. Then order something to drink with that dish. A classmate will play the part of the waiter.

Note: **Et avec ça?** means *And with that?*

Prononciation

L'accent final

In French, the rhythm is very even and the accent always falls on the *last* syllable of a word or group of words.

Répétez: **Philippe Thomas Alice Sophie Dominique**

un café	**Je voudrais un café.**
une salade	**Donnez-moi un salade.**
un chocolat	**Donne-moi un chocolat.**

ŭn chŏcŏlāt

If you want French people to understand you, the most important thing is to speak with an even rhythm and to stress the last syllable in each group of words. (Try speaking English this way: people will think you have a French accent!)

LEÇON 11

Ça fait combien?

At the café, Jean-Paul and Isabelle have talked about many things. It is now time to go. Jean-Paul calls the waiter so he can pay the check.

JEAN-PAUL: S'il vous plaît?
LE GARÇON: Oui, monsieur.
JEAN-PAUL: Ça fait combien?
LE GARÇON: Voyons, un jus d'orange, 12 francs, et une limonade, 10 francs. Ça fait 22 francs.
JEAN-PAUL: 22 francs . . . Très bien . . . Mais, euh . . . Zut! Où est mon porte-monnaie . . . ? Dis, Isabelle, prête-moi 30 francs, s'il te plaît.

JEAN-PAUL: Excuse me? (Please?)
WAITER: Yes, Sir.
JEAN-PAUL: What do I owe you? (How much does that make?)
WAITER: Let's see, one orange juice, 12 francs, and one "limonade" 10 francs. That comes to (makes) 22 francs.
JEAN-PAUL: 22 francs . . . Very well . . . But, uh . . . Darn! Where is my wallet . . . ? Hey, Isabelle, loan me 30 francs, please.

NOTE CULTURELLE

L'argent français *(French money)*

The monetary unit of France is the **franc,** which is divided into 100 **centimes.** French currency consists of bills and coins. French bills are of different sizes—the greater the value, the larger the bill: **500 francs, 200 francs, 100 francs, 50 francs,** and **20 francs.** The people represented on the bills are famous French writers, painters, and musicians.

POUR *COMMUNIQUER*

How to ask how much something costs:

C'est combien?	*How much is it?*	—**C'est combien?**
Ça fait combien?	*How much does that come to (make)?*	—**Ça fait combien?**
Ça fait . . .	*That's . . . , That comes to . . .*	—**Ça fait** 30 francs.
Combien coûte . . . ?	*How much does . . . cost?*	—**Combien coûte** le sandwich?
Il/Elle coûte . . .	*It costs . . .*	—**Il coûte** 14 francs.

How to ask a friend to lend you something:

Prête-moi . . .	*Lend me . . ., Loan me . . .*	**Prête-moi** 10 francs, s'il te plaît.

➡ Note that masculine nouns can be replaced by **il** and feminine nouns can be replaced by **elle.**

Voici **une glace.**	**Elle** coûte 8 francs.	***It*** *costs 8 francs.*
Voici **un sandwich.**	**Il** coûte 15 francs.	***It*** *costs 15 francs.*

Petit commentaire

French people of all ages love to eat out, and French restaurants have the reputation of offering the best cuisine in the world. Of course, there are all kinds of restaurants for all kinds of budgets, ranging from the simple country inn ***(l'auberge de campagne)*** *with its hearty regional food to the elegant three-star restaurant* ***(restaurant trois étoiles)*** *with its exquisite—and expensive—menu.*

1 S'il te plaît . . .

You have been shopping in Paris and discover that you did not exchange enough money. Ask a friend to loan you the following sums.

▶ 10 francs
S'il te plaît, prête-moi dix francs.

1. 20 francs
2. 30 francs
3. 45 francs
4. 60 francs
5. 75 francs
6. 80 francs
7. 85 francs
8. 90 francs
9. 95 francs

2 Décision

Before ordering at a café, Stéphanie and Émilie are checking the prices. Act out the dialogues.

▶ le chocolat

1. le thé
2. le jus d'orange
3. la salade de tomates
4. la glace à la vanille
5. le café
6. le steak-frites
7. le hot dog
8. l'omelette
9. la salade mixte
10. le jus de raisin

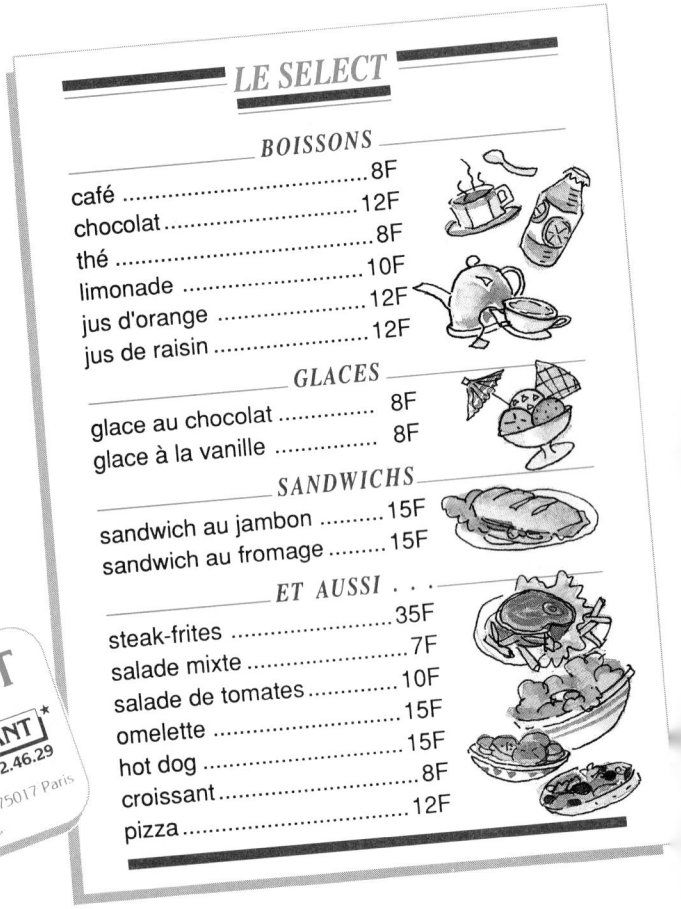

3 Ça fait combien?

You have gone to Le Select with your friends and have ordered the following items. Now you are ready to leave the café, and each one wants to pay. Check the prices on the menu for Le Select, and act out the dialogue.

▶ —Ça fait combien, s'il vous plaît?
—Ça fait 12 francs.
—Voici 12 francs.
—Merci.

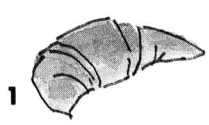

1

2

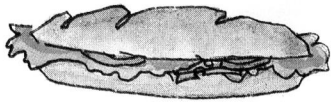

3

4

5

4 Au «Select»

You are at Le Select. Order something to eat and drink. Since you are in a hurry, ask for the check right away. Act out the dialogue with a classmate who will play the part of the waiter/waitress.

Prononciation

La consonne «r» /r/

The French consonant "**r**" is not at all like the English "**r**". It is pronounced at the back of the throat. In fact, it is similar to the Spanish "jota" sound of José.

Répétez: **Marie Paris orange Henri**
franc très croissant fromage
bonjour pour Pierre quart
Robert Richard Renée Raoul

Marie, prête-moi trente francs.

Marie

LEÇON 12

LE FRANÇAIS PRATIQUE

Le temps

It is nine o'clock Sunday morning. Cécile and her brother Philippe have planned a picnic for the whole family. Cécile is asking about the weather.

CÉCILE: Quel temps fait-il?
PHILIPPE: Il fait mauvais!
CÉCILE: Il fait mauvais?
PHILIPPE: Oui, il fait mauvais! Regarde! Il pleut!
CÉCILE: Zut, zut et zut!
PHILIPPE: !!!???
CÉCILE: Et le pique-nique?
PHILIPPE: Le pique-nique? Ah oui, le pique-nique! . . . Écoute, ça n'a pas d'importance.
CÉCILE: Pourquoi?
PHILIPPE: Pourquoi? Parce que Papa va nous inviter au restaurant.
CÉCILE: Super!

CÉCILE: *How's the weather?*
PHILIPPE: *It's bad!*
CÉCILE: *It's bad?*
PHILIPPE: *Yes, it's bad! Look! It's raining!*
CÉCILE: *Darn, darn, darn!*
PHILIPPE: *!!!???*
CÉCILE: *And the picnic?*
PHILIPPE: *The picnic? Oh yes, the picnic! . . . Listen, it's not important (that has no importance).*
CÉCILE: *Why?*
PHILIPPE: *Why? Because Dad is going to take us out (invite us) to a restaurant.*
CÉCILE: *Great!*

POUR COMMUNIQUER

How to talk about the weather:

Quel temps fait-il? *How's the weather?*

Il fait beau.

Il fait bon.

Il fait chaud.

Il fait frais.

Il fait froid.

Il fait mauvais.

Il pleut.

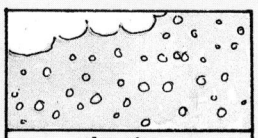
Il neige.

Les saisons *(Seasons)*

le printemps	*spring*	**au printemps**	*in (the) spring*
l'été	*summer*	**en été**	*in (the) summer*
l'automne	*fall, autumn*	**en automne**	*in (the) fall*
l'hiver	*winter*	**en hiver**	*in (the)winter*

1 Ta région

Tell Cécile what the weather is like in your part of the country.

▶ en juillet

1. en août
2. en septembre
3. en novembre
4. en janvier
5. en mars
6. en mai

2 Les quatre saisons

Describe what the weather is like in each of the four seasons in the following cities.

▶ à Miami

1. à Chicago
2. à San Francisco
3. à Denver
4. à Boston
5. à Seattle
6. à Dallas

À votre tour!

1 Isabelle et Jean-Paul

Isabelle is talking to Jean-Paul. You hear parts of their conversation. For each of Isabelle's questions, select Jean-Paul's response from the suggested answers.

1 Tu as faim?

2 Tu veux un jus de pommes?

3 Combien coûte le café au Café Français?

4 Quel temps fait-il?

5 Quelle est ta saison favorite?

a. Il fait chaud.
b. Huit francs.
c. Oui, merci, j'ai soif.
d. C'est le printemps.
e. Oui, je voudrais un sandwich.

2 Et toi?

Now Isabelle is phoning you. Answer her questions.

1. Quel temps fait-il aujourd'hui?
2. Quel temps fait-il en hiver?
3. Quelle est ta saison favorite?

3 Conversation dirigée

Stéphanie is in a café called Le Petit Bistrot. The waiter is taking her order. With a partner, compose and act out a dialogue according to the script suggested below.

le garçon		Stéphanie
greets client and asks if he may help her	→ ↙	says that she would like a croissant and asks how much an orange juice costs
answers 15 francs	→ ↙	asks for an orange juice . . . calls the waiter and asks how much she owes
says 22 francs	→ ↙	gives waiter 25 francs **(Voici . . .)**
says thank you		

4 Au café

You are in a French café. Call the waiter/waitress and order the following items. A classmate will play the part of the waiter/waitress.

▶ **—Monsieur (Mademoiselle), s'il vous plaît!**
—Vous désirez?
—Un croissant, s'il vous plaît!
(Donnez-moi un croissant, s'il vous plaît!)
(Je voudrais un croissant, s'il vous plaît!).

5 En scène

With two classmates, act out the following scene.

CHARACTERS:
You, a French friend, and the waiter in the café

SITUATION:
A French friend has been showing you around Paris. You invite your friend to a café and discover too late that you have not changed enough money. Your friend will respond to your questions.

- Ask your friend if he/she is thirsty.
- Ask if he/she wants a soft drink.
- Ask if he/she is hungry.
- Ask if he/she wants a sandwich.
- When the waiter comes, your friend orders and you ask for a croissant and a cup of hot chocolate.
- Ask the waiter how much everything is.
- Ask your friend to please lend you 20 francs.

6 La date, la saison et le temps

Look at the calendar days. For each one, give the date, the season, and the weather.

▶ **C'est le dix avril.**
C'est le printemps.
Il pleut.

ENTRACTE 3

Une chanson: Alouette

Alouette *(The Lark)* is a popular folksong of French-Canadian origin. As the song leader names the various parts of the bird's anatomy, he points to his own body. The chorus repeats the refrain with enthusiasm.

bonjour QUÉBEC

Alouette

G — A - lou - et - te, gen - tille a - lou - et - te,
D7 G

G — a - lou - et - te, je te plu - me - rai.
D7 G

G — Je te plu - me - rai la tête, je te plu - me - rai la tête.
D7 G

D7 — Et la tête, et la tête, a - lou - ette, a - lou - ette, oh!

1. Alouette, gentille, alouette,
   Alouette, je te plumerai.

   Je te plumerai la tête,
   Je te plumerai la tête.

   Et la tête—et la tête
   Alouette—Alouette
   Oh oh oh oh

2. Alouette, gentille alouette
   Alouette, je te plumerai.

   Je te plumerai le bec,
   Je te plumerai le bec.

   Et le bec—et le bec
   Et la tête—et la tête
   Alouette—Alouette
   Oh oh oh oh

3. Je te plumerai le cou . . .
4. Je te plumerai les ailes . . .
5. Je te plumerai le dos . . .
6. Je te plumerai les pattes . . .
7. Je te plumerai la queue . . .

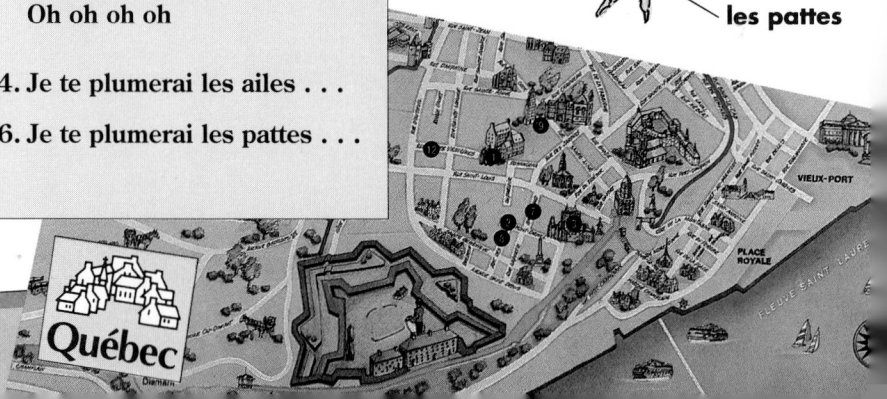

Les parties du corps

(Parts of the body)

l'oeil (les yeux)
le nez
la bouche
le bras
le ventre
la jambe
les cheveux
la tête
l'oreille
le cou
le dos
la main
le pied

Un jeu **Simon dit**

The French sometimes play a game called **Simon dit** *(Simon says)*. The rules are the same as they are in English. Everyone stands up to play.

The game leader says: **Simon dit: Les mains sur la tête!** placing her hands on her head. The other players also place their hands on their head.

Then the game leader may say: **Les mains sur le dos!** placing her hands on her back. This time, however, the other players should not move, because the game leader did not first say **Simon dit.** Any player that did move must sit down.

The game continues until only one player is left standing.

À l'école en France

BONJOUR, Nathalie!

Bonjour!
Je m'appelle Nathalie Aubin.
J'ai 15 ans et j'habite° à Savigny-sur-Orge
avec ma famille. (Savigny est
une petite° ville° à 20 kilomètres
au sud° de Paris.)
J'ai un frère, Christophe, 17 ans,
et deux soeurs, Céline, 13 ans,
et Florence, 7 ans.
Mon père est programmeur.
(Il travaille° à Paris.)
Ma mère est dentiste.
(Elle travaille à Savigny.)
Je vais au lycée Jean-Baptiste
Corot.
Je suis élève° de seconde°.
Et vous?

Nathalie

j'habite *I live* **petite** *small* **ville** *city* **sud** *south*
travaille *works* **élève** *student* **seconde** *tenth grade*

mon père

moi

ma soeur Florence

Voici ma famille.

ma mère ma soeur Céline

mon frère Christophe

Voici mon école.° Le lycée Jean-Baptiste Corot est dans° un château!°

Voici ma maison.° (C'est une maison confortable, mais° ce n'est pas un château!)

Ville de SAVIGNY-SUR-ORGE

école *school* **dans** *in* **château** *castle*
maison *house* **mais** *but*

Un jour de classe

Le matin

À la maison

Nathalie gets up every morning at seven. After a light breakfast (toasted bread with butter and jam, hot chocolate), she leaves for school.

Nathalie sur sa mobylette

Since she does not live too far from her lycée, she goes there on her moped **(sa mobylette).** Students who live farther away take the school bus.

La classe de sciences-éco

Nathalie arrives at school at about 8:25, five minutes before her first class. Today, Thursday, her first class is economics **(les sciences économiques),** which is her favorite subject.

L'après-midi

À la cantine

At 12:30, Nathalie goes to the school cafeteria **(la cantine)** for lunch. As in American schools, the food is served cafeteria-style. During lunch break, Nathalie meets with her friends from other classes.

La classe d'anglais

Classes start again at two o'clock. Today they finish at four.

Après les classes

Depending on when her last class ends, Nathalie either goes home right after school or participates in one of the many school clubs.

Le soir

Dans la salle à manger

The Aubins have dinner around 7:30. Everyone helps with the kitchen chores. Today it is Christophe's turn.

Nathalie does her homework after dinner. She usually has about one or two hours of homework every night. When she is finished, she reads or listens to cassettes for a while, then goes to bed around 11 P.M.

Nathalie dans sa chambre

L'emploi du temps

LYCÉE JEAN-BAPTISTE COROT

Étudiante: AUBIN, Nathalie

	LUNDI	MARDI	MERCREDI	JEUDI	VENDREDI	SAMEDI
8h30 à 9h30	Histoire	Allemand		Sciences économiques		Français
9h30 à 10h30	Anglais	Français	Anglais	Sciences physiques	Allemand	Français
10h30 à 11h30	Sport	Français	Sciences économiques	(13h30) Maths	Latin	Latin
11h30 à 12h30	Français	Latin	Maths	(13h30)	Sciences physiques	Histoire ou Civilisation
13h00 à 14h00						
14h00 à 15h00	Sciences physiques	Maths		Allemand		
15h00 à 16h00	Géographie	Maths		Histoire		
16h00 à 17h00	Civilisation	Anglais				

NOTE CULTURELLE

Le programme scolaire

At the lycée, all students take a certain number of required subjects. These include French, math, one foreign language, history and geography, physical sciences, natural sciences, and physical education. Depending on their career plans, French students also have to choose among certain electives: a second foreign language, economics, computer science, biology, music.

Here are some of the subjects taught in French secondary schools. How many can you identify?

le français
l'anglais
l'espagnol
l'allemand
le latin
l'histoire
la géographie
les sciences économiques
l'éducation civique *(civics)*
la musique
le dessin
l'éducation physique
les maths
la biologie
la physique
la chimie
l'informatique *(computer science)*
les sciences naturelles

ACTIVITÉS CULTURELLES

1. Look carefully at Nathalie's class schedule. You may have noted certain differences between the French and the American school systems.
   - French students have more class hours than American students. How many hours of classes does Nathalie have each week?
   - French students learn more foreign languages than American students. In France, the study of foreign languages is compulsory. What languages is Nathalie learning?
   - French students usually have Wednesday afternoon free. Does Nathalie have school on Saturday morning? on Saturday afternoon?
2. Write out your own class schedule in French.

Le lycée Jean-Baptiste Corot

un pastel de Corot

Jean-Baptiste Corot

Like many French schools, the lycée Jean-Baptiste Corot of Savigny-sur-Orge is named after a famous French person. Jean-Baptiste Corot is a 19th century painter, remembered especially for his landscapes.

The lycée Jean-Baptiste Corot is both very old and very modern. It was created in the 1950's on the grounds of a historical castle dating from the 12th century. The castle, which serves as the administrative center, is still surrounded by a moat. The lycée itself has many modern facilities which include:

- **les salles de classe** *(classrooms)*
- **la cantine** *(cafeteria)*
- **le stade** *(stadium)* **et le terrain de sport** *(playing field)*

Plan du lycée Jean-Baptiste Corot

Basket
Basket
Volley
Volley
Gymnase
PARKING
Refectoire élèves
cuisines
PARKING
DOUVE
Rue des Rossays

une salle de classe

la cantine

le terrain de sport

NOTES CULTURELLES

1 L'école secondaire

There are two types of secondary schools in France:

- **le collège,** which corresponds to the U.S. middle school (grades 6 to 9)
- **le lycée,** which corresponds to the U.S. high school (grades 10 to 12)

On the following chart, you will notice that each grade **(une classe)** is designated by a number (as in the United States): **sixième (6e), cinquième (5e), quatrième (4e),** etc. However, the progression from grade to grade is the opposite in France. The secondary school begins in France with **sixième** and ends with **terminale.**

École	Classe	Âge des élèves	Équivalent américain
Le collège	sixième (6e) cinquième (5e) quatrième (4e) troisième (3e)	11–12 ans 12–13 ans 13–14 ans 14–15 ans	*sixth grade* *seventh grade* *eighth grade* *ninth grade*
Le lycée	seconde (2e) première (1e) terminale	15–16 ans 16–17 ans 17–18 ans	*tenth grade* *eleventh grade* *twelfth grade*

2 Le bulletin de notes

At the end of each semester, French students receive a report card **(le bulletin de notes),** which must be signed by their parents. Most schools assign grades on a scale of 0 (low) to 20 (high). Most teachers also write a brief evaluation of the student's progress in each subject.

Here is a report card for the first semester.

LYCÉE J.-B. COROT 91605 SAVIGNY - SUR - ORGE CLASSE 2e

PICARD Laurent PREMIER TRIMESTRE

	NIVEAU A	B	C	D	E	Appréciations des Professeurs
Math. M. Antoine		13,5				Élève sérieux.
Sc. Phys. Mme. Durin			+ 11,2			Un premier devoir médiocre. Depuis, c'est mieux. Il faut continuer.
Sc. Nat. M. Lemaire		+ 12,5				ASSEZ BON ENSEMBLE.
Hist. et Géogr. M. Brunier	– 13					Bien.
Français M. Rivaud		11				Bon travail.
Anglais I M. Marx 16						Très bien.
Allemand II Mme. Dumet 15,2						Excellent élève.

ENSEMBLE DES RÉSULTATS : A Très satisfaisant (B) Satisfaisant C Tout juste suffisant D Insuffisant E Très insuffisant

Appréciations du Proviseur - du Proviseur Adjoint du Conseiller Principal d'Éducation - du Professeur Principal

Bon trimestre

ACTIVITÉ CULTURELLE

1. What is the name of the student?
2. What is the name of his school?
3. What grade is he in?
4. What is his best subject? What grade did he get?
5. What is his weakest subject? What grade did he get?
6. How many foreign languages is he studying? Which ones?

Expressions pour la classe

Le professeur dit . . .

à une élève | à un élève | à la classe

Regarde! *(Look!)*
Regarde la vidéo.
Écoute! *(Listen!)*
Écoute la bande *(tape).*

Parle! *(Speak!)*
Parle plus fort *(louder).*
Réponds! *(Answer!)*
Réponds à la question.
Répète! *(Repeat!)*
Répète la phrase *(sentence).*

Lis! *(Read!)*
Lis l'exercice.
Écris! *(Write!)*
Écris dans ton cahier.

Prends *(Take)*	**une feuille de papier.**
	un crayon
Ouvre *(Open)*	**ton livre.**
	la porte
Ferme *(Close)*	**ton cahier.**
	la fenêtre

Viens! *(Come!)*
Viens ici.
Va! *(Go!)*
Va au tableau.
Lève-toi! *(Stand up!)*
Assieds-toi! *(Sit down!)*

Apporte-moi *(Bring me)*	
Donne-moi *(Give me)*	**ton devoir.**
Montre-moi *(Show me)*	

Regardez!
Regardez la vidéo.
Écoutez!
Écoutez la bande.

Parlez!
Parlez plus fort.
Répondez!
Répondez à la question.
Répétez!
Répétez la phrase.

Lisez!
Lisez l'exercice.
Écrivez!
Écrivez dans vos cahiers.

Prenez	**une feuille de papier.**
	un crayon
Ouvrez	**vos livres.**
	la porte
Fermez	**vos cahiers.**
	la fenêtre

Venez!
Venez ici.
Allez!
Allez au tableau.
Levez-vous!
Asseyez-vous!

Apportez-moi	
Donnez-moi	**vos devoirs.**
Montrez-moi	

Quelques objets

un crayon

un livre

une feuille de papier

un stylo

un cahier

une cassette

un devoir

un morceau de craie

une vidéocassette

un bureau

un ordinateur

une télé

une carte

une porte

un tableau

un magnétoscope

une table

une chaise

une fenêtre

Tu dis ...

Je sais.	*I know.*
Je ne sais pas.	*I don't know.*
Je ne comprends pas.	*I don't understand.*
Que veut dire ... ?	*What does ... mean?*
Comment dit-on ... en français?	*How does one say ... in French?*

NIVEAU B

La vie de

Félicitations!

Congratulations! Now that you have learned how to meet and greet people in French, you are going to discover more about everyday life in France: **La vie de tous les jours.**

What are some of the aspects of daily life that you and your friends often talk about? You probably discuss home and family, things you own, and people you know. You talk about what you like to do, where you like to go, and what your weekend plans are. If you were going to France, you would discover that French young people are interested in the same topics.

In this second part of your book, you will learn . . .

- how to talk about your daily activities (both in school and out of school)
- how to make future plans: what you are going to do
- how to describe people you know
- how to describe objects you own
- how to talk about your home and your family
- how to express your opinions

You will also learn . . .

- how to ask your way around in a French city
- how to extend and accept invitations

In order to express yourself accurately, you will also begin to learn how the French language works: how to ask and answer questions, how to describe people, places, and things.

En avant et bon courage!

Jean-Paul Valette Rebecca M. Valette

tous les jours

UNITÉ

4

Qu'est-ce qu'on fait?

LEÇON 13 Le français pratique: Mes activités

LEÇON 14 Qui est là?

LEÇON 15 Une boum

LEÇON 16 Une interview

THÈME ET OBJECTIFS

Daily activities

In this unit, you will be talking about the things you do every day, such as working and studying, as well as watching TV and listening to the radio.

You will learn . . .

- to describe some of your daily activities
- to say what you like and do not like to do
- to ask and answer questions about where others are and what they are doing

You will also learn . . .

- to invite friends to do things with you
- to politely accept or turn down an invitation

LE FRANÇAIS PRATIQUE

LEÇON 13 Mes activités

Au cinéma
Des copains sont au cinéma.

Accent sur ... Les activités de la semaine

French teenagers, as well as their parents, put a lot of emphasis on doing well in school. On the whole, French students spend a great deal of time on their studies. French schools have a longer class day than American schools, and teachers tend to assign quite a lot of homework.

However, French teenagers do not study all the time. They also watch TV and listen to music. Many participate in various sports activities, but to a lesser extent than young Americans. On weekends, French teenagers like to go out with their friends. Some go shopping. Others go to the movies. Many enjoy dancing and going to parties. Sunday is usually a family day for visiting relatives or going for a drive in the country.

Au café
Stéphanie est au café.

Une boum
Dominique et Stéphanie sont à une boum.

Le terrain de foot au lycée Corot
Des jeunes jouent au foot.

En classe
Marc et Patrick sont en classe.

A. Préférences

How to talk about what you like and don't like to do:

Est-ce que tu aimes . . .?	*Do you like . . .?*	**Est-ce que tu aimes** parler *(to speak)* français?
J'aime . . .	*I like . . .*	Oui, **j'aime** parler français.
Je n'aime pas . . .	*I don't like . . .*	Non, **je n'aime pas** parler français.
Je préfère . . .	*I prefer . . .*	**Je préfère** parler anglais.

téléphoner *to phone*

parler français *to talk, speak French*

parler anglais *to speak English*

parler espagnol *to speak Spanish*

manger *to eat*

chanter *to sing*

danser *to dance*

nager *to swim*

1 Et toi?

Indicate what you like to do in the following situations by completing the sentences.

1. En classe,
   j'aime . . .
   mais je préfère . . .
   - étudier
   - écouter le professeur
   - parler avec *(with)* un copain
   - parler avec une copine

2. En été,
   j'aime . . .
   mais je préfère . . .
   - travailler
   - nager
   - voyager
   - jouer au volley

J'aime aussi *(also)* . . .

jouer au tennis
to play tennis

jouer au volley
to play volleyball

jouer au basket
to play basketball

jouer au foot
to play soccer

Mais *(but)* **je préfère . . .**

regarder la télé
to watch TV

écouter la radio
to listen to the radio

dîner au restaurant
to have dinner at the restaurant; to eat out

voyager
to travel

Je n'aime pas toujours *(always)* . . .

étudier
to study

travailler
to work

HAVE YOU NOTED?

1. French people like to shorten words. For example, the words **volleyball, basketball, football,** and **télévision** are often shortened to **volley, basket, foot,** and **télé.**
2. In French, **foot** (or **football**) refers to *soccer.*

3. Avec mes *(my)* copains,
   j'aime . . .
   mais je préfère . . .
   - chanter
   - manger
   - écouter la radio
   - jouer au basket
4. Avec ma famille,
   j'aime . . .
   mais je préfère . . .
   - voyager
   - regarder la télé
   - jouer à «Trivial Pursuit»
   - dîner au restaurant
5. À la maison *(At home)*,
   j'aime . . .
   mais je préfère . . .
   - étudier
   - téléphoner
   - manger
   - écouter mon walkman

2 Tu aimes ou tu n'aimes pas?

Say whether or not you like to do the following things.

▶ parler français?

1. parler anglais?
2. étudier?
3. danser?
4. chanter?
5. jouer au basket?
6. jouer au tennis?
7. regarder la télé?
8. dîner au restaurant?
9. manger?
10. travailler?
11. écouter la radio?
12. téléphoner?

3 Préférences

Ask your classmates if they like to do the following things.

▶ **—Est-ce que tu aimes téléphoner?**
—Oui, j'aime téléphoner. (Non, je n'aime pas téléphoner.)

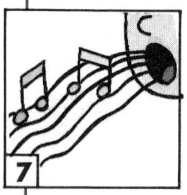

4 Dialogue

Philippe is asking Hélène if she likes to do certain things. She replies that she prefers to do other things. Play both roles. Note: "??" means you can invent an answer.

▶ PHILIPPE: **Est-ce que tu aimes nager?**
HÉLÈNE: **Oui, mais je préfère jouer au tennis.**

B. Souhaits *(Wishes)*

How to talk about what you want, would like, and do not want to do:

Je veux . . .	*I want . . .*	**Je veux** parler français.
Je voudrais . . .	*I would like . . .*	**Je voudrais** voyager en France.
Je ne veux pas . . .	*I don't want . . .*	**Je ne veux pas** étudier aujourd'hui.

5 Ce soir *(Tonight)*

Say whether or not you want to do the following things tonight.

▶ étudier?
Oui, je veux étudier.
(Non, je ne veux pas étudier.)

1. parler français?
2. travailler?
3. jouer au ping-pong?
4. chanter?
5. danser?
6. regarder la télé?
7. écouter la radio?
8. dîner avec une copine?
9. parler à *(to)* mon frère?
10. téléphoner à mon cousin?

6 Weekend

Caroline and her friends are discussing their weekend plans. What do they say they would like to do?

▶ CAROLINE: **Je voudrais jouer au tennis.**

7 Trois souhaits *(Three wishes)*

Read the list of suggested activities and select the three that you would like to do most.

parler français	voyager avec ma cousine
parler espagnol	voyager en France
parler avec *(with)* Oprah Winfrey	chanter comme *(like)* Bruce Springsteen
dîner avec le Président	jouer au tennis avec Steffi Graf
dîner avec Tom Cruise	jouer au basket comme Michael Jordan

▶ **Je voudrais parler espagnol.**
Je voudrais chanter comme Bruce Springsteen.
Je voudrais voyager en France.

C. Invitations

How to invite a friend:

Est-ce que tu veux . . .?	*Do you want to . . . ?*	**Est-ce que tu veux** jouer au tennis?
Est-ce que tu peux . . .?	*Can you . . . ?*	**Est-ce que tu peux** parler à mon copain?
avec moi/toi	*with me/you*	Est-ce que tu veux dîner **avec moi?**

How to accept an invitation:

Oui, bien sûr . . .	*Yes, of course . . .*	
Oui, merci . . .	*Yes, thanks . . .*	
Oui, d'accord . . .	*Yes, all right, okay . . .*	
je veux bien.	*I'd love to.*	**Oui, bien sûr, je veux bien.**
je veux bien . . .	*I'd love to . . .*	**Oui, merci, je veux bien** dîner avec toi.

How to turn down an invitation:

Je regrette, mais	*I'm sorry, but*	**Je regrette, mais je ne peux pas**
je ne peux pas . . .	*I can't . . .*	dîner avec toi.
Je dois . . .	*I have to, I must . . .*	**Je dois** étudier.

8 Invitations

Imagine a French exchange group is visiting your school. Invite the following French students to do things with you. They will accept. (Your classmates will play the parts of the students.)

▶ Monique / dîner

1. Éric / parler français
2. Philippe / étudier
3. Céline / jouer au tennis
4. Anne / manger une pizza
5. Jean-Claude / chanter
6. Caroline / danser

9 Conversation

Ask your classmates if they want to do the following things. They will answer that they cannot and explain what they have to do.

▶ jouer au tennis? (étudier)
—**Est-ce que tu veux jouer au basket?**
—**Non, je ne peux pas. Je dois étudier.**

1. jouer au volley? (travailler)
2. jouer au ping-pong? (téléphoner à ma cousine)
3. étudier avec moi? (étudier avec ma copine)
4. dîner avec moi? (dîner avec ma famille)
5. nager? (jouer au foot à deux heures)

À votre tour!

1 Créa-dialogue

Ask your classmates if they want to do the following things with you. They will answer that they cannot and will give one of the excuses in the box.

▶ jouer au tennis

1. jouer au basket
2. manger une pizza
3. regarder la télé
4. jouer au ping-pong
5. dîner au restaurant

Excuses:

étudier
travailler
téléphoner à une copine
dîner avec ma cousine
parler avec ma mère
chanter avec la chorale *(choir)*

2 Conversation dirigée

Philippe is phoning Stéphanie. Write out their conversation according to the directions. You may want to act out the dialogue with a classmate.

Philippe		Stéphanie
asks Stéphanie how she is	→	answers that she is fine
asks her if she wants to eat out	←	asks at what time
says at 8 o'clock	→	says that she is sorry but that she has to study
says it is too bad (**Dommage!**)	←	

3 Expression personnelle

What we like to do often depends on the circumstances. Complete the sentences below saying what you like and don't like to do in the following situations.

▶ En hiver . . .
En hiver, j'aime regarder la télé.
J'aime aussi jouer au basket.
Je n'aime pas nager.

1. En été . . .
2. En automne . . .
3. Le samedi *(On Saturdays)* . . .
4. Le dimanche . . .
5. Le soir *(In the evening)* . . .
6. En classe . . .
7. Avec mes *(my)* amis . . .
8. Avec ma famille . . .

4 Composition

Write three things that you like to do and three things that you do not like to do.

▶ J'aime jouer au volley.
Je n'aime pas jouer au foot.

5 Correspondance

This summer, you are going to spend two weeks in France. Your pen pal Philippe has written, asking what you like and don't like to do on vacation (**en vacances**). Write a postcard answering his questions.

▶

Cher Philippe,
En vacances, j'aime . . .

PHILIPPE RAYMOND
12 AV. VICTOR HUGO
PARIS 75116
FRANCE

LEÇON 14 Qui est là?

It is Wednesday afternoon. Pierre is looking for his friends but cannot find anyone. Finally he sees Hélène at the Café Bellevue and asks her where everyone is.

PIERRE:	Où est Jacqueline?	*Where*
HÉLÈNE:	Elle est à la maison.	*at home*
PIERRE:	Et Jean-Claude? Il est là?	*here*
HÉLÈNE:	Non, il n'est pas là.	
PIERRE:	Où est-il?	
HÉLÈNE:	Il est en ville avec une copine.	*in town*
PIERRE:	Et Nicole et Sandrine? Est-ce qu'elles sont ici?	*here*
HÉLÈNE:	Non, elles sont au restaurant.	
PIERRE:	Alors, qui est là?	*So*
HÉLÈNE:	Moi, je suis ici.	
PIERRE:	C'est vrai, tu es ici! Eh bien, puisque tu es là, je t'invite au cinéma. D'accord?	*true / since* *I'll invite you to the movies*
HÉLÈNE:	Super! Pierre, tu es un vrai copain!	*real*

Compréhension

Indicate where the following people are by selecting the appropriate completions.

1. Jacqueline est . . . a) au café
2. Jean-Claude est . . . b) à la maison
3. Nicole et Sandrine sont . . . c) en ville
4. Hélène et Pierre sont . . . d) au restaurant

NOTE CULTURELLE

Le mercredi après-midi

French high school students do not have classes on Wednesday afternoons. They use this free time to go out with their friends or to catch up on their homework. For some students, Wednesday afternoon is also the time for music and dance lessons as well as sports club activities. However, in contrast to the United States, many French schools have classes on Saturday mornings.

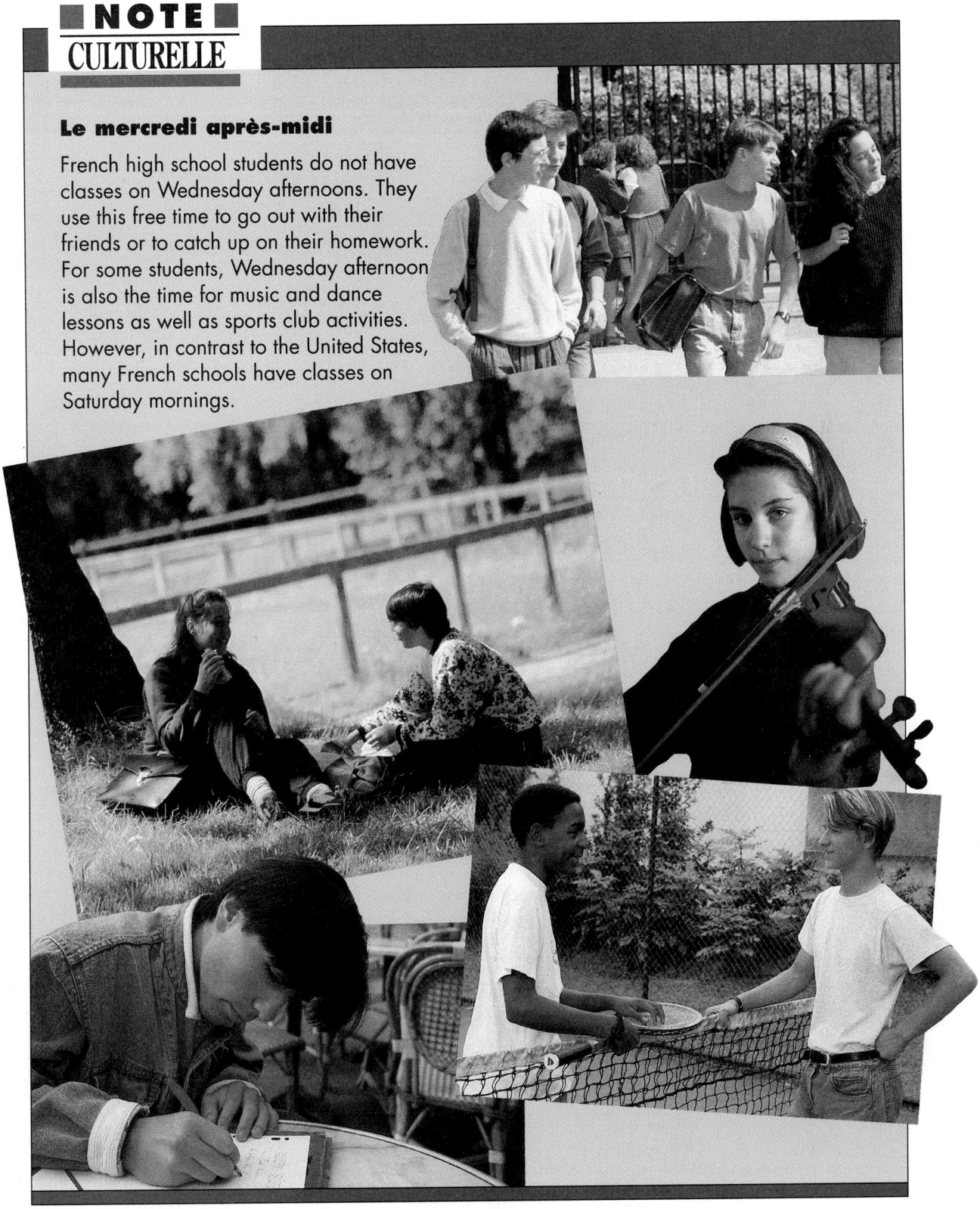

A. Le verbe *être* et les pronoms sujets

Être *(to be)* is the most frequently used verb in French. Note the forms of **être** in the chart below.

	être	*to be*	
SINGULAR	je **suis** tu **es** il/elle **est**	*I am* *you are* *he/she is*	Je **suis** américain. Tu **es** canadienne. Il **est** anglais.
PLURAL	nous **sommes** vous **êtes** ils/elles **sont**	*we are* *you are* *they are*	Nous **sommes** à Paris. Vous **êtes** à San Francisco. Ils **sont** à Genève.

➡ Note the liaison in the **vous**-form:

Vous êtes français?

➡ Note the expression **être d'accord** *(to agree)*:

—Tu **es d'accord** avec moi? — *Do you agree with me?*

— Oui, je **suis d'accord!** — *Yes, I agree.*

TU or *VOUS?*

When talking to ONE person, the French have two ways of saying *you*:

- **tu** ("familiar *you*") is used to talk to someone your own age (or younger) or to a member of your family
- **vous** ("formal *you*") is used when talking to anyone else

When talking to TWO or more people, the French use **vous.**

> ***Learning about language***
>
> The words **je** *(I)*, **tu** *(you)*, **il** *(he)*, **elle** *(she)*, etc. are called SUBJECT PRONOUNS.
>
> - SINGULAR pronouns refer to one person (or object).
> - PLURAL pronouns refer to two or more people (or objects).
>
> The VERB **être** *(to be)* is IRREGULAR because its forms do not follow a predictable pattern.
>
> A chart showing the subject pronouns and their corresponding verb forms is called a CONJUGATION.

> REMINDER: You should use . . .
> - **vous** to address your teacher
> - **tu** to address a classmate

ILS or *ELLES?*

The French have two ways of saying *they:*

- **ils** refers to two or more males or to a mixed group of males and females
- **elles** refers to two or more females

1 En France

The following students are on vacation in France. Which cities are they in?

▶ Alice . . . à Nice. **Alice est à Nice.**

1. Philippe . . . à Toulon.
2. Nous . . . à Paris.
3. Vous . . . à Marseille.
4. Je . . . à Lyon.
5. Tu . . . à Tours.
6. Michèle et Francine . . . à Lille.
7. Éric et Vincent . . . à Strasbourg.
8. Ma cousine . . . à Toulouse.
9. Mon copain . . . à Bordeaux.

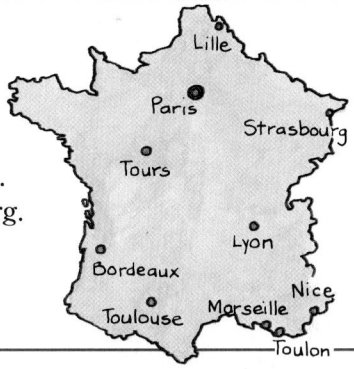

Vocabulaire: *Où?*

Où est Cécile? *Where is Cécile?*

Elle est . . .

ici *(here)*
à Paris *(in Paris)*
en classe *(in class)*
en vacances *(on vacation)*
au café *(at the café)*
à la maison *(at home)*
là *(here, there)*
à Boston
en ville *(downtown, in town, in the city)*
en France *(in France)*
au restaurant
là-bas *(over there)*
à Québec
au cinéma *(at the movies)*

2 À Nice

Catherine is spending her summer vacation in Nice at the home of her pen pal Stéphanie Lambert. Catherine has met many different people and is asking them various questions. Complete her questions with **Tu es** or **Vous êtes,** as appropriate.

▶ *(Stéphanie's brother)* . . . en vacances?
Tu es en vacances?

▶ *(Monsieur Lambert)* . . . de *(from)* Tours?
Vous êtes de Tours?

1. *(Mélanie, a friend of Stéphanie's)* . . . canadienne?
2. *(Olivier, Stéphanie's boyfriend)* . . . souvent *(often)* avec Stéphanie?
3. *(Monsieur Tardif, the neighbor)* . . . en vacances?
4. *(the mailman)* . . . de Nice?
5. *(Frédéric, Stéphanie's young cousin)* . . . souvent à Nice?
6. *(a woman in the park)* . . . française?
7. *(a little girl at the beach)* . . . en vacances?
8. *(a man reading* Time *magazine)* . . . américain?

3 Où sont-ils?

Corinne is wondering if some of the people she knows are in certain places. Tell her she is right, using **il, elle, ils,** or **elles** in your answers.

▶ —Ta cousine est à Chicago?
—Oui, elle est à Chicago.

▶ —Pierre et Vincent sont au café?
—Oui, ils sont au café.

1. Stéphanie est à Lyon?
2. Monsieur Thomas est à San Francisco?
3. Suzanne et Monique sont à Genève?
4. Cécile et Charlotte sont au café?
5. Ta soeur est en ville?
6. Ton cousin est en vacances?
7. Claire, Alice et Éric sont au cinéma?
8. Monsieur et Madame Joli sont à Montréal?

4 Où?

You want to know where certain people are. A classmate will answer you on the basis of the illustrations.

▶ **—Où est Céline?**
—Elle est à New York.

B. Les questions à réponse affirmative ou négative

The sentences on the left are statements. The sentences on the right are questions. These questions are called YES/NO QUESTIONS because they can be answered by *yes* or *no.* Note how the French questions begin with **est-ce que.**

STATEMENTS	YES/NO QUESTIONS	
Stéphanie est ici.	**Est-ce que** Stéphanie est ici?	*Is Stéphanie here?*
Tu es français.	**Est-ce que** tu es français?	*Are you French?*
Paul et Marc sont au café.	**Est-ce que** Paul et Marc sont au café?	*Are Paul and Marc at the café?*
Tu veux dîner avec moi.	**Est-ce que** tu veux dîner avec moi?	*Do you want to have dinner with me?*

Yes/no questions can be formed according to the pattern:

est-ce que + STATEMENT?	**Est-ce que** Pierre est ici?
↓	
est-ce qu' (+ VOWEL SOUND)	**Est-ce qu'**il est en ville?

➡ In yes/no questions, the voice goes up at the end of the sentence.

Est-ce que Paul et Florence sont au café?

➡ In casual conversation, yes/no questions can be formed without **est-ce que** simply by letting your voice rise at the end of the sentence.

Tu es français? Cécile est en ville?

OBSERVATION: When you expect someone to agree with you, another way to form a yes/no question is to add the tag **n'est-ce pas** at the end of the sentence.

Tu es américain, **n'est-ce pas?**	*You are American,* ***aren't you?***
Tu aimes parler français, **n'est-ce pas?**	*You like to speak French,* ***don't you?***
Vous êtes d'accord, **n'est-ce pas?**	*You agree,* ***don't you?***

5 Nationalités

You are attending an international music camp. Ask about the nationalities of the other participants.

▶ Marc/canadien? **Est-ce que Marc est canadien?**

1. Jim/américain?
2. Luisa/mexicaine?
3. Paul et Philippe/français?
4. tu/canadien?
5. vous/anglais?
6. Anne/française?
7. Ellen et Carol/américaines?

Expressions pour la conversation

How to answer a yes/no question:

Oui!	*Yes!*	**Non!**	*No!*
Mais oui!	*Sure!*	**Mais non!**	*Of course not!*
Bien sûr!	*Of course!*		
Peut-être . . .	*Maybe . . .*		

6 Conversation

Ask your classmates the following questions. They will answer, using an expression from **Expressions pour la conversation.**

▶ Ton cousin est français?

1. Ta mère est à la maison?
2. Ta cousine est en France?
3. Ton copain est en classe?
4. Tu veux dîner avec moi?
5. Tu veux jouer au tennis avec moi?

C. La négation

Compare the affirmative and negative sentences below:

AFFIRMATIVE	NEGATIVE	
Je **suis** américain.	Je **ne suis pas** français.	*I'**m not** French.*
Nous **sommes** en classe.	Nous **ne sommes pas** en vacances.	*We **are not** on vacation.*
Claire **est** là-bas.	Elle **n'est pas** ici.	*She **is not** here.*
Vous **êtes** à Paris.	Vous **n'êtes pas** à Lyon.	*You **are not** in Lyon.*
Tu **es** d'accord avec moi.	Tu **n'es pas** d'accord avec Marc.	*You **do not** agree with Marc.*

Negative sentences are formed as follows:

SUBJECT + **ne** + VERB + **pas** . . . ↓ **n'** (+ VOWEL SOUND)	Éric et Anne **ne** sont **pas** là. Michèle **n'**est **pas** avec moi.

7 Non!

Answer the following questions negatively.

▶ —Est-ce que tu es français (française)?
—**Non, je ne suis pas français (française).**

1. Est-ce que tu es canadien (canadienne)?
2. Est-ce que tu es à Québec?
3. Est-ce que tu es à la maison?
4. Est-ce que tu es au café?
5. Est-ce que tu es en vacances?
6. Est-ce que tu es au cinéma?

8 D'accord

It is raining. François suggests to his friends that they go to the movies. Say who agrees and who does not, using the expression **être d'accord.**

▶ ☹ Philippe

▶ ☺ Hélène

1. ☺ nous
2. ☺ je
3. ☹ tu
4. ☺ Patrick et Marc
5. ☹ Claire et Stéphanie
6. ☹ vous
7. ☺ ma copine
8. ☹ mon frère

Vocabulaire: Mots utiles *(Useful words)*

à	*at*	Je suis **à** la maison **à** dix heures.
	in	Nous sommes **à** Paris.
de	*from*	Vous êtes **de** San Francisco.
	of	Voici une photo **de** Paris.
et	*and*	Anne **et** Sophie sont en vacances.
ou	*or*	Qui est-ce? Juliette **ou** Sophie?
avec	*with*	Philippe est **avec** Pauline.
pour	*for*	Je veux travailler **pour** Monsieur Martin.
mais	*but*	Je ne suis pas français, **mais** j'aime parler français.

➡ **De** becomes **d'** before a vowel sound:
Patrick est **de** Lyon. François est **d'**Annecy.

9 Le mot juste *(The right word)*

Complete the sentences below with the word in parentheses that fits logically.

1. Monsieur Moreau est en France. Aujourd'hui, il est . . . Lyon. (à/de)
2. Martine est canadienne. Elle est . . . Montréal. (de/et)
3. Florence n'est pas ici. Elle est . . . Jean-Claude. (et/avec)
4. Alice . . . Paul sont au restaurant. (avec/et)
5. Jean-Pierre n'est pas à la maison. Il est au café . . . au cinéma. (ou/et)
6. J'aime jouer au tennis . . . je ne veux pas jouer avec toi. (ou/mais)
7. Je dois travailler . . . mon père. (pour/à)

10 Être ou ne pas être *(To be or not to be)*

We cannot be in different places at the same time. Express this according to the model.

▶ Aline est en ville. (ici)
Aline n'est pas ici.

1. Frédéric est là-bas. (à la maison)
2. Nous sommes en classe. (au restaurant)
3. Tu es à Nice. (à Toulon)
4. Vous êtes au café. (au cinéma)
5. Jérôme est avec Sylvie. (avec Catherine)
6. Juliette et Sophie sont avec Éric. (avec Marc)

Prononciation /a/

La voyelle /a/

chat

The letter "**a**" alone always represents the sound /a/ as in the English word *ah*. It never has the sound of "*a*" as in English words like *class, date,* or *cinema*.

Répétez: **chat ça va à la là-bas avec ami voilà**
classe café salade dame date Madame Canada

Anne est au Canada avec Madame Laval.

À votre tour!

1 Allô!

Jacques is phoning some friends. Match his questions on the left with his friends' answers on the right.

1. Où es-tu?
2. Où est ta soeur?
3. Est-ce que ton frère est à la maison?
4. Tes parents sont en vacances, n'est-ce pas?
5. Ta soeur est avec une copine?

a. Non, il est au cinéma.
b. Oui, elles sont au restaurant.
c. Je suis à la maison.
d. Elle est en classe.
e. Oui! Ils sont à Paris.

2 Où sont-ils?

Read what the following people are saying and decide where they are.

▶ Anne et Éric sont au café.

▶ **Anne et Éric**

1. nous

2. les touristes

3. vous

4. tu

5. Paul

3 Créa-dialogue

You are working for a student magazine in France. Your assignment is to interview tourists who are visiting Paris. Ask them where they are from. (Make sure to address the people appropriately as **tu** or **vous.**) Remember: The symbol "??" means you may invent your own responses.

Nationalité	Villes *(Cities)*
▶ anglaise	Londres? *(London)* Liverpool

▶ — **Bonjour. Vous êtes anglaise?**
— **Oui, je suis anglaise.**
— **Est-ce que vous êtes de Londres?**
— **Mais non, je ne suis pas de Londres. Je suis de Liverpool.**

Nationalité	Villes
1 américaine	New York? Washington
2 canadien	Québec? Montréal
3 française	Paris? Nice
4 mexicain	Mexico? Puebla
5 ??	?? ??
6 ??	?? ??

4 Composition: Et toi?

Write a short paragraph about yourself and your friends.

1. Say what city you are from. **(Je suis de . . .)**
2. Say what city your father or your mother is from. **(Mon père / ma mère est de . . .)**
3. Say where one of your friends is from. **(Mon copain / ma copine . . .)**
4. Name an activity you like to do with a friend. **(J'aime . . . avec . . .)**
5. Name an activity you want to do with two friends. **(Je veux . . .)**
6. Name an activity you would like to do with one of your relatives. **(Je voudrais . . .)**

5 Composition: Personnellement

On a separate piece of paper, write where you are and where you are not at each of the following times.

▶ à 9 heures du matin
- à 4 heures
- à 7 heures du soir
- samedi
- dimanche
- en juillet

LEÇON 15

Une boum

Jean-Marc has been invited to a party. He is trying to decide whether to bring Béatrice or Valérie. First he talks to Béatrice.

JEAN-MARC:	Dis, Béatrice, tu aimes danser?	*Hey*
BÉATRICE:	Bien sûr, j'aime danser!	
JEAN-MARC:	Est-ce que tu danses bien?	
BÉATRICE:	Oui, je danse très, très bien.	*very well*
JEAN-MARC:	Et ta cousine Valérie? Est-ce qu'elle danse bien?	
BÉATRICE:	Non, elle ne danse pas très bien.	
JEAN-MARC:	Alors, c'est Valérie que j'invite à la boum.	*So / that / party*
BÉATRICE:	Mais pourquoi elle? Pourquoi pas moi?	*why*
JEAN-MARC:	Écoute, Béatrice, je ne sais pas danser! Alors, je préfère inviter une fille qui ne danse pas très bien. C'est normal, non?	*don't know how / So*

Compréhension: Vrai ou faux?

Read the following statements and say whether they are true (**C'est vrai!**) or false (**C'est faux!**).

1. Béatrice aime danser.
2. Elle danse bien.
3. Valérie danse très bien.
4. Jean-Marc invite Béatrice.
5. Il invite Valérie.

NOTE CULTURELLE

Une boum

On weekends, French teenagers like to go to parties that are organized at a friend's home. Often the guests contribute something to the buffet: sandwiches or soft drinks. There is also a lot of music and dancing. (French teenagers love to dance!)

These informal parties have different names according to the age group of the participants. For students at a **collège** (or junior high), a party is known as **une boum.** For older students at a **lycée** (or high school), it is called **une soirée.**

A. Les verbes en *-er:* le singulier

Many French verbs end in **-er** in the infinitive. Most of these verbs are conjugated like **parler** *(to speak)* and **habiter** *(to live)*. Note the forms of the present tense of these verbs in the singular. Pay attention to their endings.

> ***Learning about language***
> The basic form of the VERB is the INFINITIVE:
> **jouer** *(to play)* **travailler** *(to work)*
> In French dictionaries, verbs are listed by their infinitives.

INFINITIVE	**parler**	**habiter**	ENDINGS
STEM	**parl-**	**habit-**	
PRESENT TENSE (SINGULAR)	Je **parle** français. Tu **parles** anglais. Il / Elle **parle** espagnol.	J' **habite** à Paris. Tu **habites** à Boston. Il / Elle **habite** à Madrid.	**-e** **-es** **-e**

The present tense forms of **-er** verbs consist of two parts:

STEM + ENDING

- The STEM does not change. It is the infinitive minus **-er:**
  parler **parl-** **habiter** **habit-**
- The ENDINGS change with the subject:
  je → **-e** **tu** → **-es** **il / elle** → **-e**

➡ The above endings are silent.

➡ **Je** becomes **j'** before a vowel sound.
je parle **j'**habite

> ***Learning about language***
> Verbs conjugated like **parler** and **habiter** follow a *predictable pattern*.
> They are called REGULAR VERBS.

1 Curiosité

At the party, Olivier wants to learn more about Isabelle. She answers his questions affirmatively. Play both roles.

▶ parler anglais?

1. parler espagnol?
2. habiter à Paris?
3. étudier ici?
4. jouer au volley?
5. jouer au basket?
6. chanter?

Vocabulaire: Les verbes en *-er*

Verbs you already know:

chanter	*to sing*	**nager**	*to swim*
danser	*to dance*	**parler**	*to speak, talk*
dîner	*to have dinner*	**regarder**	*to watch, look at*
écouter	*to listen (to)*	**téléphoner**	*to phone, call*
étudier	*to study*	**travailler**	*to work*
jouer	*to play*	**voyager**	*to travel*
manger	*to eat*		

New verbs:

aimer	*to like*	Tu **aimes** Paris?
habiter	*to live*	Philippe **habite** à Toulouse?
inviter	*to invite*	J'**invite** un copain.
organiser	*to organize*	Sophie **organise** une **boum** *(party)*.
visiter	*to visit (places)*	Hélène **visite** Québec.

➡ **Regarder** has two meanings:

to look (at) Paul **regarde** Cécile.
to watch Cécile **regarde** la télé.

➡ Note the construction **téléphoner à:**

Hélène **téléphone**	**à**	Marc.
Hélène calls	. . .	*Marc.*

➡ Note the constructions with **regarder** and **écouter:**

Philippe **regarde**	. . .	Alice.
Philippe looks	*at*	*Alice.*

Alice **écoute**	. . .	le professeur.
Alice listens	*to*	*the teacher.*

2 Quelle activité?

Describe what the following people are doing by completing the sentences with one of the verbs below. Be logical in your choice of activity.

chanter écouter parler travailler manger voyager regarder inviter

1. Je . . . un sandwich. Tu . . . une pizza.
2. Tu . . . anglais. Je . . . français.
3. Éric . . . la radio. Claire . . . un compact (un CD).
4. Jean-Paul . . . la télé. Tu . . . un match de tennis.
5. M. Simon . . . en *(by)* bus. Mme Dupont . . . en train.
6. Nicolas . . . Marie à la boum. Tu . . . Alain.
7. Mlle Thomas . . . dans *(in)* un hôpital. Je . . . dans un supermarché *(supermarket)*.
8. Mick Jagger . . . bien. Est-ce que tu . . . bien?

3 Le télescope

Curious Georges has set up a telescope to observe what his neighbors are doing. Describe each person's activity.

▶ **Monsieur Thomas dîne.**

4 Où sont-ils?

You want to know where the following people are. A classmate will answer, telling you where the people are and what they are doing.

▶ Jacques? (en classe/étudier)

1. Pauline? (au restaurant/dîner)
2. Véronique? (à la maison/téléphoner)
3. Mme Dupont? (en ville/travailler)
4. M. Lemaire? (en France/voyager)
5. Jean-Claude? (à Paris/visiter la tour Eiffel)
6. André? (au Tennis Club/jouer au tennis)
7. Alice? (à l'Olympic Club/nager)

B. Les verbes en *-er:* le pluriel

Note the plural forms of **parler** and **habiter,** paying attention to the endings.

INFINITIVE	**parler**	**habiter**	ENDINGS
STEM	**parl-**	**habit-**	
PRESENT TENSE (PLURAL)	Nous **parlons** français. Vous **parlez** anglais. Ils/Elles **parlent** espagnol.	Nous **habitons** à Québec. Vous **habitez** à Chicago. Ils/Elles **habitent** à Caracas.	**-ons** **-ez** **-ent**

➡ In the present tense, the plural endings of **-er** verbs are:

nous → **-ons** vous → **-ez** ils/elles → **-ent**

➡ The **-ent** ending is silent.

➡ Note the liaison when the verb begins with a vowel sound:

Nous étudions. Vous invitez Thomas. Ils habitent en France. Elles aiment Paris.

OBSERVATION: When the infinitive of the verb ends in **-ger,** the **nous**-form ends in **-geons.**

nager: nous na**geons** manger: nous man**geons** voyager: nous voya**geons**

5 Qui?

Stéphanie is speaking to or about her friends. Complete her sentences with **tu, elle, vous,** or **ils.**

▶ . . . étudient à Toulouse.
Ils étudient à Toulouse.

1. . . . habitez à Tours.
2. . . . aime Paris.
3. . . . étudiez à Tours.
4. . . . aiment danser.
5. . . . organisent une boum.
6. . . . parlez espagnol.
7. . . . téléphone à Jean-Pierre.
8. . . . invites un copain.
9. . . . dîne avec Cécile.
10. . . . invitent Monique.

6 À la boum

At a party, Olivier is talking to two Canadian students, Monique and her friend. Monique answers yes to his questions.

▶ parler français?

1. parler anglais?
2. habiter à Québec?
3. étudier à Montréal?
4. voyager en France?
5. voyager en train?
6. visiter Paris?
7. aimer Paris?
8. aimer la France?

7 Le camp français

At summer camp, everything is organized according to a schedule. Describe the activities of the following campers by completing the sentences according to the illustrations.

▶ À cinq heures, Alice et Marc . . . **À cinq heures, Alice et Marc jouent au volley.**

1. À neuf heures, nous . . .
2. À quatre heures, vous . . .
3. À huit heures, Véronique et Pierre . . .
4. À sept heures, nous . . .
5. À trois heures, Thomas et François . . .
6. À six heures, vous . . .

8 Un voyage à Paris

A group of American students are visiting Paris. During their stay, they do all of the following things:

voyager en bus → *visiter la tour Eiffel* → téléphoner à un copain → *dîner au restaurant* → inviter une copine → *écouter un opéra*

Describe the trips of the following people.

▶ Jim **Il voyage en bus, il visite la tour Eiffel . . .**

1. Linda 2. Paul et Louise 3. nous 4. vous

C. Le présent des verbes en *-er:* forme affirmative et forme négative

FORMS

Compare the affirmative and negative forms of **parler.**

AFFIRMATIVE	NEGATIVE
je **parle** tu **parles** il/elle **parle**	je **ne parle pas** tu **ne parles pas** il/elle **ne parle pas**
nous **parlons** vous **parlez** ils/elles **parlent**	nous **ne parlons pas** vous **ne parlez pas** ils/elles **ne parlent pas**

REMEMBER: The negative form of the verb follows the pattern:

SUBJECT + **ne** + VERB + **pas** ↓ **n'** (+ VOWEL SOUND)	Il **ne** travaille **pas** ici. Je **n'**invite **pas** Pierre.

Il ne travaille pas.

Ils n'écoutent pas.

Elle ne chante pas bien.

USES

In the present tense, French verbs have several English equivalents:

Je **joue** au tennis. { *I* ***play*** *tennis.*
I ***do play*** *tennis.*
I ***am playing*** *tennis.* }

Je **ne joue pas** au tennis. { *I* ***do not play*** *tennis. (I* ***don't*** *play tennis.)*
I ***am not playing*** *tennis. (I'****m not playing*** *tennis.)* }

Studying French helps you better appreciate how the English language works.

9 Non!

One cannot do everything. From the following list of activities, select at least three that you do *not* do.

▶ **Je ne joue pas au bridge.**

- parler espagnol
- étudier à Paris
- parler italien
- habiter à Québec
- danser le tango
- étudier le japonais
- jouer au hockey
- nager en hiver
- jouer au water-polo
- dîner avec le prof
- jouer au bridge
- travailler dans un restaurant

10 Pas aujourd'hui

Today the following people are tired and are not doing what they usually do. Express this according to the model.

▶ Pierre joue au tennis.
Aujourd'hui, il ne joue pas au tennis.

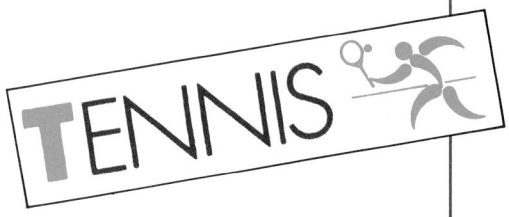

1. Je joue au foot.
2. Tu étudies.
3. Madame Simonet travaille.
4. Vous dînez à la maison.
5. Marc téléphone à Martine.
6. Nous nageons.
7. Jacques et Florence étudient.

11 Un jeu: Weekend!

On weekends, people like to do different things. For each person, pick an activity and say what that person does. Select another activity and say what that person does not do.

▶ **Antoine et Isabelle dansent.**
Ils ne regardent pas la télé.

je
tu
ma cousine
nous
Antoine et Isabelle
Monsieur Leblanc
Madame Jolivet
vous
le professeur

Vocabulaire: Mots utiles

bien	*well*	Je joue **bien** au tennis.
très bien	*very well*	Je ne chante pas **très bien.**
mal	*badly, poorly*	Tu joues **mal** au volley.
beaucoup	*a lot, much, very much*	Paul aime **beaucoup** voyager.
un peu	*a little, a little bit*	Nous parlons **un peu** français.
souvent	*often*	Charles invite **souvent** Nathalie.
toujours	*always*	Je travaille **toujours** en été.
aussi	*also, too*	Je téléphone à Marc. Je téléphone **aussi** à Véronique.
maintenant	*now*	J'étudie **maintenant.**
rarement	*rarely, seldom*	Vous voyagez **rarement.**

➡ In French, the above expressions *never* come *between* the subject and the verb. They usually come *after* the verb. Compare their positions in French and English.

Nous parlons **toujours** français.	*We **always** speak French.*
Tu joues **bien** au tennis.	*You play tennis **well.***

12 Expression personnelle

Complete the following sentences with an expression from the list below.

bien | mal | très bien | toujours | souvent | rarement | un peu | beaucoup

1. Je chante . . .
2. Je nage . . .
3. Je regarde . . . la télé.
4. Je mange . . .
5. Je voyage . . . en bus.
6. Le prof parle . . . français.
7. Nous parlons . . . français en classe.
8. Les Rolling Stones chantent . . .
9. Michael Jordan joue . . . au basket.
10. Les Yankees jouent . . . au baseball.

Expressions pour la conversation

How to express approval or regret:

Super!	*Terrific!*	Tu parles français? **Super!**
Dommage!	*Too bad!*	Tu ne joues pas au tennis? **Dommage!**

13 Conversation

Ask your classmates if they do the following things. Then express approval or regret, according to their answers.

▶ parler français? —**Est-ce que tu parles français?**
—**Oui, je parle français. (Non, je ne parle pas français.)**
—**Super! (Dommage!)**

1. parler espagnol?
2. jouer au tennis?
3. danser bien?
4. voyager beaucoup?
5. dîner souvent au restaurant?
6. inviter souvent ton copain?

D. La construction: verbe + infinitif

Note the use of the infinitive in the following sentences.

J'aime **parler** français.	*I like **to speak** French. I like **speaking** French.*
Nous aimons **voyager.**	*We like **to travel.** We like **traveling.***
Tu n'aimes pas **étudier.**	*You don't like **to study.** You don't like **studying.***
Ils n'aiment pas **danser.**	*They don't like **to dance.** They don't like **dancing.***

To express what they like and don't like to do, the French use these constructions:

SUBJECT + PRESENT TENSE + INFINITIVE . . . of **aimer**	SUBJECT + **n'** + PRESENT TENSE + **pas** + INFINITIVE . . . of **aimer**
Nous **aimons** **voyager.**	Nous **n'aimons pas** **voyager.**

➡ Note that in this construction, the verb **aimer** may be affirmative or negative:
AFFIRMATIVE: Jacques **aime** voyager. NEGATIVE: Philippe **n'aime pas** voyager.

➡ The above construction is used in questions: Est-ce que Paul **aime voyager?**

OBSERVATION: The infinitive is also used after the following expressions:

Je préfère . . .	*I prefer . . .*	**Je préfère travailler.**
Je voudrais . . .	*I would like . . .*	**Je voudrais voyager.**
Je (ne) veux (pas) . . .	*I (don't) want . . .*	**Je veux jouer** au foot.
Est-ce que tu veux . . .	*Do you want . . .*	**Est-ce que tu veux danser?**
Je (ne) peux (pas) . . .	*I can (I can't) . . .*	**Je ne peux pas dîner** avec toi.
Je dois . . .	*I have to . . .*	**Je dois étudier.**

14 Dialogue

Ask your classmates if they like to do the following things.

▶ chanter?
—Est-ce que tu aimes chanter?
—Oui, j'aime chanter. (Non, je n'aime pas chanter.)

1. étudier?
2. voyager?
3. téléphoner?
4. danser?
5. parler français en classe?
6. nager en été?
7. nager en hiver?
8. travailler le week-end *(on weekends)*?

15 Une excellente raison *(An excellent reason)*

The following people are doing certain things. Say that they like these activities.

▶ Thomas voyage. **Il aime voyager.**

1. Monique chante.
2. Charles étudie la musique.
3. Henri téléphone.
4. Isabelle organise une boum.
5. Marc et Sophie nagent.
6. Annie et Vincent dansent.
7. Lise et Rose jouent au frisbee.
8. Éric et Denis écoutent la radio.
9. Nous travaillons.
10. Nous parlons espagnol.
11. Vous regardez la télé.
12. Vous mangez.

Prononciation

Les voyelles /i/ et /u/

/u/ **où?** /i/ **ici!**

The vowel sounds /i/ and /u/ are easy to say. Remember to pronounce the French "**i**" as in **Mimi** and not as in the English *him*.

Répétez:

/i/ **ici Philippe il Mimi Sylvie visite**
Philippe visite Paris avec Sylvie.

/u/ **où nous vous écoute joue toujours**
Vous jouez au foot avec nous?

À votre tour!

1 Allô!

Sophie is phoning some friends. Match her questions on the left with her friends' answers on the right.

1. Est-ce que Marc est canadien?
2. Est-ce que tu joues au tennis?
3. Ton frère est à la maison?
4. Ta mère est en vacances?
5. Tu invites Christine et Juliette à la boum?

a. Non, elle travaille.
b. Oui, mais pas très bien.
c. Bien sûr! Elles aiment beaucoup danser.
d. Oui, il habite à Montréal.
e. Non, il dîne au restaurant avec un copain.

2 Créa-dialogue

Find out how frequently your classmates do the following activities. They will respond using one of the expressions on the scale.

NON	OUI				
	un peu	→	souvent	→	beaucoup

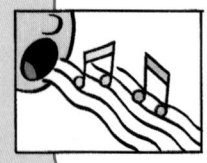

▶ — Robert, est-ce que tu joues au tennis?
— Non, je ne joue pas au tennis.
— Est-ce que tu écoutes la radio?
— Oui, j'écoute souvent la radio.

3 Qu'est-ce qu'ils font?

(What do they do?)

Look at what the following students have put in their lockers and say what they like to do.

4 Message illustré

Marc wrote about certain activities, using pictures. On a separate sheet, write out his description replacing these pictures with the missing words.

À la maison, ma soeur Catherine  à une copine. Mon frère Éric  . En général, nous  à sept heures et demie. Après° le dîner, mes° parents  . Moi, j'  pour la classe de français.

En vacances, nous  . Je 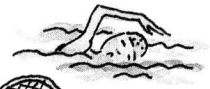 . Éric et Catherine  . Parfois° mes parents  au restaurant.

Après *After* **mes** *my* **Parfois** *Sometimes*

5 Point de vue personnel

Select one of the following situations. On a separate sheet of paper, write two things you do and one thing you do not do in that situation. Use complete sentences.

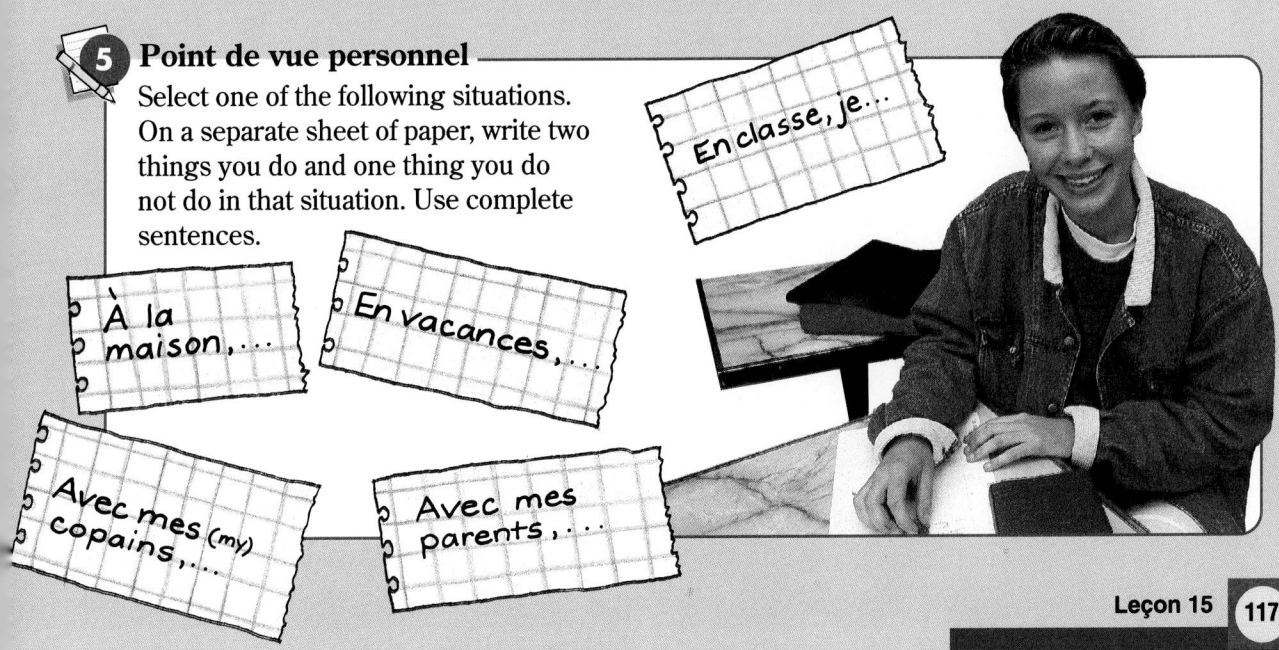

LEÇON 16

Une interview

Nicolas is a reporter for *La Gazette des Étudiants,* the student newspaper. He has decided to write an article on the foreign students who attend his school. Today he is interviewing Fatou, a student from Senegal.

NICOLAS:	Bonjour, Fatou. Est-ce que je peux te poser quelques questions?	*ask you some questions*
FATOU:	Oui, bien sûr.	
NICOLAS:	Tu es sénégalaise, n'est-ce pas?	*Senegalese*
FATOU:	Oui, je suis sénégalaise.	
NICOLAS:	Où est-ce que tu habites?	
FATOU:	Je suis de Dakar, mais maintenant j'habite à Paris avec ma famille.	
NICOLAS:	Pourquoi est-ce que vous habitez à Paris?	*Why*
FATOU:	Parce que ma mère travaille pour l'Unesco.	*Because*
NICOLAS:	Est-ce que tu aimes Paris?	
FATOU:	J'adore Paris.	
NICOLAS:	Qu'est-ce que tu fais le weekend?	*What do you do on weekends?*
FATOU:	Ça dépend! Je regarde la télé ou je joue au tennis avec mes copains.	*That* *my*
NICOLAS:	Merci beaucoup, Fatou.	
FATOU:	C'est tout?	*all*
NICOLAS:	Oui, c'est tout!	

NOTES CULTURELLES

1 Le Sénégal

Senegal is a country in western Africa, whose capital is Dakar. Its population includes seventeen different tribes, all speaking their own dialects. Because of the historical and cultural ties between Senegal and France, French has been adopted as the official language.

Most of the people of Senegal are Muslims. Some common names are **Awa** and **Fatou** (for girls), **Babacar** and **Mamadou** (for boys).

FATOU:	Bon. Alors, maintenant c'est mon tour! Est-ce que je peux te poser une question?	*So / turn*
NICOLAS:	Bien sûr!	
FATOU:	Qu'est-ce que tu fais samedi?	
NICOLAS:	Euh . . . je ne sais pas.	*I don't know*
FATOU:	Alors, est-ce que tu veux aller à un concert de musique africaine?	*to go*
NICOLAS:	Avec qui?	
FATOU:	Avec moi, bien sûr!	
NICOLAS:	D'accord! Où? Quand? Et à quelle heure?	*When*

2 L'Unesco

UNESCO (United Nations Educational Scientific and Cultural Organization) was founded in 1946 to promote international cooperation in education, science, and the arts. The organization has its headquarters in Paris and is staffed by people from all member countries.

Compréhension: Vrai ou faux?

Read the following statements and say whether they are true (**C'est vrai!**) or false (**C'est faux!**).

1. Fatou est française.
2. Elle habite à Paris.
3. Le père de Fatou travaille pour l'Unesco.
4. Le weekend, Fatou aime jouer au tennis.
5. Nicolas invite Fatou à un concert.
6. Fatou accepte l'invitation.

A. Les questions d'information

The questions below ask for specific information and are called INFORMATION QUESTIONS. The INTERROGATIVE EXPRESSIONS in heavy print indicate what kind of information is requested.

—**Où** est-ce que tu habites?	***Where** do you live?*
—J'habite **à Nice.**	*I live **in Nice.***
—**À quelle heure** est-ce que vous dînez?	***At what time** do you eat dinner?*
—Nous dînons **à sept heures.**	*We eat **at seven.***

In French, information questions may be formed according to the pattern:

INTERROGATIVE EXPRESSION	+ **est-ce que**	+ SUBJECT	+ VERB . . . ?
À quelle heure	**est-ce que**	vous	travaillez?

➡ **Est-ce que** becomes **est-ce qu'** before a vowel sound.
Quand **est-ce qu'**Alice et Roger dînent?

➡ In information questions, your voice rises on the interrogative expression and then falls until the last syllable.

Quand est-ce que tu travailles?

À quelle heure est-ce que vous dînez?

OBSERVATION: In casual conversation, French speakers frequently form information questions by placing the interrogative expression at the end of the sentence. The voice rises on the interrogative expression.

Vous habitez **où?**

Vous dînez **à quelle heure?**

Vocabulaire: Expressions interrogatives

où	*where?*	**Où** est-ce que vous travaillez?
quand?	*when?*	**Quand** est-ce que ton copain organise une boum?
à quelle heure?	*at what time?*	**À quelle heure** est-ce que tu regardes la télé?
comment?	*how?*	**Comment** est-ce que tu chantes? Bien ou mal?
pourquoi?	*why?*	—**Pourquoi** est-ce que tu étudies le français?
parce que	*because*	—**Parce que** je veux voyager en France.

➡ **Parce que** becomes **parce qu'** before a vowel sound.
Juliette invite Olivier **parce qu'**il danse bien.

1 Le Club International

The president of the International Club wants to know where some of the members are from. The secretary tells her where each one lives.

▶ Sylvie (à Québec)
LA PRÉSIDENTE: **Où est-ce que Sylvie habite?**
LE SECRÉTAIRE: **Elle habite à Québec.**

1. Jacques (à Montréal)
2. Awa (à Dakar)
3. Marc et Frédéric (à Toulouse)
4. Jean-Pierre (à Genève)
5. Sophie et Michèle (à Nice)
6. Isabelle (à Paris)

2 Curiosité

At a party in Paris, Nicolas meets Béatrice, a Canadian student. He wants to know more about her. Play both roles.

▶ où / habiter? (à Québec)
NICOLAS: **Où est-ce que tu habites?**
BÉATRICE: **J'habite à Québec.**

1. où/étudier? (à Montréal)
2. où/travailler? (dans [*in*] une pharmacie)
3. quand/parler français? (toujours)
4. quand/parler anglais? (souvent)
5. comment/jouer au tennis? (bien)
6. comment/danser? (très bien)
7. pourquoi/être en France? (parce que j'aime voyager)
8. pourquoi/être à Paris? (parce que j'ai [*I have*] un copain ici)

Expression pour la conversation

How to express surprise or mild doubt:

Ah bon? *Oh? Really?* —Stéphanie organise une boum.
—**Ah bon?** Quand?

3 Au téléphone

When Philippe phones his cousin Michèle, he likes to tell her what his plans are. She asks him a few questions. Play both roles.

▶ organiser une boum (quand? samedi)

1. organiser un pique-nique (quand? dimanche)
2. dîner avec Pauline (quand? lundi)
3. dîner avec Caroline (où? au restaurant Belcour)
4. regarder «Batman» (à quelle heure? à 9 heures)
5. jouer au tennis (quand ? demain)
6. inviter Brigitte (où? à un concert)
7. parler espagnol (comment? assez bien)
8. étudier l'italien (pourquoi? je veux voyager en Italie)

4 Questions personnelles

1. Où est-ce que tu habites? *(name of your city)*
2. Où est-ce que tu étudies? *(name of your school)*
3. À quelle heure est-ce que tu dînes?
4. À quelle heure est-ce que tu regardes la télé?
5. Quand est-ce que tu nages?
6. Quand est-ce que tu joues au tennis? (en mai? en juillet?)
7. Comment est-ce que tu chantes? (bien? très bien? mal?)
8. Comment est-ce que tu nages?

B. Les expressions interrogatives avec *qui*

To ask about PEOPLE, French speakers use the following interrogative expressions:

qui?	*who(m)?*	**Qui** est-ce que tu invites au concert?
à qui? **de qui?**	*to who(m)?* *about who(m)?*	**À qui** est-ce que tu téléphones? **De qui** est-ce que vous parlez?
avec qui? **pour qui?**	*with who(m)?* *for who(m)?*	**Avec qui** est-ce que Pierre étudie? **Pour qui** est-ce que Laure organise la boum?

To ask *who is doing something,* French speakers use the construction:

qui + VERB . . . ?	
Qui habite ici?	***Who** lives here?*
Qui organise la boum?	***Who** is organizing the party?*

5 Précisions *(Details)*

Anne is telling Hélène what certain people are doing. She asks for more details. Play both roles.

▶ Alice dîne. (avec qui? avec une copine)

1. Jean-Pierre téléphone. (à qui? à Sylvie)
2. Frédéric étudie. (avec qui? avec un copain)
3. Madame Masson parle. (à qui? à Madame Bonnot)
4. Monsieur Lambert travaille. (avec qui? avec Monsieur Dumont)
5. Juliette danse. (avec qui? avec Georges)
6. François parle à Michèle. (de qui? de toi)

6 Un sondage *(A poll)*

Take a survey to find out how your classmates spend their free time. Ask who does the following things.

▶ écouter la radio
Qui écoute la radio?

1. voyager souvent
2. aimer chanter
3. nager
4. aimer danser
5. regarder la télé
6. jouer au tennis
7. jouer au foot
8. travailler
9. regarder les clips *(MTV)*
10. parler italien
11. étudier beaucoup
12. visiter souvent New York

7 Questions

Prepare short dialogues with your classmates, using the information in the illustrations.

▶ **—Où est-ce que tu dînes?**
—Je dîne à la maison.

C. *Qu'est-ce que?*

Note the use of the interrogative expression **qu'est-ce que** *(what)* in the questions below.

Qu'est-ce que tu regardes?	Je regarde un match de tennis.
Qu'est-ce qu'Alice mange?	Elle mange une pizza.

To ask *what people are doing,* the French use the following construction:

qu'est-ce que + SUBJECT + VERB + . . . ?	**Qu'est-ce que** tu fais?
↓ **qu'est-ce qu'** (+ VOWEL SOUND)	**Qu'est-ce qu'**elle fait?

8 La Boutique-Musique

People in Column A are at the Boutique-Musique, a local music shop. Use a verb from Column B to ask what they are listening to or looking at. A classmate will answer you, using an item from Column C.

A	B	C
tu	écouter?	une guitare
vous	regarder?	un poster
Alice		un compact (CD) de jazz
Éric		une cassette de rock
Antoine et Claire		un album de Paul Simon

D. Le verbe *faire*

Faire *(to do, make)* is one of the most useful French verbs. It is an IRREGULAR verb since it does not follow a predictable pattern. Note the forms of **faire** in the present tense.

faire *(to do, make)*	
je **fais**	Je **fais** un sandwich.
tu **fais**	Qu'est-ce que tu **fais** maintenant?
il/elle **fait**	Qu'est-ce que ton copain **fait** samedi?
nous **faisons**	Nous **faisons** une pizza.
vous **faites**	Qu'est-ce que vous **faites** ici?
ils/elles **font**	Qu'est-ce qu'elles **font** pour la boum?

Vocabulaire: Expressions avec *faire*		
faire un match	*to play a game (match)*	Mes cousins **font un match** de tennis.
faire une promenade	*to go for a walk*	Caroline **fait une promenade** avec Olivier.
faire un voyage	*to take a trip*	Ma copine **fait un voyage** en France.
faire attention	*to pay attention*	Est-ce que tu **fais attention** quand le professeur parle?

9 La boum de Juliette

Juliette's friends are helping her prepare food for a party. Use the verb **faire** to say what everyone is doing.

▶ Je . . . une crêpe.

1. Nous . . . une salade.
2. Tu . . . une salade de fruits.
3. Vous . . . une tarte *(pie)*.
4. Cécile et Marina . . . un gâteau *(cake)*.
5. Christine . . . une pizza.
6. Marc . . . un sandwich.
7. Patrick et Thomas . . . une omelette.
8. Pierre et Karine . . . une quiche.

10 Qu'est-ce qu'ils font?

Read the descriptions below and say what the people are doing. Use the verb **faire** and an expression from the list below. Be logical.

un voyage *une promenade* *une pizza* *un match* *attention*

▶ Madame Dumont est en Chine.
Elle fait un voyage.

1. Nicolas travaille dans *(in)* un restaurant.
2. Nous sommes en ville.
3. Hélène et Jean-Paul jouent au tennis.
4. Je suis dans la cuisine *(kitchen)*.
5. Marc est dans le train Paris–Nice.
6. Vous jouez au volley.
7. Je suis dans le parc.
8. Monsieur Lambert visite Tokyo.
9. Nous écoutons le prof.

E. L'interrogation avec inversion

Learning about language

In conversational French, questions are usually formed with **est-ce que.** However, when the subject of the sentence is a pronoun, French speakers often use INVERSION, that is, they invert or reverse the order of the subject pronoun and the verb.

REGULAR ORDER: **Vous parlez** français. (SUBJECT VERB)

INVERSION: **Parlez-vous** anglais? (VERB SUBJECT)

Look at the two sets of questions below. They both ask the same thing. Compare the position of the subject pronouns in heavy print.

Est-ce que **tu** parles anglais?	Parles-**tu** anglais?	*Do you speak English?*
Est-ce que **vous** habitez ici?	Habitez-**vous** ici?	*Do you live here?*
Où est-ce que **nous** dînons?	Où dînons-**nous?**	*Where are we having dinner?*
Où est-ce qu'**il** est?	Où est-**il?**	*Where is he?*

Inverted questions are formed according to the patterns:

YES / NO QUESTION	VERB / SUBJECT PRONOUN . . . ?
	Voyagez-vous souvent?

INFORMATION QUESTION	INTERROGATIVE EXPRESSION + VERB / SUBJECT PRONOUN . . . ?
	Avec qui travaillez-vous demain?

➡ In inversion, the verb and the subject pronoun are connected by a hyphen.

OBSERVATION: In inversion, liaison is required before **il/elle** and **ils/elles.** If a verb in the singular ends on a vowel, the letter "**t**" is inserted between the verb and the subject pronoun so that liaison can occur:

Où travaille-**t**-il?	Où travaille-**t**-elle?
Avec qui dîne-**t**-il?	Avec qui dîne-**t**-elle?

11 Conversation

Get better acquainted with your classmates by asking them a few questions. Use inversion.

▶ où / habiter? —**Où habites-tu?**
—**J'habite à (Boston).**

1. à quelle heure / dîner?
2. à quelle heure / regarder la télé?
3. avec qui / parler français?
4. à qui / téléphoner souvent?
5. comment / nager?
6. avec qui / étudier?

Prononciation /y/

La voyelle /y/

Super!

The vowel sound /y/ – represented by the letter "**u**" – does not exist in English. Here is a helpful trick for producing this new sound.

First say the French word **si.** Then round your lips as if to whistle and say **si** with rounded lips: /sy/. Now say **si-per.** Then round your lips as you say the first syllable: **super!**

Répétez: /y/ **super tu étudie bien sûr**
Lucie Luc
Tu étudies avec Lucie.

▶ ▶

À votre tour!

1 Allô!

Awa is phoning some friends. Match her questions on the left with her friends' answers on the right.

1. Qu'est-ce que tu fais?
2. Qu'est-ce que vous faites samedi?
3. Où est ton père?
4. Quand est-ce que tu veux jouer au tennis avec moi?
5. Qui est-ce que tu invites au cinéma?
6. Pourquoi est-ce que tu étudies l'anglais?

a. Il fait une promenade.
b. Ma cousine Alice.
c. Dimanche. D'accord?
d. J'étudie.
e. Nous faisons un match de tennis.
f. Parce que je voudrais habiter à New York.

2 Les questions

The following people are answering questions. Read what they say and figure out what questions they were asked.

▶ **Comment est-ce que tu chantes?**

1

2

3

4

5

6

3 Créa-dialogue

Ask your classmates what they do on different days of the week. Carry out conversations similar to the model. Note: "??" means you can invent your own answers.

▶ —Qu'est-ce que tu fais lundi?
—Je joue au tennis.
—Ah bon? À quelle heure est-ce que tu joues?
—À deux heures.
—Et avec qui?
—Avec Anne-Marie.

▶	lundi	mardi	mercredi	jeudi	vendredi	samedi	dimanche
ACTIVITÉ						??	??
À QUELLE HEURE?	2 heures	6 heures	??	??	??	??	??
AVEC QUI?	avec Anne-Marie	avec un copain	??	??	??	??	??

4 Faisons connaissance!

(Let's get acquainted!)

Get better acquainted with a classmate that you don't know very well. Ask questions in French. For instance:

- Where does he/she live?
- Does he/she study much at home?
- Does he/she speak French at home? (with whom?)
- Does he/she watch TV? (at what time?)
- Does he/she like to phone? (whom? [**à qui?**])

5 Interview

A famous rock star is visiting the United States. You are going to interview her for your school paper. Write out five questions you would want to ask the singer, addressing her as **vous.** For example, you may want to know . . .

- where she lives in France
- where she is singing
- why she is visiting your city
- how she is traveling
- how (well) she speaks English

6 Curiosité

Imagine that a French friend has just made the following statements. For each one, write down three or four related questions you could ask him or her.

ENTRACTE 4

Vive la différence!

Les activités quotidiennes

Nous sommes américains, français, anglais, canadiens . . . Nos° cultures ont° beaucoup de points communs, mais elles ne sont pas identiques.

Parlons° de la vie quotidienne.° Nous faisons les mêmes choses,° mais souvent nous faisons ces° choses un peu différemment.° Voici plusieurs° questions. Répondez° à ces questions. À votre avis,° quelles° sont les réponses des jeunes Français?°

1 Quel jour de la semaine est-ce que vous préférez?
- le lundi
- le vendredi
- le samedi
- le dimanche

Et les Français, quel jour est-ce qu'ils préfèrent?

2 Pendant° la semaine, qu'est-ce que vous préférez faire quand vous n'étudiez pas?
- Je préfère regarder la télé.
- Je préfère lire.°
- Je préfère jouer au basket.
- Je préfère téléphoner à mes° copains.

Et les jeunes Français, qu'est-ce qu'ils préfèrent faire?

3 Voici quatre sports. Quel sport est-ce que vous pratiquez le plus?°
- Je nage.
- Je joue au basket.
- Je fais du jogging.
- Je joue au football.

Et les jeunes Français, quel sport est-ce qu'ils pratiquent le plus?

4 À quelle heure est-ce que vous dînez en général?
- entre° cinq heures et demie et six heures
- entre six heures et sept heures
- entre sept heures et huit heures
- après huit heures

Et les Français, à quelle heure est-ce qu'ils dînent?

5 En moyenne,° combien d'heures° par jour° est-ce que vous regardez la télé?
- une heure
- deux heures
- trois heures
- quatre heures ou plus°

Et les jeunes Français? Combien d'heures par jour est-ce qu'ils regardent la télé?

6 Qu'est-ce que vous préférez regarder à la télé?
- les sports
- les films
- la publicité°
- les feuilletons°

Et les jeunes Français, qu'est-ce qu'ils préfèrent regarder?

Et les Français?
1. Ils préfèrent le samedi. 2. Ils préfèrent regarder la télé. 3. Ils jouent au football. 4. Ils dînent entre sept heures et huit heures. 5. Ils regardent la télé deux heures par jour. 6. Ils préfèrent regarder les films.

Nos *Our* **ont** *have* **Parlons** *Let's talk* **vie quotidienne** *daily life* **mêmes choses** *same things* **ces** *these* **différemment** *differently* **plusieurs** *several* **Répondez** *Answer* **À votre avis** *In your opinion* **quelles** *what* **jeunes Français** *young French people* **Pendant** *During* **lire** *to read* **mes** *my* **le plus** *the most* **entre** *between* **En moyenne** *On the average* **combien d'heures** *how many hours* **par jour** *per day* **plus** *more* **publicité** *commercials* **feuilletons** *series*

EN FRANCE

À la télé, ce weekend

In France, TV viewers have a choice of six main channels: ***TF1, Antenne 2, FR3, La 5, M6,*** *and* ***Canal Plus.*** *(People who want to watch* ***Canal Plus*** *need to have a special decoding machine for which they pay a monthly fee.)*

Note that in TV listings, times are expressed using a 24-hour clock. In this system, 8 P.M. is ***20.00 (vingt heures)****; 10 P.M. is* ***22.00 (vingt-deux heures)****.*

Imagine that you are spending a month in Paris with a French family. This Friday and Saturday you have decided to stay home and watch TV. Look at the program listings at the right.

- Which programs would you like to watch on Friday? When do they start?
- Which programs would you choose on Saturday evening? When do they start?
- Your French hosts are soccer fans. What program would they want to watch and when? Which teams are playing? (Locate these cities on the map of France.)
- What program is featured on **Antenne 2** on Saturday evening? Who are the guests on this program? Do you know any of them?
- How many different movies are being shown over the weekend? How many of these movies are American? Which movie would you choose to see? At what time and on which channel?
- You are interested in watching a French TV series. Which program would you select? On which channel? According to its title, what kind of a series do you think it is?

SÉLECTION DE LA SEMAINE	VEN	SAM
	**20.30** VARIÉTÉS **SALUT L'ARTISTE** Sketches de **Thierry Le Luron** **22.05** DOCUMENT **HISTOIRES NATURELLES**	**20.35** SPECTACLE **HOLIDAY ON ICE** **Mis en scène par Jérôme Savary** **22.10** SÉRIE **DANS LA CHALEUR DE LA NUIT**
	**20.35** SÉRIE **HÔTEL DE POLICE** **LE GENTIL MONSIEUR** **de Claude Barrois** avec Cécile Magnet **23.20** FILM **ALICE DANS LES VILLES** **de Wim Wenders**	**20.40** VARIÉTÉS **CHAMPS-ÉLYSÉES** Invités: Elton John, Isabelle Adjani, Tom Cruise **22.25** SÉRIE **MÉDECINS DE NUIT**
	**21.30** SÉRIE **LE MASQUE** **MADEMOISELLE EVELYNE** **de Jean-Louis Fournier** **23.45** CONCERT **MUSIQUES, MUSIQUE**	**20.35** JEUNESSE **SAMDYNAMITE** **DESSINS ANIMÉS** Série : **BATMAN** **22.25** ENTRETIEN **LE DIVAN** **Pierre Dumayet**
	**20.30** FILM **MON PROF EST UN EXTRA-TERRESTRE** **de Dave De Coteau** **22.15** SÉRIE **DEUX FLICS À MIAMI**	**20.30** FILM TV **OPÉRATION COMMANDO** **de Ted Kaplan** avec D. Stephen, R. Kristoff **22.25** SÉRIE **DEUX FLICS À MIAMI**
	**20.30** FILM TV **COPACABANA** **de Warris Hussein** avec Barry Manilow, Annette O'Toole **22.05** THÉATRE **LE SEXE FAIBLE**	**20.35** FILM TV **L'ÉCLOSION DES MONSTRES** **de J. Piquer Simon** avec Yan Sera **22.20** SÉRIE **LE COMTE DE MONTE-CRISTO**
	**20.30** FOOTBALL **CAEN - TOULOUSE** Championnat de France 28e journée **22.40** FILM **AFTER HOURS** **de Martin Scorsese**	**20.30** FILM **ALIENS, LE RETOUR** **de James Cameron** avec Sigourney Weaver **22.45** FILM **UNE NUIT À L'ASSEMBLÉE NATIONALE** **de Jean-Pierre Mocky**

Entre amis: Bonjour, Patrick!

Qu'est-ce que vous aimez faire? Dans° une lettre, Patrick répond° à cette question. Voici la lettre de Patrick.

Bonjour!

Je m'appelle Patrick Lacaze. J'ai 14 ans. J'habite à Tours avec ma famille. Je suis élève° de troisième.° J'étudie beaucoup, mais je n'étudie pas tout le temps.° Voici ce que° j'aime faire.

J'aime les boums parce que j'adore danser.

J'aime la musique. J'aime surtout° le rock. J'aimerais° jouer de la guitare, mais je ne sais pas.°

J'aime les sports. En hiver je skie et en été je nage et je joue au tennis. (Je ne suis pas un champion, mais je joue assez° bien.) J'aime jouer au basket, mais je préfère jouer au foot. (J'aime jouer au babyfoot, mais ce n'est pas un sport.) J'aime faire des promenades à vélo° le weekend avec mes copains.

J'aime mon école.° J'aime surtout l'anglais parce que le prof est sympa.° (Il s'appelle Mr. Ross, mais il est très gentil.°) Je n'aime pas trop° les maths.

À la maison, j'aime regarder la télé. J'adore les séries américaines! J'aime aussi écouter mes cassettes.

J'aime téléphoner à ma copine, mais je ne téléphone pas souvent. (Mon père n'aime pas ça.°)

J'aime jouer aux jeux° sur le Minitel!

Et vous, qu'est-ce que vous aimez faire? Répondez-moi° vite.°

Amicalement,°
Patrick Lacaze

Dans *In* **répond** *answers* **élève** *student* **troisième** *ninth grade* **tout le temps** *all the time* **ce que** *what* **surtout** *especially* **aimerais** *would like* **je ne sais pas** *I don't know how* **assez** *rather* **promenades à vélo** *bike rides* **école** *school* **sympa** *nice* **gentil** *nice* **trop** *too much* **ça** *that* **jeux** *games* **Répondez-moi** *Answer me* **vite** quickly **Amicalement** *Cordially (In friendship)*

NOTES CULTURELLES

1 Tours

Tours is an attractive city located about 150 miles southwest of Paris. It is the capital of Touraine, an area of France known for its beautiful castles.

2 Le babyfoot

Babyfoot is a tabletop soccer game in which two teams of two people each try to score goals by manipulating rows of toy players. **Babyfoot** is very popular among French teenagers, who play it in cafés or in youth clubs.

Comment lire *(Reading hints)*

GETTING THE MEANING

When you read French, try to understand the meaning. Don't look for a word-for-word English translation for each sentence.

- Sometimes the two languages use different constructions.

  Je m'appelle . . . *(I call myself . . .)* *My name is . . .*

- Sometimes French uses some words that English leaves out.

  J'aime le rock. *I love rock.*
  J'aime jouer de la guitare. *I like to play the guitar.*

- And sometimes French leaves out words that English uses.

  Je suis élève de troisième. *I am a student in ninth grade.*

- Word order may also be different.

  des promenades à vélo *bike rides*

Enrichissez votre vocabulaire

COGNATES

You have already discovered that there are many words in French that look like English words and have similar meanings. These are called COGNATES. Cognates let you increase your vocabulary effortlessly. But be sure to pronounce them the French way!

- Sometimes the spelling is the same, or almost the same.

  la radio *radio*
  un champion *champion*

- Sometimes the spelling is a little different.

  américain *American*

Activité

Read the letter from Patrick again and find five more French-English cognates.

Activité: Une lettre à Patrick

You are writing a letter to Patrick in which you introduce yourself and explain what you like to do. You may tell him:

- if you like music (and what kind)
- what sports you like to do in fall or winter
- what sports you like to do in spring or summer
- what you like to do at home
- whether or not you like French and math
- what you like to do on weekends
- what programs you like to watch on TV

You may start your letter with the words:
Mon cher Patrick,
(My dear Patrick)
and end it with:
Amicalement,

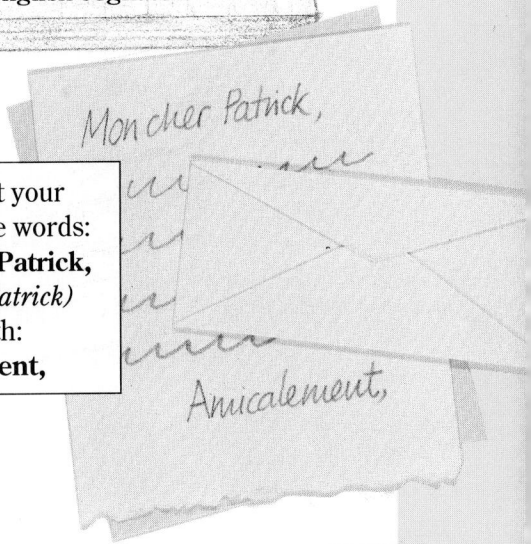

NOTE CULTURELLE

Le Minitel

If you lived in Paris and wanted to find the phone number or address of a friend, you wouldn't call information. You would turn to your **Minitel.** The **Minitel** is a small computer terminal connected to the telephone. By entering certain codes, you can gain access to a large variety of services. The most popular is the **annuaire électronique** (*computerized phone directory*).

However, the **Minitel** has much more to offer. You can check plane and train schedules, reserve theater tickets, and send electronic messages. For recreation, there are all sorts of games sponsored by various companies. If you answer a certain number of questions correctly, for example, you can win prizes like a pair of movie tickets or even a trip abroad.

But there is a catch! Although the **Minitel** terminals are distributed free of charge, users are billed each month according to the types of services used and time spent on the line. Because the **Minitel** may become expensive, French parents insist on limiting its use.

Variétés

Cinq portraits

Cinq jeunes parlent de ce qu'ils font,° mais ils ne révèlent pas leur° identité. Est-ce que vous pouvez° identifier chacun?° Lisez° les paragraphes suivants° et faites correspondre° chaque° paragraphe à une photo.

Moussa Dembila
Abidjan, Côte d'Ivoire

Catherine Miguel
Bordeaux, France

Laurent Arnold
Genève, Suisse

Isabelle Lamy
Trois Îlets, Martinique

Denis Lévêque
Montréal, Québec

1 Je ne suis pas français, mais je parle français. Je parle anglais aussi, mais je préfère parler français. J'aime les sports. Je joue au volley et au basket, mais mon sport préféré° est le hockey. Je m'appelle . . .

2 Je suis française, mais je n'habite pas à Paris. J'habite dans une île tropicale. Au lycée, j'étudie beaucoup. Mon sujet préféré est la biologie. (Je voudrais être médecin.°) J'aime la musique. J'aime beaucoup le reggae et j'adore chanter. J'aime les sports. Je nage souvent. Là où j'habite je peux nager en toute saison.° Je m'appelle . . .

3 Je n'habite pas à Paris. J'habite dans° une grande° ville° à 600 kilomètres de Paris. Je suis élève° dans un lycée. J'étudie beaucoup. Mes sujets préférés sont l'espagnol, la gymnastique, le français et la musique. J'aime beaucoup le jazz et le rock. J'adore danser. Je m'appelle . . .

4 Je n'habite pas en France, mais un jour je voudrais étudier à Paris. J'habite en Afrique. Je suis élève au Collège Moderne du Plateau. J'étudie l'anglais, les maths et la physique. Mon ambition est d'être architecte. Je m'appelle . . .

5 J'habite dans un petit° pays° européen. Dans mon pays les gens° parlent des langues différentes. Moi, je parle français. En classe j'étudie l'anglais et l'allemand.° J'aime voyager. Je voudrais visiter le Canada. Ma cousine Christine habite là-bas. Je m'appelle . . .

ce qu'ils font *what they do* **leur** *their* **pouvez** *can* **chacun** *each one* **Lisez** *Read* **suivants** *following* **faites correspondre** *match* **chaque** *each* **préféré** *favorite* **médecin** *doctor* **en toute saison** *all year round (in any season)* **dans** *in* **grande** *large* **ville** *city* **élève** *student* **petit** *small* **pays** *country* **gens** *people* **allemand** *German*

UNITÉ

5

Le monde personnel et familier

LEÇON 17 Le français pratique: Les personnes et les objets

LEÇON 18 Vive la différence!

LEÇON 19 Le copain de Mireille

LEÇON 20 La voiture de Roger

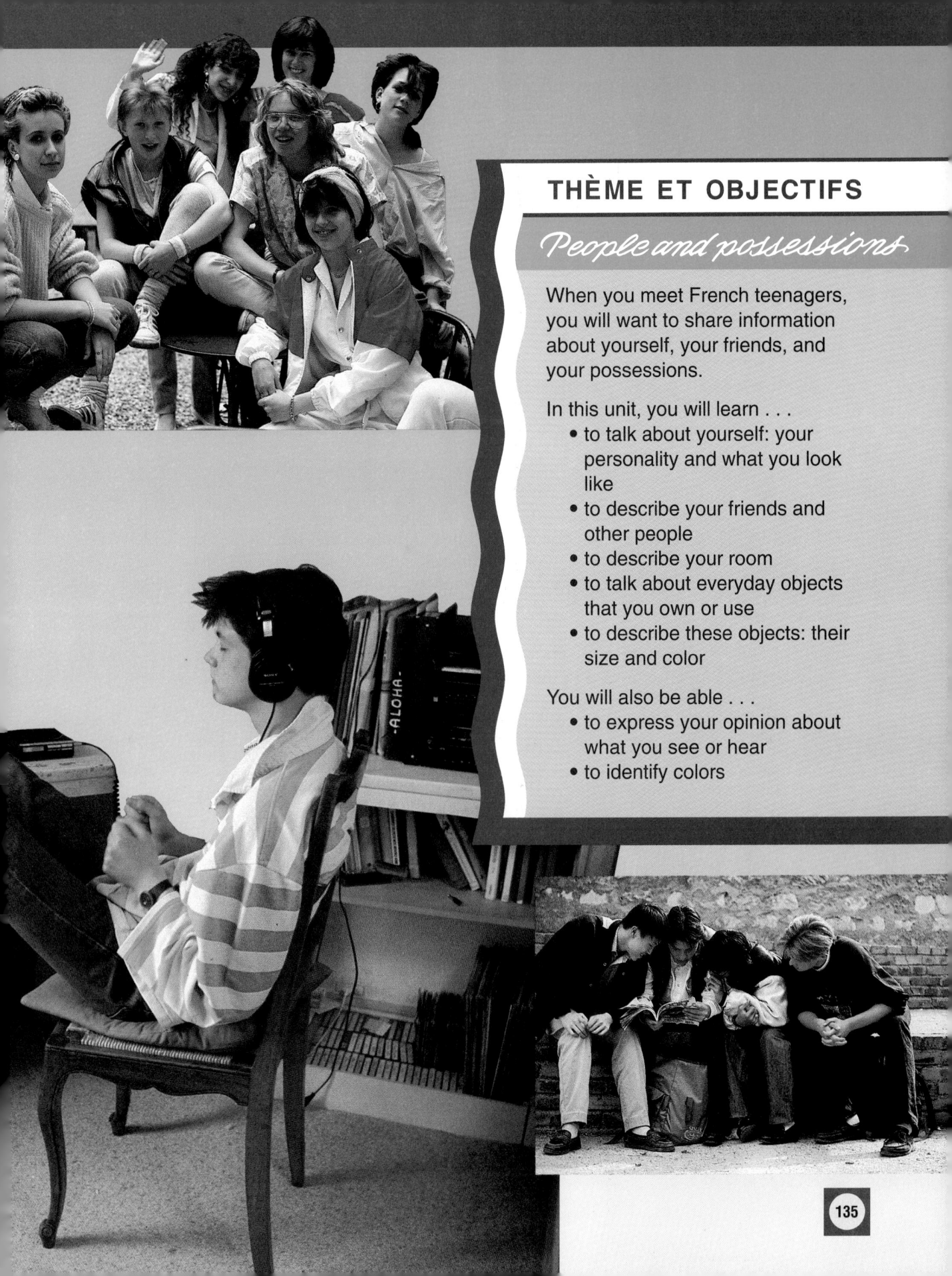

THÈME ET OBJECTIFS

People and possessions

When you meet French teenagers, you will want to share information about yourself, your friends, and your possessions.

In this unit, you will learn . . .

- to talk about yourself: your personality and what you look like
- to describe your friends and other people
- to describe your room
- to talk about everyday objects that you own or use
- to describe these objects: their size and color

You will also be able . . .

- to express your opinion about what you see or hear
- to identify colors

LE FRANÇAIS PRATIQUE

LEÇON 17

Les personnes et les objets

Accent sur . . . Les Français

France has a population of 55 million people. France is a European country, but its population includes people of many different ethnic backgrounds and cultural origins. There are many French citizens whose families have come from North Africa and French-speaking West Africa, as well as from Vietnam, Laos, and Cambodia.

- France is a country of Catholic tradition, but it also has:
  — the largest Jewish population of Western Europe (about 600,000 people).
  — the largest Muslim population of Western Europe (about five million people).
- France is a young country. Thirty percent of its population is under the age of 20.
- French young people tend to be idealists. They believe in freedom and democracy. They also believe in friendship and family. In fact, they rank these values far above money and material success.
- French young people in general have a positive attitude toward Americans. They like American music and would enjoy visiting the United States.
- Because language study is required in French secondary schools, many French teenagers can communicate in a second language, such as English or German.

Au Café Montparnasse
Stéphanie parle avec ses amis.

Chez le marchand de glaces
Philippe est chez le marchand de glaces avec une copine.

À Paris
Des jeunes font une promenade sur les Champs-Élysées.

Chez des amis
Stéphanie écoute des disques avec un copain.

A. La description des personnes

How to describe someone:

Qui est-ce?
C'est un copain.

Comment s'appelle-t-il?
Il s'appelle Marc.

Quel âge a-t-il?
Il a seize ans.

Comment est-il?
Il est petit.
Il est blond.

Qui est-ce?
C'est une copine.

Comment s'appelle-t-elle?
Elle s'appelle Sophie.

Quel âge a-t-elle?
Elle a quinze ans.

Comment est-elle?
Elle est grande.
Elle est brune.

Les personnes

une **personne**

un **étudiant** *(student)*
un **élève** *(pupil)*
un **camarade** *(classmate)*

un **homme** *(man)*
un **professeur,** un **prof** *(teacher)*
un **voisin** *(neighbor)*

une **personne**

une **étudiante**
une **élève**
une **camarade**

une **femme** *(woman)*
un **professeur,** une **prof**
une **voisine**

➡ **Une personne** is always feminine whether it refers to a male or female person.

➡ **Un professeur** is always masculine whether it refers to a male or female teacher. However, in casual French, one distinguishes between **un prof** (male) and **une prof** (female).

La description physique

Il est . . .

grand | **petit** | **brun** | **blond** | **beau** *handsome, good-looking* | **jeune** *young*

Elle est . . .

grande | **petite** | **brune** | **blonde** | **belle** *beautiful* / **jolie** *pretty* | **jeune**

1 Oui ou non?

Describe the people below in affirmative or negative sentences.

▶ Michael Jordan / petit?
Michael Jordan n'est pas petit.

▶ Cher / grande?
Cher est grande.

1. Larry Bird / grand?
2. Tom Cruise / blond?
3. Dracula / beau?
4. mon copain / brun?
5. mon père / petit?
6. mon voisin / jeune?
7. la princesse Diana / belle?
8. Jane Fonda / jeune?
9. Oprah Winfrey / grande?
10. ma copine / petite?
11. ma mère / brune?
12. ma voisine / jolie?

2 Vacances à Québec

You spent last summer in Quebec and have just had your photographs developed. Describe each of the people, giving name, approximate age, and two or three characteristics.

blond(e)	petit(e)
brun(e)	beau (belle)
grand(e)	jeune

▶ **Il s'appelle Alain.**
Il est brun.
Il a seize ans.
Il n'est pas grand.
Il est petit.

▶ **Alain**

1. Anne-Marie

2. Jean-Pierre

3. Claire

4. Mademoiselle Lévêque

5. Madame Paquette

6. Monsieur Beliveau

B. Les objets

How to identify something:

Qu'est-ce que c'est?	*What is it? What's that?*	—**Qu'est-ce que c'est?**
C'est . . .	*It's . . . , That's . . .*	—**C'est** une radio.

How to say that you know or do not know:

Je sais.	*I know.*
Je ne sais pas.	*I don't know.*

How to point out something:

—**Regarde ça.**	*Look at that.*
—**Quoi?**	*What?*
—**Ça,** là-bas.	*That, over there.*

Quelques objets *(A few objects)*

un objet

un stylo

un crayon

un livre

un disque

un compact (un CD)

un sac

une chose *(thing)*

une raquette

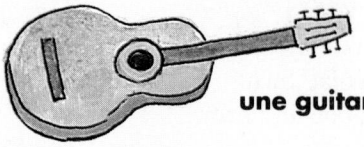
une guitare

une affiche

une cassette

DO YOU REMEMBER?

In French, the names of objects are MASCULINE or FEMININE.

Masculine objects can be introduced by **un** or **le (l')**: **un disque, le disque, l'objet.**

Feminine objects can be introduced by **une** or **la (l')**: **une cassette, la cassette, l'affiche.**

3 Qu'est-ce que c'est?

Ask a classmate to identify the following objects.

4 S'il te plaît

Ask a classmate to give you the following objects.

▶ **— S'il te plaît, donne-moi la cassette.**
— Voilà la cassette.
— Merci.

C. Les possessions personnelles

How to talk about things you have:

Est-ce que tu as . . . ?	*Do you have . . . ?*	—**Est-ce que tu as** un sac?
Oui, j'ai . . .	*Yes, I have . . .*	—**Oui, j'ai** un sac.

Quelques objets

un vélo (une bicyclette)

un scooter

un téléphone

un walkman

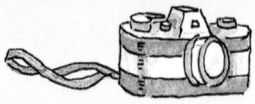
un appareil-photo

un magnétophone

un ordinateur

une voiture (une auto)

une moto

une mobylette

une montre

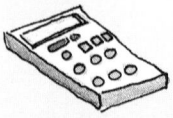
une calculatrice

une radio

une radiocassette

une télé

une chaîne stéréo

How to ask if an object works:

—Est-ce que la radio **marche?**	*Does the radio **work?***
—Oui, elle **marche.**	*Yes, it works.*

➡ The verb **marcher** has two meanings:

for people:
to walk — Nous **marchons.**

for things:
to work, to run — Le scooter ne **marche** pas bien.

DO YOU REMEMBER?

Masculine nouns can be replaced by **il.**
Le vélo marche.
Il marche.

Feminine nouns can be replaced by **elle.**
La voiture marche.
Elle marche.

5 Et toi?

1. J'ai . . .
   (Name 3 objects you own.)
2. Je voudrais . . .
   (Name 3 things you would like to have.)
3. Pour Noël / Hanoukka, je voudrais . . .
   (Name 2 gifts you would like to receive.)

6 Joyeux anniversaire
(Happy birthday)

For your birthday, a rich aunt is giving you the choice between different possible gifts. Indicate your preferences.

▶ vélo ou scooter?

1. mobylette ou moto?
2. montre ou radio?
3. appareil-photo ou walkman?
4. radiocassette ou chaîne stéréo?
5. télé ou ordinateur?
6. magnétophone ou calculatrice?

7 Qu'est-ce que tu as?

Philippe asks Christine if she has the following objects. She says that she does. Play both roles.

▶ PHILIPPE: **Est-ce que tu as une guitare?**
CHRISTINE: **Oui, j'ai une guitare.**

8 Est-ce qu'il marche bien?

Tell your classmates that you own the following objects. They will ask you if the objects are working. Answer according to the illustrations.

▶ **—J'ai un vélo.**
—Est-ce qu'il marche bien?
—Non, il ne marche pas.

▶ **—J'ai une télé.**
—Est-ce qu'elle marche bien?
—Oui, elle marche très bien.

D. Ma chambre *(My room)*

How to talk about what there is in a place:

il y a	*there is* *there are*	Dans *(In)* ma chambre, **il y a** une télé. Dans le garage, **il y a** deux voitures.
est-ce qu'il y a . . . ?	*is/are there . . . ?*	**Est-ce qu'il y a** un ordinateur dans la classe?
qu'est-ce qu'il y a . . . ?	*what is there . . . ?*	**Qu'est-ce qu'il y a** dans le garage?

How to say where something or someone is:

9 Qu'est-ce qu'il y a?

Describe the various objects that are in the pictures.

1. Sur la table, il y a . . .
2. Sous le lit, il y a . . .
3. Dans le garage, il y a . . .

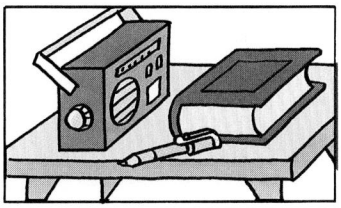

10 Ma chambre

Describe the various objects (pieces of furniture and personal belongings) that are in your room.

▶ **Il y a une radio, . . .**
Il y a aussi . . .

11 Où est le téléphone?

Michèle is looking for the telephone. Jean-Claude tells her where it is.

▶ MICHÈLE: **Où est le téléphone?**
JEAN-CLAUDE: **Il est sur la table.**

12 C'est étrange! *(It's strange!)*

Funny things sometimes happen. Describe these curious happenings by selecting an item from Column A and putting it in one of the places listed in Column B.

▶ **Il y a un éléphant sous le lit!**

▶ Il y a . . .

A	B
un rhinocéros	dans la classe
un éléphant	sur le bureau
une girafe	sous la table
un crabe	sous le lit
une souris *(mouse)*	derrière la porte
un ami de King Kong	sur la tour Eiffel
un extra-terrestre	dans le jardin *(garden)*
	devant le restaurant

13 La chambre de Nicole

Florence wants to borrow a few things from Nicole's room. Nicole tells her where each object is.

▶ la raquette

1. la télé
2. la guitare
3. le livre
4. le vélo
5. l'ordinateur
6. le sac
7. la radio
8. le compact
9. la cassette

14 Pauvre Monsieur Vénard *(Poor Mr. Vénard)*

Today Monsieur Vénard left on vacation, but he soon ran out of luck. Describe the four cartoons by completing the sentences below.

Le voyage de Monsieur Vénard

1. M. Vénard est ___ la voiture.

2. M. Vénard est ___ la voiture.

3. M. Vénard est ___ la voiture.

4. La contractuelle° est ___ la voiture.

la contractuelle *meter maid*

À votre tour!

1 Créa-dialogue

Daniel is showing Nathalie his recent photographs, and she is asking questions about the various people. Create similar dialogues and act them out in class.

▶ **un copain**

Éric/14

▶ **—Qui est-ce?**
—C'est un copain.
—Comment s'appelle-t-il?
—Il s'appelle Eric.
—Quel âge a-t-il?
—Il a quatorze ans.

1. une cousine	2. un camarade	3. une camarade	4. un voisin	5. une voisine	6. un professeur

Valérie/20	**Philippe Boucher/13**	**Nathalie Masson/15**	**Monsieur Dumas/70**	**Madame Smith/51**	**Monsieur Laval/35**

2 Conversation dirigée

Olivier is visiting his new friend Valérie. Act out the dialogue according to the instructions.

Olivier

asks Valérie if she has a boom box	→ ↙	answers affirmatively
asks her if it works well	→ ↙	says that it works very well and asks why
says he would like to listen to his new **(sa nouvelle)** cassette	→	says that the boom box is on the table in the living room **(le salon)**

Valérie

3 Mes possessions

Imagine that your family is going to move to another city. Prepare for the move by making a list of the objects you own. Use a separate sheet of paper.

4 Composition: Un objet

Write a short paragraph describing a real or an imaginary object. You may want to include a picture. (Use only vocabulary that you know.) You may begin your sentences with the following phrases:

▶ Voici mon/ma ...
Il/Elle est ...
Il/Elle marche (ne marche pas) ...

LEÇON 18

Vive la différence!

We are not necessarily like our friends. Caroline, a French girl from Montpellier, describes herself. She also talks about her friend Jean-Pierre.

Je m'appelle Caroline.	Il s'appelle Jean-Pierre.
J'habite à Montpellier.	Il habite à Strasbourg.
J'ai des frères.	Il n'a pas de frère, mais il a des soeurs.
J'ai un chien.	Il n'a pas de chien, mais il a deux horribles chats.
J'ai un scooter.	Il a une moto.
J'aime le cinéma.	Il préfère le théâtre.
J'aime les films de science-fiction.	Il préfère les westerns.
J'aime les sports.	Il préfère la musique.
J'étudie l'anglais.	Il étudie l'espagnol.

Jean-Pierre et moi, nous sommes très différents . . . mais nous sommes copains.

C'est l'essentiel, non?

Compréhension

Answer the questions below with the appropriate names: **Caroline, Jean-Pierre,** or **Caroline et Jean-Pierre.**

1. Qui habite en France?
2. Qui a des soeurs?
3. Qui n'a pas de frère?
4. Qui a un animal domestique?
5. Qui aime jouer au volley?
6. Qui préfère écouter un concert?
7. Qui étudie une langue *(language)?*

Et toi?

Describe yourself and your best friend by completing the sentences below with a phrase of your choice.

1. J'ai . . . Mon copain (ma copine) a . . .	• un frère • une soeur	• des frères • des soeurs
2. J'ai . . . Mon copain (ma copine) a . . .	• un chien • un chat	• un perroquet *(parrot)* • un poisson rouge *(goldfish)*
3. J'ai . . . Mon copain (ma copine) a . . .	• un vélo • une moto	• un scooter • une mobylette
4. J'aime . . . Mon copain (ma copine) aime . . .	• le cinéma • le théâtre	• la musique • les sports
5. Je préfère . . . Mon copain (ma copine) préfère . . .	• les westerns • les comédies	• les films d'aventures • les films de science-fiction
6. J'étudie . . . Mon copain (ma copine) étudie . . .	• l'espagnol • le français	• l'italien • l'allemand *(German)*
7. Mon ami(e) et moi, nous sommes . . .	• assez *(rather)* différent(e)s • très différent(e)s	• assez semblables *(similar)* • très semblables

NOTE CULTURELLE

Montpellier et Strasbourg

Montpellier and Strasbourg are two very different cities.

- Montpellier is a city of about 200,000 inhabitants located in southern France near the Mediterranean. It is an important university center with a School of Medicine founded in 1221.
- Strasbourg, a city of 250,000 inhabitants, is the capital of the French province of Alsace. Because of its location near Germany and Switzerland, it has always been an international city. Strasbourg is now the seat of important European institutions.

A. Le verbe *avoir*

The verb **avoir** *(to have, to own)* is irregular. Note the forms of this verb in the present tense.

avoir	*to have*	
j' **ai** tu **as** il/elle **a**	*I have* *you have* *he/she has*	J'**ai** une copine à Québec. Est-ce que tu **as** un frère? Philippe **a** une cousine à Paris.
nous **avons** vous **avez** ils/elles **ont**	*we have* *you have* *they have*	Nous **avons** un ordinateur. Est-ce que vous **avez** une moto? Ils n'**ont** pas ton appareil-photo.

➡ There is liaison in the forms: **nous avons, vous avez, ils ont, elles ont.**

Vocabulaire: Expressions avec *avoir*		
avoir faim	*to be hungry*	J'**ai faim.** Et toi, est-ce que tu **as faim?**
avoir soif	*to be thirsty*	Paul **a soif.** Sylvie n'**a** pas **soif.**
avoir . . . ans	*to be . . . (years old)*	J'**ai** 14 **ans.** Le prof **a** 35 **ans.**

1 Les voitures

The people below own cars made in the countries where they live. Match each car with its owner.

▶ Monsieur Sato habite à Tokyo.

Il a une Toyota.

une Alfa Roméo
une Jaguar
une Renault
une Chevrolet
une Volvo
une Mercedes
une Toyota

1. Tu habites à Boston.
2. Vous habitez à Munich.
3. Madame Ericson habite à Stockholm.
4. J'habite à Paris.
5. Nous habitons à Oxford.
6. Mes cousines habitent à Rome.

2 Expression personnelle

How old are the following people? Complete the sentences below. If you don't know the exact age, make a guess.

1. J'ai . . .
2. *(The student on your right)* Tu as . . .
3. *(The teacher)* Vous . . .
4. Mon copain . . .
5. Ma copine . . .
6. La voisine . . .

3 Faim ou soif?

You are at a party with your classmates. Offer them the following foods and beverages. They will accept or refuse by saying whether they are hungry or thirsty.

1. une crêpe
2. un soda
3. un hamburger
4. un jus d'orange
5. un croissant
6. un jus de raisin
7. une pizza
8. un Perrier

▶ un sandwich
▶ une limonade

Tu veux un sandwich?

Oui, merci! J'ai faim.

(Non, merci! Je n'ai pas faim.)

Tu veux une limonade?

Oui, merci! J'ai soif.

(Non, merci! Je n'ai pas soif.)

B. Les noms et les articles: masculin et féminin

NOUNS

- Nouns designating PEOPLE
  Nouns that designate male persons are almost always *masculine:*
  un garçon **un ami**
  Nouns that designate female persons are almost always *feminine:*
  une fille **une amie**

> ***Learning about language***
> NOUNS are words that designate people, animals, objects, and things.
> In French, all nouns have GENDER: they are either MASCULINE or FEMININE.

➡ EXCEPTIONS:
une personne is always feminine (even when it refers to a male)
un professeur is always masculine (even when it refers to a woman)

- Nouns designating ANIMALS, OBJECTS, and THINGS
  There is no systematic way to determine whether these nouns are masculine or feminine. Therefore, it is very important to learn these nouns with their articles.

MASCULINE:	**un** disque	**un** vélo	**un** ordinateur
FEMININE:	**une** cassette	**une** moto	**une** affiche

ARTICLES

Note the forms of the articles in the chart below.

INDEFINITE ARTICLE	MASCULINE	FEMININE	
	un *a, an*	**une** *a, an*	**un** garçon **une** fille
DEFINITE ARTICLE	**le** *the*	**la** *the*	**le** garçon **la** fille

> ***Learning about language***
> Nouns are often introduced by ARTICLES. In French, ARTICLES have the *same* gender as the nouns they introduce.

➡ Both **le** and **la** become **l'** before a vowel sound:
le garçon **l'ami**
la fille **l'amie**

> ***Learning about language***
> Nouns may be replaced by PRONOUNS. In French, PRONOUNS have the *same* gender as the nouns they replace.

PRONOUNS

Note the forms of the pronouns in the chart below.

MASCULINE	**il** *he* *it*	Où est **le** garçon? Où est **le** disque?	**Il** est en classe. **Il** est sur la table.
FEMININE	**elle** *she* *it*	Où est **la** fille? Où est **la** voiture?	**Elle** est en ville. **Elle** est là-bas.

4 Les célébrités

You and Jean-Pierre have been invited to a gala dinner attended by many American celebrities. Jean-Pierre asks you who each person is. Answer him using **un** or **une,** as appropriate.

▶ Connie Chung / journaliste

1. Peter Jennings / journaliste
2. Michelle Pfeiffer / actrice
3. Tom Cruise / acteur
4. Lily Tomlin / comédienne
5. Cher / chanteuse *(singer)*
6. Michael Jordan / athlète
7. Eddie Murphy / comédien
8. Michael Jackson / chanteur

5 Sur la table ou sous la table?

Caroline is looking for the following objects. Cécile tells her where each one is: on or under the table.

▶ walkman
CAROLINE: **Où est le walkman?**
CÉCILE: **Le walkman? Il est sur la table.**

1. ordinateur
2. sac
3. affiche
4. calculatrice
5. raquette
6. disque
7. radiocassette
8. télé

C. Les noms et les articles: le pluriel

Compare the singular and plural forms of the articles and nouns in the sentences below.

SINGULAR	PLURAL
Tu as **le disque?**	Tu as **les disques?**
Qui est **la fille** là-bas?	Qui sont **les filles** là-bas?
Voici **un livre.**	Voici **des livres.**
J'invite **une copine.**	J'invite **des copines.**

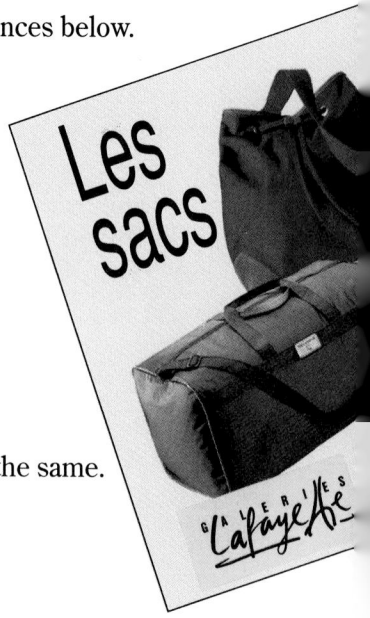

PLURAL NOUNS

In written French, the plural of most nouns is formed as follows:

SINGULAR NOUN + **s** = PLURAL NOUN

- ➡ If the noun ends in **-s** in the singular, the singular and plural forms are the same.
  Voici **un Français.** Voici **des Français.**
- ➡ In spoken French, the final **-s** of the plural is always silent.
- ➡ NOTE: **des gens** *(people)* is always plural. Compare:

une personne	*person*	Qui est **la personne** là-bas?
des gens	*people*	Qui sont **les gens** là-bas?

SINGULAR AND PLURAL ARTICLES

The forms of the articles are summarized in the chart below.

	SINGULAR	PLURAL		
DEFINITE ARTICLE	**le (l')** *the* **la (l')**	**les** *the*	**les** garçons **les** filles	**les** ordinateurs **les** affiches
INDEFINITE ARTICLE	**un** *a, an* **une**	**des** *some*	**des** garçons **des** filles	**des** ordinateurs **des** affiches

➡ There is liaison after **les** and **des** when the next word begins with a vowel sound.

➡ **Des** corresponds to the English article *some.* While *some* is often omitted in English, **des** MUST be expressed in French. Contrast:

Il y a *There are*	**des** *some*	**livres sur la table.** *books on the table.*

Je dîne avec *I'm having dinner with*	**des** . . .	**amis.** *friends.*

6 Pluriel, s'il vous plaît

Give the plurals of the following nouns.

▶ un copine
des copines

▶ l'ami
les amis

1. un copain
2. une amie
3. un homme
4. une femme
5. un vélo
6. une affiche
7. le voisin
8. l'élève
9. la cousine
10. le livre
11. l'ordinateur
12. la voiture

7 Shopping

You are in a department store in Montpellier looking for the following items. Ask the salesperson if he or she has these items. The salesperson will answer affirmatively.

▶ **—Pardon, monsieur (madame). Est-ce que vous avez des sacs?**
—Bien sûr, nous avons des sacs.

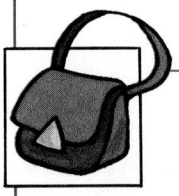

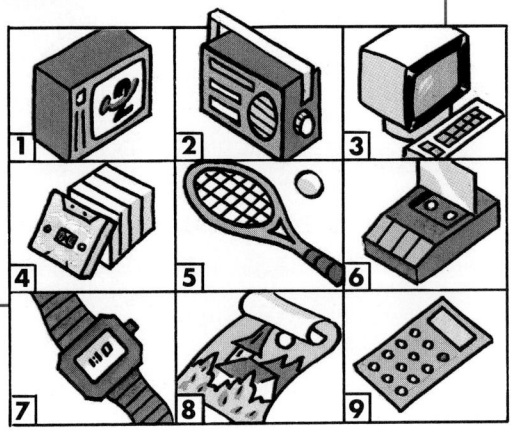

8 Qu'est-ce qu'il y a?

Explain what there is in the following places. Complete the sentences with **il y a** and a noun from the box. Be sure to use the appropriate articles: **un, une, des.** Be logical. Often several choices are possible.

▶ Dans le garage, . . .

1. Sur le bureau, . . .
2. À la boum, . . .
3. Dans la classe, . . .
4. Au café, sur la table, . . .
5. Dans ma chambre, . . .
6. Dans le laboratoire de maths, . . .

limonade stylo livres affiches moto professeur lit croissants voitures filles ordinateur garçons élèves table

D. L'article indéfini dans les phrases négatives

Compare the forms of the indefinite article in affirmative and negative sentences.

AFFIRMATIVE	NEGATIVE	
Tu as **un** vélo?	Non, je n'ai **pas de** vélo.	*No, I don't have a bike.*
Est-ce que Paul a **une** radio?	Non, il n'a **pas de** radio.	*No, he doesn't have a radio.*
Vous invitez **des** copains demain?	Non, nous n'invitons **pas de** copains.	*No, we are not inviting any friends.*

After a NEGATIVE verb:

pas + un, une, des becomes **pas de**

➡ Note that **pas de** becomes **pas d'** before a vowel sound.

Alice a un ordinateur.	Paul n'a **pas d'**ordinateur.
J'ai des amis à Québec.	Je n'ai **pas d'**amis à Montréal.

➡ The negative form of **il y a** is **il n'y a pas:**

Dans ma chambre, il y a une radio.	**Il n'y a pas de** télé.	*There is no TV.*
il y a des affiches.	**Il n'y a pas de** photos.	*There are no photographs.*

➡ After **être,** the articles **un, une,** and **des** do NOT change.

Philippe est un voisin.	Éric n'est **pas un** voisin.
Ce sont des vélos.	Ce ne sont **pas des** mobylettes.

9 Possessions

Ask your classmates if they own the following.

▶ un ordinateur

(Non, je n'ai pas d'ordinateur.)

1. un appareil-photo
2. une moto
3. une mobylette
4. une clarinette
5. des disques de jazz
6. des affiches
7. un boa
8. un alligator
9. des hamsters

10 Oui et non

One cannot have everything. Say that the following people do not have what is indicated in parentheses.

▶ Paul a un vélo. (un scooter)
Il n'a pas de scooter.

1. Julien a un scooter. (une voiture).
2. J'ai une radio. (une télé)
3. Vous avez des cassettes. (des compacts)
4. Vous avez des frères. (une soeur)
5. Nous avons un chien. (des chats)
6. Tu as des copains à Bordeaux. (des copains à Lyon)
7. Marc a un oncle à Québec. (un oncle à Montréal)
8. Nathalie a des cousins à San Francisco. (des cousins à Los Angeles)

11 Le grenier *(The attic)*

Your friend is cleaning the attic. Ask if the following items are up there. Your friend (a classmate) will answer according to the illustration.

▶ une raquette?
—**Est-ce qu'il y a une raquette?**
—**Non, il n'y a pas de raquette.**

1. des vélos?
2. une guitare?
3. des livres?
4. un magnétophone?
5. des disques?
6. des cassettes?
7. une télé?
8. une radiocassette?
9. un bureau?
10. une table?

Expression pour la conversation

How to contradict a negative statement or question:

Si! *Yes!* —Tu n'as pas de chaîne stéréo?
—**Si!** J'ai une chaîne stéréo.

12 Contradictions!

Contradict all of the following negative statements.

▶ Tu ne parles pas anglais! **Si, je parle anglais!**

1. Tu ne parles pas français!
2. Tu n'étudies pas!
3. Tu ne joues pas au basket!
4. Tu n'aimes pas les sports!
5. Tu n'aimes pas la musique!
6. Tu n'écoutes pas le professeur!

E. L'usage de l'article défini dans le sens général

In French, the definite article **(le, la, les)** is used more often than in English. Note its use in the following sentences.

J'aime **la musique.**	*(In general) I like* ***music.***
Tu préfères **le tennis** ou **le golf?**	*(Generally) do you prefer* ***tennis*** *or* ***golf?***
Pauline aime **les westerns.**	*(In general) Pauline likes* ***westerns.***
Nous aimons **la liberté.**	*(In general) we love* ***liberty.***

The definite article **(le, la, les)** is used to introduce ABSTRACT nouns, or nouns used in a GENERAL or COLLECTIVE sense.

J'❤ le français

13 Expression personnelle

Say how you feel about the following things, using one of the suggested expressions.

Je n'aime pas . . .
J'aime un peu . . .
J'aime beaucoup . . .

▶ **Je n'aime pas la violence.**

la musique	**le français**	**la violence**	**le théâtre**
la nature	**les maths**	**l'injustice**	**le cinéma**
les sports	**les sciences**	**la liberté**	**la danse**
le camping			**la photo** *(photography)*

14 C'est évident! *(It's obvious!)*

Read about the following people and say what they like. Choose the appropriate item from the list. (Masculine nouns are in blue. Feminine nouns are in red.)

▶ Cécile écoute des cassettes.
Cécile aime la musique.

art *cinéma* *danse* *français* *musique* *nature* *tennis*

1. Jean-Claude a une raquette.
2. Vous faites une promenade dans la forêt.
3. Les touristes visitent un musée *(museum)*.
4. Tu regardes un film.
5. Nous étudions en classe de français.
6. Véronique et Roger sont dans une discothèque.

F. L'usage de l'article défini avec les jours de la semaine

Compare the following sentences.

REPEATED EVENTS	SINGLE EVENT
Le samedi, je dîne avec des copains.	**Samedi,** je dîne avec mon cousin.
(On) Saturdays *(in general), I have dinner with friends.*	***(On) Saturday*** *(that is, this Saturday), I am having dinner with my cousin.*

To indicate a repeated or habitual event, French uses the construction:

le + DAY OF THE WEEK

➡ When an event happens only once, no article is used.

15 Questions personnelles

1. Est-ce que tu étudies le samedi?
2. Est-ce que tu dînes au restaurant le dimanche? Si *(If)* oui, avec qui?
3. Est-ce que tu as une classe de français le lundi? le mercredi?
4. Est-ce que tu regardes les matchs de football américain le samedi? le dimanche?
5. Quel programme de télé est-ce que tu regardes le vendredi? le jeudi?
6. Est-ce que tu travailles? Où? *(Name of place or store)* Quand?

16 L'emploi du temps

	LUNDI	MARDI	MERCREDI	JEUDI	VENDREDI
9 h	français	physique	sciences	biologie	
10 h		histoire		maths	anglais
11 h	maths	sciences	anglais		français

The following students all have the same morning schedule. Complete the sentences accordingly.

▶ **Nous avons une classe de français le lundi . . .**

1. J'ai une classe de maths _____.
2. Tu as une classe de sciences _____.
3. Jacques a une classe de physique _____.
4. Thérèse a une classe d'histoire _____.
5. Vous avez une classe de biologie _____.
6. Les élèves ont une classe d'anglais _____.

Prononciation

Les articles *le* et *les*

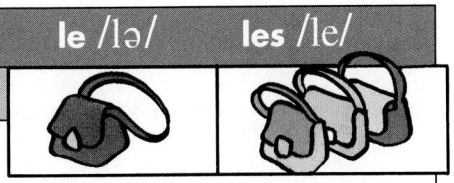

Be sure to distinguish between the pronunciation of **le** and **les.** In spoken French, that is often the only way to tell the difference between a singular and a plural noun.

Répétez:						
	/lə/	**le**	**le sac**	**le vélo**	**le disque**	**le copain**	**le voisin**
	/le/	**les**	**les sacs**	**les vélos**	**les disques**	**les copains**	**les voisins**

À votre tour!

1 Allô!

Jean-Marc is phoning some friends. Match his questions on the left with his friends' answers on the right.

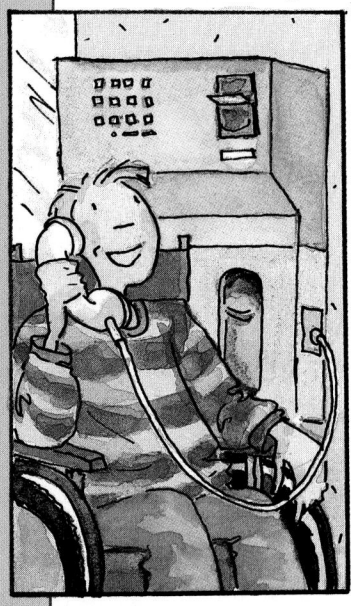

1. Quel âge a ton copain?
2. Est-ce qu'Éric a un scooter?
3. Où est l'appareil-photo?
4. Tu as des cassettes?
5. Est-ce que tu aimes étudier l'anglais?
6. Tu as soif?

a. Oui, mais je n'ai pas de magnétophone.
b. Il est sur la table.
c. Quatorze ans.
d. Oui, je voudrais une limonade.
e. Oui, mais je préfère l'espagnol.
f. Non, mais il a une moto.

2 Un sondage

A French consumer research group wants to know what things American teenagers own. Conduct a survey in your class asking who has the objects on the list. Count the number of students who raise their hands for each object, and report your findings on a separate piece of paper.

Qui a des cassettes?... Quinze élèves ont des cassettes.

3 Créa-dialogue

Ask your classmates if they like the following things. Then ask if they own the corresponding object.

▶ le tennis

1. la musique	2. le jogging	3. les maths	4. la photo	5. les matchs de baseball	6. l'exercice

▶ —Tu aimes le tennis?
—Oui, j'aime le tennis.
(Non, je n'aime pas le tennis.)

—Tu as une raquette?
—Oui, j'ai une raquette.
(Non, je n'ai pas de raquette.)

4 Quelle est la différence?

Sophie went away with her family for the weekend and she took some of her belongings with her. Describe what is in her room on Friday and what is missing on Saturday.

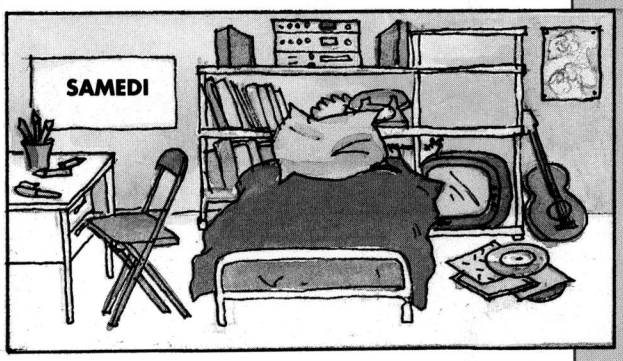

▶ Il y a . . .

▶ Il n'y a pas de . . .

5 Inventaire *(Inventory)*

Write a short paragraph naming two things that may be found in each of the following places. Also indicate one thing that is usually not found in that place.

▶ Dans le salon, il y a une télé et des chaises. Il n'y a pas de lit.

- dans ma chambre
- dans mon sac
- dans le garage
- dans la rue *(street)*
- sur la table

6 Composition: Ma semaine

In a short paragraph, describe what you do (or do not do) regularly on various days of the week. Select three days and two different activities for each day. Use only vocabulary that you know.

▶ Le lundi, j'ai une classe de français. Je regarde « La roue de la fortune » (Wheel of Fortune) à la télé.

Le samedi, je n'étudie pas. Je dîne au restaurant avec mon copain.

LEÇON 19

Le copain de Mireille

Nicolas and Jean-Claude are having lunch at the school cafeteria. Nicolas is looking at the students seated at the other end of their table.

NICOLAS: Regarde la fille là-bas!
JEAN-CLAUDE: La fille blonde?
NICOLAS: Oui! Qui est-ce?
JEAN-CLAUDE: C'est Mireille Labé.
NICOLAS: Elle est mignonne! *cute*
JEAN-CLAUDE: Elle est aussi amusante, intelligente et sympathique. *fun / nice*
NICOLAS: Est-ce qu'elle a un copain?
JEAN-CLAUDE: Oui, elle a un copain.
NICOLAS: Il est sympathique?
JEAN-CLAUDE: Oui . . . Très sympathique!
NICOLAS: Et intelligent?
JEAN-CLAUDE: Aussi!
NICOLAS: Dommage! . . . Qui est-ce?
JEAN-CLAUDE: C'est moi!
NICOLAS: Euh . . . oh . . . Excuse-moi et félicitations! *congratulations*

Compréhension

1. Qui est-ce que Nicolas regarde?
2. Comment s'appelle la fille?
3. Est-ce qu'elle est jolie?
4. Est-ce qu'elle a d'autres *(other)* qualités?
5. Est-ce qu'elle a un copain?
6. Qui est le copain de Mireille *(Mireille's boyfriend)?*

NOTE CULTURELLE

L'amitié *(Friendship)*

For the French, friendship is very important. On the scale of personal values, it ranks first — before family, freedom, justice, love, and money.

What qualities do French young people expect in their friends? As in the United States, friends must be fun to be with, since French teenagers like to do things as a group with their **bande de copains.** Friends should be helpful and understanding because when French teenagers have a problem, they tend to talk to their friends before talking to their parents. And, of course, friends must be loyal, because the French tend to remain close to their high school friends for the rest of their lives.

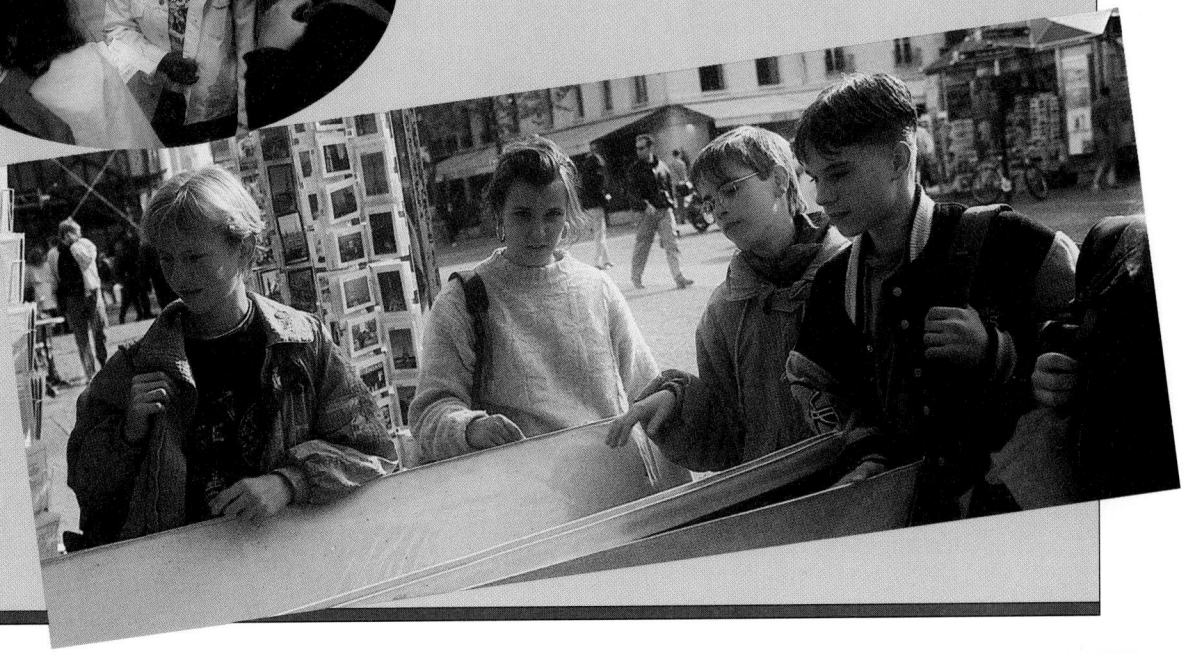

A. Les adjectifs: masculin et féminin

Compare the forms of the adjectives in heavy print as they describe masculine and feminine nouns.

MASCULINE	FEMININE
Le scooter est **petit.**	La voiture est **petite.**
Patrick est **intelligent.**	Caroline est **intelligente.**
L'ordinateur est **moderne.**	La télé est **moderne.**

In written French, feminine adjectives are usually formed as follows:

MASCULINE ADJECTIVE + **-e** = FEMININE ADJECTIVE

➡ If the masculine adjective ends in **-e,** there is no change in the feminine form.

Jérôme est **timide.** Juliette est **timide.**

➡ Adjectives that follow the above patterns are called REGULAR adjectives. Those that do not are called IRREGULAR adjectives. For example:

Marc est **beau.** Sylvie est **belle.**
Paul est **canadien.** Marie est **canadienne.**

NOTE: French dictionaries list adjectives by their masculine forms. For irregular adjectives, the feminine form is indicated in parentheses.

NOTES DE PRONONCIATION:

- If the masculine form of an adjective ends in a silent consonant, that consonant is pronounced in the feminine form.
- If the masculine form of an adjective ends in a vowel or a pronounced consonant, the masculine and feminine forms sound the same.

DIFFERENT PRONUNCIATION		SAME PRONUNCIATION	
petit	petite	timide	timide
blond	blonde	joli	jolie
français	française	espagnol	espagnole

Learning about language

ADJECTIVES are words that describe people, places, and things.

In French, MASCULINE adjectives are used with masculine nouns, and FEMININE adjectives are used with feminine nouns. This is called NOUN-ADJECTIVE AGREEMENT.

1 Vive la différence!

People can be friends and yet be quite different. Describe the girls named in parentheses, indicating that they are not like their friends.

▶ Jean-Claude est brun. (Nathalie)
Nathalie n'est pas brune.

1. Jean-Louis est blond. (Carole)
2. Paul est petit. (Mireille)
3. Éric est beau. (Marthe)
4. Jérôme est grand. (Louise)
5. Michel est riche. (Émilie)
6. André est français. (Lisa)
7. Antonio est espagnol. (Céline)
8. Bill est américain. (Julie)

Vocabulaire: La description

ADJECTIFS		Voici Jean-Claude.	Voici Mireille.
amusant	*amusing, fun*	Il est **amusant.**	Elle est **amusante.**
intelligent	*intelligent*	Il est **intelligent.**	Elle est **intelligente.**
intéressant	*interesting*	Il est **intéressant.**	Elle est **intéressante.**
méchant	*mean, nasty*	Il n'est pas **méchant.**	Elle n'est pas **méchante.**
bête	*silly, dumb*	Il n'est pas **bête.**	Elle n'est pas **bête.**
sympathique	*nice, pleasant*	Il est **sympathique.**	Elle est **sympathique.**
timide	*timid*	Il est **timide.**	Elle n'est pas **timide.**
gentil (gentille)	*nice, kind*	Il est **gentil.**	Elle est **gentille.**
mignon (mignonne)	*cute*	Il est **mignon.**	Elle est **mignonne.**
sportif (sportive)	*athletic*	Il est **sportif.**	Elle est **sportive.**

ADVERBES		
assez	*rather*	Nous sommes **assez** intelligents.
très	*very*	Vous n'êtes pas **très** sportifs!

2 Oui ou non?

In your opinion, do the following people have the suggested traits? (Note: These traits are given in the masculine form only.)

▶ le prince Charles / intéressant. ▶

1. le Président / sympathique?
2. Steffi Graf / sportif?
3. ma copine / gentil?
4. Vanna White / mignon?
5. Oprah Winfrey / intelligent?
6. Einstein / bête?
7. Eddie Murphy / amusant?
8. le prof / méchant?

3 Descriptions

Select one of the following characters. Using words from the **Vocabulaire,** describe this character in two affirmative or negative sentences.

▶ Frankenstein
Il est très méchant.
Il n'est pas très mignon.

1. Tarzan
2. King Kong
3. Big Bird
4. Batman
5. Miss Piggy
6. Wonder Woman
7. Charlie Brown
8. Blanche-Neige *(Snow White)*
9. Garfield
10. Snoopy

4 L'idéal

Now you have the chance to describe your ideal people. Use two adjectives for each one.

1. Le copain idéal est . . . et . . .
2. La copine idéale est . . . et . . .
3. Le professeur idéal est . . . et . . .
4. L'étudiant idéal est . . . et . . .
5. L'étudiante idéale est . . . et . . .

B. Les adjectifs: le pluriel

Compare the forms of the adjectives in heavy print as they describe singular and plural nouns.

SINGULAR	PLURAL
Paul est **intelligent** et **timide.**	Paul et Éric sont **intelligents** et **timides.**
Alice est **intelligente** et **timide.**	Alice et Claire sont **intelligentes** et **timides.**

In written French, plural adjectives are usually formed as follows:

SINGULAR ADJECTIVE + **-s** = PLURAL ADJECTIVE

➡ If the masculine singular adjective already ends in **-s,** there is no change in the plural form.

Patrick est **français.** Patrick et Daniel sont **français.**
BUT: Anne est **française.** Anne et Alice sont **françaises.**

NOTE DE PRONONCIATION: Because the final **-s** of plural adjectives is silent, singular and plural adjectives sound the same.

SUMMARY: Forms of regular adjectives

	MASCULINE	FEMININE	*also:*
SINGULAR	– **grand**	-e **grand<u>e</u>**	timide timide
PLURAL	-s **grand<u>s</u>**	-es **grand<u>es</u>**	français français<u>es</u>

5 Une question de personnalité

Indicate whether or not the following people exhibit the personality traits in parentheses. (These traits are given in the masculine singular form only. Make the necessary agreements.)

▶ Alice et Thérèse aiment parler en public. (timide?)

1. Claire et Valérie sont très populaires. (amusant?)
2. Robert et Jean-Luc n'aiment pas danser. (timide?)
3. Catherine et Martine aiment jouer au foot. (sportif?)
4. Laure et Gisèle ont un «A» en français. (intelligent?)
5. Thomas et Vincent n'aiment pas le jogging. (sportif?)
6. Les voisins n'aiment pas parler avec nous. (sympathique?)

Vocabulaire: Les adjectifs de nationalité

américain	*American*	**italien (italienne)**	*Italian*
mexicain	*Mexican*	**canadien (canadienne)**	*Canadian*
français	*French*	**japonais**	*Japanese*
anglais	*English*	**chinois**	*Chinese*
espagnol	*Spanish*		
suisse	*Swiss*		

➡ Words that describe nationality are adjectives and take adjective endings.

Monsieur Katagiri est **japonais.**
Kumi et Michiko sont **japonaises.**

Expression pour la conversation

How to introduce a conclusion:

alors *so, then* —J'habite à Québec.
—**Alors,** tu es canadien!

6 Quelle nationalité?

Your classmate wants to know more about the following people: where they live and what their nationality is. Act out the dialogues.

▶ —Où habitent Janet et Barbara?
—Elles habitent à San Francisco.
—Alors, elles sont américaines?
—Mais oui, elles sont américaines.

▶ Janet et Barbara	1. Jim et Bob	2. Laure et Céline
San Francisco	Liverpool	Toulouse
américain	anglais	français
3. Luisa et Teresa	**4. Éric et Vincent**	**5. ??**
Madrid	Montréal	??
espagnol	??	??

7 Les nationalités

Read the descriptions of the following people and give their nationalities.

▶ Silvia et Maria sont étudiantes à Rome.
Elles sont italiennes.

1. Lise et Nathalie étudient à Québec.
2. Michael et Dennis sont de Liverpool.
3. Luis et Paco étudient à Madrid.
4. Isabel et Carmen travaillent à Acapulco.
5. Yoko et Liliko sont étudiantes à l'université de Tokyo.
6. Monsieur et Madame Chen habitent à Beijing.
7. Jean-Pierre et Claude sont de Genève.
8. Françoise et Sylvie travaillent à Paris.

C. La place des adjectifs

Note the position of the adjectives in the sentences on the right.

Philippe a une voiture.	Il a une voiture **anglaise.**
Denise invite des copains.	Elle invite des copains **américains.**
Voici un livre.	Voici un livre **intéressant.**
J'ai des amies.	J'ai des amies **sympathiques.**

In French, adjectives usually come AFTER the noun they modify, according to the pattern:

ARTICLE +	NOUN +	ADJECTIVE
une	voiture	**française**
des	copains	**intéressants**

8 Préférences personnelles

For each person or object below, choose among the characteristics in parentheses. Indicate your preference.

▶ avoir un copain (sympathique, intelligent, sportif)
Je préfère avoir un copain intelligent.

1. avoir une copine (amusante, mignonne, intelligente)
2. avoir un professeur (gentil, intelligent, amusant)
3. avoir des voisins (sympathiques, intéressants, riches)
4. avoir une voiture (moderne, confortable, rapide)
5. avoir une calculatrice (japonaise, américaine, française)
6. avoir une montre (suisse, japonaise, française)
7. dîner dans un restaurant (italien, chinois, français)
8. regarder un film (intéressant, amusant, intelligent)
9. travailler avec des personnes (gentilles, amusantes, sérieuses)
10. faire un voyage avec des gens (amusants, riches, sympathiques)

9 Qui se ressemble . . .

(Birds of a feather . . .)

Say that the following people have friends, relatives, or acquaintances with the same personality or nationality.

▶ Claire est anglaise. (un copain)
Elle a un copain anglais.

1. Jean-Pierre est sympathique. (des cousines)
2. La prof est intelligente. (des étudiants)
3. Madame Simon est intéressante. (des voisines)
4. Alice est américaine. (des copines)
5. Véronique est amusante. (un frère)
6. Michel est sportif. (une soeur)
7. Pedro est espagnol. (des camarades)
8. Antonio est mexicain. (une copine)
9. Bernard est sportif. (un voisin)

Birds of a feather flock together.

10 Préférences internationales

Choose an item from Column A and indicate your preference as to country of origin by choosing an adjective from Column B. Be sure to make the necessary agreement.

	A	B
	la musique	anglais
	la cuisine	américain
	les voitures	français
Je préfère . . .	les ordinateurs	mexicain
	les appareils-photo	chinois
	les compacts	japonais
	les restaurants	italien

Prononciation

Les consonnes finales

/-/ /d/

As you know, when the last letter of a word is a consonant, that consonant is often silent. But when a word ends in "**e**," the consonant before it is pronounced. As you practice the following adjectives, be sure to distinguish between the masculine and the feminine forms.

blond

blonde

	MASCULINE ADJECTIVE *(no final consonant sound)*		FEMININE ADJECTIVE *(final consonant sound)*
Répétez:	**blond**	/d/	**blonde**
	grand		**grande**
	petit	/t/	**petite**
	amusant		**amusante**
	français	/z/	**française**
	anglais		**anglaise**
	américain	/n/	**américaine**
	canadien		**canadienne**

À votre tour!

1 Allô!

Valérie is phoning some friends. Match her questions on the left with her friends' answers on the right.

1. Ton frère aime jouer au foot?
2. Cécile et Sophie sont mignonnes, n'est-ce pas?
3. Pourquoi est-ce que tu invites Olivier?
4. Tu aimes la classe?
5. Tu as des cousins?

a. Oui, et intelligentes aussi!
b. Parce qu'il est amusant et sympathique.
c. Oui, j'ai un professeur très intéressant.
d. Oui, il est très sportif.
e. Oui, mais ils ne sont pas très sympathiques.

2 Créa-dialogue

With your classmates, talk about the people of different nationalities you may know or objects you may own.

▶ —J'ai des cousins mexicains.
—Ils sont mignons?
—Oui, ils sont très mignons.

1. une voisine	2. un prof	3. des copines	4. un livre	5. une voiture
blond?	sympathique?	mignon?	intéressant?	grand?

3 Une invitation

A French friend has invited you to go to a party with his/her cousin. You want to know as much as you can about this cousin. You may first ask your friend the cousin's name and age.

Then ask as many questions as you can about the cousin's physical appearance and personality traits. Act out your conversation with a classmate.

4 Avis de recherche

(Missing person's bulletin)

The two people in the pictures below have been reported missing. Describe each one as well as you can, using your imagination. Mention:

- the (approximate) age of the person
- the way he/she looks
- personality traits
- other features or characteristics

5 Composition: Descriptions

Describe one of the following well-known French people in a short paragraph, giving the person's name, profession, and approximate age. Also briefly describe the person's physical appearance.

Isabelle Adjani (actrice)

Yannick Noah (athlète)

Jean-Jacques Goldman (chanteur)

François Mitterrand (président)

6 Composition: Rencontres

Select two people whom you would like to meet (a man and a woman). These people may be famous singers, actors or actresses, sports figures, politicians, professional people, community leaders, etc. Describe each person (physical traits and personality), using either affirmative or negative sentences.

LEÇON 20

La voiture de Roger

Dans la rue, il y a une voiture rouge. *street / red*
C'est une petite voiture. C'est une voiture de sport.
Dans la rue, il y a aussi un café. Au café, il y a un jeune homme.
Il s'appelle Roger.
C'est le propriétaire de la voiture rouge. *owner*

Une jeune fille entre dans le café. *enters*
Elle s'appelle Véronique.
C'est l'amie de Roger. *Roger's friend*
Véronique parle à Roger.

VÉRONIQUE: Tu as une nouvelle voiture, n'est-ce pas? *new*
ROGER: Oui, j'ai une nouvelle voiture.
VÉRONIQUE: Est-ce qu'elle est grande ou petite?
ROGER: C'est une petite voiture.
VÉRONIQUE: De quelle couleur est-elle?
ROGER: C'est une voiture rouge.
VÉRONIQUE: Est-ce que c'est une voiture italienne?
ROGER: Oui, c'est une voiture italienne. Mais dis donc, Véronique, tu es vraiment très curieuse! *hey there* *really*
VÉRONIQUE: Et toi, tu n'es pas assez curieux! *curious enough*
ROGER: Ah bon? Pourquoi?
VÉRONIQUE: Pourquoi?! . . . Regarde la contractuelle là-bas! *meter maid*
ROGER: Ah, zut alors!

Compréhension

1. Qu'est-ce qu'il y a dans la rue?
2. Est-ce que la voiture est grande?
3. Comment s'appelle le jeune homme?
4. Où est-il?
5. Comment s'appelle la jeune fille?
6. De quelle couleur est la voiture?

NOTE CULTURELLE

Les Français et l'auto

France is one of the leading producers of automobiles in the world. The two major automakers are **Renault** and **Peugeot.** They manufacture a variety of models ranging from sports cars to mini-vans and buses.

To obtain a driver's license in France, you must be eighteen years old and pass a very difficult driving test. French teenagers can, however, begin to drive at the age of sixteen, as long as they take lessons at an accredited driving school **(auto-école)** and are accompanied by an adult.

On the whole, because cars (even used cars) are expensive to buy and maintain, few French teenagers have cars. Instead, many get around on two-wheelers: motorcycles, scooters, and mopeds.

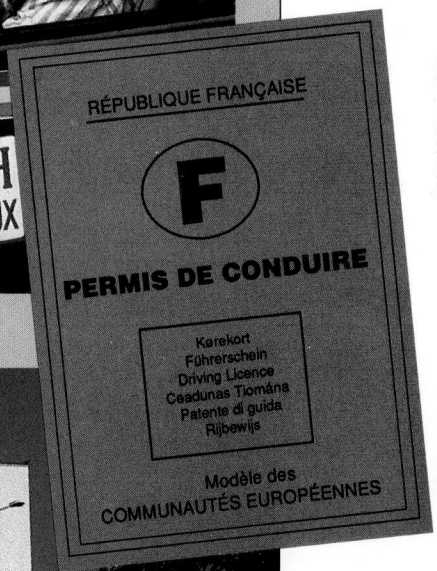

A. Les couleurs

Note the form and position of the color words in the following sentences:

Alice a un vélo **bleu.**	*Alice has a **blue** bicycle.*
Nous avons des chemises **bleues.**	*We have **blue** shirts.*

Names of colors are ADJECTIVES and take adjective ENDINGS. Like most descriptive adjectives, they come *after* the noun.

Vocabulaire: Les couleurs

De quelle couleur . . . ? *What color . . . ?* —**De quelle couleur** est la moto?
—Elle est rouge.

blanc (blanche)	noir (noire)	bleu (bleue)	rouge (rouge)	jaune (jaune)	vert (verte)	gris (grise)	marron (marron)	orange (orange)	rose (rose)

➡ The colors **orange** and **marron** are INVARIABLE. They do not take any endings.

un sac **orange** — des sacs **orange**
un tee-shirt **marron** — une chemise **marron**

1 De quelle couleur?

Ask your classmates to name the colors of things they own. (They may invent answers.)

▶ ta chambre?

1. ta bicyclette?
2. ton tee-shirt?
3. ton appareil-photo?
4. ta montre?
5. ta raquette de tennis?
6. ton livre de français?
7. ton livre d'anglais?
8. ton chien (chat)?

2 Possessions

Ask what objects or pets the following people own. A classmate will answer, giving the color.

▶ —**Est-ce que Monsieur Thomas a une voiture?**
—**Oui, il a une voiture bleue.**

3 L'arche de Noé

Noah's ark has just landed. Give the colors of the animals as they get off the ship.

▶ le chien **Le chien est blanc.**

1. le chat
2. l'éléphant *(m.)*
3. la panthère
4. le zèbre
5. le flamant
6. le cardinal
7. le lion
8. le perroquet

B. La place des adjectifs avant le nom

Compare the position of the adjectives in the following sentences.

Voici une voiture **française.**	Voici une **petite** voiture.
Paul est un garçon **intelligent.**	Pierre est un **beau** garçon.

▌ A few adjectives like **petit** and **beau** come BEFORE the noun they modify.

➡ The article **des** often becomes **de** before an adjective. Compare:
des voitures → **de** petites voitures

Vocabulaire: Les adjectifs qui précèdent le nom

beau (belle)	*beautiful, handsome*	Regarde la **belle** voiture!
joli	*pretty*	Qui est la **jolie** fille avec André?
grand	*big, large, tall*	Nous habitons dans un **grand** appartement.
petit	*little, small, short*	Ma soeur a un **petit** ordinateur.
bon (bonne)	*good*	Tu es un **bon** copain.
mauvais	*bad*	Patrick est un **mauvais** élève.

➡ There is a LIAISON after the above adjectives when the noun which follows begins with a vowel sound. Note that in liaison:

- the "**d**" of **grand** is pronounced /t/: **un grand appartement**
- **bon** is pronounced like **bonne: un bon élève**

4 Opinions personnelles

Give your opinion about the following people and things, using the adjectives **bon** or **mauvais.**

▶ Meryl Streep est (une) actrice *(actress)*.
Meryl Streep est une bonne actrice (une mauvaise actrice).

1. *Rambo* est un film.
2. Le «Bill Cosby Show» est un programme de télé.
3. Whitney Houston est (une) chanteuse *(singer)*.
4. Steve Martin est (un) acteur.
5. Cybil Shepherd est (une) actrice.
6. Dracula est une personne.
7. McDonald's est un restaurant.
8. Les Yankees sont une équipe *(team)* de baseball.
9. Les Lakers sont une équipe de basket.
10. Je suis [un(e)] élève.

Expressions pour la conversation

How to get someone's attention:

Dis!	*Say! Hey!*	**Dis,** Éric, est-ce que tu as une voiture?
Dis donc!	*Hey there!*	**Dis donc,** est-ce que tu veux faire une promenade avec moi?

5 Dialogue

Christine asks her cousin Thomas if he has certain things. He responds affirmatively, describing each one. Play both roles.

▶ un ordinateur (petit)

▶ une voiture (anglaise)

1. une télé (petite)
2. une guitare (espagnole)
3. un vélo (rouge)
4. une calculatrice (petite)
5. un sac (grand)
6. des livres (intéressants)
7. une copine (amusante)
8. une mobylette (bleue)
9. une montre (belle)
10. un copain (bon)
11. une cousine (jolie)
12. une radio (japonaise)

C. *Il est* ou *c'est?*

When describing a person or thing, French speakers use two different constructions, **il est (elle est)** and **c'est.**

		Il est + ADJECTIVE **Elle est** + ADJECTIVE	**C'est** + ARTICLE + NOUN (+ ADJECTIVE)
Roger	*He is . . .*	**Il est** amusant.	**C'est** un copain. **C'est** un copain amusant.
Véronique	*She is . . .*	**Elle est** sportive.	**C'est** une amie. **C'est** une bonne amie.
un scooter	*It is . . .*	**Il est** joli.	**C'est** un scooter français. **C'est** un bon scooter.
une voiture	*It is . . .*	**Elle est** petite.	**C'est** une voiture anglaise. **C'est** une petite voiture.

➡ Note the corresponding plural forms:

(Pierre et Marc) *They are . . .* **Ils sont** amusants. **Ce sont** des copains.
(Claire et Anne) *They are . . .* **Elles sont** timides. **Ce sont** des copines.

➡ In negative sentences, **c'est** becomes **ce n'est pas.**

Ce n'est pas un mauvais élève. *He's not a bad student.*
Ce n'est pas une Peugeot. ***It's*** *not a Peugeot.*

➡ **C'est** is also used with names of people

C'est Véronique. **C'est** Madame Lamblet.

6 Descriptions

Complete the following descriptions with **Il est, Elle est,** or **C'est,** as appropriate.

A. Roger

1. _____ grand.
2. _____ brun.
3. _____ un garçon sympathique.
4. _____ un mauvais élève.

B. Véronique

5. _____ une fille brune.
6. _____ une amie sympathique.
7. _____ très amusante.
8. _____ assez grande.

C. La voiture de Roger

9. _____ une voiture moderne.
10. _____ une petite voiture.
11. _____ rouge.
12. _____ très rapide.

D. Le scooter de Véronique

13. _____ bleu et blanc.
14. _____ très économique.
15. _____ un joli scooter.
16. _____ assez confortable.

D. Les expressions impersonnelles avec *c'est*

Note the use of **c'est** in the following sentences.

J'aime parler français.	**C'est** intéressant.	*It's interesting.*
Je n'aime pas travailler le weekend.	**Ce n'est pas** amusant.	*It's no(t) fun.*

To express an opinion on a general topic, the French use the construction:

C'est / **Ce n'est pas** } + MASCULINE ADJECTIVE

Vocabulaire: Opinions

C'est . . . *It's . . . , That's . . .*
Ce n'est pas . . . *It's not . . . , That's not . . .*

vrai	*true*	**chouette**	*neat*
faux	*false*	**super**	*great*
		extra	*terrific*
facile	*easy*	**pénible**	*a pain, annoying*
difficile	*hard, difficult*	**drôle**	*funny*

➡ To express an opinion, the French also use adverbs like **bien** and **mal.**

C'est bien.	*That's good.*	Tu étudies? **C'est bien.**
C'est mal.	*That's bad.*	Alain n'étudie pas. **C'est mal.**

7 Vrai ou faux?

Imagine that your little sister is talking about where certain cities are located. Tell her whether her statements are right or wrong.

1. Paris est en Italie.
2. Los Angeles est en Californie.
3. Genève est en Italie.
4. Dakar est en Afrique.
5. Fort-de-France est au Canada.
6. Québec est en France.

8 Opinion personelle

Ask your classmates if they like to do the following things. They will answer, using an expression from the **Vocabulaire.**

▶ parler français

(Non, c'est difficile!)

1. téléphoner
2. parler en public
3. nager
4. danser
5. voyager
6. dîner en ville
7. regarder le «Bill Cosby Show»
8. étudier le weekend
9. écouter la musique classique

Prononciation

ch /ʃ/

Les lettres «ch»

The letters "**ch**" are usually pronounced like the English "*sh.*"

Répétez: **chien chat chose marche chouette chocolat affiche**
Michèle a un chat et deux chiens.

chien

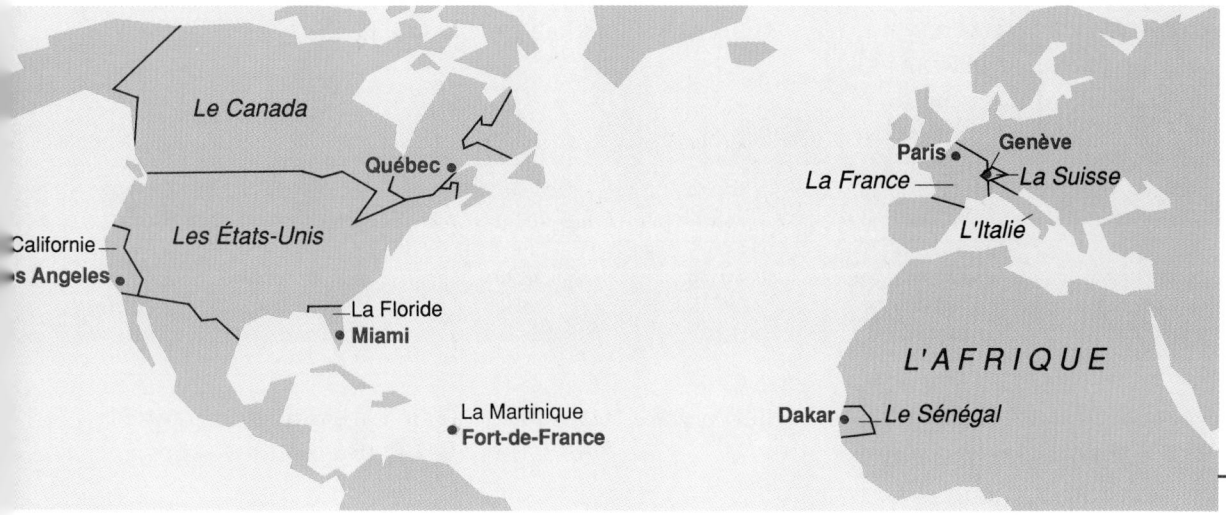

À votre tour!

1 Allô!

Christophe is phoning some friends. Match his questions on the left with his friends' answers on the right.

1. De quelle couleur est ton vélo?
2. Ta raquette est bleue?
3. Tu aimes regarder la télé?
4. C'est un magazine français?
5. Philippe n'aime pas parler en public?

a. Non, il est canadien.
b. C'est vrai! Il est très timide.
c. Non, elle est blanche.
d. Oui, c'est amusant.
e. Il est vert.

2 Créa-dialogue

There has been a burglary in the rue Saint-Pierre. By walkie-talkie, two detectives are describing what they see. Play both roles.

(le)	1. (la)	2. (la)	3. (le)	4. (le)	5. (la)
CAFÉ	PHARMACIE	LIBRAIRIE	Restaurant	CINÉMA	fontaine
grande ou petite?	rouge ou bleue?	grande ou petite?	brun ou blond?	anglais ou français?	noir ou jaune?

▶ DÉTECTIVE 1: **Qu'est-ce qu'il y a devant le café?**
DÉTECTIVE 2: **Il y a une voiture.**

DÉTECTIVE 1: **Elle est grande ou petite?**
DÉTECTIVE 2: **C'est une petite voiture.**

3 Faisons connaissance!

Try to find out which students have the same interests you do. Select two activities you enjoy from Column A and ask a classmate if he/she likes to do them. Your classmate will answer yes or no, using an appropriate expression from Column B.

A	B
chanter	chouette
danser	super
nager	extra
téléphoner	amusant
voyager	intéressant
jouer au foot	pénible
jouer au volley	drôle
organiser des boums	difficile
parler avec les voisins	facile
parler français en classe	
dîner au restaurant	

4 Composition: La chambre de Véronique

Look at the picture of Véronique's room. Write a short paragraph in which you describe five of the following items. You may want to mention color or size **(grand? petit?),** and perhaps give your opinion **(joli? beau? drôle? bon?,** etc.)

la chambre
la porte
le lit
la table
la chaise
la radiocassette
la guitare
l'affiche

▶ **La chambre de Véronique est bleue et blanche. Elle a un grand lit. . . .**

5 Composition: Ma chambre

Write a short description of your own room: real or imaginary. Use only vocabulary that you know. You may use the suggestions about Véronique's room as a guide.

ENTRACTE 5

Vive la différence!

Le monde personnel

Parlons° de votre monde° personnel. Répondez aux questions suivantes.° D'après° vous, quelles sont les réponses des jeunes Français en général à ces° questions?

1 Combien de télés est-ce qu'il y a chez vous?°

- zéro
- une
- deux
- trois ou plus°

Et dans une maison française typique, combien est-ce qu'il y a de télés?

2 Combien de livres est-ce qu'il y a chez vous?

- dix
- cinquante
- cent
- plus de° cent cinquante

Et dans une maison française typique, combien de livres est-ce qu'il y a?

3 Dans la classe de français, quel est le pourcentage d'élèves qui ont un walkman?

- moins de° 25% (vingt-cinq pour cent)
- entre° 26% et 50%
- entre 51% et 75%
- entre 76% et 100% (cent pour cent)

Selon° vous, quel est le pourcentage de jeunes Français qui ont un walkman?

4 En général, comment sont vos relations avec vos parents?

- très bonnes
- bonnes
- assez bonnes
- mauvaises

Et en France, comment sont les relations entre parents et enfants?°

5 Quand vous avez une chose importante à discuter° (par exemple, un problème personnel), à qui est-ce que vous préférez parler?

- à votre frère ou à votre soeur
- à votre père ou à votre mère
- à un copain ou à une copine
- à un professeur

Et les jeunes Français, à qui est-ce qu'ils préfèrent parler de leurs° problèmes?

6 En général, qu'est-ce que vous pensez° de vos professeurs?

- Ils sont «cool».
- Ils sont compréhensifs.°
- Ils sont sévères.°
- Ils sont sympathiques.

Et les élèves français, qu'est-ce qu'ils pensent de leurs professeurs?

7 Quelle est la chose la plus° importante dans votre vie?°

- l'argent°
- l'amitié°
- l'indépendance
- les études°

Et pour les jeunes Français, quelle est la chose la plus importante?

Et les Français?

1. La majorité des familles françaises ont seulement *(only)* une télé. 2. Les Français aiment lire *(to read)*. Ils ont en moyenne *(on the average)* plus de cent livres par famille. 3. 41% (quarante et un pour cent) 4. La majorité des jeunes Français ont de très bonnes relations avec leurs parents. 5. En général, ils préfèrent parler avec un copain ou une copine. 6. En général, ils pensent que leurs professeurs sont sympathiques. 7. C'est l'amitié.

Parlons *Let's talk* **monde** *world* **suivantes** *following* **D'après** *According to* **ces** *these* **chez vous** *in your home* **plus** *more* **plus de** *more than* **moins de** *less than* **entre** *between* **Selon** *According to* **enfants** *children* **discuter** *to discuss* **leurs** *their* **pensez** *think* **compréhensifs** *understanding* **sévères** *strict* **la plus** *the most* **vie** *life* **argent** *money* **amitié** *friendship* **études** *studies*

EN FRANCE

La mobylette

Because mopeds or cyclomoteurs are easy and fun to drive, they are very popular with French teenagers. During the week, many students go to school on their mopeds. On weekends, they take their mopeds to go downtown or to go for a ride in the country with their friends.

Although the term mobylette is a trade name, students tend to use the term (or its shortened form mob) to refer to any type of moped. In France, you can drive a mobylette at age 14, and the only restrictions are that you must wear a helmet and cannot exceed 45 kilometers per hour.

Look at the ads on the right. Which moped would you like to have? Describe it using words that you know. (What color is it? What country is it from? Is it big or small?)

Entre amis: Bonjour, Brigitte!

Chers° copains américains,

Je m'appelle Brigitte Lavie. J'ai quatorze ans. Voici ma photo. Je ne suis pas très grande, mais je ne suis pas petite. Je suis de taille° moyenne.° Je suis brune mais j'ai les yeux° verts. Je suis sportive. J'aime le ski, le jogging et la danse moderne.

J'habite à Toulouse avec ma famille. Mon père travaille dans l'industrie aéronautique. Il est ingénieur.° Ma mère travaille dans une banque. Elle est directrice° du personnel.

J'ai une soeur et un frère. Ma petite soeur s'appelle Ariane. Elle a cinq ans. Elle est très mignonne. Mon frère s'appelle Jérôme. Il a treize ans. Il est pénible. J'ai un chien. Il s'appelle Attila mais il est très gentil. (Il est plus gentil que° mon frère!) J'ai aussi deux poissons rouges.° Ils n'ont pas de nom.°

J'ai une chaîne stéréo et des quantités de compacts. J'ai aussi une moblyette. Le weekend, j'adore faire des promenades° à moblyette avec mes copains. J'ai beaucoup de copains, mais je n'ai pas de « petit copain ».° Ça n'a pas d'importance!° Je suis heureuse° comme ça!°

Amitiés,
Brigitte

Chers *Dear* **taille** *size* **moyenne** *average* **yeux** *eyes* **ingénieur** *engineer* **directrice** *director* **plus gentil que** *nicer than* **poissons rouges** *goldfish* **nom** *name* **faire des promenades** *go for rides* **petit copain** *boyfriend* **Ça n'a pas d'importance!** *It doesn't matter!* **heureuse** *happy* **comme ça** *like that*

NOTE CULTURELLE

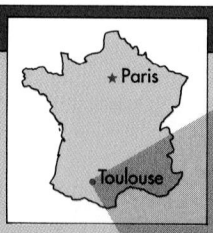

Toulouse

Toulouse, with a population of over half a million people, is the center of the French aeronautic and space industry. It is in Toulouse that the Airbus planes and the Ariane rockets are being built in cooperation with other European countries.

Comment lire

GUESSING FROM CONTEXT

- As you read French, try to guess the meanings of unfamiliar words before you look at the English equivalents. Often the context provides good hints. For example, Brigitte writes:

  Je ne suis pas très grande, mais je ne suis pas petite.
  Je suis de taille moyenne.

  She is neither tall nor short. She must be about average:

  de taille moyenne = *of medium height or size*

- Sometimes you know what individual words in an expression mean, but the phrase does not seem to make sense. Then you have to guess at the real meaning. For example, Brigitte writes that she has:

  deux poissons rouges *??red fish??*

  If you guessed that these are most likely *goldfish,* you are right!

Enrichissez votre vocabulaire

MORE ON COGNATES

- Some words are PARTIAL COGNATES. The English word may help you remember the regular meaning. For example:

gentil	looks like	*gentle*	but means	*nice*
grand	looks like	*grand*	but means	*tall, big*
j'adore	looks like	*I adore*	but means	*I love*

- Some cognates are spelled differently in the two languages. Knowing cognate patterns makes it easier to identify new words. For example:

FRENCH	ENGLISH	FRENCH	ENGLISH
-ique	*-ic*	**aéronautique**	*aeronautic, aeronautical*
-ique	*-ical*	**typique**	*typical*
-té	*-ty*	**quantité**	*quantity*

Activité

Can you identify the English equivalents of the following French words?

la musique classique, une personne dynamique, un film comique, une guitare électrique, une société, une activité, une possibilité, la curiosité, la beauté

Comment écrire *(to write)* **une lettre**

Begin with: *(to a boy)* **Cher** **Cher Patrick,**
(to a girl) **Chère** **Chère Brigitte,**

End with: **Amicalement,** *(In friendship,)*
Amitiés, *(Best regards,)*

Activité: Une lettre à Brigitte

Write a letter to Brigitte in which you describe yourself and your family. You may tell her:

- your name and how old you are
- if you are tall or short
- if you like sports
- if you have brothers and sisters (If so, give their names and ages.)
- if you have pets (If so, say what type and give their names.)
- a few things you own
- a few things you like to do with your friends

Variétés

Petit catalogue des compliments et des insultes

LES ANIMAUX ET LE LANGAGE

Selon° toi, est-ce que les animaux ont une personnalité? Pour les Français, les animaux ont des qualités et des défauts,° comme° nous. Devine° comment on° complète les phrases suivantes° en français.

1 Philippe n'aime pas étudier. Il préfère dormir.° Il est paresseux° comme° . . .

un tigre

un chat

un lézard

2 Charlotte adore parler. Elle est bavarde° comme . . .

une poule

une pie

un lion

3 Isabelle est une excellente élève. Elle a une mémoire extraordinaire. Elle a la mémoire d' . . .

un éléphant

un hippopotame

un kangourou

4 Le petit frère de Christine est jeune, mais il est très intelligent. Il est malin° comme . . .

un cheval

un singe

une girafe

5 Où est Jacques? Il n'est pas prêt!° Oh là là! Il est lent° comme . . .

une tortue

un poisson

un rhinocéros

6 Nicole a très, très faim. Elle a une faim de (d') . . .

lion

ours

loup

Voici les réponses:
1. un lézard 2. une pie 3. un éléphant 4. un singe 5. une tortue 6. loup

Selon According to **défaults** *shortcomings* **comme** *like* **Devine** *Guess* **on** *one* **phrases suivantes** *following sentences* **dormir** *to sleep* **paresseux** *lazy* **comme** *as* **bavarde** *talkative* **malin** *clever* **prêt** *ready* **lent** *slow*

UNITÉ

6 En ville

LEÇON 21 Le français pratique: La ville et la maison

LEÇON 22 Weekend à Paris

LEÇON 23 Au Café de l'Univers

LEÇON 24 Mes voisins

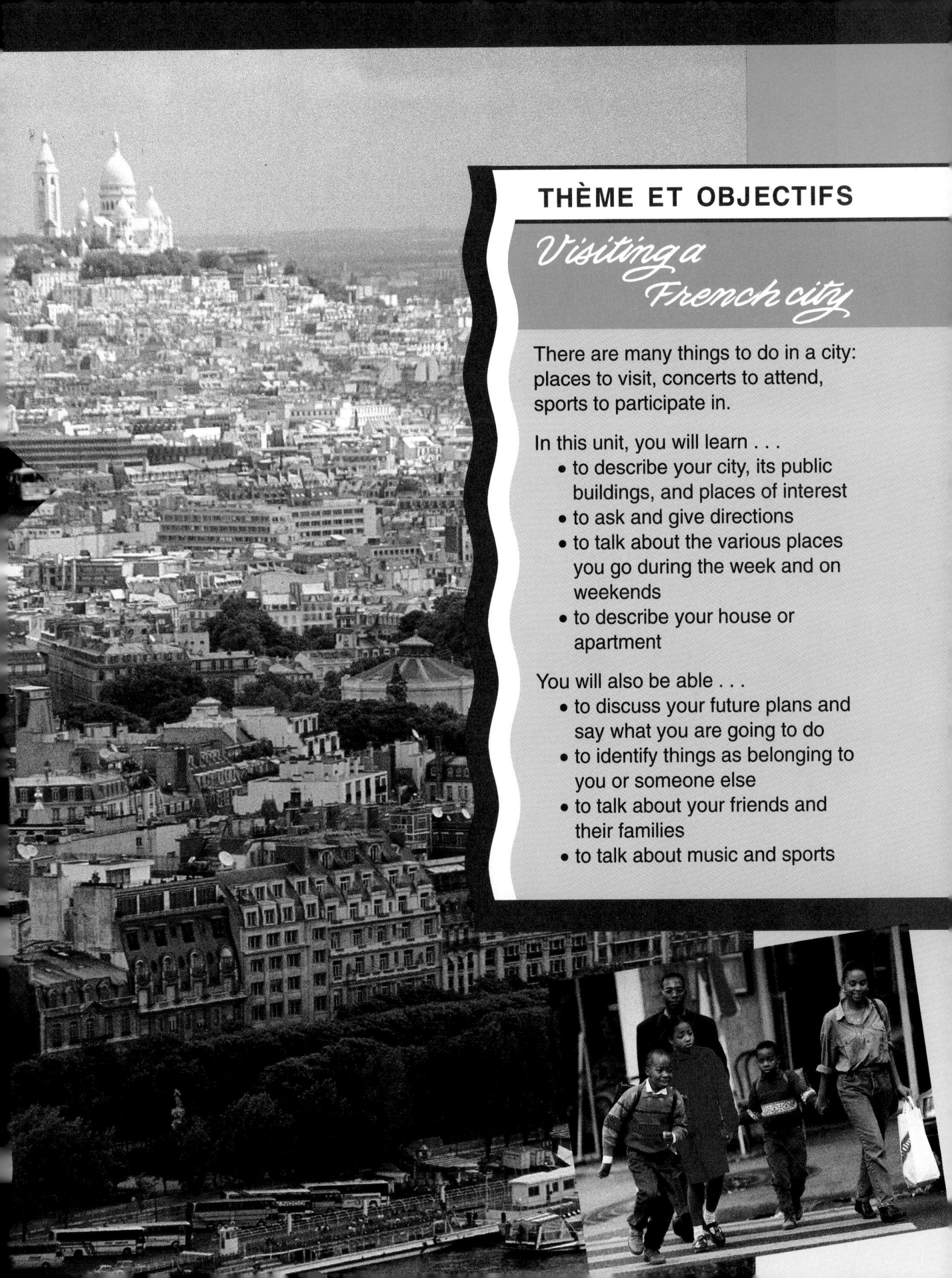

THÈME ET OBJECTIFS

Visiting a French city

There are many things to do in a city: places to visit, concerts to attend, sports to participate in.

In this unit, you will learn . . .

- to describe your city, its public buildings, and places of interest
- to ask and give directions
- to talk about the various places you go during the week and on weekends
- to describe your house or apartment

You will also be able . . .

- to discuss your future plans and say what you are going to do
- to identify things as belonging to you or someone else
- to talk about your friends and their families
- to talk about music and sports

LEÇON 21

LE FRANÇAIS PRATIQUE

La ville et la maison

Accent sur . . . Les villes françaises

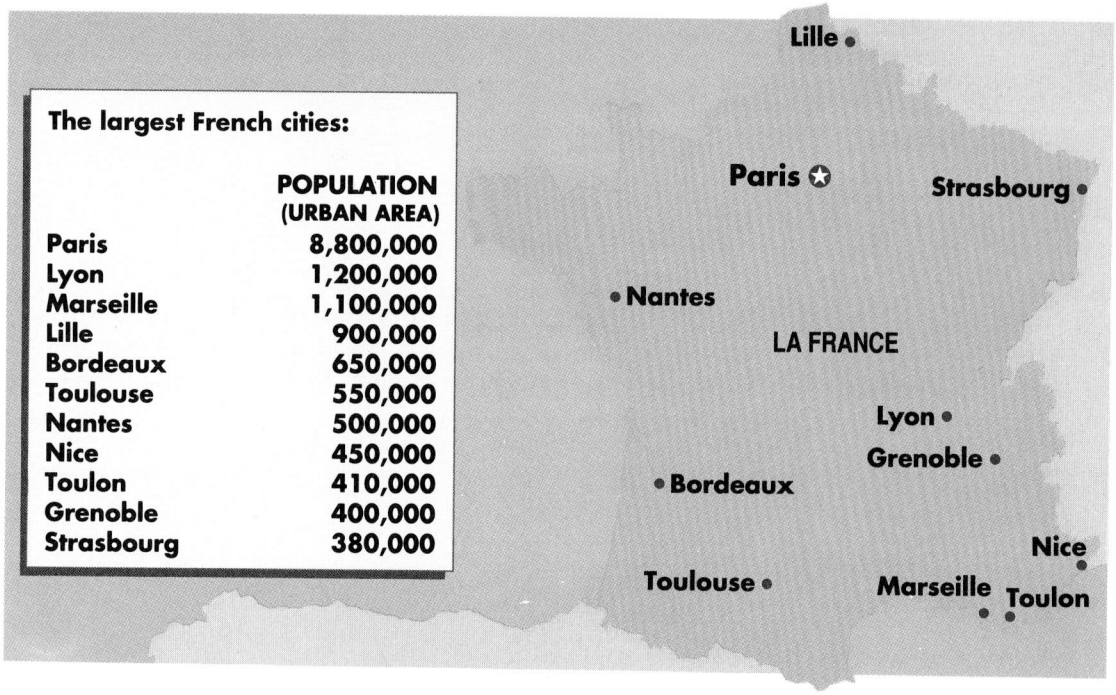

The largest French cities:

	POPULATION (URBAN AREA)
Paris	8,800,000
Lyon	1,200,000
Marseille	1,100,000
Lille	900,000
Bordeaux	650,000
Toulouse	550,000
Nantes	500,000
Nice	450,000
Toulon	410,000
Grenoble	400,000
Strasbourg	380,000

- Today 80% of the French population lives in cities and their surrounding suburbs.
- French cities have a long history. Paris, Lyon, and Marseille, the three largest French cities, were founded well over two thousand years ago! Many cities have a historical district with houses and monuments dating back several centuries. At the same time, French cities also appear very modern, with growing numbers of new houses and modern office buildings.
- French cities differ in architectural style from region to region because of their geographical location and their historical background. However, they also share many common features.

Here are some of the places you may see when you visit a French city:

- **La gare**
  For French people, the train is a rapid and inexpensive means of travel. In general, the railroad station is located near the center of the city or town. The station **(la gare)** offers many useful services to travelers: an information desk, a bicycle rental agency, and a place to check luggage.

- **La poste**
  There are many things you can do in a French post office **(la poste)** besides buying stamps. You can make long-distance phone calls. You can deposit and withdraw money with special postal checking accounts. In many post offices you can use the **Minitel.**

- **Les magasins**
  Although supermarkets and grocery chain stores now exist all over France, most French people still love to shop at the local bakery **(la boulangerie),** the pastry shop **(la pâtisserie),** the butcher shop **(la boucherie),** the grocery store **(l'épicerie),** etc.

- **Le parc**
  The city park **(le parc public)** or public garden **(le jardin public)** is the place where French young people come at noon or after class to walk around or to sit on chairs and talk. The colorful flower beds and shrubbery of the public parks reflect the French love of nature and beauty. This is the Jardin du Luxembourg in Paris.

- **Le château**
  Many French cities were built around a medieval castle **(un château),** which offered protection against enemy attack. This is the castle of Angers built in the XIIIth century.

A. Où habites-tu?

How to talk about where one lives:

Où habites-tu?

J'habite
- à Tours.
- à Villeneuve
- dans **une grande ville** *(city, town)*
- dans **un petit village**
- dans **un joli quartier** *(neighborhood)*
- dans **une rue** *(street)* intéressante

Quelle est **ton adresse?**

J'habite
- 32, **avenue** Victor Hugo.
- 14, **rue** La Fayette
- 50, **boulevard** Wilson

NOTE CULTURELLE

Le nom des rues

In France, streets are often named after famous people, especially writers, artists, and politicians.

- Victor Hugo (1802–1885), novelist and poet, is best known for his monumental novel *Les Misérables*.
- La Fayette (1757–1834) played an important role in the American and French Revolutions.
- Woodrow Wilson (1856–1924) is remembered as the United States President who sent American troops to help French forces fight against Germany during World War I (1914–1918).

1 Expression personnelle

Describe where you live by completing the following sentences.

1. J'habite à . . .
2. Ma ville est (n'est pas) . . . (grande? petite? moderne? jolie?)
   Mon village est (n'est pas) . . . (grand? petit? joli?)
3. Mon quartier est (n'est pas) . . . (intéressant? joli? moderne?)
4. Mon adresse est . . .
5. Ma ville favorite est . . .
6. Un jour, je voudrais visiter . . . *(name of city)*

2 Interview

You are a French journalist writing an article about living conditions in the United States. Interview a classmate and find out the following information.

1. Where does he/she live?
2. Is his/her city large or small?
3. Is his/her city pretty?
4. What is his/her address?

B. Ma ville

How to talk about one's hometown:

3 Ton quartier

Say whether the following places are located in the area where you live. If so, you may want to give the name of the place.

▶ école **Il y a une école. Elle s'appelle «Washington School». (Il n'y a pas d'école.)**

1. restaurant
2. cinéma
3. église
4. centre commercial
5. bibliothèque
6. café
7. plage
8. supermarché
9. hôpital
10. parc
11. stade
12. musée
13. hôtel
14. piscine
15. théâtre

4 À Montréal

You are visiting your friend Pauline in Montreal. For each of the situations below, decide where you would like to go. Ask Pauline if there is such a place in her neighborhood.

▶ You are hungry.

1. You want to have a soft drink.
2. You want to see a movie.
3. You want to swim a few laps.
4. You want to run on a track.
5. You want to read a book about Canada.
6. You want to see a French play.
7. You want to buy some fruit and crackers.
8. You want to see an art exhibit.
9. You want to play frisbee on the grass.
10. You slipped and you're afraid you sprained your ankle.

aux Anciens Canadiens
RESTAURANT

LE GRILL 183 ST-PAUL EST 397-1044

LE BISTROT DU GRILL

- Steak frites Salade $5,95
- Poulet rôti frites, salade $5,95

CHANSON FRANÇAISE
jeu., ven. et sam. dès 21h.
AMBIANCE GARANTIE

LE RESTAURANT
CUISINE FRANÇAISE

Atmosphère chaleureuse
Vieille maison du 17e siècle
LA PLUS BELLE TERRASSE DU VIEUX-MONTRÉAL

C. Pour demander un renseignement *(information)*

How to ask for directions:

Pardon, | monsieur. Où est l'hôtel Normandie?
Excusez-moi, | madame
mademoiselle

Il est dans la rue Jean Moulin.

Où est-ce qu'il y a un café?

Il y a un café | **rue** Saint Paul. — **une rue**
boulevard Masséna — **un boulevard**
avenue de Lyon — **une avenue**

Où est-ce? *(Where is it?)*
Est-ce que c'est **loin** *(far)*?

Non, ce n'est pas loin.
C'est **près** *(nearby)*.

C'est | **à gauche** *(to the left)*. — **Tournez** | à gauche.
à droite *(to the right)* — à droite
tout droit *(straight ahead)* — **Continuez** tout droit.

Merci beaucoup!

5 En ville

A tourist who is visiting a French city asks a local resident how to get to the following places. Act out the dialogues.

▶ **— Pardon, mademoiselle (monsieur). Où est le Café de la Poste?**
— Le Café de la Poste? Il est dans la rue Pascal.
— Où est-ce?
— Continuez tout droit!
— Merci, mademoiselle (monsieur).

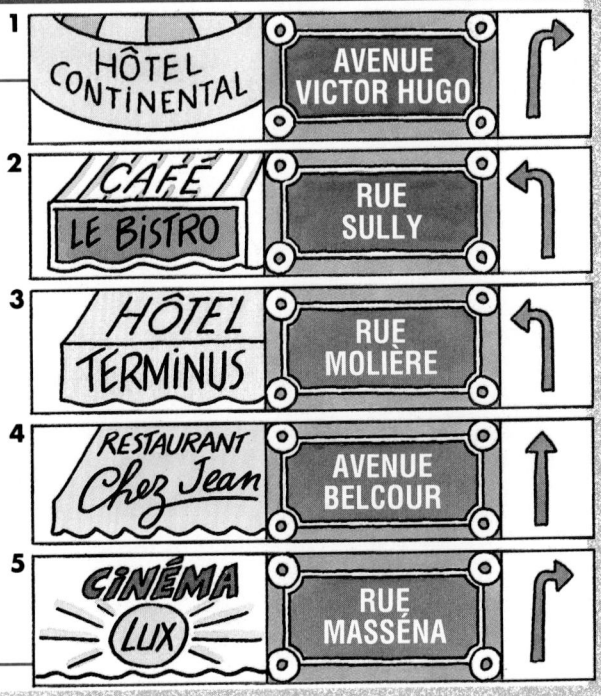

D. Ma maison

How to describe one's home:

J'habite dans | **une maison** *(house).*
un appartement
un immeuble *(apartment building)*

Ma maison / mon appartement est | **moderne.**
confortable

Ma chambre est | **en haut** *(upstairs).*
en bas *(downstairs)*

La maison

le garage

une chambre

les toilettes

une salle de bains

une salle de bains

le jardin

une chambre

une chambre

la cuisine

les toilettes

la salle à manger

le salon

6 Ma maison

Describe your home by completing the following sentences.

1. J'habite dans . . . (une maison? un appartement?)
2. Mon appartement est . . . (grand? petit? confortable? joli?)
   Ma maison est . . . (grande? petite? confortable? jolie?)
3. La cuisine est . . . (grande? petite? moderne?)
4. La cuisine est peinte *(painted)* en . . . (jaune? vert? gris? blanc? ??)
5. Ma chambre est peinte en . . . (bleu? rose? ??)
6. Dans le salon, il y a . . . (une télé? un sofa? des plantes vertes? ??)
7. En général, nous dînons dans . . . (la cuisine? la salle à manger?)
8. Ma maison / mon appartement a . . . (un jardin? un garage? ??)

7 En haut ou en bas?

Imagine you live in a two-story house. Indicate where the following rooms are located.

▶ ma chambre

1. la cuisine
2. la salle à manger
3. les toilettes
4. la salle de bains
5. la chambre de mes *(my)* parents
6. le salon

8 Où sont-ils?

From what the following people are doing, guess where they are — in or around the house.

▶ Madame Martin répare *(is repairing)* la voiture.
Elle est dans le garage.

1. Nous dînons.
2. Tu regardes la télé.
3. Antoine et Juliette jouent au frisbee.
4. J'étudie le français.
5. Monsieur Martin prépare le dîner.
6. Henri se lave *(is washing up)*.
7. Ma soeur téléphone à son copain.

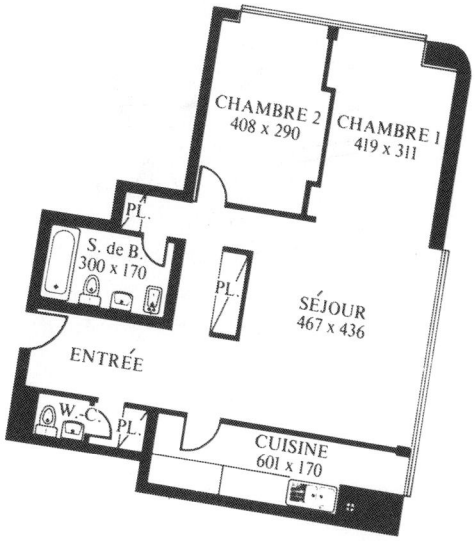

À votre tour!

1 La bonne réponse

Match the questions on the left with the appropriate answers on the right.

1. Pardon, mademoiselle, où est le supermarché?
2. Est-ce que Jacques est à la bibliothèque?
3. Ta voiture est au garage?
4. Est-ce que vous dînez dans la salle à manger?
5. Est-ce qu'il y a une piscine dans la ville où tu habites?

a. Non, dans la cuisine.
b. Non, mais il y a une belle plage.
c. Oui, il regarde des magazines anglais.
d. Non, elle est dans la rue.
e. C'est tout droit!

2 Créa-dialogue

You have just arrived in Villeneuve, where you will spend the summer. Ask a pedestrian where you can find the places represented by the symbols. He (She) will give you the location of each place, according to the map on page 197.

▶ —Pardon, monsieur (madame). Où est-ce qu'il y a un hôtel?
—Il y a un hôtel avenue de Bordeaux.
—Est-ce que c'est loin?
—Non, c'est près.
—Merci beaucoup!

3 Où est-ce?

Now you have been in Villeneuve for several weeks and are familiar with the city. You meet a tourist on the avenue de Bordeaux at the place indicated on the map. The tourist asks you where certain places are and you indicate how to get there.

▶ l'hôpital Sainte Anne

Villeneuve
musée La Salle
piscine municipale
magasin de sport
boulevard de la République
rue Jean Moulin
rue du Commerce
restaurant Le Matador
stade
rue Danton
rue Jean Moulin
hôtel Armor
avenue de Bordeaux
hôpital Sainte Anne
Ciné-Rex
Café Dupont
rue Danton
rue Pascal
boulevard de la République
Église St-Louis
bibliothèque municipale
avenue de Bordeaux
rue Saint-Louis
rue Danton
supermarché Casino
parc de la ville
X
Vous êtes ici.

4 Mon quartier

Describe your neighborhood, listing five places and giving their names.

▶ **Dans mon quartier, il y a un supermarché. C'est le supermarché Casino.**

1. le musée La Salle
2. le supermarché Casino
3. l'hôtel Armor
4. le restaurant Le Matador
5. l'église Saint Louis

5 Composition: La maison idéale

Briefly describe your dream house. You may use the following adjectives to describe the various rooms: **grand, petit, moderne, confortable, joli,** as well as colors. If you wish, sketch and label a floor plan.

Modernes et confortables . . .
SUPERBES VILLAS
à partir de 995.000 F
Près toutes commodités
Écoles, lycées, commerces, R.E.R. à 10 mn.

LEÇON 22

Weekend à Paris

Aujourd'hui c'est samedi.
Les élèves ne vont pas en classe. *are not going*
Où est-ce qu'ils vont alors?
Ça dépend!

Thomas va au café. *is going*
Il a un rendez-vous avec une copine. *date*

Florence et Karine vont aux Champs-Élysées.
Elles vont regarder les magasins de mode. *fashion*
Après, elles vont aller au cinéma. *Afterward / to go*

Daniel va chez son copain Laurent. *to the house of / his*
Les garçons vont jouer au ping-pong.
Après, ils vont aller au musée des sciences de la Villette.
Ils vont jouer avec les machines électroniques.

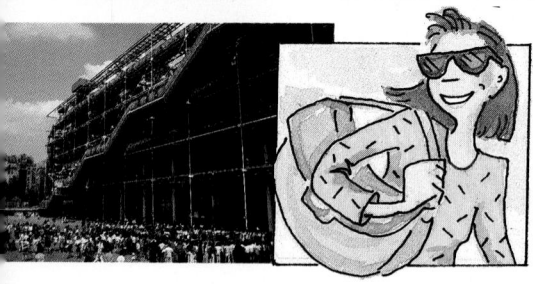

Béatrice a un grand sac et des lunettes de soleil. *sunglasses*
Est-ce qu'elle va à un rendez-vous secret?
Non! Elle va au Centre Pompidou.
Elle va regarder les acrobates.
Et après, elle va écouter un concert.

Et Jean-François? Qu'est-ce qu'il va faire aujourd'hui?
Est-ce qu'il va visiter le Centre Pompidou?
Est-ce qu'il va regarder les acrobates?
Est-ce qu'il va écouter un concert?
Hélas, non! *Alas (Unfortunately)*
Il va rester à la maison. *to stay*
Pourquoi? Parce qu'il est malade. *sick*
Pauvre Jean-François! *Poor*
Il fait si beau dehors! *so / outside*

Compréhension

1. Quel jour est-ce aujourd'hui?
2. Pourquoi est-ce que Thomas va au café?
3. Avec qui est-ce que Florence va au cinéma?
4. Où va Daniel?
5. Qu'est-ce que Daniel et Laurent font d'abord *(first)*?
6. Où va Béatrice?
7. Pourquoi est-ce que Jean-François ne va pas en ville?
8. Quel temps fait-il aujourd'hui?

NOTE CULTURELLE

À Paris

Paris offers many attractions for people of all ages. Here are some places particularly popular with young people.

Le parc de la Villette

This spacious park on the outskirts of Paris is home to a new modern science museum with its hundreds of hands-on exhibits. Also located on the grounds is Le Zénith, a large music hall that frequently features rock concerts.

Le Centre Pompidou

This immense cultural center, also known as Beaubourg, is dedicated to modern art. It has a large media library where young people have access to all types of audio-visual equipment. On the large plaza in front of the building, one can listen to reggae and jazz bands or watch mimes, jugglers, and acrobats.

Les Champs-Élysées

The Champs-Élysées is a wide avenue with elegant shops, movie theaters, and popular cafés.

A. Le verbe *aller*

Aller *(to go)* is the only IRREGULAR verb that ends in **-er.** Note the forms of **aller** in the present tense.

aller	*to go*	J'aime **aller** au cinéma.
je **vais** tu **vas** il/elle **va**	*I go, I am going* *you go, you are going* *he/she goes, he/she is going*	Je **vais** à un concert. **Vas**-tu à la boum? Paul **va** à l'école.
nous **allons** vous **allez** ils/elles **vont**	*we go, we are going* *you go, you are going* *they go, they are going*	Nous **allons** au café. Est-ce que vous **allez** là-bas? Ils ne **vont** pas en classe.

➡ Remember that **aller** is used in asking people how they feel.

Ça **va?** — Oui, ça **va.**
Comment **vas**-tu? — Je **vais** bien, merci.
Comment **allez**-vous? — Très bien.

➡ **Aller** is used in many common expressions.

To encourage someone to do something:
Vas-y! *Come on! Go ahead! Do it!*

To tell someone to go away:
Va-t'en! *Go away!*

To tell friends to start doing something:
Allons-y! *Let's go!*

1 Les vacances

The following students at a boarding school in Nice are going home for vacation. Indicate to which of the cities they are going, according to the luggage tags shown below.

▶ Jean-Michel est canadien.

1. Je suis suisse.
2. Charlotte est américaine.
3. Nous sommes italiens.
4. Tu es français.
5. Vous êtes espagnols.
6. Michiko est japonaise.
7. Mike et Shelley sont anglais.
8. Ana et Carlos sont mexicains.

2 Jamais le dimanche!

(Never on Sunday!)

On Sundays, French students do not go to class. They all go somewhere else. Express this according to the model.

▶ Philippe/au cinéma
Le dimanche, Philippe ne va pas en classe.
Il va au cinéma.

1. nous / au café
2. vous / en ville
3. Céline et Michèle / à un concert
4. Jérôme / au restaurant
5. je / à un match de foot
6. tu / à la piscine

B. La préposition *à; à* + l'article défini

The preposition **à** has several meanings:

in	Patrick habite **à** Paris.	*Patrick lives **in** Paris.*
at	Nous sommes **à** la piscine.	*We are **at** the pool.*
to	Est-ce que tu vas **à** Toulouse?	*Are you going **to** Toulouse?*

CONTRACTIONS

Note the forms of **à** + DEFINITE ARTICLE in the sentences below.

Voici **le** café.	Marc est **au** café.	Corinne va **au** café.
Voici **les** Champs-Élysées.	Tu es **aux** Champs-Élysées.	Je vais **aux** Champs-Élysées.
Voici **la** piscine.	Anne est **à la** piscine.	Éric va **à la** piscine.
Voici **l'**hôtel.	Je suis **à l'**hôtel.	Vous allez **à l'**hôtel.

The preposition **à** contracts with **le** and **les,** but not with **la** and **l'.**

CONTRACTION	NO CONTRACTION		
à + le → **au**	à + la = **à la**	**au** cinéma	**à la** piscine
à + les → **aux**	à + l' = **à l'**	**aux** Champs-Élysées	**à l'**école

➡ There is liaison after **aux** when the next word begins with a vowel sound.

Le professeur parle **aux** (z) **élèves.** Je téléphone **aux** (z) **amis** de Claire.

3 Dans la rue

Two friends meet in the street and talk about where they are going.

4 Préférences

Ask your classmates about their preferences. Be sure to use contractions when needed.

▶ aller à (le concert ou le théâtre?)

1. dîner à (la maison ou le restaurant)?
2. étudier à (la bibliothèque ou la maison)?
3. nager à (la piscine ou la plage)?
4. regarder un match de foot à (la télé ou le stade)?
5. aller à (le cinéma ou le musée)?

(Je préfère aller au théâtre.)

5 À Paris

You are living in Paris. A friend asks you where you are going and why. Act out the dialogues with a classmate.

▶ **—Où vas-tu?**
—Je vais à l'Opéra.
—Pourquoi?
—Parce que j'aime le ballet classique.

OÙ?	POURQUOI?
▶ l'Opéra	J'aime le ballet classique.
1. l'Alliance Française	J'ai une classe de français.
2. le Centre Pompidou	J'aime l'art moderne.
3. le musée d'Orsay	C'est un musée intéressant.
4. les Champs-Élysées	J'ai un rendez-vous là-bas.
5. la tour Eiffel	Il y a une belle vue *(view)* sur Paris.
6. le Zénith	Il y a un concert de rock.
7. la Villette	Il y a une exposition *(exhibit)* intéressante.
8. le stade de Bercy	Il y a un match de foot.

6 Où vont-ils?

Read what the following people like to do. Then say where each one is going by choosing the appropriate place from the list.

▶ Daniel aime danser.
Il va à la discothèque.

1. Corinne aime l'art moderne.
2. Jean-François aime manger.
3. Delphine aime les westerns.
4. Marina aime nager.
5. Éric aime regarder les magazines.
6. Denise aime faire des promenades.
7. Philippe aime la musique.
8. Alice aime le football.
9. Cécile aime le shopping.

le stade
la bibliothèque
le cinéma
le centre commercial
la discothèque
le musée
le parc
le restaurant
la plage
le concert

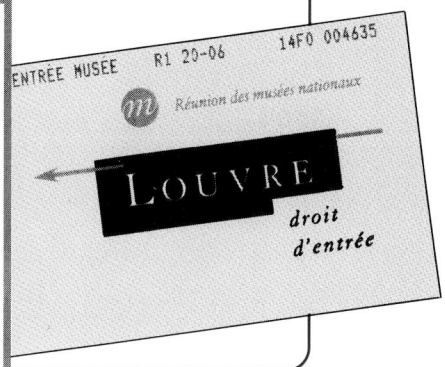

Vocabulaire: En ville

Quelques endroits où aller

un endroit	*place*	**une boum**	*party*
un concert	*concert*		
un film	*movie*		
un pique-nique	*picnic*		
un rendez-vous	*date, appointment*		

VERBES

arriver	*to arrive, come*	**J'arrive** à l'école à 9 heures.
rentrer	*to go back, come back*	À quelle heure **rentres**-tu à la maison?
rester	*to stay*	Les touristes **restent** à l'hôtel.

EXPRESSIONS

à pied	*on foot*	**en voiture**	*by car*	**en métro**	*by subway*
à vélo	*by bicycle*	**en bus**	*by bus*	**en taxi**	*by taxi*
		en train	*by train*		

faire une promenade à pied *to go for a walk*
faire une promenade à vélo *to go for a ride (by bike)*
faire une promenade en voiture *to go for a drive*

7 Questions personnelles

1. En général, à quelle heure est-ce que tu arrives à l'école?
2. À quelle heure est-ce que tu rentres à la maison? Qu'est-ce que tu fais quand tu rentres à la maison?
3. Comment vas-tu à l'école? à pied, à vélo, en voiture ou en bus?
4. Le weekend, est-ce que tu restes à la maison? Où vas-tu?
5. Comment vas-tu à la piscine? à la plage? au cinéma?
6. Est-ce que tu aimes faire des promenades à pied? Où vas-tu? avec qui?
7. Est-ce que tu aimes faire des promenades à vélo? Où vas-tu?
8. En général, est-ce que tu aimes regarder les films à la télé? Quels films est-ce que tu préfères? (films d'action? films de science-fiction? comédies?)
9. Quand tu as un rendez-vous avec un copain ou une copine, où allez-vous?
10. Est-ce que tu fais *(go on)* des pique-niques? où?

C. La préposition *chez*

Note the use of **chez** in the following sentences.

Paul est **chez Céline.**	*Paul is* ***at Céline's (house).***
Je dîne **chez un copain.**	*I am having dinner* ***at a friend's (home).***
Nathalie va **chez Juliette.**	*Nathalie is going* ***to Juliette's (apartment).***
Tu vas **chez ta cousine.**	*You are going* ***to your cousin's (place).***

The French equivalent of *to* or *at someone's (house, home)* is the construction:

chez + PERSON	**chez** Béatrice	**chez** ma cousine

➡ Note the interrogative expression: **chez qui?**

Chez qui vas-tu? ***To whose house*** *are you going?*

8 En vacances

When we are on vacation, we often like to visit friends and relatives. Say where the following people are going.

▶ Claire / Marc
Claire va chez Marc.

1. Hélène / Jérôme
2. Jean-Paul / Lucie
3. tu / un copain
4. Corinne / une cousine
5. vous / des copines à Québec
6. nous / un cousin à Paris

9 Weekend

On weekends, we often like to visit friends and do things together. Say how the following people are spending Sunday afternoon.

▶ Cécile / jouer au ping-pong / Robert

1. Nathalie / aller / Béatrice
2. Claire / dîner / des cousins
3. Éric / jouer au croquet / Sylvie
4. Marc / écouter des disques / un copain
5. Jean-Pierre / regarder la télé / une copine
6. Catherine / jouer au Monopoly / François

D. La construction *aller* + l'infinitif

The following sentences describe what people are *going to do.* Note how the verb **aller** is used to describe these FUTURE events.

Nathalie **va nager.**	*Nathalie **is going to swim.***
Paul et Marc **vont jouer** au tennis.	*Paul and Marc **are going to play** tennis.*
Nous **allons rester** à la maison.	*We **are going to stay** home.*
Je **vais aller** en ville.	*I **am going to go** downtown.*

To express the NEAR FUTURE, the French use the construction:

PRESENT of **aller** + INFINITIVE

➡ In negative sentences, the construction is:

SUBJECT + **ne** + PRESENT of **aller** + **pas** + INFINITIVE . . .				
Sylvie	**ne**	va	**pas**	écouter le concert avec nous.

➡ Note the interrogative forms:

Qu'est-ce que tu vas faire?	***What are you going** to do?*
Quand est-ce que vous allez rentrer?	***When are you going** to come back?*

Learning about language

To talk about FUTURE plans and intentions, French and English frequently use similar verbs: **aller** *(to be going to).*

10 Tourisme

Say where the following people are going this summer and what they are going to visit.

▶ Monique (à Paris / le Louvre)
Monique va à Paris. Elle va visiter le Louvre.

1. Alice (à New York / la statue de la Liberté)
2. nous (en Égypte / les pyramides)
3. vous (à Rome / le Colisée)
4. tu (à la Nouvelle Orléans / le Vieux Carré)
5. je (à San Francisco / Chinatown)
6. les élèves (à San Antonio / l'Alamo)
7. Madame Lambert (à Beijing / la Cité interdite *[Forbidden City]*)
8. les touristes (à Kyoto / les temples)

11 Qu'est-ce que tu vas faire?

Ask your classmates if they are going to do the following things this weekend.

▶ étudier

1. travailler
2. écouter la radio
3. regarder la télé
4. nager
5. inviter des amis
6. aller à une boum
7. jouer au tennis
8. rester à la maison
9. faire une promenade à vélo

(Non, je ne vais pas étudier.)

12 Un jeu: Descriptions

Choose a person from Column A and say where the person is, what he or she has, and what he or she is going to do. Use the verbs **être, avoir,** and **aller** with the phrases in columns B, C, and D. How many logical descriptions can you make?

A	B (être)	C (avoir)	D (aller)
tu	sur le court	des livres	chanter
Monique	à la bibliothèque	un vélo	manger un sandwich
je	au salon	30 francs	étudier
les amis	en vacances	une télé	faire une promenade
nous	à la boum	une chaîne stéréo	regarder un film
vous	à la maison	une guitare	faire un match
	au café	une raquette	écouter des cassettes

▶ **Monique est en vacances. Elle a un vélo. Elle va faire une promenade.**

Prononciation

Les semi-voyelles /w/ et /j/

In French, the semi-vowels /w/ and /j/ are pronounced very quickly, almost like consonants.

Répétez:

/w/ **oui chouette Louise**

/wa/, /wɛ̃/ **moi toi pourquoi voiture loin**

Chouette! La voiture de Louise n'est pas loin.

/j/ **bien chien radio piano Pierre Daniel violon pied étudiant**

Pierre écoute la radio avec Daniel.

oui

très bien

À votre tour!

1 Allô!

Anne is calling Jérôme. Match Jérome's answers with Anne's questions. Then act out the dialogue with a friend.

1. Tu restes chez toi samedi?
2. Qu'est-ce que vous allez faire?
3. Est-ce que vous allez aller au cinéma?
4. À quelle heure est-ce que tu vas rentrer?

a. À dix heures.
b. Peut-être! Il y a un très bon film au Rex.
c. Nous allons faire une promenade en ville.
d. Non, j'ai un rendez-vous avec Christine.

2 Créa-dialogue

As you are going for a walk in town, you meet several friends. Ask them where they are going and what they are going to do there.

OÙ?	ACTIVITÉ
	dîner avec un copain

▶ —Salut, Alison. Ça va?
—Oui, ça va!
—Où vas-tu?
—Je vais au restaurant.
—Ah bon? Qu'est-ce que tu vas faire là-bas?
—Je vais dîner avec un copain.
—Avec qui?
—Avec Chris.

OÙ?	ACTIVITÉ
1 	manger une pizza
2 	faire une promenade
3 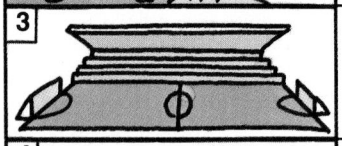	jouer au foot
4 	nager
5 	jouer au volley
6 	travailler
7 	??

3 Conversation libre

Have a conversation with a classmate. Ask your classmate questions about what he / she plans to do on the weekend. Try to find out as much as possible, using yes / no questions.

▶ Est-ce que tu vas rester à la maison?

Non, je ne vais pas rester à la maison.

Est-ce que tu vas aller en ville?

Oui, je vais aller en ville.

Est-ce que tu vas au cinéma?

Oui, je vais au cinéma.

(Non, je ne vais pas au cinéma.)

4 Qu'est-ce que vous allez faire?

Leave a note for your friend Jean-Marc, telling him three things that you and your friends are going to do tonight and three things that you are going to do this weekend.

Jean-Marc
Ce soir (Tonight)
1. Nous allons...
2.
3.
Ce weekend
1.
2.
3.

5 Bonnes résolutions

Imagine that it is January 1 and you are making up New Year's resolutions. On a separate sheet of paper, describe six of your resolutions by saying what you are going to do and what you are not going to do in the coming year.

▶

1 JANVIER
1. Je vais toujours parler français en classe.
2. Je ne vais pas être pénible avec mes copains...

LEÇON 23

Au Café de l'Univers

Où vas-tu après les classes?	*after*
Est-ce que tu vas directement chez toi?	*straight / home*
Monique, elle, ne va pas directement chez elle.	*to her house*
Elle va au Café de l'Univers avec ses copines Anne-Marie et Estelle.	
Elle vient souvent ici avec elles.	*comes*
À la table de Monique, la conversation est toujours très animée.	*lively*
De quoi parlent les filles aujourd'hui?	*About what*
Est-ce qu'elles parlent de l'examen d'histoire?	*history test*
du problème de maths?	
de la classe de sciences?	
Non!	
Est-ce qu'elles parlent du weekend prochain?	*next*
des vacances?	
Non plus!	*Not that either.*
Est-ce qu'elles parlent du nouveau copain de Marie-Claire?	*new*
de la cousine de Pauline?	
des amis de Véronique?	
Pas du tout!	*Not at all!*
Aujourd'hui, les filles parlent d'un sujet beaucoup plus important!	*subject / more*
Elles parlent du nouveau prof d'anglais! (C'est un jeune professeur américain. Il est très intéressant, très amusant, très sympathique … et surtout il est très mignon!)	*above all*

Compréhension

1. Où va Monique après les classes?
2. Avec qui est-ce qu'elle va au café?
3. Qu'est-ce que les filles font au café?
4. Est-ce qu'elles parlent de l'école?
5. Est-ce qu'elles parlent des activités du weekend?
6. De quelle *(which)* personne parlent-elles aujourd'hui?
7. De quelle nationalité est le professeur d'anglais?
8. Comment est-il?

Et toi?

Describe what you do by completing the following sentences.

1. En général, après les classes,
   je vais . . .
   je ne vais pas . . .

   - à la bibliothèque
   - au café
   - chez mes *(my)* copains
   - directement chez moi

2. Avec mes copains,
   je parle . . .
   je ne parle pas . . .

   - de la classe de français
   - des examens
   - du prof de français
   - du weekend

3. Avec mes parents,
   je parle . . .
   je ne parle pas . . .

   - de l'école
   - de mes notes *(grades)*
   - de la classe de français
   - de mes copains

4. Avec mon frère ou ma soeur,
   je parle . . .
   je ne parle pas . . .

   - de mes copains
   - de mes problèmes
   - du weekend
   - des vacances

NOTE CULTURELLE

Au café

For French teenagers, the café is much more than just a place to have a soft drink or a sandwich. Some go there to study, others go to listen to music, to play electronic games **(le flipper),** or to make a phone call. Most students, however, go to their favorite café after class or on weekends to meet their friends and simply talk.

A French café usually consists of two parts: **l'intérieur** (the indoor section) and **la terrasse** (the outdoor section which often occupies part of the sidewalk). In spring and summer, **la terrasse** is the ideal spot to enjoy the sun and to watch the people passing by.

A. Le verbe *venir*

The verb **venir** *(to come)* is irregular. Note the forms of **venir** in the present tense.

venir	Nous allons **venir** avec des amis.
je **viens** tu **viens** il / elle **vient**	Je **viens** avec toi. Est-ce que tu **viens** au cinéma? Monique ne **vient** pas avec nous.
nous **venons** vous **venez** ils / elles **viennent**	Nous **venons** à cinq heures. À quelle heure **venez**-vous à la boum? Ils **viennent** de Paris, n'est-ce pas?

➡ **Revenir** *(to come back)* is conjugated like **venir.**

—À quelle heure **revenez**-vous?
—Nous **revenons** à dix heures.

➡ Note the interrogative expression: **d'où?** *(from where?)*

D'où viens-tu? ***Where** do you come **from?***

1 Tu viens?

Tell a friend where you are going and ask him or her to come along.

▶ au restaurant

(Non, je ne viens pas.)

1. au café
2. à la bibliothèque
3. à la piscine
4. au supermarché
5. au centre commercial
6. au magasin de disques
7. au stade
8. en classe

2 Le pique-nique de Monique

Monique has invited friends to a picnic. Say who is coming and who is not.

▶ Philippe (non)
Philippe ne vient pas.

1. Alice (oui)
2. Jean-Pierre (non)
3. Paul et Caroline (oui)
4. vous (non)
5. je (oui)
6. nous (non)
7. tu (non)
8. les copines d'Alice (oui)
9. le prof d'anglais (oui)

You may think French verbs are hard to learn because they have several forms. French students, on the other hand, have a hard time with English verbs because so many are made up of two words. For example, they may know the words *get* and *keep*, but then they have to learn the meanings of *get up, get out, get on,* and these meanings are different from *keep up, keep out, keep on,* etc.

B. La préposition *de; de* + l'article défini

The preposition **de** has several meanings:

from	Nous venons **de** la bibliothèque.	*We are coming **from** the library.*
of	Quelle est l'adresse **de** l'école?	*What is the address **of** the school?*
about	Je parle **de** mon copain.	*I am talking **about** my friend.*

CONTRACTIONS

Note the forms of **de** + DEFINITE ARTICLE in the sentences below.

Voici **le** café.	Marc vient **du** café.
Voici **les** Champs-Élysées.	Nous venons **des** Champs-Élysées.
Voici **la** piscine.	Tu reviens **de la** piscine.
Voici **l'**hôtel.	Les touristes arrivent **de l'**hôtel.

The preposition **de** contracts with **le** and **les,** but not with **la** and **l'.**

CONTRACTION	NO CONTRACTION		
de + le → **du**	de + la = **de la**	**du** café	**de la** plage
de + les → **des**	de + l' = **de l'**	**des** magasins	**de l'**école

➡ There is liaison after **des** when the next word begins with a vowel sound.

Où sont les livres **des** (z) **étudiants?**

3 Rendez-vous

The following students live in Paris. On a Saturday afternoon they are meeting in a café. Say where each one is coming from.

▶ Jacques: le musée d'Orsay

1. Sylvie: le Louvre
2. Isabelle: le parc de la Villette
3. Jean-Paul: le Centre Pompidou
4. François: le Quartier latin
5. Cécile: l'avenue de l'Opéra
6. Nicole: la tour Eiffel
7. Marc: le jardin du Luxembourg
8. André: les Champs-Élysées
9. Pierre: les Galeries Lafayette
10. Corinne: la rue Bonaparte

4 D'où viens-tu?

During vacation, Philippe goes out every day. When he gets home, his sister Cécile asks him where he is coming from.

▶ mardi

1. lundi
2. mercredi
3. vendredi
4. dimanche
5. samedi
6. jeudi

▶

LUNDI	le restaurant
MARDI	le théâtre
MERCREDI	la bibliothèque
JEUDI	l'opéra
VENDREDI	le concert
SAMEDI	le pique-nique de Monique
DIMANCHE	la boum de Christine

Vocabulaire: Les sports, les jeux et la musique

Les sports		Les instruments de musique	
le foot(ball)	**le volley(ball)**	**le piano**	**la flûte**
le basket(ball)	**le tennis**	**le violon**	**la guitare**
le ping-pong	**le baseball**	**le saxo(phone)**	**la clarinette**
		le clavier *(keyboard)*	**la batterie** *(drums)*

Les jeux *(games)*

les échecs *(chess)* **les dames** *(checkers)*
le Monopoly **les cartes** *(cards)*

VERBES

jouer à + **le, la, les** + SPORT or GAME	*to play*	Nous **jouons au** tennis.
jouer de + **le, la, les** + INSTRUMENT	*to play*	Alice **joue du** piano.

5 Activités

Ask your classmates if they play the following instruments and games.

▶ —Est-ce que tu joues au ping-pong?
—Oui, je joue au ping-pong.
(Non, je ne joue pas au ping-pong.)

▶ —Est-ce que tu joues du piano?
—Oui, je joue du piano.
(Non, je ne joue pas du piano.)

C. Les pronoms accentués

In the answers to the questions below, the nouns in heavy print are replaced by pronouns. These pronouns are called STRESS PRONOUNS. Note their forms.

—François dîne avec **Florence?**	*Is François having dinner with **Florence?***
—Oui, il dîne avec **elle.**	*Yes, he is having dinner with **her.***
—Tu parles de **Jean-Paul?**	*Are you talking about **Jean-Paul?***
—Non, je ne parle pas de **lui.**	*No, I'm not talking about **him.***

FORMS

(SUBJECT PRONOUNS)	STRESS PRONOUNS	(SUBJECT PRONOUNS)	STRESS PRONOUNS
(je)	**moi**	(nous)	**nous**
(tu)	**toi**	(vous)	**vous**
(il)	**lui**	(ils)	**eux**
(elle)	**elle**	(elles)	**elles**

USES

Stress pronouns are used:

- to reinforce a subject pronoun

  Moi, je parle français. — *I speak French.*
  Vous, vous parlez anglais. — *You speak English.*

- after **c'est** and **ce n'est pas**

  —C'est Paul là-bas?
  —Non ce n'est pas **lui.** — *No, it's not **him.***

- in short sentences where there is no verb

  —Qui parle français ici?
  —**Moi!** — ***I do!***

- before and after **et** and **ou**

  Lui et moi, nous sommes copains. — ***He and I,** (we) are friends.*

- After prepositions such as **de, avec, pour, chez**

  Voici Marc et Paul. Je parle souvent **d'eux.** — *I often talk **about them.***
  Voici Isabelle. Je vais au cinéma **avec elle.** — *I go to the movies **with her.***
  Voici M. Mercier. Nous travaillons **pour lui.** — *We work **for him.***

  ➡ Note the meaning of **chez** + STRESS PRONOUN:

  Je vais **chez moi.** — *I am going **home.***
  Paul étudie **chez lui.** — *Paul is studying **at home.***

  Tu viens **chez nous?** — *Are you coming **to our house?***
  Je suis chez Alice. Je dîne **chez elle.** — *I am having dinner **at her place.***

Expression pour la conversation

How to contradict someone:

Pas du tout! *Not at all!* —Vous êtes français?
Definitely not! —**Pas du tout!** Nous sommes italiens!

6 Mais, pas du tout!

You are not good at guessing the identities of the following people. A classmate will indicate that you are wrong.

▶ —C'est Tarzan?
—Mais, pas du tout!
Ce n'est pas lui!

▶ **Tarzan?**

7 Samedi soir *(Saturday night)*

On Saturday night, some people stay home and others do not. Read what the following people are doing and say whether or not they are at home.

▶ Alice étudie.
Elle est chez elle.

▶ Paul va au cinéma.
Il n'est pas chez lui.

1. François regarde la télé.
2. Jacqueline va au café.
3. Marc et Pierre dînent au restaurant.
4. Hélène et Pauline écoutent des disques.
5. Les voisins font une promenade.
6. Je travaille avec mon père.
7. Tu vas au théâtre.
8. Nous allons à la bibliothèque.
9. Tu prépares le dîner.

Expression pour la conversation

How to express surprise:

Vraiment?! *Really?!* —C'est Batman.
—**Vraiment?**

8 Commérage *(Gossip)*

Thomas likes to gossip. Act out the dialogues between him and his friend Sandrine.

▶ Marina dîne avec Jean-Pierre.

1. Éric dîne avec Alice.
2. Thérèse va chez Paul.
3. Jérôme est au cinéma avec Delphine.
4. Monsieur Mercier travaille pour Mademoiselle Duval.
5. Philippe travaille pour le voisin.
6. Marc et Vincent dansent avec Mélanie et Juliette.

9 Questions personnelles

Use stress pronouns in your answers.

1. Est-ce que tu étudies souvent avec tes *(your)* copains?
2. Est-ce que tu vas souvent chez ta cousine?
3. Est-ce que tu travailles pour les voisins?
4. Est-ce que tu parles français avec ton père?
5. Est-ce que tu vas souvent au cinéma avec tes copines?
6. Est-ce que tu restes chez toi le weekend?
7. Est-ce que tu restes chez toi pendant *(during)* les vacances?

D. La construction: nom + *de* + nom

Compare the word order in French and English.

J'ai une raquette.	C'est une **raquette de tennis.**	*It's a* ***tennis racket.***
Paul a une voiture.	C'est une **voiture de sport.**	*It's a* ***sports car.***

When one noun is used to modify another noun, the French construction is:

MAIN NOUN + **de** + MODIFYING NOUN	**une classe de français**
↓ **d'** (+ VOWEL SOUND)	**une classe d'espagnol**

➡ In French, the main noun comes *first.* In English, the main noun comes second.

➡ There is no article after **de.**

10 Précisions

Complete the following sentences with an expression consisting of **de** + underlined noun.

▶ J'aime le sport. J'ai une voiture . . .

1. Claire aime le ping-pong. Elle a une raquette . . .
2. Nous adorons le jazz. Nous écoutons un concert . . .
3. Jacques aime la musique classique. Il écoute un programme . . .
4. Vous étudiez l'anglais. Vous avez un livre . . .
5. Tu étudies le piano. Aujourd'hui, tu as une leçon . . .
6. Thomas et Paul aiment l'espagnol. Ils ont une bonne prof . . .
7. Je regarde mes photos. J'ai un album . . .

Prononciation

Les voyelles /ø/ et /œ/

/ø/ /œ/

deux **neuf**

The letters "**eu**" and "**oeu**" represent vowel sounds that do not exist in English but that are not very hard to pronounce.

Répétez:

/ø/ **deux eux je veux je peux un peu jeux il pleut Tu peux aller chez eux.**

/œ/ **neuf soeur heure professeur jeune Ma soeur arrive à neuf heures.**

À votre tour!

1 Conversation

Saturday afternoon, Henri meets Stéphanie downtown. Match Henri's questions with Stéphanie's answers. Then act out the conversation with a classmate.

1. Salut, Stéphanie! D'où viens-tu?
2. Et où vas-tu maintenant?
3. Tu ne veux pas venir au cinéma avec moi?
4. Ah bon? Pourquoi?

a. J'ai un examen d'anglais lundi.
b. Du supermarché.
c. Je rentre chez moi.
d. Je ne peux pas. Je dois étudier.

2 Créa-dialogue

Ask your classmates whom they are going to visit and what they are going to do. Then decide if you are going to come along.

CHEZ QUI?	Jean-Claude
ACTIVITÉ	

▶ — Où vas-tu?
— Je vais chez Jean-Claude. Tu viens?
— Ça dépend! Qu'est-ce que tu vas faire chez lui?
— Nous allons jouer au ping-pong.
— D'accord, je viens!
(Non, je ne viens pas.)

CHEZ QUI?	1. Françoise	2. Corinne et Claire	3. Nicolas et Patrick	4. mon cousin	5. ma cousine	6. des copains
ACTIVITÉ						

3 Retour à la maison

This afternoon, the following people went downtown. Say which places they are coming from.

▶ Nous venons de l'école.

▶ nous

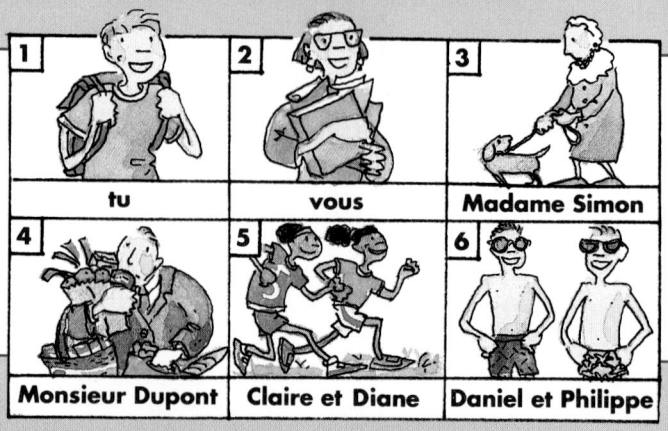

4 Message illustré

Frédéric likes to use illustrations in his diary. Transcribe what he has written about himself and others, replacing the pictures with the corresponding missing words.

Je joue . J'aime aussi aller .

Ma soeur Catherine joue très bien . Elle est musicienne aussi. Elle joue et .

Mon frère Marc préfère jouer . Tiens, voilà ma copine Stéphanie. Elle vient . Elle joue très bien .

5 Une lettre à Sandrine

In a recent letter, Sandrine, your French pen pal, mentioned various hobbies she enjoys. In a short letter, tell her …

- which sports you play
- which musical instruments you play
- which games you play

Chère Sandrine,
J'aime beaucoup les sports. Je joue au…

LEÇON 24

Mes voisins

Bonjour!
Je m'appelle Frédéric Mallet.
J'habite à Versailles avec ma famille.
Nous habitons dans un immeuble de six étages.
Voici mon immeuble et voici mes voisins.

building
floors
my

Monsieur Lacroche habite au sixième étage avec sa femme. Ils sont musiciens. Lui, il joue du piano et elle, elle chante. Oh là là, quelle musique!

sixth
what

Mademoiselle Jolivet habite au cinquième étage avec son oncle et sa tante.

fifth / her
her

Paul, mon meilleur ami, habite au quatrième étage avec sa soeur et ses parents.

best
fourth / his
his

Mademoiselle Ménard habite au troisième étage avec son chien Pomme, ses deux chats Fritz et Arthur, son perroquet Coco et son canari Froufrou. (Je pense que c'est une personne très intéressante, mais mon père pense qu'elle est un peu bizarre.)

third
parrot
think / that

Monsieur et Madame Boutin habitent au deuxième étage avec leur fils et leurs deux filles.

second / their
son
daughters

Et qui habite au premier étage?
C'est un garçon super-intelligent, super-cool et très sympathique! Et ce garçon . . . c'est moi!

Compréhension

1. Où habite Frédéric?
2. Combien *(How many)* d'étages est-ce qu'il y a dans l'immeuble où il habite?
3. Quelle est la profession des Lacroche?
4. Comment s'appelle le meilleur ami de Frédéric?
5. Combien d'animaux a Mademoiselle Ménard?
6. Qui est Pomme?
7. Qui sont Fritz et Arthur?
8. Selon toi *(In your opinion)*, est-ce que Mademoiselle Ménard est une personne bizarre ou intéressante?
9. Quel est le numéro *(number)* de l'étage où habite Frédéric?
10. Est-ce que Frédéric habite en haut ou en bas de l'immeuble?

NOTES CULTURELLES

1 Versailles

Versailles is a city of about 100,000 inhabitants, located about 15 miles southwest of Paris. Its famous **château,** built for King Louis XIV (1638–1715), welcomes four million visitors every year. It is the third most visited monument in France (after the Pompidou Center and the Eiffel Tower).

2 La vie en appartement

Most French people in urban areas live in apartments. Newer high-rise apartment buildings have been built in the suburbs. In the cities, however, apartment houses are traditionally no more than six or seven stories high. (This is because, historically, there were no elevators.) The ground floor, which often houses stores and shops, is known as **le rez-de-chaussée** (literally, "level with the street"). The next floor, **le premier étage** (or "first" floor above the street), corresponds to the American second floor. Similarly, **le deuxième étage** corresponds to our third floor, etc. The top floor of older buildings used to consist of individual rooms, one per apartment. These original maid's rooms often became student rooms. In recent years, as elevators were installed in these buildings, the top-floor rooms frequently have been combined to form new apartments.

A. La possession avec *de*

Note the words in heavy print:

Voici une moto.	C'est la moto **de Frédéric.**	*It's **Frédéric's** motorcycle.*
Voici un vélo.	C'est le vélo **de Sophie.**	*It's **Sophie's** bike.*

To express POSSESSION, French speakers use the construction:

le/la/les + NOUN + **de** + OWNER ↓ **d'** (+ VOWEL SOUND)	la radio **de** Thomas les disques **de** Claire la maison **d'**Émilie

➡ The same construction is used to express RELATIONSHIP:

C'est **le copain de Daniel.** — *That's **Daniel's friend.***
C'est **la mère de Paul.** — *That's **Paul's mother.***

➡ Remember that **de** contracts with **le** and **les:**

Pomme est le chien **du voisin.** — *Pomme is **the neighbor's** dog.*
Voici la chambre **des enfants.** — *Here is **the children's** room.*

➡ While English often indicates possession with *s,* French always uses **de.**

la copine **de Monique** — ***Monique's** friend (the friend **of Monique**)*

1 Présentations *(Introductions)*

Imagine that you are hosting a party in France. Introduce the following people.

▶ Marc (cousin / Sylvie)

1. Carole (cousine / Jacques)
2. Michel (copain / Caroline)
3. Philippe (camarade / Charles)
4. Robert (frère / Guillaume)
5. Marina (copine / Paul)
6. Pauline (amie / Éric)
7. Thomas (frère / Christine)
8. Alice (soeur / Karine)

2 Échanges

The following friends have decided to trade a few of their possessions. On a separate sheet of paper, write out what each person has, once the exchange has been completed.

Vocabulaire: La famille

la famille *(family)*

les grands-parents
- **le grand-père** — **la grand-mère**

les parents *(parents)*
- **le père** — **la mère**
- **le mari** *(husband)* — **la femme** *(wife)*

les enfants *(children)*
- **un enfant** — **une enfant**
- **le frère** — **la soeur**
- **le fils** *(son)* — **la fille** *(daughter)*

les parents *(relatives)*
- **l'oncle** — **la tante** *(aunt)*
- **le cousin** — **la cousine**

3 La famille de Frédéric

Frédéric has drawn his family tree. Study it and explain the relationships between the people below.

▶ Éric / Isabelle Vidal
Éric est le fils d'Isabelle Vidal.

1. Véronique / Frédéric
2. Martine Mallet / Véronique
3. Albert et Suzanne Mallet / Frédéric
4. Isabelle Vidal / Frédéric Mallet
5. François Mallet / Martine Mallet
6. Isabelle Vidal / Maurice Vidal
7. François Mallet / Suzanne Mallet
8. Catherine / Maurice Vidal
9. Véronique / Éric
10. Frédéric / Catherine

▶ Marc a la guitare d'Alice et . . .

B. Les adjectifs possessifs: *mon, ton, son*

Learning about language

French, like English, shows possession and relationship with POSSESSIVE ADJECTIVES:

ma voiture *(**my** car)*, **mon** père *(**my** father)*

In French, possessive adjectives AGREE with the nouns they introduce.

Note the forms of the possessive adjectives in the chart below:

		SINGULAR		PLURAL			
(POSSESSOR)		MASCULINE	FEMININE				
(je)	*my*	**mon**	**ma**	**mes**	**mon** frère	**ma** soeur	**mes** copains
(tu)	*your*	**ton**	**ta**	**tes**	**ton** oncle	**ta** tante	**tes** cousins
(il)	*his*	**son**	**sa**	**ses**	**son** père	**sa** mère	**ses** parents
(elle)	*her*	**son**	**sa**	**ses**	**son** père	**sa** mère	**ses** parents

➡ The feminine singular forms **ma, ta, sa** become **mon, ton, son** before a vowel sound.

une amie **mon** amie **ton** amie **son** amie
une auto **mon** auto **ton** auto **son** auto

➡ There is liaison after **mon, ton, son, mes, tes, ses** when the next word begins with a vowel sound.

mon oncle **mes** amis

➡ The choice between **son, sa,** and **ses** depends on the gender (masculine or feminine) and the number (singular or plural) of the noun that *follows*. It does NOT depend on the gender of the possessor (that is, whether the owner is male or female). Compare:

	un vélo	une radio	des cassettes
 Voici Frédéric.	 Voici son vélo. (his bike)	 Voici sa radio. (his radio)	 Voici ses cassettes. (his cassettes)
 Voici Sophie.	 Voici son vélo. (her bike)	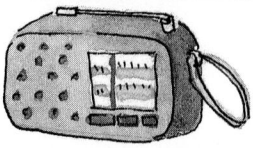 Voici sa radio. (her radio)	 Voici ses cassettes. (her cassettes)

4 Marc et Hélène

Marc Pertout never knows where his things are. Fortunately, his friend Hélène Sétout knows. Play both roles.

▶ le vélo / dans le garage

1. les cassettes / ici
2. la raquette / là-bas
3. la montre / sur toi
4. les livres / dans le sac
5. la radio / sur le bureau
6. les tee-shirts / sous le lit
7. le chien / derrière la porte
8. l'appareil-photo / dans la chambre

5 Invitations

Each of the following people is bringing a friend or relative to the school party. Say whom each person is inviting, using the appropriate possessive adjectives.

▶ Michel / la copine
Michel invite sa copine.

1. André / la cousine
2. Jean-Claude / la soeur
3. Marie-Noëlle / les frères
4. Pascal / l'amie Sophie
5. Monique / les cousins
6. Nathalie / l'ami Marc
7. Georges / l'amie Cécile
8. Paul / l'amie Thérèse
9. Isabelle / les copains

6 Chez Marie et Christophe Boutin

Items 1 to 8 belong to Marie. Items 9 to 16 belong to Christophe. Point these things out.

Marie

▶ le vélo **C'est son vélo.**

1. le walkman
2. le sac
3. le chien
4. l'album
5. la radiocassette
6. la guitare
7. les disques
8. les cassettes

Christophe

▶ les disques **Ce sont ses disques.**

9. la guitare
10. la chaîne stéréo
11. le chat
12. la mobylette
13. les livres
14. la montre
15. les photos
16. les skis

Expression pour la conversation

How to question a statement or express a doubt:

Tu es sûr(e)? *Are you sure?* —C'est mon pantalon *(pants)*!
—**Tu es sûr?**

7 Après la boum

Last night Frédéric and Paul gave a party. They realize that their friends left certain things behind. Frédéric thinks he knows what belongs to whom.

▶ le sac / Claire

FRÉDÉRIC: **Voici le sac de Claire.**
PAUL: **Tu es sûr?**
FRÉDÉRIC: **Mais oui, c'est son sac!**

1. le sac / Jean-Pierre
2. la guitare / Antoine
3. l'appareil-photo / Cécile
4. le walkman / Stéphanie
5. les livres / Philippe
6. le chapeau *(hat)* / Thomas
7. la cassette / Roger
8. les compacts / Corinne

C. Les adjectifs possessifs: *notre, votre, leur*

Note the forms of the possessive adjectives in the chart below:

(POSSESSOR)		SINGULAR	PLURAL		
(nous)	*our*	**notre**	**nos**	**notre** prof	**nos** livres
(vous)	*your*	**votre**	**vos**	**votre** ami	**vos** copains
(ils / elles)	*their*	**leur**	**leurs**	**leur** radio	**leurs** disques

➡ There is liaison after **nos, vos, leurs** when the next word begins with a vowel sound.

nos amis **vos** amies **leurs** ordinateurs

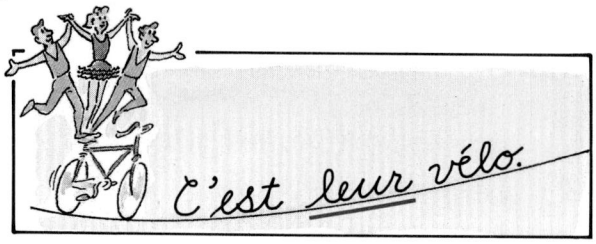

8 Aux Galeries Lafayette

At the Galeries Lafayette department store, a customer is looking for various things. The person at the information desk indicates where they can be found. Play both roles.

▶ les disques / là-bas

1. les livres / à gauche
2. les affiches / à droite
3. le restaurant / en haut
4. le garage / en bas
5. les ordinateurs / ici
6. la cafétéria / tout droit

9 Les millionnaires

Imagine you are showing a millionaire's estate to French visitors.

▶ la maison
Voici leur maison.

1. la piscine
2. la Cadillac
3. les chiens
4. le parc
5. l'hélicoptère
6. les courts de tennis

10 En famille

We often do things with our family. Complete each sentence with a possessive adjective: **son, sa, ses, leur,** or **leurs.**

▶ **Pascal joue au tennis avec sa cousine.**
▶ **Éric et Paul jouent au Monopoly avec leurs cousins.**

1. Frédéric dîne chez ... oncle.
2. André dîne chez ... grands-parents.
3. Caroline et Paul vont chez ... grand-mère.
4. Mlle Vénard fait une promenade avec ... chien.
5. Antoine va à la piscine avec ... soeur.
6. Stéphanie et Céline vont au cinéma avec ... parents.
7. M. et Mme Boutin voyagent avec ... fille.
8. Mme Denis visite Paris avec ... fils, Marc et Frédéric.
9. M. Mallet est à Québec avec ... femme.

D. Les nombres ordinaux

Learning about language

Numbers like *first, second, third, fourth, fifth* are used to rank persons or things—to put them in a given order.
They are called ORDINAL NUMBERS.
In English, most ordinal numbers end in *-th*.

Compare the following regular numbers and the ordinal numbers in French:

(2)	deux	**deuxième**	Février est le **deuxième** mois de l'année.
(3)	trois	**troisième**	Mercredi est le **troisième** jour de la semaine.
(4)	quatre	**quatrième**	J'habite au **quatrième** étage *(floor)*.
(12)	douze	**douzième**	Qui habite au **douzième** étage?

To form ordinal numbers, the French use the following pattern:

NUMBER (minus final **-e,** if any) + **-ième**						
(6)	six	:	**six**	+ **-ième**	→	**sixième**
(11)	onze	:	**onz-**	+ **-ième**	→	**onzième**

➡ EXCEPTIONS: **un (une)** → **premier (première)**
cinq → **cinquième**
neuf → **neuvième**

➡ Ordinal numbers are adjectives and come BEFORE the noun.

11 La course *(The race)*

Frédéric and his friends are participating in a five-kilometer race. Announce the order of arrival of the following runners.

▶ Paul (6)

1. Frédéric (4)
2. Jérôme (7)
3. Christophe (8)
4. Sophie (2)
5. Christine (1)
6. Claire (10)
7. Karine (11)
8. Olivier (12)

▶▶▶▶▶▶▶▶▶▶▶▶▶▶▶▶▶▶▶

Prononciation

Les voyelles /o/ et /ɔ/

/o/

vélo

/ɔ/

téléphone

The French vowel /o/ is pronounced with more tension than in English. It is usually the last sound in a word.

Répétez: /o/ **vélo radio nos vos eau château chaud**
Nos vélos sont au château.

The French vowel /ɔ/ occurs in the middle of a word. Imitate the model carefully.

Répétez: /ɔ/ **téléphone école Nicole notre votre copain prof dommage**
Comment s'appelle votre prof?

À votre tour!

1 Allô!

Émilie is on the phone with Bernard. Match Émilie's questions with Bernard's answers. Then act out the dialogue with a classmate.

1. Avec qui est-ce que tu vas au cinéma?
2. C'est le cousin de Monique?
3. Tu connais leurs parents?
4. Ils sont canadiens, n'est-ce pas?

a. Non, c'est son frère.
b. Bien sûr, ils sont très sympathiques.
c. Avec mon copain Marc.
d. Non, mais leurs voisins sont de Québec.

2 Créa-dialogue

We often identify objects by their color. Create conversations with your classmates according to the model.

▶ —C'est le vélo de Paul?
—Non, ce n'est pas son vélo.
—Tu es sûr?
—Mais oui. Son vélo est bleu.

3 Faisons connaissance

You want to know more about certain relatives and acquaintances (friends, neighbors, teachers, etc.) of your classmates. Ask a classmate three questions: each question will be about a different person. You may want to use some of the following suggestions:

OUI/NON	INFORMATION
parler français?	où/habiter?
avoir une voiture?	quel âge/avoir?
aimer les sports?	où/travailler?
travailler beaucoup?	à quelle école/étudier?
voyager souvent?	quand/venir chez toi?

4 Composition: Ma famille

Select five people in your family and write one to three sentences about each person.

Ma cousine s'appelle Barbara. Elle habite à San Francisco. Elle a treize ans.

5 Arbre généalogique *(Family tree)*

On a separate sheet of paper, draw your own (real or imaginary) family tree. Label the people and indicate their relationships to you.

Vive la différence!

Les loisirs

Parlons° de vos loisirs.° Répondez aux questions suivantes.° Selon° vous, quelles sont les réponses des jeunes Français en général à ces questions?

1 Qu'est-ce que vous préférez faire quand vous n'étudiez pas?
- aller au cinéma
- aller dans les magasins
- pratiquer un sport
- jouer avec les jeux vidéo

Selon vous, qu'est-ce que les jeunes Français préfèrent faire?

2 Quand vous allez au cinéma, quels films est-ce que vous préférez voir?°
- les films de science-fiction
- les films d'aventures
- les comédies
- les films d'horreur

Selon vous, quels sont les films préférés des jeunes Français?

3 Combien de fois° par an° est-ce que vous allez au concert?
- jamais°
- une fois ou deux
- de trois à six fois
- sept fois ou plus°

Et les jeunes Français, combien de fois vont-ils au concert en moyenne° par an?

4 Voici quatre acteurs américains très célèbres° en France. Quel est votre acteur préféré?
- Tom Cruise
- Jack Nicholson
- Robert Redford
- Dustin Hoffman

Selon vous, qui est l'acteur américain préféré des Français?

5 Quelle musique est-ce que vous préférez écouter?
- les chansons folkloriques°
- le rock
- le jazz
- la musique classique

Selon vous, quelle est la musique préférée des jeunes Français?

6 Quels livres est-ce que vous préférez lire?°
- les biographies
- les livres de science-fiction
- les livres d'aventures
- les albums de bandes dessinées°

Selon vous, quels sont les livres préférés des jeunes Français?

7 Quelle est votre dépense° principale?
- Je vais au concert.
- Je vais au cinéma ou au restaurant.
- J'achète° des cassettes ou des compacts.
- J'achète des vêtements.°

Et pour les jeunes Français, quelle est leur dépense principale?

Et les jeunes Français?

1. Ils préfèrent aller au cinéma. 2. Ils préfèrent les comédies. 3. Ils vont au concert en moyenne six fois par an. 4. Leur acteur américain préféré est Dustin Hoffman. 5. Ils préfèrent le rock. 6. Ils préfèrent les albums de bandes dessinées. 7. Ça dépend. Les garçons vont au cinéma ou au restaurant. Les filles achètent des vêtements.

Parlons *Let's talk* **loisirs** *leisure activities* **suivantes** *following* **Selon** *According to* **voir** *to see* **fois** *times* **par an** *per year* **jamais** *never* **plus** *more* **en moyenne** *on the average* **célèbres** *famous* **chansons folkloriques** *folksongs* **lire** *to read* **bandes dessinées** *comics, cartoons* **dépense** *expense* **achète** *buy* **vêtements** *clothes*

EN FRANCE

Vive la musique!

Est-ce que vous préférez écouter votre groupe favori à la radio ou dans une salle de concert? Regardez bien ces documents.

- Quel groupe est-ce qu'on peut écouter à la radio? Quels jours et à quelle heure?
- Est-ce que vous connaissez° ce groupe? Est-ce que vous avez leurs disques? Aimez-vous leur musique?

- Quand a lieu° le concert? Où?
- À quelle heure est-ce que le concert commence?°
  À quelle heure est-ce qu'il finit?°
- Quel est le numéro de téléphone pour réserver les billets?°
- Qui sont les «stars» de ce concert? Quelles stars est-ce que vous connaissez? Qui est votre star préférée?
- Est-ce que vous aimeriez° aller à ce concert? Pourquoi ou pourquoi pas?

connaissez *know* **a lieu** *does . . . take place* **commence** *does . . . begin* **finit** *does . . . end* **billets** *tickets* **aimeriez** *would like*

Entre amis: Interview avec Karine Legoff

Karine Legoff est élève dans un lycée° français. En mars, elle a passé° deux semaines aux États-Unis avec un programme d'échange.° Nous avons interviewé° Karine pendant° son séjour.° Voici les réponses de Karine à nos questions.

École

En France, comment vas-tu à l'école?	À pied, généralement.°
À quelle heure arrives-tu le matin?	À huit heures.
À quelle heure rentres-tu chez toi le soir?	Ça dépend des° jours. En général, à 5 heures 30 ou à 6 heures.
Où déjeunes-tu?°	Je déjeune à la cantine° du lycée.

Sports

Quels sports pratiques-tu à l'école?	Je joue au volley.
Et en dehors de° l'école?	Je joue au tennis.
Où?	Au club de la ville.

Loisirs

Est-ce que tu vas au cinéma?	Oui, de temps en temps.°
Combien de fois par mois?°	Une ou deux fois.
Qui sont tes acteurs préférés?	Christophe Lambert, Gérard Depardieu. Aussi Dustin Hoffman.
Et tes actrices préférées?	Isabelle Adjani, Emmanuelle Béart.
Est-ce que tu vas au concert?	Oui, mais pas très souvent.
Où vas-tu?	Ça dépend! Au Zénith, au parc des Princes.
Qui sont tes groupes ou tes chanteurs° préférés?	The Police, U2, Tracy Chapman.
Est-ce que tu joues d'un instrument?	Non.
Est-ce que tu vas à des boums?	Oui, de temps en temps.
Où et quand?	Chez des amis. Généralement le samedi soir.

Les États-Unis

Quelles sont tes impressions des États-Unis?	J'aime le pays° et les gens.
Pourquoi?	C'est un pays très dynamique et très ouvert.° Les gens sont francs, communicatifs et honnêtes avec eux-mêmes.° Les Américains sont très cool!
Qu'est-ce que tu n'aimes pas?	La nourriture.°

lycée *high school* **a passé** *spent* **échange** *exchange* **avons interviewé** *interviewed* **pendant** *during* **séjour** *stay* **généralement** *generally* **Ça dépend des** *It depends on the* **déjeunes-tu** *do you have lunch* **cantine** *cafeteria* **en dehors de** *outside of* **de temps en temps** *from time to time* **fois par mois** *times a month* **chanteurs** *singers* **pays** *country* **ouvert** *open* **eux-mêmes** *themselves* **nourriture** *food*

Comment lire
SOUNDING FRENCH

As you read the interview over, try to think how the new words sound in French.

- Remember to put the accent on the LAST syllable of a word or phrase.

  programme **acteur préféré** **communicatif**

- Remember that many final consonants are silent.

  sport **Zénith** **maths** **instrument**

If you think of the right French pronunciation as you read, you will be prepared to recognize these words when you hear them spoken.

Enrichissez votre vocabulaire
SUFFIXES

You can expand your reading vocabulary easily by learning to recognize common suffixes (or endings).

	FRENCH	ENGLISH		
(ADJECTIVE +)	**-ment**	*-ly*	**généralement**	*generally*
(VERB STEM +)	**-ant**	*-ing*	**amusant**	*amusing*
(VERB STEM +)	**-é**	*-ed*	**préféré**	*preferred*

Activité
Can you identify the English equivalents of the following French words?

- **normalement** **finalement** **rarement** **rapidement** **sûrement**
- **intéressant** **alarmant** **terrifiant** **charmant**
- **importé** **occupé** **limité** **marié**

Activité: Une interview
Interview a classmate about his / her school life and leisure activities. Use Karine's interview as a point of departure.

Activité: Une lettre à Karine
Write Karine a letter about yourself. Using her responses to the interview as a model, tell her about your school, the sports you play, your leisure-time activities, as well as your impressions of France and the French people.

Variétés

Les jeunes Français et le cinéma américain

En général, les jeunes Français aiment beaucoup les films américains. (Quand ils parlent anglais, ils peuvent° voir° ces films en «version originale».) Voici une liste de films qui ont eu° beaucoup de succès en France. Est-ce que vous pouvez° identifier ces films? Lisez° le titre° français de chaque° film. Faites correspondre° le titre de ce film avec le titre américain.

TITRES FRANÇAIS

1. ***Blanche-Neige***
2. ***Le parrain***
3. ***Un prince à New York***
4. ***Un poisson nommé Wanda***
5. ***E.T. l'extra-terrestre***
6. ***Le retour du Jedi***
7. ***Les aventuriers de l'arche perdue***
8. ***Rencontres du troisième type***
9. ***Les dents de la mer***
10. ***Danse avec les loups***
11. ***La guerre des étoiles***
12. ***Indiana Jones et la dernière croisade***
13. ***Qui veut la peau de Roger Rabbit?***
14. ***Le retour de la panthère rose***

TITRES AMÉRICAINS

A. *Jaws*
B. *Star Wars*
C. *E.T. The Extra Terrestrial*
D. *Close Encounters of the Third Kind*
E. *Indiana Jones and the Last Crusade*
F. *The Return of the Jedi*
G. *Coming to America*
H. *The Godfather*
I. *Raiders of the Lost Ark*
J. *Dances with Wolves*
K. *A Fish Called Wanda*
L. *The Return of the Pink Panther*
M. *Who Framed Roger Rabbit?*
N. *Snow White and the Seven Dwarfs*

peuvent *can* **voir** *see* **ont eu** *had* **pouvez** *can* **Lisez** *Read* **titre** *title* **chaque** *each*
Faites correspondre *Match*

UN FILM D'AVENTURES *américain*

20.30 DURÉE : 2h00

FILM AMÉRICAIN DE STEVEN SPIELBERG

LES AVENTURIERS DE L'ARCHE PERDUE

777

SCÉNARIO DE LAWRENCE KASDAN - MUSIQUE DE JOHN WILLIAMS

Indiana Jones ..... **Harrison Ford**
Marion Ravenhood ..... **Karen Allen**
Dietrich ..... **Wolf Kahler**
Belloq ..... **Paul Freeman**
Toht ..... **Ronald Lacey**
Sallah ..... **John Rhys-Davies**

Indiana Jones (Harrison Ford) est en compétition avec Belloq (Paul Freeman)

Ce film américain a eu° beaucoup de succès en France.

- Est-ce que vous avez vu° ce film? Où? à la télévision? au cinéma? sur vidéocassette?
- Quel est le titre anglais du film?
- Qui est le directeur du film?
- Qui est l'acteur principal?
- Qui sont les autres acteurs?
- Qui est le compositeur de la musique?
- Combien de temps dure° le film?

NOTE CULTURELLE

Au cinéma

Le samedi, les jeunes Français adorent aller au cinéma. C'est pour eux l'occasion de voir° un bon film et aussi d'être avec leurs copains. En général, ils vont au cinéma pour voir des films récents. Leurs films préférés sont les films comiques. Ils aiment aussi les films d'aventures, les films de science-fiction et les films policiers.°

Beaucoup de jeunes vont aussi au cinéclub de leur école ou de la ville où ils habitent. Là ils peuvent° voir les «grands classiques» du cinéma. Ces grands classiques sont des films anciens° réalisés° par des cinéastes° français ou étrangers.°

a eu *had* **Est-ce que vous avez vu** *Did you see* **dure** *does . . . last* **de voir** *to see* **films policiers** *detective movies* **peuvent** *can* **anciens** *old* **réalisés** *made* **cinéastes** *filmmakers* **étrangers** *foreign*

À PARIS

Bonjour, Paris!

QUELQUES FAITS

- Paris est la capitale de la France.
- Paris est une très grande ville. La ville de Paris a deux millions d'habitants. La région parisienne a dix millions d'habitants. Quinze pour-cent (15%) des Français habitent dans la région parisienne.
- Paris est situé° sur la Seine. Ce fleuve° divise° la ville en deux parties: la rive° droite (au nord) et la rive gauche (au sud).
- Administrativement, Paris est divisé en vingt arrondissements.°
- Paris est une ville très ancienne.° Elle a plus de° deux mille° ans.
- Paris est aussi une ville moderne et dynamique. C'est le centre économique, industriel et commercial de la France.
- Avec ses musées, ses théâtres, ses bibliothèques, ses écoles d'art, Paris est un centre culturel et artistique très important.
- Avec ses nombreux° monuments et ses larges avenues, Paris est une très belle ville. Pour beaucoup de gens, c'est la plus° belle ville du monde.° Chaque année,° des millions de touristes visitent Paris.

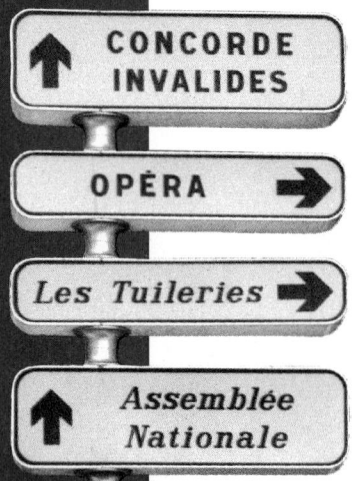

situé *located* **fleuve** *river* **divise** *divides*
rive *(river)bank* **arrondissements** *districts* **ancienne** *old*
plus de *more than* **mille** *thousand* **nombreux** *many*
la plus *the most* **monde** *world* **Chaque année** *Each year*

pte DAUPHINE
PORTE MAILLOT
Place
Victor Hugo

FRANCE

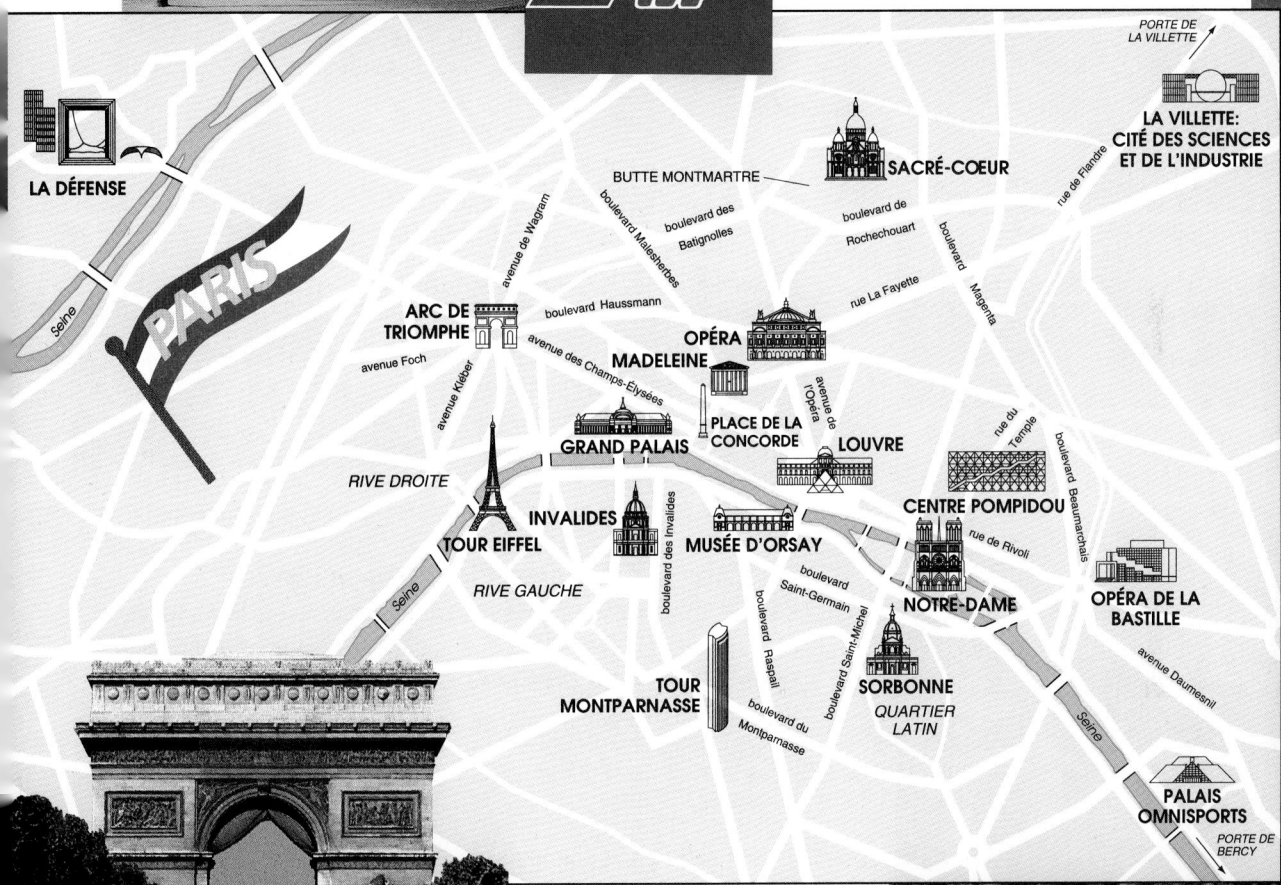
PORTE DE LA VILLETTE
LA VILLETTE: CITÉ DES SCIENCES ET DE L'INDUSTRIE
LA DÉFENSE
BUTTE MONTMARTRE
SACRÉ-CŒUR
rue de Flandre
boulevard de Rochechouart
boulevard des Batignolles
boulevard Malesherbes
avenue de Wagram
boulevard Magenta
rue La Fayette
boulevard Haussmann
ARC DE TRIOMPHE
avenue Foch
avenue Kléber
avenue des Champs-Élysées
OPÉRA
MADELEINE
avenue de l'Opéra
PLACE DE LA CONCORDE
GRAND PALAIS
LOUVRE
rue du Temple
boulevard Beaumarchais
RIVE DROITE
INVALIDES
TOUR EIFFEL
boulevard des Invalides
MUSÉE D'ORSAY
CENTRE POMPIDOU
rue de Rivoli
Seine
RIVE GAUCHE
boulevard Saint-Germain
boulevard Raspail
boulevard Saint-Michel
NOTRE-DAME
OPÉRA DE LA BASTILLE
avenue Daumesnil
TOUR MONTPARNASSE
boulevard du Montparnasse
SORBONNE
QUARTIER LATIN
Seine
PALAIS OMNISPORTS
PORTE DE BERCY

Moulin Rouge
PARIS à la CARTE
TEL. (1) 47 42 31 63

Le PARIS *traditionnel*

1 Notre-Dame

Notre-Dame est la cathédrale de Paris. Elle est située au centre de Paris sur une île,° l'île de la Cité. Notre-Dame a été construite° aux treizième et quatorzième siècles.°

2 La tour Eiffel

Pour beaucoup de gens, la tour Eiffel est le symbole de Paris. Cette° immense tour de fer° a trois cent mètres de haut.° Elle a été construite en 1889 (dix-huit cent quatre-vingt-neuf) par l'ingénieur Gustave Eiffel. Du sommet de la tour Eiffel, on° a une très belle vue sur Paris.

3 L'Arc de Triomphe et les Champs-Élysées

L'Arc de Triomphe est un monument qui° commémore les victoires de Napoléon (1769–1821). Ce monument est situé en haut° des Champs-Élysées. Les Champs-Élysées sont une très grande et très belle avenue avec beaucoup de cinémas, de cafés, de magasins et de boutiques élégantes.

4 Le Sacré-Coeur

Le Sacré-Coeur est une église de pierre° blanche qui domine Paris. Cette église est située sur la butte° Montmartre. Montmartre est un quartier pittoresque. Les artistes viennent ici pour peindre° et les touristes viennent pour regarder les artistes. Si vous voulez° avoir un souvenir personnel de Paris, allez à Montmartre et demandez à° un artiste de faire votre portrait.

île *island* **a été construite** *was built* **siècles** *centuries* **Cette** *This* **fer** *iron*
a trois cent mètres de haut *is 300 meters high* **on** *one* **qui** *which* **en haut** *at the top*
pierre *stone* **butte** *hill* **peindre** *to paint* **voulez** *want* **demandez à** *ask*

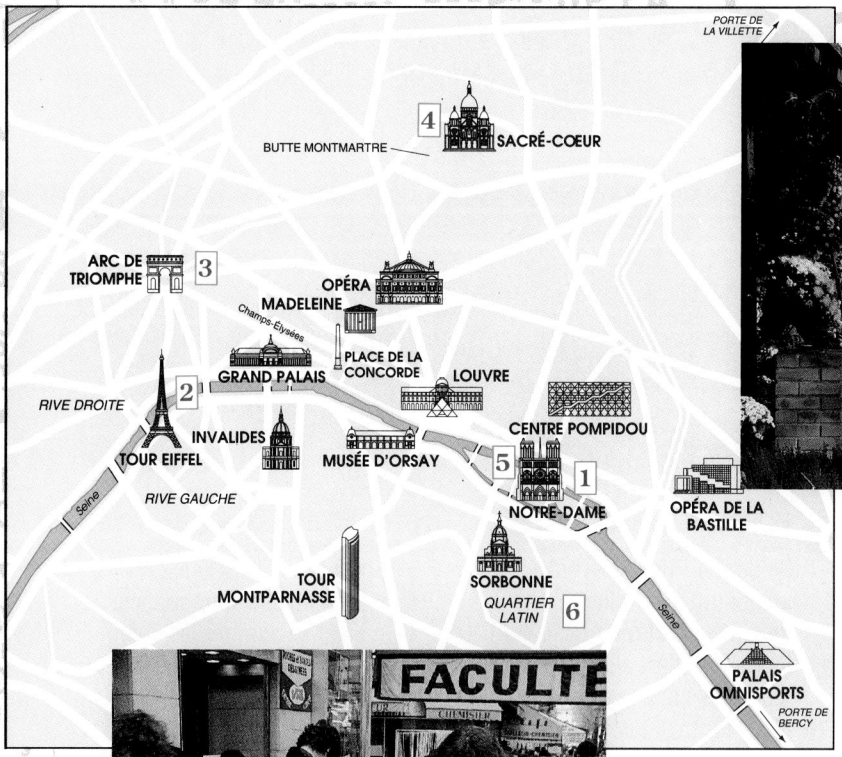

5 Le Marché aux fleurs

Ce° marché° est situé près de Notre-Dame. Ici on trouve° toutes° sortes de fleurs° et de plantes vertes. À Paris il y a beaucoup d'autres° marchés spécialisés: marché aux oiseaux,° marché aux timbres° et, bien sûr, le fameux Marché aux puces.°

6 Le Quartier latin

Le Quartier latin est le quartier des étudiants. C'est un quartier très animé avec des cafés, des cinémas, des librairies et des restaurants exotiques et bon marché.° Pourquoi est-ce que ce quartier s'appelle «Quartier latin»? Parce qu'autrefois° les étudiants parlaient° latin ici.

ACTIVITÉ CULTURELLE

Imaginez que vous passez une journée° à Paris. Où allez-vous aller le matin? Où allez-vous aller l'après-midi? Choisissez deux endroits à visiter et expliquez° votre choix.°

Ce *This* **marché** *market* **trouve** *finds* **toutes** *all* **fleurs** *flowers* **d'autres** *other* **oiseaux** *birds* **timbres** *stamps* **Marché aux puces** *flea market* **bon marché** *inexpensive* **autrefois** *in the past* **parlaient** *used to speak* **passez une journée** *are spending the day* **expliquez** *explain* **choix** *choice*

Le nouveau PARIS

❶ Le Louvre et la pyramide du Louvre

Le Louvre est une ancienne° résidence royale transformée en musée. C'est dans ce° musée que se trouve° la fameuse «Mona Lisa». On entre dans le Louvre par° une pyramide de verre.° Cette pyramide moderne a été construite° par l'architecte américain I.M. Pei. Avec sa pyramide, le Louvre est le symbole du nouveau° Paris, à la fois° moderne et traditionnel.

❷ Le Centre Pompidou

Le Centre Pompidou est le monument le plus° visité de Paris. C'est un musée d'art moderne. C'est aussi une bibliothèque, une cinémathèque et un centre audio-visuel. À l'extérieur,° sur l'esplanade, il y a des musiciens, des mimes, des acrobates, des jongleurs° . . . Un peu plus loin,° il y a une place° avec des fontaines, un bassin° et des sculptures mobiles.

❸ Le musée d'Orsay

Autrefois,° c'était° une gare.° Aujourd'hui, c'est un musée. On vient ici admirer les chefs-d'oeuvre° des grands peintres° et sculpteurs français du dix-neuvième siècle.° On peut,° par exemple, admirer les oeuvres° de Monet, de Renoir et de Toulouse-Lautrec. À l'extérieur, il y a des sculptures qui représentent les cinq continents.

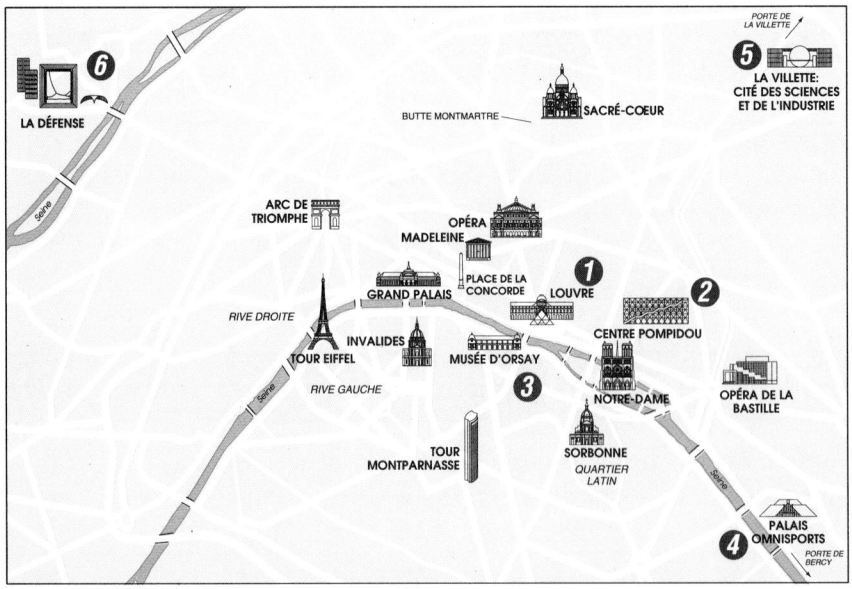

ancienne *former* **ce** *this* **se trouve** *is located* **par** *by* **verre** *glass* **a été construite** *was built* **nouveau** *new* **à la fois** *at the same time* **le plus** *the most* **À l'extérieur** *Outside* **jongleurs** *jugglers* **plus loin** *farther away* **place** *square* **bassin** *ornamental pool* **Autrefois** *Formerly* **c'était** *it used to be* **gare** *train station* **chefs-d'oeuvre** *masterpieces* **peintres** *painters* **siècle** *century* **peut** *can* **oeuvres** *works*

4 Le palais Omnisports de Bercy

Sport ou musique? Bercy est le nouveau stade de Paris. C'est aussi une immense salle° de concert. On vient ici écouter et applaudir les vedettes° de la chanson° française . . . et de la chanson américaine.

5 Le parc de la Villette

Le parc de la Villette est un lieu° de récréation pour les jeunes de tout âge.° On trouve ici des parcs d'enfants,° des terrains de jeu° et différentes° constructions ultra-modernes.

- Le Zénith est une salle de concert où viennent les vedettes du monde° entier.
- Le Géode est un omni-cinéma avec un écran° circulaire géant.
- La Cité des sciences et de l'industrie est un grand musée scientifique où les jeunes peuvent° faire leurs propres° expériences° et jouer avec toutes sortes de gadgets électroniques.

6 La Défense et son arche

La Défense est le nouveau centre d'affaires° situé à l'ouest de Paris. Chaque° jour, des milliers° de Parisiens viennent travailler dans ses gratte-ciel° de verre. Il y a aussi des magasins, des cinémas, des restaurants et une patinoire.° Récemment,° une immense arche a été construite pour commémorer le deux centième anniversaire de la Révolution française.

ACTIVITÉ CULTURELLE

Vous êtes à Paris pour une semaine. Pendant votre séjour, vous voulez faire les choses suivantes. Dites où vous allez pour cela.

Quand?	Pourquoi?	Où?
▶ lundi	voir *(to see)* une exposition d'art moderne	??
mardi	voir une exposition sur les lasers	??
mercredi	voir la «Mona Lisa»	??
jeudi	voir un match de basket	??
vendredi	voir une exposition sur Toulouse-Lautrec	??
samedi	aller dans les magasins et faire du shopping	??

▶ **Lundi, je voudrais voir une exposition d'art moderne. Je vais au Centre Pompidou.**

salle *hall* **vedettes** *stars* **chanson** *song* **lieu** *place* **de tout âge** *of all ages* **parcs d'enfants** *playgrounds* **terrains de jeu** *playing fields* **différentes** *several* **monde** *world* **écran** *screen* **peuvent** *can* **propres** *own* **expériences** *experiments* **affaires** *business* **Chaque** *Each* **des milliers** *thousands* **gratte-ciel** *skyscrapers* **patinoire** *skating rink* **Récemment** *Recently*

Salut, les amis!

Je m'appelle Jean-Marc Lacoste. Je suis parisien. J'habite rue Racine. C'est une petite rue du Quartier latin. Notre appartement est situé au quatrième étage° d'un vieil° immeuble. L'immeuble est très ancien (il n'y a pas d'ascenseur°), mais notre appartement est moderne et confortable.

Je vais à l'École Alsacienne où je suis élève de seconde. En général, je vais là-bas en bus. Quand il fait beau, je prends° ma mob,° ou bien° je vais à pied. C'est assez loin, mais j'adore marcher.

En semaine, j'ai beaucoup de travail et je n'ai pas le temps° de sortir.° Le weekend, c'est différent. Qu'est-ce que je fais? Ça dépend! Quand j'ai de l'argent,° je vais au concert. Le weekend prochain,° j'espère aller au Zénith écouter le groupe Indochine. Quand je n'ai pas d'argent, je vais au Centre Pompidou. Là, au moins,° le spectacle° est gratuit.°

J'aime aussi me promener° dans mon quartier avec mes copains. Il y a toujours quelque chose° à faire au Quartier latin. On° va au cinéma. On va dans les magasins de disques pour écouter les nouveaux albums. On va dans les librairies° pour regarder les vieux livres et les bandes dessinées.° On va au café. Là, on regarde les gens qui passent dans la rue. Parfois,° on rencontre° des filles...

Et vous, quand est-ce que vous allez venir à Paris? Bientôt,° j'espère. Je vous attends!°

Amitiés,°

Jean-Marc

étage *floor* **vieil** *old* **ascenseur** *elevator* **prends** *take* **mob** *moped* **ou bien** *or else* **temps** *time*
sortir *go out* **argent** *money* **prochain** *next* **au moins** *at least* **spectacle** *show* **gratuit** *free*
me promener *to go for walks* **quelque chose** *something* **On** *We* **librairies** *bookstores*
bandes dessinées *comics* **Parfois** *Sometimes* **rencontre** *meet* **Bientôt** *Soon*
Je vous attends! *I'm expecting you!* **Amitiés** *In friendship*

PARIS *en* BATEAU-MOUCHE

Comment visiter Paris? On peut° visiter Paris en taxi, mais c'est cher.° On peut prendre° le bus. C'est amusant, mais la circulation° à Paris est souvent difficile. On peut prendre le métro. C'est pratique, rapide et bon marché,° mais on ne voit rien.°

Pourquoi ne pas faire une promenade° en bateau-mouche?° Les bateaux-mouches sont des bateaux modernes et confortables qui circulent sur la Seine. Pendant° la promenade, on peut prendre des photos et admirer les monuments le long de° la Seine. Le soir, on peut voir les monuments illuminés!

ACTIVITÉ CULTURELLE

Vous faites une promenade en bateau-mouche.

- Combien coûte le billet?
- Quels° monuments est-ce que vous pouvez° voir?

On peut *One can* **cher** *expensive* **prendre** *take* **circulation** *traffic* **bon marché** *inexpensive* **ne voit rien** *sees nothing* **Pourquoi ne pas faire une promenade** *Why not take a ride* **bateau-mouche** *sight-seeing boat* **Pendant** *During* **le long de** *along* **Quels** *Which* **pouvez** *can*

UNITÉ

7 Le shopping

LEÇON 25 Le français pratique: L'achat des vêtements

LEÇON 26 Rien n'est parfait!

LEÇON 27 Un choix difficile

LEÇON 28 Alice a un job

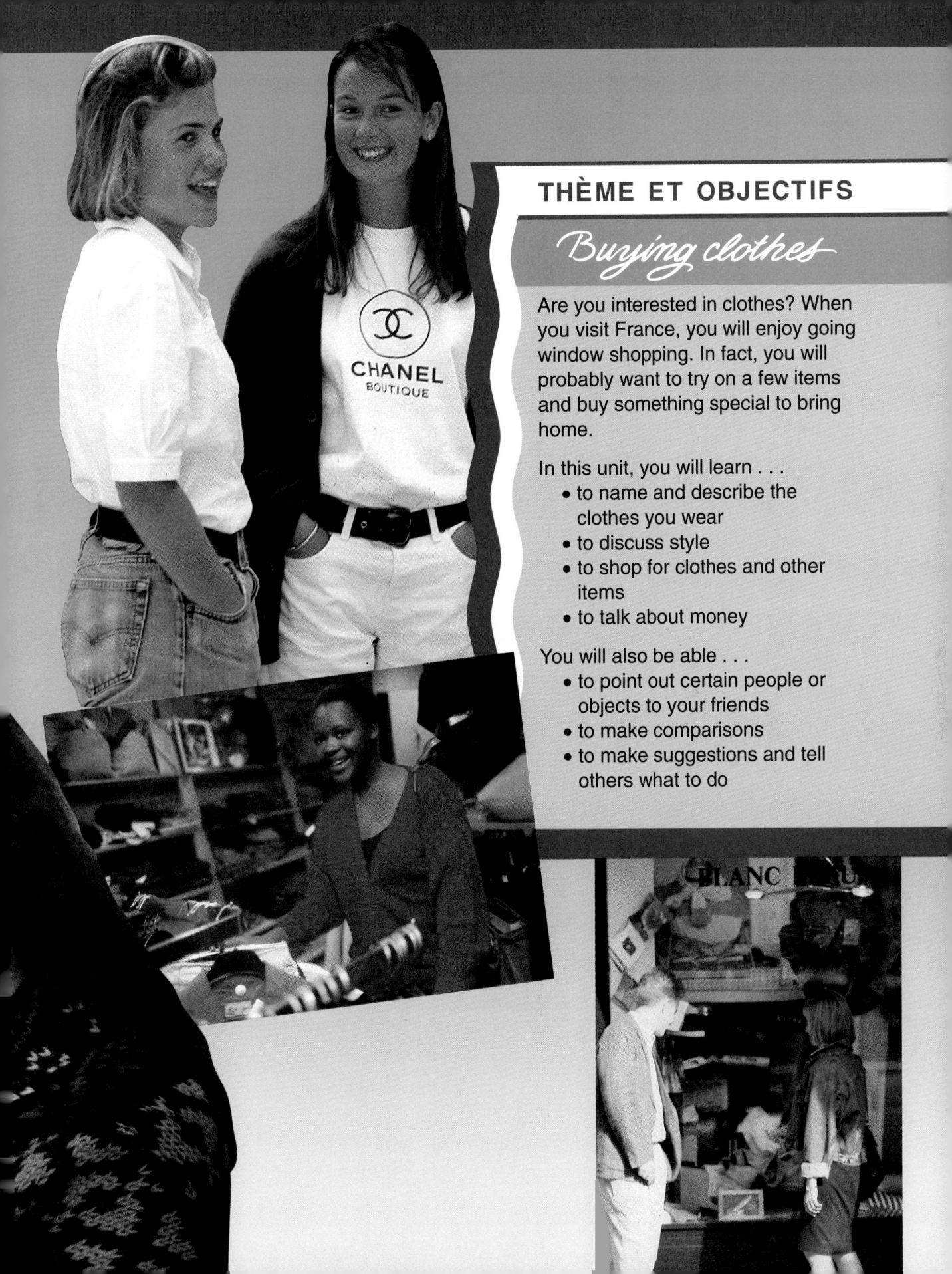

THÈME ET OBJECTIFS

Buying clothes

Are you interested in clothes? When you visit France, you will enjoy going window shopping. In fact, you will probably want to try on a few items and buy something special to bring home.

In this unit, you will learn . . .

- to name and describe the clothes you wear
- to discuss style
- to shop for clothes and other items
- to talk about money

You will also be able . . .

- to point out certain people or objects to your friends
- to make comparisons
- to make suggestions and tell others what to do

LEÇON 25

L'achat des vêtements

LE FRANÇAIS PRATIQUE

Accent sur . . . L'élégance française

French people like to look good. Young people are generally well-informed about fashions and trends. They like to be in style, even if their clothes are casual and not too expensive. Many well-known fashion design houses started in Paris: Christian Dior, Chanel, Yves Saint-Laurent, Pierre Cardin, Sonia Rykiel.

Depending on their budgets, French young people may buy their clothes at:

- **une boutique de soldes** *(discount shop)*
- **un grand magasin** *(department store)*
- **une boutique de vêtements** *(clothing store)*
- **le Marché aux puces** *(flea market)*

- **Un grand magasin**
  A large Parisian department store, the **Galeries Lafayette** has branches in other French cities. It offers a wide variety of clothing, from modestly priced items to more expensive designer labels.

- **Une boutique de vêtements**
  There are several **Céline** shops in Paris. They sell relatively expensive designer clothes.

- **Une boutique de soldes**
  At a discount store called the **Mouton à cinq pattes,** you can find jeans and casual clothes at good prices.

- **Une maison de couture**
  One of the most famous French fashion design houses is that of **Christian Dior.** Every season it presents a new collection which influences fashion trends all over the world. Christian Dior sells original designer dresses at very high prices, but also markets a more affordable line of clothes under its ready-to-wear label.

- **Le Marché aux puces**
  At the **Marché aux puces,** you can find all types of used clothes, from hats of the 1930's to old military uniforms.

A. Les vêtements

How to talk about shopping for clothes:

Où vas-tu?

Je vais | dans **une boutique** *(shop)*.
| dans **un magasin** *(store)*
| dans **un grand magasin** *(department store)*

Qu'est-ce que tu vas **acheter** *(to buy)*?

Je vais acheter **des vêtements** *(clothes)*.

Les vêtements

Pour hommes et femmes

un chapeau
un blouson
une veste
un manteau
un pull
un pantalon
un imper
(un imperméable)
un jean
une chemise
un polo
des chaussettes
(une chaussette)

➡ Nouns that end in **-eau** in the singular end in **-eaux** in the plural.

un chap**eau** des chap**eaux** un mant**eau** des mant**eaux**

acheter	*to buy*	Je vais **acheter** une cravate.
porter	*to wear*	Qu'est-ce que tu vas **porter** demain?
mettre	*to put on, wear*	Oh là là, il fait froid. Je vais **mettre** un pull.

➡ **Mettre** is irregular. (Its forms are presented in Leçon 26.)

1 Shopping

Below are the names of several Paris stores. Using the illustrations as a guide, talk to a classmate about where you are going shopping and what you plan to buy.

▶ —Où vas-tu?
—Je vais au Monoprix.
—Qu'est-ce que tu vas acheter?
—Je vais acheter une chemise.

▶ (au) MONOPRIX

1. (au) PRINTEMPS

2. (au) BON MARCHÉ

3. (au) PRISUNIC

4. (chez) CÉLINE

5. (aux) GALERIES LAFAYETTE

6. (chez) BURBERRY

7. (chez) DIOR

8. (à) LA SAMARITAINE

2 Quels vêtements?

What we wear often depends on the circumstances: where we are, what we will be doing, what the weather is like. Complete the following sentences with the appropriate items of clothing.

1. Aujourd'hui, je porte...
2. Le professeur porte...
3. L'élève à ma gauche porte...
4. L'élève à ma droite porte...
5. Quand je vais à une boum, je porte...
6. Quand je vais dans un restaurant élégant, je porte...
7. S'il pleut *(If it rains)* demain, je vais mettre...
8. S'il fait chaud demain, je vais mettre...
9. Si *(If)* je vais en ville samedi, je vais mettre...
10. Si je vais à un concert dimanche, je vais mettre...

B. D'autres vêtements et accessoires

Les chaussures

les chaussures (une chaussure)

des tennis (une tennis)

des bottes (une botte)

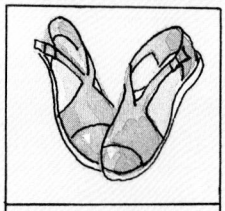
des sandales (une sandale)

des baskets (une basket)

Les vêtements de sport

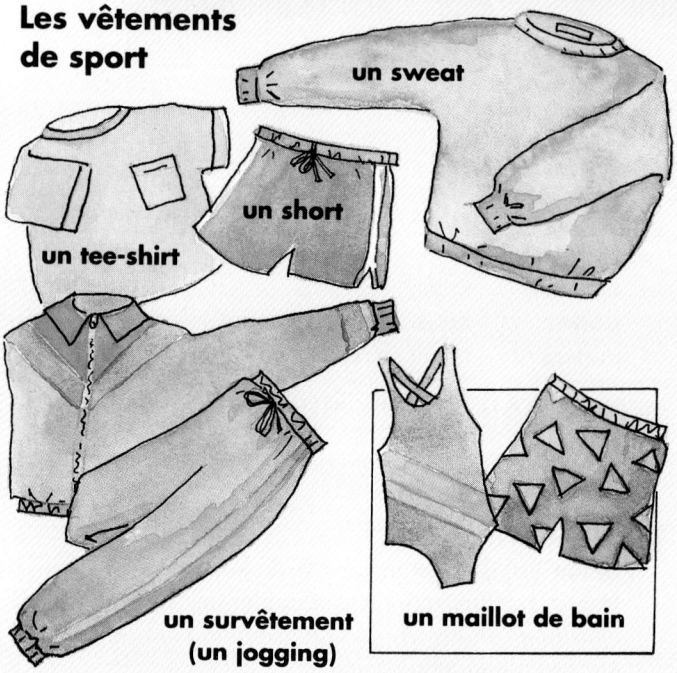
un sweat
un short
un tee-shirt
un survêtement (un jogging)
un maillot de bain

Les accessoires

une ceinture

des lunettes

des lunettes de soleil

3 À la plage de Deauville

You are spending the summer vacation in Deauville, a popular ocean resort in Normandy. Describe what you and your friends are wearing.

▶ Paul 1. Anne 2. Sophie 3. Michel 4. Catherine 5. moi

▶ Paul porte un maillot de bain . . .

4 Qu'est-ce que tu portes?

Ask your classmates what they wear in the following circumstances. Let them use their imagination.

▶ jouer au tennis

1. aller à la piscine
2. aller à la plage
3. jouer au basket
4. travailler dans le jardin
5. aller au gymnase *(gym)*
6. faire une promenade dans la forêt *(forest)*
7. faire une promenade dans la neige *(snow)*

5 Un jeu

When you see what people are wearing, you can often tell what they are going to do. How many different logical sentences can you make in five minutes? Follow the model below.

A	B	C
André	un maillot de bain	nager
Sylvie	des lunettes de soleil	aller à la plage
Paul et Éric	un short	aller à un concert
Michèle et Anne	des chaussettes blanches	jouer au tennis
	un sweat	jouer au volley
	un pantalon très chic	jouer au football
	des chaussures noires	aller à la campagne *(country)*
	des bottes	faire du jogging *(to jog)*
	un costume *(suit)*	dîner en ville
	une robe	

6 Joyeux anniversaire!

The following people are celebrating their birthdays. Find a present for each person by choosing an item of clothing from pages 248, 249, or 250.

1. Pour mon père (ma mère), je vais acheter, ...
2. Pour ma grand-mère (mon grand-père), ...
3. Pour ma petite cousine Chantal (10 ans), ...
4. Pour mon grand frère Guillaume (18 ans), ...
5. Pour le professeur, ...
6. Pour mon meilleur *(best)* ami, ...
7. Pour ma meilleure amie, ...

C. Dans un magasin

How to get help from a salesperson:

Pardon, monsieur (madame).

Vous désirez *(May I help you),* **monsieur? madame mademoiselle**

Je cherche *(I'm looking for)* . . . un pantalon.

Quel est le prix *(What is the price)* du pantalon?
Combien *(How much)* **coûte** le pantalon?
Combien est-ce qu'il coûte?
Il coûte 200 francs.

Je cherche . . . une veste.

Quel est le prix de la veste?
Combien coûte la veste?
Combien est-ce qu'elle coûte?
Elle coûte 300 francs.

How to discuss clothes with a friend:

Qu'est-ce que tu penses du pantalon vert?
(What do you think of . . . ?)
Comment trouves-tu le pantalon vert?
(What do you think of . . . ?)

Qu'est-ce que tu penses de la veste verte?
Comment trouves-tu la veste verte?

Il est	**joli.**	Elle est	**jolie.**
	élégant		**élégante**
	super		**super**
	chouette *(terrific)*		**chouette**
	à la mode *(in style)*		**à la mode**
Il est	**moche** *(plain, ugly).*	Elle est	**moche.**
	démodé *(out of style)*		**démodée**
Il est **trop** *(too)*	**petit.**	Elle est **trop**	**petite.**
	grand *(big)*		**grande**
	court *(short)*		**courte**
	long *(long)*		**longue**
Il est	**cher** *(expensive).*	Elle est	**chère.**
	bon marché *(cheap)*		**bon marché**

➡ **Super** and **bon marché** are INVARIABLE. They do not take adjective endings.
La robe rouge est **super.** Les chaussures blanches sont **bon marché.**

VERBES

chercher	*to look for*	Je **cherche** un jean.
coûter	*to cost*	Les chaussures **coûtent** 300 francs.
penser	*to think*	Qu'est-ce que tu **penses** de cette *(this)* robe?
penser que	*to think (that)*	Je **pense qu'**elle est super!
trouver	*to find*	Je ne **trouve** pas ma veste.
	to think of	Comment **trouves**-tu mes lunettes de soleil?

➡ The verb **penser** is often used alone.
Tu **penses?** *Do you think so?* Je **ne pense pas.** *I don't think so.*

Les nombres de 100 à 1000							
100	**cent**	200	**deux cents**	500	**cinq cents**	800	**huit cents**
101	**cent un**	300	**trois cents**	600	**six cents**	900	**neuf cents**
102	**cent deux**	400	**quatre cents**	700	**sept cents**	1000	**mille**

7 Au Marché aux puces

You are at the Paris flea market looking for clothes with a French friend. Explain why you are not buying the following items. Use your imagination ... and expressions from the **Vocabulaire.**

▶ **— Tu vas acheter le blouson?**
— Non, je ne pense pas.
— Pourquoi pas?
— Il est trop grand.

▶ 

8 C'est combien?

You are at the Printemps, a department store in Paris. Ask a salesperson how much the various items cost.

▶ 

À votre tour!

1 La bonne réponse

You are in a French department store. Match the questions on the left with the appropriate answers on the right.

1. Vous désirez, monsieur?	a. Mon pantalon gris et ma veste bleue.
2. Est-ce que tu vas acheter le survêtement bleu?	b. 900 francs.
3. Comment trouves-tu les lunettes de soleil?	c. Je cherche une cravate.
4. Combien coûte l'imper?	d. Non, il est trop cher.
5. Qu'est-ce que tu vas mettre pour aller au restaurant?	e. Elles sont chouettes.

2 Créa-dialogue

You are at Place Bonaventure in Montreal looking at clothes in various shops. You like what the salesperson shows you and ask how much each item costs. React to the price.

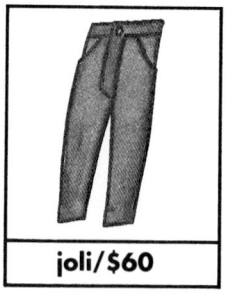

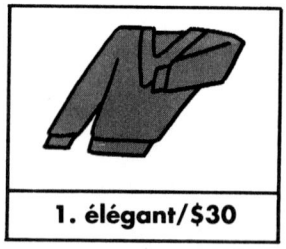

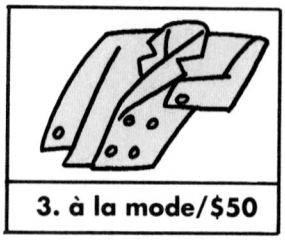

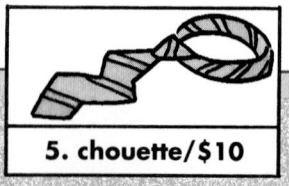

▶ —Vous désirez, monsieur (mademoiselle)?
—Je cherche un pantalon.
—Comment trouvez-vous le pantalon gris?
—Il est joli. Combien est-ce qu'il coûte?
—Soixante dollars.
—Oh là là, il est cher!
(Il est bon marché.)

3 Conversation dirigée

Sophie and Christophe are shopping in a department store. Act out their conversation in French.

Sophie				Christophe
	asks Christophe what he is looking for	→ ←	answers that he is looking for a tie	
	asks him what he thinks of the yellow tie	→ ←	says that it is pretty but adds that he is going to buy the blue tie	
	asks how much it costs	⇄	answers 25 francs	
	says that it is inexpensive but adds that the tie is out of style			

4 Qu'est-ce qui ne va pas? *(What's wrong?)*

The people in the pictures below are not very good shoppers. Describe what is wrong with each of the items they bought.

Monsieur Dupont

Édouard

▶ **Le chapeau de Monsieur Dupont est trop grand.**

5 Les valises

Imagine that you are spending a year in Paris. On two different weekends, you have been invited by families of your classmates to visit their homes. On the first weekend, you will visit Nice and go sailing in the Mediterranean. For the second weekend, you have been invited to go skiing at Chamonix in the French Alps. Prepare your suitcases for the two trips, listing the items you will take with you.

▶ un maillot de bain
deux shorts

un jean
un pull

6 À l'aéroport

Next week you are going to Paris for the first time on an exchange program. At the airport, you will be met by your host family. They do not have a picture of you. Describe yourself in a short note, telling what you look like and what you are going to wear.

▶ Je vais arriver à Paris par le vol (flight) Air France 070.
Je suis...
Je vais porter...

LEÇON 26 Rien n'est parfait!

Cet après-midi, Frédéric et Jean-Claude vont acheter des vêtements. Ils vont acheter ces vêtements dans un grand magasin. Ce magasin s'appelle Le Bon Marché.

This
these / This

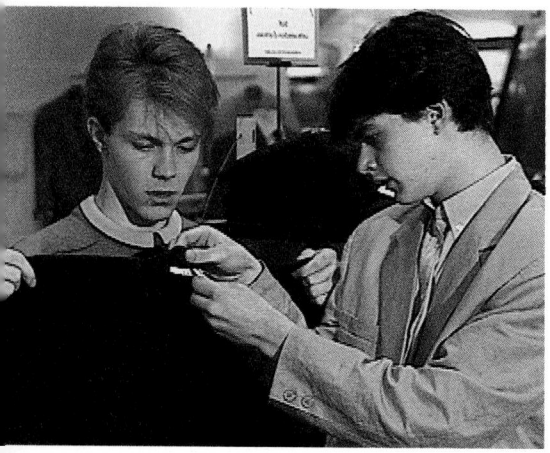

Scène 1.
Frédéric et Jean-Claude regardent les pulls.

FRÉDÉRIC: Regarde! Comment trouves-tu ce pull?
JEAN-CLAUDE: Quel pull? *Which*
FRÉDÉRIC: Ce pull bleu.
JEAN-CLAUDE: Il est chouette.
FRÉDÉRIC: C'est vrai, il est très chouette.
JEAN-CLAUDE: *(qui regarde le prix)* Il est aussi très cher.
FRÉDÉRIC: Combien est-ce qu'il coûte?
JEAN-CLAUDE: Six cents francs.
FRÉDÉRIC: Six cents francs! Quelle horreur! *What a scandal!*

NOTE CULTURELLE

Le grand magasin

Many people consider the department store **(le grand magasin)** to be a typically American institution. However, it is a Frenchman, Aristide Boucicaut (1810–1877), who is generally credited with its creation. Monsieur Boucicaut's idea was to satisfy his Paris customers by offering them a large selection of good quality items at inexpensive prices. When he opened his new store in 1852, he appropriately named it Au Bon Marché. His success was soon imitated, leading to the creation in Paris of more department stores: Printemps, Galeries Lafayette, Samaritaine. These well-known stores still exist today and have branches in cities across France.

Scène 2.
Maintenant Frédéric et Jean-Claude regardent les vestes.

FRÉDÉRIC: Quelle veste est-ce que tu préfères?
JEAN-CLAUDE: Je préfère cette veste jaune. Elle est très élégante et elle n'est pas très chère.
FRÉDÉRIC: Oui, mais elle est trop grande pour toi!
JEAN-CLAUDE: Dommage!

Scène 3.
Marc est au rayon des chaussures. Quelles chaussures est-ce qu'il va acheter? *department*

JEAN-CLAUDE: Alors, quelles chaussures est-ce que tu achètes?
FRÉDÉRIC: J'achète ces chaussures noires. Elles sont très confortables ... et elles ne sont pas chères. Regarde, elles sont en solde. *on sale*
JEAN-CLAUDE: C'est vrai, elles sont en solde ... mais elles ne sont plus à la mode. *are no longer*
FRÉDÉRIC: Hélas, rien n'est parfait! *too bad/nothing is perfect*

Compréhension

1. Où vont Frédéric et Jean-Claude cet après-midi?
2. Qu'est-ce qu'ils vont faire?
3. Qu'est-ce qu'ils regardent d'abord *(first)?*
4. Combien coûte le pull bleu?
5. Quelle *(What)* est la réaction de Frédéric?
6. Qu'est-ce que Jean-Claude pense de la veste jaune?
7. Pourquoi est-ce qu'il n'achète pas la veste?
8. Qu'est-ce que Frédéric pense des chaussures noires?
9. Pourquoi est-ce qu'il n'achète pas les chaussures?

A. Les verbes *acheter* et *préférer*

Verbs like **acheter** *(to buy)* end in: **e** + CONSONANT + **-er.**
Verbs like **préférer** *(to prefer)* end in: **é** + CONSONANT + **-er.**

Note the forms of these two verbs in the chart, paying attention to:

- the **e** of the stem of **acheter**
- the **é** of the stem of **préférer**

INFINITIVE	acheter	préférer
PRESENT	J' **achète** une veste. Tu **achètes** une cravate. Il/Elle **achète** un imper.	Je **préfère** la veste bleue. Tu **préfères** la cravate jaune. Il/Elle **préfère** l'imper gris.
	Nous **achetons** un jean. Vous **achetez** un short. Ils/Elles **achètent** un pull.	Nous **préférons** le jean noir. Vous **préférez** le short blanc. Ils/Elles **préfèrent** le pull rouge.

➡ Verbs like **acheter** and **préférer** take regular endings and have the following changes in the stem:

acheter e → è
préférer é → è
} in the **je, tu, il,** and **ils** forms of the present

1 Achats *(Purchases)*

What we buy depends on how much money we have. Complete the sentences below with **acheter** and one or more of the items from the list.

1. Avec dix dollars, tu ...
2. Avec quinze dollars, j' ...
3. Avec trente dollars, nous ...
4. Avec cinquante dollars, Jean-Claude ...
5. Avec cent dollars, vous ...
6. Avec quinze mille dollars, mes parents ...
7. Avec ?? dollars, mon cousin ...
8. Avec ?? dollars, j' ...

une voiture

des chaussures

une cravate

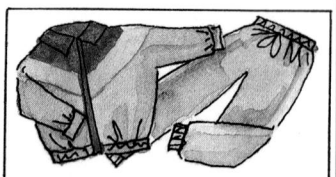
un survêtement

des lunettes de soleil

un polo

une veste

un compact

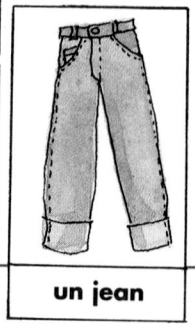
un jean

??

Vocabulaire: Verbes comme *(like)* ***acheter et préférer***

acheter	*to buy*	Qu'est-ce que tu **achètes?**
amener	*to bring (a person)*	François **amène** sa copine à la boum.
préférer	*to prefer*	**Préfères-**tu le manteau ou l'imper?
espérer	*to hope*	J'**espère** visiter Paris en été.

➡ In French, there are two verbs that correspond to the English *to bring:*

amener + PEOPLE — J'**amène** une copine au pique-nique.
apporter + THINGS — J'**apporte** des sandwichs au pique-nique.

2 Pique-nique

Everyone is bringing someone or something to the picnic. Complete the sentences below with the appropriate forms of **amener** or **apporter.**

▶ **Nous amenons un copain. Marc apporte des sandwichs.**

1. Tu . . . ta guitare.
2. Philippe . . . sa soeur.
3. Nous . . . nos voisins.
4. Vous . . . un dessert.
5. Michèle . . . des sodas.
6. Antoine et Vincent . . . leur cousine.
7. Raphaël . . . ses cassettes.
8. Mon cousin . . . sa copine.
9. J' . . . ma radiocassette.

3 Expression personnelle

Complete the sentences below with one of the suggested options or an expression of your choice. Note: You may wish to make some of the sentences negative.

1. Quand je vais à un pique-nique, j'amène . . . (ma petite soeur, mes voisins, mon chien, ??)
   J'apporte . . . (mon walkman, mon livre de français, des sandwichs, ??)
2. Quand je vais à une boum, j'amène . . . (des copains, une copine, ma grand-mère, ??)
   J'apporte . . . (des sandwichs, ma guitare, mes cassettes, ??)
3. Le weekend, je préfère . . . (étudier, aller au cinéma, rester à la maison, ??)
   Ce *(This)* weekend, j'espère . . . (travailler, avoir un rendez-vous avec un copain ou une copine, jouer au volley, ??)
4. Pendant *(During)* les vacances, j'espère . . . (rester à la maison, trouver un job, voyager, ??)
   Un jour, j'espère . . . (visiter la France, parler français, aller à l'université, être millionnaire, ??)

B. L'adjectif démonstratif *ce*

Learning about language

DEMONSTRATIVE ADJECTIVES *(this, that)* are used to point out specific people or things.

In French, the demonstrative adjective **ce** always agrees with the noun it introduces.

Note the forms of the demonstrative adjective **ce** in the chart below.

	SINGULAR *(this, that)*	PLURAL *(these, those)*		
MASCULINE	**ce** ↓ **cet** (+ VOWEL SOUND)	**ces**	**ce** blouson **cet** homme	**ces** blousons **ces** hommes
FEMININE	**cette**	**ces**	**cette** veste **cette** amie	**ces** vestes **ces** amies

- There is liaison after **cet** and **ces** when the next word begins with a vowel sound.
- To distinguish between a person or an object that is close by and one that is further away, the French sometimes use **-ci** or **-là** after the noun.

Philippe achète **cette chemise-ci.** *Philippe is buying* ***this shirt*** *(over here).*
François achète **cette chemise-là.** *François is buying* ***that shirt*** *(over there).*

4 À la Samaritaine

Marc and Nathalie are at the Samaritaine department store. Marc likes everything that Nathalie shows him. Play both roles.

▶ une robe (jolie)
NATHALIE: **Regarde cette robe!**
MARC: **Elle est jolie!**

1. un imper (élégant)
2. des bottes (à la mode)
3. une cravate (chouette)
4. un survêtement (super)
5. des livres (amusants)
6. un ordinateur (super)
7. une télé (moderne)
8. une ceinture (jolie)
9. des sandales (jolies)

Expression pour la conversation

How to emphasize a question or remark:

Eh bien! *Well!* —**Eh bien,** est-ce que tu viens en ville avec nous?
—**Eh bien,** non!

5 Différences d'opinion

Whenever they go shopping together, Éric and Brigitte cannot agree on what they like. Play both roles.

▶ un short

1. une chemise
2. un blouson
3. des chaussures
4. des lunettes
5. des disques
6. une affiche
7. un stylo
8. un ordinateur

C. L'adjectif interrogatif *quel?*

The interrogative adjective **quel** *(what? which?)* is used in questions. It agrees with the noun it introduces and has the following forms:

	SINGULAR	PLURAL		
MASCULINE	**quel**	**quels**	**Quel** garçon?	**Quels** cousins?
FEMININE	**quelle**	**quelles**	**Quelle** fille?	**Quelles** copines?

➡ Note the liaison after **quels** and **quelles** when the next word begins with a vowel sound.
Quelles affiches est-ce que tu préfères?

6 Vêtements d'été

You are shopping for the following items before going on a summer trip to France. A friend is asking you which ones you are buying. Identify each item by color.

▶ **une jupe/ jaune**

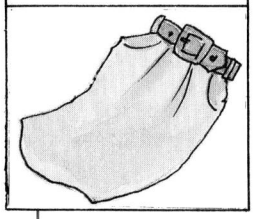

1. un maillot de bain/ bleu

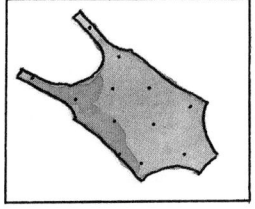

2. des chaussettes/ vertes

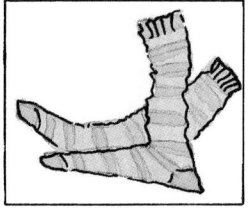

3. un pantalon/ noir

4. une veste/ bleue

5. des chaussures/ blanches

6. des sandales/ brunes

7. un sweat/ gris

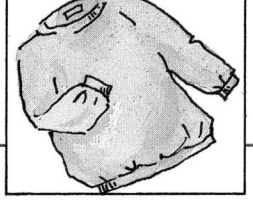

8. une chemise/ orange

9. un pull/ rouge

7 Questions personnelles

1. À quelle école vas-tu?
2. Dans quel magasin achètes-tu tes vêtements?
3. Dans quel magasin achètes-tu tes chaussures?
4. Quels disques aimes-tu écouter?
5. Quels programmes aimes-tu regarder à la télé?
6. Quel est ton restaurant préféré?

D. Le verbe *mettre*

The verb **mettre** *(to put, place)* is irregular. Note its forms in the chart below.

INFINITIVE	**mettre**	
PRESENT	je **mets** tu **mets** il / elle **met**	nous **mettons** vous **mettez** ils / elles **mettent**

➡ In the singular forms, the "**t**" of the stem is silent. The "**t**" is pronounced in the plural forms.

➡ The verb **mettre** has several English equivalents:

to put, place	Je **mets** mes livres sur la table.
to put on, wear	Caroline **met** une robe rouge.
to turn on	Nous **mettons** la télé.

8 Où?

Say where the people of Column A put the objects of Column B, by choosing a place from Column C. Be logical! ▶

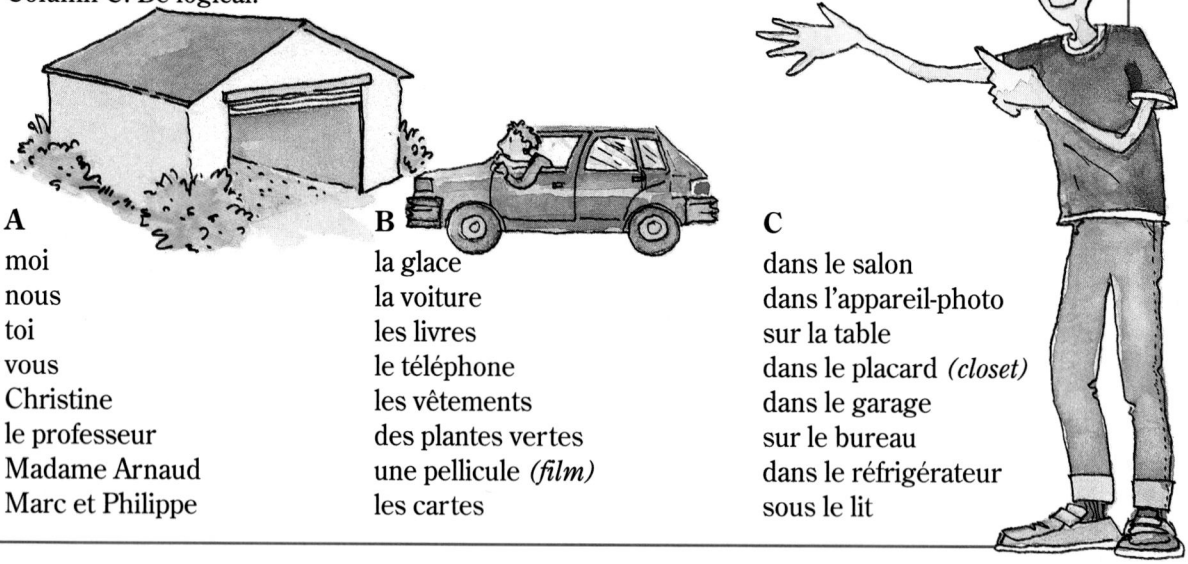

A	B	C
moi	la glace	dans le salon
nous	la voiture	dans l'appareil-photo
toi	les livres	sur la table
vous	le téléphone	dans le placard *(closet)*
Christine	les vêtements	dans le garage
le professeur	des plantes vertes	sur le bureau
Madame Arnaud	une pellicule *(film)*	dans le réfrigérateur
Marc et Philippe	les cartes	sous le lit

Où mettre...
vos vêtements?
vos livres?
les cartes?

GALERIES Lafayette

Meubles et lampes: 4ème étage

9 Questions personnelles

1. Est-ce que tu mets la radio quand tu étudies?
2. Chez vous, est-ce que vous mettez la télé quand vous dînez?
3. Est-ce que tu mets des lunettes de soleil quand tu vas à la plage?
4. Où est-ce que tes parents mettent leur voiture? (dans le garage? dans la rue?)
5. Quels programmes de télé est-ce que tu mets le dimanche? le samedi?
6. Quels disques (ou quelles cassettes) est-ce que tu mets quand tu vas à une boum?
7. Quels vêtements est-ce que tu mets quand il fait froid?
8. Quels vêtements est-ce que tu mets quand tu joues au basket?

Prononciation

Les lettres «e» et «è»

e = /ə/

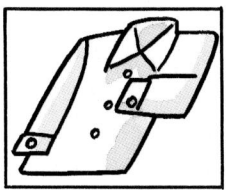

chemise

e = /ɛ/

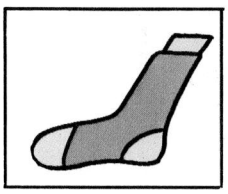

chaussette

è = /ɛ/

chère

Practice pronouncing "**e**" within a word:

- /ə/ (as in **je**) [. . . "**e**" + *one* CONSONANT + VOWEL]
  Répétez: **chemise regarder Denise Renée petit venir**

  Note that in the middle of a word the /ə/ is sometimes silent.
  achéter achétons amener samedi rarement avenue
- /ɛ/ (as in **elle**) [. . . "**e**" + *two* CONSONANTS + VOWEL]
  Répétez: **chaussette veste quelle cette rester professeur raquette**

Now practice pronouncing "**è**" within a word:

- /ɛ/ (as in **elle**) [. . . "**è**" + *one* CONSONANT + VOWEL]
  Répétez: **chère père mère achète amènent espère deuxième**

À votre tour!

1 La bonne réponse

Alice is talking to her cousin Jérôme. Match Alice's questions with Jérôme's answers. Act out the dialogue with a classmate.

Alice

1. Je vais à la boum de Delphine. Et toi?
2. Tu amènes une copine?
3. Qu'est-ce que vous allez apporter?
4. Qu'est-ce que tu vas mettre?

a. Oui, Christine.
b. Mon pull jaune et mon blouson marron.
c. Nous allons acheter des pizzas.
d. Moi aussi.

Jérôme

2 Créa-dialogue

Ask your classmates what they think about the following. They will answer affirmatively or negatively.

▶ — Comment trouves-tu cette fille?
— Quelle fille?
— Cette fille-là!
— Eh bien, je pense qu'elle est jolie.
(Elle n'est pas jolie.)

▶ jolie?

1. intéressants?

2. sympathique?

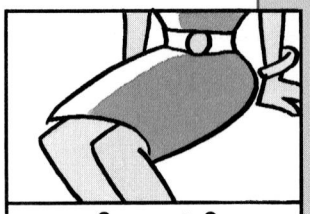

3. courte?

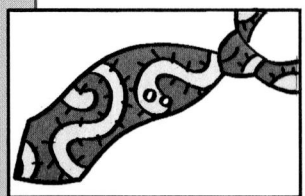

4. moche?

5. bon marché?

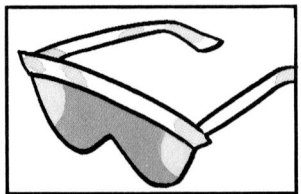

6. ??

7. ??

3 Shopping

You and a friend are shopping by catalog. Choose an object and tell your friend what you are buying. Identify it by color and explain why you like it.

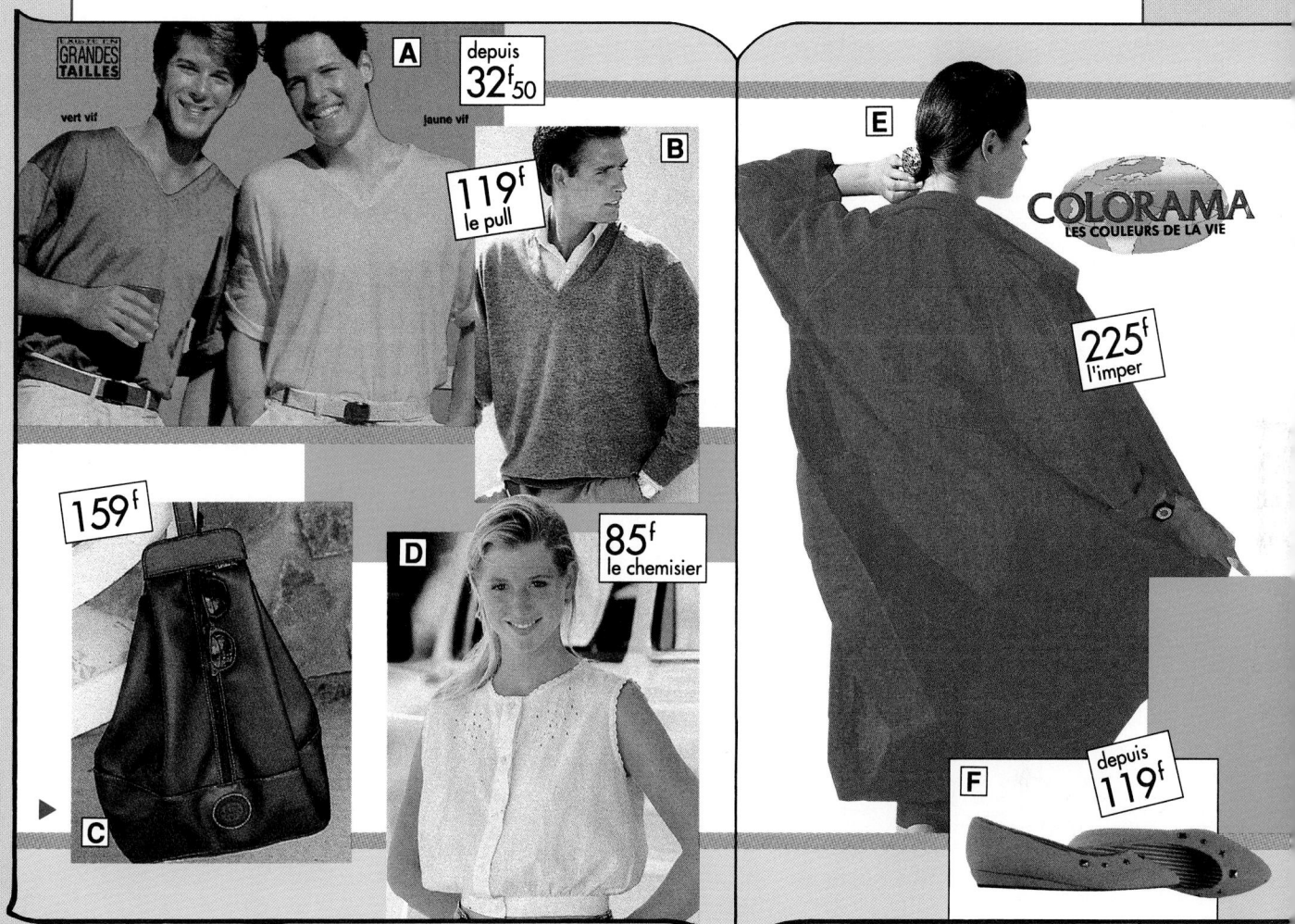

▶ — Je vais acheter un sac.
— Quel sac?
— Ce sac noir.
— Pourquoi?
— Parce qu'il est joli.

4 Composition: La boum

You have been invited to a party by a French friend. In a short paragraph, describe . . .

- what clothes you are going to wear
- whom you are going to bring along
- what things (food? records? cassettes?) you are going to bring

LEÇON 27

Un choix difficile

Dans un mois, Delphine va aller au mariage de sa cousine. Elle va acheter une nouvelle robe pour cette occasion. Pour cela, elle va dans une boutique de mode avec sa copine Véronique. Il y a beaucoup de jolies robes dans cette boutique.

Delphine hésite entre une robe jaune et une robe rouge. Quelle robe est-ce que Delphine va choisir? Ah là là, le choix n'est pas facile.

new

is hesitating / between

to choose / choice

Scène 1.

VÉRONIQUE: Alors, quelle robe est-ce que tu choisis?

DELPHINE: Eh bien, finalement je choisis la robe rouge. Elle est plus jolie que la robe jaune.

VÉRONIQUE: C'est vrai, elle est plus jolie . . . mais la robe jaune est moins chère et elle est plus grande. Regarde. La robe rouge est trop petite pour toi.

DELPHINE: Mais non, elle n'est pas trop petite.

VÉRONIQUE: Bon, écoute, essaie-la!

finally

prettier than

less / larger

NOTE CULTURELLE

Le choix de vêtements

Since clothes are more expensive in France than in the United States and because budgets are limited, French teenagers are very careful when buying clothes. They spend a lot of time window shopping, comparing (brands, labels, and prices), and discussing with their friends what is in or out of fashion, before finally deciding what to buy. In general, French teenagers would rather buy one item of good quality than several of lesser quality. Of course, this item has to be the right one!

Scène 2.

Delphine sort de la cabine d'essayage. *comes out / fitting room*

DELPHINE: C'est vrai, la robe rouge est plus petite mais ce n'est pas un problème. *smaller*

VÉRONIQUE: Pourquoi?

DELPHINE: Parce que j'ai un mois pour maigrir. *to lose weight*

VÉRONIQUE: Et si tu grossis? *if / gain weight*

DELPHINE: Toi, tais-toi! *be quiet*

Compréhension

1. Où vont Delphine et Véronique?
2. Qu'est-ce que Delphine va acheter?
3. Pourquoi?
4. Delphine hésite entre deux robes. De quelle couleur sont-elles?
5. Quelle robe est-ce qu'elle choisit?
6. Pourquoi est-ce qu'elle préfère la robe rouge?
7. Selon (*According to*) Véronique, quel est le problème de la robe rouge?
8. Qu'est-ce que Delphine doit *(must)* faire pour porter la robe?

A. Les verbes réguliers en *-ir*

Many French verbs end in *-ir*. Most of these verbs are conjugated like **finir** *(to finish)*. Note the forms of this verb in the present tense, paying special attention to the endings.

INFINITIVE	**finir**	STEM (infinitive minus **-ir**)	ENDINGS
PRESENT	Je **finis** à deux heures. Tu **finis** à une heure. Il/Elle **finit** à cinq heures. Nous **finissons** à midi. Vous **finissez** à une heure. Ils/Elles **finissent** à minuit.	**fin-**	**-is** **-is** **-it** **-issons** **-issez** **-issent**

➡ Note that all final consonants are silent.

1 Le marathon de Paris

Not everyone who enters the Paris marathon finishes. Say which of the following runners finish the marathon and which do not.

▶ Philippe (non) **Philippe ne finit pas.**

1. moi (oui)
2. toi (non)
3. nous (oui)
4. vous (non)
5. Éric (oui)
6. Stéphanie (non)
7. Frédéric et Marc (non)
8. Anne et Cécile (oui)

Vocabulaire: Verbes réguliers en *-ir*

choisir	*to choose*	Quelle veste **choisis**-tu?
finir	*to finish*	Les classes **finissent** à midi.
grossir	*to gain weight, get fat*	Marc **grossit** parce qu'il mange beaucoup.
maigrir	*to lose weight, get thin*	Je **maigris** parce que je ne mange pas beaucoup.
réussir	*to succeed*	Tu vas **réussir** parce que tu travailles!
réussir à un examen	*to pass an exam*	Nous **réussissons à nos examens.**

2 Le régime *(Diet)*

Read about the following people. Then say whether they are gaining weight or losing weight. Use the verbs **grossir** and **maigrir.**

▶ Philippe mange beaucoup de pizzas. **Il grossit.**

1. Vous faites des exercices.
2. Nous allons souvent au gymnase.
3. Vous êtes inactifs.
4. Je mange des carottes.
5. Monsieur Moreau adore la bonne cuisine.
6. Vous n'êtes pas très sportifs.
7. Ces personnes mangent trop *(too much)*.
8. Je nage, je joue au volley et je fais des promenades.

3 Questions personnelles

1. À quelle heure finissent les classes aujourd'hui?
2. À quelle heure finit la classe de français?
3. Quand finit l'école cette année *(year)?*
4. Tu es invité(e) au restaurant ou au cinéma. Où choisis-tu d'aller?
5. Quand tu vas au cinéma avec ta famille, qui choisit le film?
6. En général, est-ce que tu réussis à tes examens? Est-ce que tu vas réussir à l'examen de français?
7. Est-ce que tes copains réussissent aussi?

B. Les adjectifs *beau, nouveau* et *vieux*

The adjectives **beau** *(beautiful, good-looking),* **nouveau** *(new),* and **vieux** *(old)* are irregular. Note their forms and their position.

		beau	nouveau	vieux
SINGULAR	MASC.	le **beau** manteau (le **bel** imper)	le **nouveau** manteau (le **nouvel** imper)	le **vieux** manteau (le **vieil** imper)
	FEM.	la **belle** veste	la **nouvelle** veste	la **vieille** veste
PLURAL	MASC.	les **beaux** manteaux	les **nouveaux** manteaux	les **vieux** manteaux
	FEM.	les **belles** vestes	les **nouvelles** vestes	les **vieilles** vestes

➡ The adjectives **beau, nouveau,** and **vieux** usually come BEFORE the noun. If the noun begins with a vowel sound, there is liaison between the adjective and the noun.

les **nouveaux** ordinateurs les **belles** affiches les **vieux** impers

➡ In the masculine singular, the liaison forms **bel, nouvel,** and **vieil** are used before a vowel sound. Note that **vieil** is pronounced like **vieille:**

un **vieil** imper une **vieille** robe

4 La collection de printemps

Mod Boutique is presenting its spring collection. You are impressed by the new clothes and accessories. Point them out to a French friend, using the appropriate forms of **beau.**

▶ une chemise
Regarde la belle chemise!

1. une robe
2. un pantalon
3. des jeans
4. des blousons
5. un imper
6. des sandales
7. un manteau
8. un chapeau

5 Différences d'opinion

François is showing the new things he bought to his sister Valérie. She prefers his old things. Play both roles.

▶ des chaussures

1. un polo
2. des lunettes de soleil
3. un imper
4. des affiches
5. une veste
6. une montre
7. un ordinateur
8. des baskets
9. un survêtement

C. La comparaison avec les adjectifs

Note how COMPARISONS are expressed in French.

Cet imper est **plus cher que** ce manteau.	*... more expensive than ...*
Cette jupe est **plus jolie que** cette robe.	*... prettier than ...*
Paul est **moins sportif que** Patrick.	*... less athletic than ...*
Il est **moins amusant que** lui.	*... less amusing than ...*
Je suis **aussi grand que** toi.	*... as tall as ...*
Tu **n'**es **pas aussi timide que** moi.	*... not as timid as ...*

To make comparisons with adjectives, the French use the following constructions:

+ **plus**	+ ADJECTIVE (+ **que** . . .)	**plus cher (que)**	*more expensive (than)*
– **moins**		**moins cher (que)**	*less expensive (than)*
= **aussi**		**aussi cher (que)**	*as expensive (as)*

➡ Note the irregular **plus**-form of **bon** *(good):*

plus + **bon(ne)** → **meilleur(e)** *(better)*

Ta cassette est **bonne,** mais ma cassette est **meilleure.**

But: Cette cassette est **moins bonne que** ce disque.
Est-ce que les Red Sox sont **aussi bons que** les Yankees?

➡ There is liaison after **plus** and **moins** when the next word begins with a vowel sound.

Cette robe-ci est **plus élégante.** Ce livre-là est **moins intéressant.**

➡ In comparisons, the adjective always agrees with the noun (or pronoun) it describes.

La jupe est plus **chère** que le chemisier.

Les vestes sont moins **chères** que les manteaux.

➡ In comparisons with people, STRESS PRONOUNS are used after **que.**

Paul est plus petit **que moi.** Je suis plus grand **que lui.**

6 Comparaisons

How much do you think the following pairs of items cost? Give your opinion, saying whether the first one is more expensive, less expensive, or as expensive as the second one.

▶ une guitare/une raquette — **Une guitare est plus (moins, aussi) chère qu'une raquette.**

1. un vélo/un scooter
2. une mobylette/une moto
3. une pizza/un sandwich
4. une télé/un ordinateur
5. des chaussures/des sandales
6. un pantalon/une robe
7. des bottes/des tennis
8. un sweat/un maillot de bain
9. des chaussettes/des collants
10. des lunettes de soleil/une montre

Expression pour la conversation

How to introduce a personal opinion:

à mon avis . . . *in my opinion . . .* **À mon avis,** le français est facile.

7 Expression personnelle

Compare the following by using the adjectives suggested. Give your personal opinion.

▶ le tennis/intéressant/le ping-pong

1. le basket/intéressant/le foot
2. l'anglais/facile/le français
3. la classe de français/amusant/ la classe d'anglais
4. la ville de New York/beau/ la ville de Chicago
5. la Floride/beau/la Californie
6. les Yankees/bon/les Red Sox
7. les Celtics/bon/les Lakers
8. les Cowboys/bon/les Saints
9. la cuisine américaine/bon/ la cuisine française
10. les voitures japonaises/bon/ les voitures américaines
11. les filles/intelligent/les garçons
12. les Américains/intelligent/ les Français

8 Et toi?

Use the appropriate stress pronouns in answering the questions below.

▶ —Es-tu plus grand(e) que ton copain?
—**Oui, je suis plus grand(e) que lui.**
(Non, je suis moins grand(e) que lui.)
(Je suis aussi grand(e) que lui.)

1. Es-tu plus grand(e) que ta mère?
2. Es-tu aussi riche que Donald Trump?
3. Es-tu plus sportif (sportive) que tes cousins?
4. Es-tu plus intelligent(e) qu'Einstein?

Prononciation

Les lettres «ill» **ill /j/**

In the middle of a word, the letters "**ill**" almost always represent the semi-vowel /j/ which is like the "**y**" of *yes*.

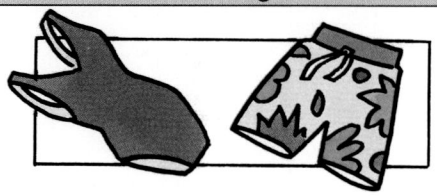

maillot

Répétez: **maillot travaillez oreille vieille fille famille juillet**
En juillet, Mireille va travailler pour sa vieille tante.

At the end of a word, the sound /j/ is sometimes spelled **il.**

Répétez: **appareil-photo vieil travail** *(job)*
Mon oncle a un vieil appareil-photo.

EXCEPTION: The letters **ill** are pronounced /il/ in the following words:

Répétez: **ville village mille Lille**

À votre tour!

1 La bonne réponse

François and Stéphanie are shopping. Match François's questions with Stéphanie's answers. You may act out the dialogue with a friend.

François

1. Tu aimes cette veste verte?
2. Combien est-ce qu'elle coûte?
3. Alors, qu'est-ce que tu vas choisir?
4. Et qu'est-ce que tu penses de cette veste rouge?

a. 600 francs.
b. À mon avis, elle est moins jolie.
c. Oui, mais elle est très chère.
d. La veste bleue. Elle est meilleur marché et elle est aussi élégante.

Stéphanie

2 Créa-dialogue

With a classmate, prepare a dialogue comparing the items in one of the following pictures. Use the suggested verb and some of the suggested adjectives.

▶ —Tu choisis la voiture rouge ou la voiture noire?
—Je choisis la voiture rouge.
—Pourquoi?
—Parce qu'elle est plus petite et moins chère.

▶ **choisir**

petit/grand/confortable/rapide/cher

1. acheter

petit/grand/cher/bon

2. préférer

joli/confortable/cher/bon

3. choisir

petit/grand/mignon/joli

4. amener

mignon/amusant/intelligent
intéressant/sympathique

5. inviter

??

3 Choix personnels

Select two people or two items in each of the following categories and ask a classmate to indicate which one he / she prefers. You may ask your classmate to explain why.

▶ *2 actors*

(plus beau, plus jeune . . .)

CATEGORIES:

▶ *2 actors*
- *2 actresses*
- *2 singers (male)*
- *2 singers (female)*
- *2 baseball teams*
- *2 cities*
- *2 restaurants in your town*
- *2 stores in your town*

4 Composition: Portrait comparatif

Write a description of yourself, comparing yourself to six other people (your friends, your family, well-known personalities, etc.) You may use some of the following adjectives:

grand petit jeune vieux amusant
intelligent bête sportif sympathique
timide élégant beau joli mignon

▶ Je suis moins sportif (sportive) que Michael Jordan (Steffi Graff).

5 Composition: Comparaisons personnelles

Choose a friend or relative about your age. Give this person's name and age. Then, in a short paragraph, compare yourself to that person in terms of physical appearance and personality traits.

▶ Mon cousin s'appelle Patrick. Il a quinze ans. Je suis plus jeune que lui, mais il est moins grand que moi...

LEÇON 28 Alice a un job

Alice a un nouveau job. Elle travaille dans un magasin hifi. Dans ce magasin, on vend toutes sortes de choses: des chaînes stéréo, des mini-chaînes, des radiocassettes . . . On vend aussi des cassettes et des compacts.

one, they / sell(s) / all
compact stereos

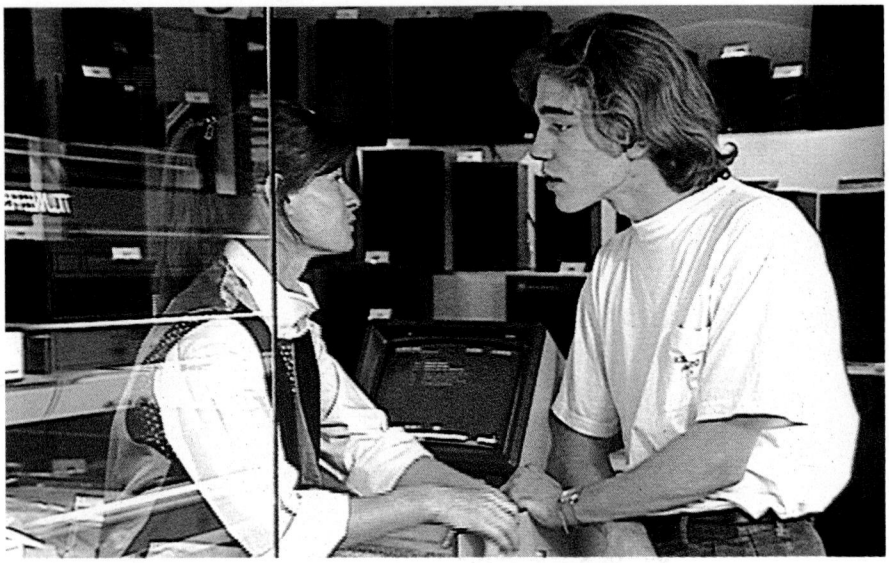

Un jour, son cousin Jérôme lui rend visite.

comes to visit her

JÉRÔME: Salut, ça va?
ALICE: Oui, ça va.
JÉRÔME: Et ce nouveau job?
ALICE: C'est super.
JÉRÔME: Qu'est-ce qu'on vend dans ton magasin?
ALICE: Eh bien, tu vois, on vend toutes sortes de matériel hifi. . . Moi, je vends des mini-chaînes. *see*
JÉRÔME: Tu es bien payée? *paid*
ALICE: Non, on n'est pas très bien payé, mais on a des réductions sur l'équipement stéréo et sur les compacts.
JÉRÔME: Qu'est-ce que tu vas faire avec ton argent? *money*
ALICE: Je ne sais pas . . . J'ai envie de voyager cet été. *feel like*
JÉRÔME: Tu as de la chance. Moi aussi, j'ai envie de voyager, mais je n'ai pas d'argent. *are lucky*
ALICE: Écoute, Jérôme, si tu as besoin d'argent, fais comme moi. *need / do as I do*
JÉRÔME: Comment? *What?*
ALICE: Cherche un job! *Find*

Compréhension

1. Où travaille Alice?
2. Qu'est-ce qu'elle vend?
3. Qu'est-ce qu'elle espère faire cet été?
4. Pourquoi est-ce que Jérôme ne va pas voyager?
5. Qu'est-ce que Jérôme doit *(must)* faire pour avoir de l'argent?

NOTE CULTURELLE

L'argent des jeunes

Do you have a job? Do you have an older brother or sister who works in a supermarket or a restaurant? In the United States, many teenagers work to earn money. Because French labor laws restrict the type of work that young people can do, few French teenagers have regular jobs. (In addition, during the school year most families expect their children to concentrate on their studies.)

It is, however, more and more common for young people in France to earn money by babysitting or doing odd jobs in the neighborhood, such as washing cars or walking dogs. Some (lucky ones) work a few hours a week in stores owned by a relative or a friend of the family.

On the whole, most French teenagers must rely on the generosity of their parents for their spending money. How much they receive depends on particular circumstances, such as how well they do in school, how much they help at home, and obviously, how much their parents can afford. On the average, the allowance of a fifteen-year-old is about 200 francs (or $35) per month.

Vocabulaire: L'argent

NOMS

l'argent *(m.)*	*money*	**une pièce** *coin*
un billet	*bill, paper money*	

ADJECTIFS

riche ≠ **pauvre**	*rich ≠ poor*

VERBES

dépenser	*to spend*	Je n'aime pas **dépenser** mon argent.
gagner	*to earn,*	Je **gagne** 10 dollars par *(per)* jour.
	to win	Tu joues bien. Tu vas **gagner** le match.
payer	*to pay, pay for*	Qui va **payer** aujourd'hui?

EXPRESSIONS

combien + VERB	*how much*	**Combien** coûte ce disque?
combien de + NOUN	*how much*	**Combien d'**argent as-tu?
	how many	**Combien de** disques as-tu?
avoir besoin de + NOUN	*to need*	J'**ai besoin de** 5 dollars.
+ INFINITIVE	*to need to, have to*	J'**ai besoin d'**étudier.
avoir envie de + NOUN	*to want*	J'**ai envie d'**une pizza.
+ INFINITIVE	*to feel like, want to*	J'**ai envie de** manger.

➡ Verbs like **payer** that end in **-yer,** have the following stem change:

y → **i** in the **je, tu, il, ils** forms of the verb

je **paie** tu **paies** il/elle **paie** ils/elles **paient**

But: nous payons vous payez

L'ARGENT NE FAIT PAS LE BONHEUR

Money does not buy happiness.

1 Combien?

Ask your classmates how many of the following they have.

▶ des disques —**Combien de disques as-tu?**
—**J'ai vingt disques.**
(Je n'ai pas de disques.)

1. des frères
2. des soeurs
3. des compacts
4. des affiches
5. des tee-shirts
6. des jeans
7. des billets de un dollar
8. des pièces de dix cents

2 Qu'est-ce que tu as envie de faire?

Ask your classmates if they feel like doing the following things.

▶ aller au cinéma

1. aller au restaurant
2. manger une pizza
3. aller à la piscine
4. parler français
5. étudier
6. visiter Paris
7. jouer au Frisbee
8. acheter une moto
9. faire une promenade
10. aller à la bibliothèque

3 Au restaurant

The following students are in a restaurant in Quebec. Say what they feel like buying and estimate how much money they need.

▶ Hélène / une pizza
Hélène a envie d'une pizza. Elle a besoin de cinq dollars.

1. Marc / un sandwich
2. nous / une glace
3. moi / un soda
4. toi / un jus d'orange
5. vous / une salade
6. mes copains / un steak

4 Questions personnelles

1. Est-ce que tu as un job? Où est-ce que tu travailles? Combien est-ce que tu gagnes par *(per)* heure? par semaine?
2. Quand tu vas au cinéma, qui paie? toi ou ton copain (ta copine)?
3. Combien est-ce que tu paies quand tu achètes un hamburger? une pizza? une glace?
4. Est-ce que tu as des pièces dans ta poche *(pocket)?* quelles pièces?
5. Qui est représenté sur le billet de un dollar? sur le billet de cinq dollars? sur le billet de dix dollars?
6. Est-ce que tu préfères dépenser ou économiser *(to save)* ton argent? Pourquoi?
7. Est-ce que tu espères être riche un jour? Pourquoi?

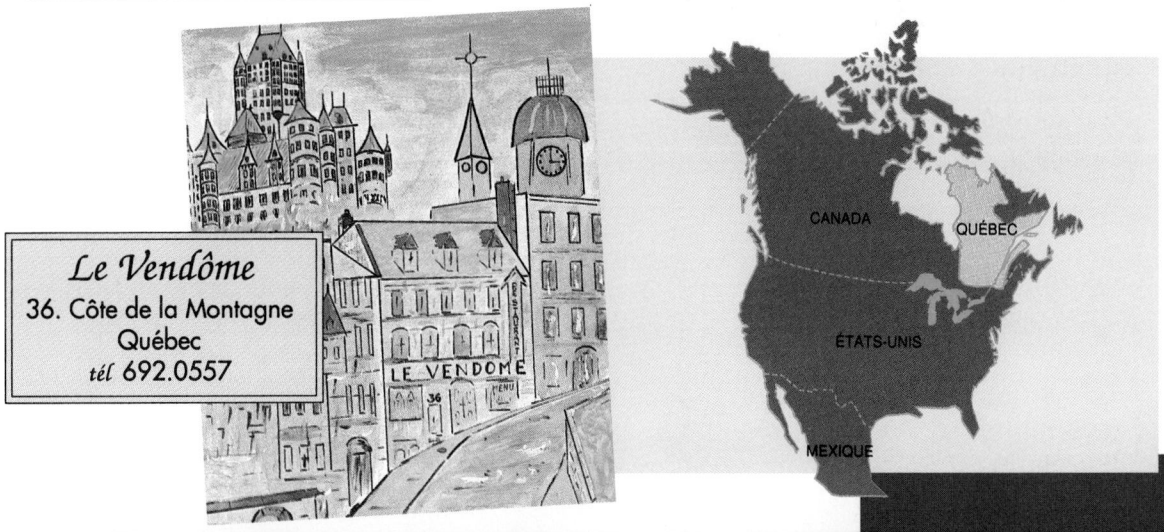

Le Vendôme
36, Côte de la Montagne
Québec
tél 692.0557

A. Le pronom *on*

Note the use of the subject pronoun **on** in the sentences below.

Qu'est-ce qu'**on** vend ici?	*What do **they** (do **you**) sell here?*
Où est-ce qu'**on** achète ce magazine?	*Where does **one** (do **people**) buy that magazine?*
En France, **on** parle français.	*In France, **people (you, they)** speak French.*

The pronoun **on** is used in GENERAL statements, according to the construction:

on + **il/elle-** form of verb	**On** travaille beaucoup.	***One*** *works a lot.* ***They*** *work a lot.* ***You*** *work a lot.* ***People*** *work a lot.*

➡ There is liaison after **on** when the next word begins with a vowel sound.
Est-ce qu'**on** invite Stéphanie à la boum?

➡ In conversation, **on** is often used instead of **nous:**

—Est-ce qu'**on** dîne à la maison?	*Are **we** having dinner at home?*
—Non, on **va** au restaurant.	*No, **we** are going to the restaurant.*

5 Ici on parle . . .

Imagine you have won a grand prize of a world tour. Say which of the following languages is spoken in each of the cities that you will be visiting.

▶ Acapulco

1. Québec
2. Boston
3. Madrid
4. Bruxelles
5. Genève
6. Tokyo
7. Buenos Aires
8. Londres *(London)*
9. Rome
10. Beijing

anglais *français* **espagnol** italien **japonais** **chinois**

Did you know that more and more French companies are investing in the United States? There may be places where you can use French right in your home state!

Expression pour la conversation

How to indicate approval:

C'est une bonne idée! *That's a good idea!*

6 Projets de weekend

Suggest possible weekend activities to your classmates. They will let you know whether they think each idea is a good one or not.

▶ jouer au baseball?

1. étudier?
2. aller à la bibliothèque?
3. aller à la plage?
4. téléphoner au professeur?
5. faire une promenade à vélo?
6. aller dans les magasins?
7. acheter des vêtements?
8. écouter des disques?

7 En Amérique et en France

A French student and an American student are comparing certain aspects of life in their own countries. Play both roles.

▶ jouer au baseball (au foot)

1. parler anglais (français)
2. étudier le français (l'anglais)
3. dîner à six heures (à huit heures)
4. manger des hamburgers (des omelettes)
5. voyager souvent en avion *(by plane)* (en train)
6. skier dans le Colorado (dans les Alpes)
7. aller à l'école le mercredi après-midi (le samedi matin)
8. chanter «la Bannière étoilée» *("The Star-Spangled Banner")* («la Marseillaise»)

8 Expression personnelle

Describe what you, your friends, and your relatives generally do. Complete the following sentences according to your personal routine.

1. À la maison, on dîne . . . (à quelle heure?)
2. À la télé, on regarde . . . (quel programme?)
3. À la cafétéria de l'école, on mange . . . (quoi?)
4. En été, on va . . . (où?)
5. Le weekend, avec mes copains, on va . . . (où?)
6. Avec mes copains, on joue . . . (à quel sport?)
7. On a une classe de français . . . (quels jours?)
8. On a un examen de français . . . (quel jour?)

B. Les verbes réguliers en *-re*

Many French verbs end in **-re**. Most of these are conjugated like **vendre** *(to sell)*. Note the forms of this verb in the present tense, paying special attention to the endings.

INFINITIVE	**vendre**	STEM (infinitive minus **-re**)	ENDINGS
PRESENT	Je **vends** ma raquette. Tu **vends** ton scooter. Il/Elle/On **vend** son ordinateur. Nous **vendons** nos disques. Vous **vendez** vos cassettes. Ils/Elles **vendent** leur voiture.	**vend-**	**-s** **-s** **—** **-ons** **-ez** **-ent**

➡ The "**d**" of the stem is silent in the singular forms, but it is pronounced in the plural forms.

Vocabulaire: Verbes réguliers en *-re*

attendre	*to wait, wait for*	Pierre **attend** Michèle au café.
entendre	*to hear*	Est-ce que tu **entends** la radio?
perdre	*to lose, waste*	Jean-Claude **perd** le match.
rendre visite à	*to visit (a person)*	Je **rends visite à** mon oncle.
répondre à	*to answer*	Nous **répondons à** la question du prof.
vendre	*to sell*	À qui **vends**-tu ton vélo?

➡ There are two French verbs that correspond to the English verb *to visit.*

visiter (+ PLACES)	Nous **visitons** Québec.
rendre visite à (+ PEOPLE)	Nous **rendons visite à** nos cousins canadiens.

9 Rendez-vous

The following people have been shopping and are now waiting for their friends at a café. Express this, using the appropriate forms of the verb **attendre**.

▶ Jérôme (Michèle) **Jérôme attends Michèle.**

1. nous (nos copains)
2. vous (vos cousines)
3. moi (Christophe)
4. toi (Anne)
5. Olivier et Éric (Claire et Sophie)
6. les étudiants (les étudiantes)
7. Jacques et moi, nous (Pauline et Hélène)
8. Annette et toi, vous (Jean-Marc)
9. on (notre copine)

10 Qui

Who is doing what? Answer the following questions, using the suggested subjects.

1. Qui perd le match? (toi, vous, Alice)
2. Qui rend visite à Pierre? (Patrick, Corinne et Hélène, toi)
3. Qui entend l'avion *(plane)?* (moi, vous, les voisins)
4. Qui vend des disques? (on, ce magasin, ces boutiques, moi)
5. Qui attend le bus? (les élèves, le professeur, on, vous)
6. Qui répond au professeur? (toi, nous, les élèves)

11 Qu'est-ce qu'ils font?

Read about the following people. Then complete each sentence with the appropriate form of one of the verbs from the list. Be logical!

1. Guillaume est patient. Il ... ses amis.
2. Vous êtes à Paris. Vous ... à vos cousins français.
3. Tu joues mal. Tu ... le match.
4. Je suis dans ma chambre. J' ... un bruit *(noise)* curieux.
5. Les élèves sont en classe. Ils ... aux questions du professeur.
6. Jacqueline travaille dans une boutique. Elle ... des robes.
7. On est au café. On ... nos copains.

attendre **entendre** perdre rendre visite **répondre** vendre

C. L'impératif

Compare the French and English forms of the imperative in the sentences below.

Écoute ce disque!	***Listen*** *to this record!*
Ne vendez pas votre voiture!	***Don't sell*** *your car!*
Allons au cinéma!	***Let's go*** *to the movies!*

Learning about language

The IMPERATIVE is used to make suggestions and to give orders and advice. The commands or suggestions may be affirmative or negative.

Note the forms of the imperative in the chart below.

INFINITIVE	**parler**	**finir**	**vendre**	**aller**
IMPERATIVE				
(tu)	**parle**	**finis**	**vends**	**va**
(vous)	**parlez**	**finissez**	**vendez**	**allez**
(nous)	**parlons**	**finissons**	**vendons**	**allons**

For regular verbs and most irregular verbs, the forms of the imperative are the same as the corresponding forms of the present tense.

➡ EXCEPTION: For all **-er** verbs, including **aller,** the **-s** of the **tu-** form is dropped in the imperative. Compare.

Tu **parles** anglais.	**Parle** français, s'il te plaît!
Tu **vas** au café.	**Va** à la bibliothèque!

➡ The negative imperative is formed as follows:

ne + VERB + **pas** ...	**Ne choisis pas** ce blouson.

12 Mais oui!

You have organized a party at your home. Juliette offers to do the following. You accept.

▶ apporter une pizza?

1. faire une salade?
2. inviter nos copains?
3. acheter des croissants?
4. apporter des cassettes?
5. choisir des disques de danse?
6. venir à huit heures?

13 L'ange et le démon

(The angel and the devil)

Véronique is wondering whether she should do certain things. The angel gives her good advice. The devil gives her bad advice. Play both roles.

▶ étudier les verbes
Étudie les verbes.
N'étudie pas les verbes.

1. téléphoner à ta tante
2. attendre tes copains
3. faire attention en classe
4. aller à l'école
5. finir la leçon
6. écouter tes professeurs
7. mettre *(set)* la table
8. inviter tes amis
9. rendre visite à ta grand-mère
10. choisir des copains sympathiques
11. acheter un cadeau *(gift)* pour ton frère
12. réussir à l'examen

14 Oui ou non?

For each of the following situations, give your classmates advice as to what to do and what not to do. Be logical.

▶ Nous sommes en vacances. (étudier? voyager?)
N'étudiez pas! Voyagez!

1. Nous sommes à Paris. (parler anglais? parler français?)
2. C'est dimanche. (aller à la bibliothèque? aller au cinéma?)
3. Il fait beau. (rester à la maison? faire une promenade?)
4. Il fait froid. (mettre un pull? mettre un tee-shirt?)
5. Il est onze heures du soir. (rester au café? rentrer à la maison?)
6. Il fait très chaud. (aller à la piscine? regarder la télé?)

15 L'esprit de contradiction *(Disagreement)*

Make suggestions to your friends about things to do. Your friends will not agree and will suggest something else.

▶ aller au cinéma (à la plage)

1. jouer au tennis (au volley)
2. écouter la radio (des disques)
3. regarder la télé (un film vidéo)
4. dîner au restaurant (à la maison)
5. inviter Michèle (Sophie)
6. organiser un pique-nique (une boum)
7. faire des sandwichs (une pizza)
8. aller au musée (à la bibliothèque)
9. faire une promenade à pied (en voiture)
10. rendre visite à nos voisins (à nos copains)

Prononciation — an, en /ã/

Les lettres «an» et «en»

The letters "**an**" and "**en**" represent the nasal vowel /ã/. Be sure not to pronounce the sound "**n**" after the vowel.

enfant

Répétez:

/ã/ **enfant an manteau collants grand élégant**
André mange un grand sandwich.

/ã/ **enfant en argent dépenser attends entend vend envie**
Vincent dépense rarement son argent.

André mange un grand sandwich.

À votre tour!

1 La bonne réponse

Anne is talking to Jean-François. Match Anne's questions with Jean-François's answers. You may act out the conversation with a classmate.

Anne

1. Est-ce que tu rends visite à tes cousins ce weekend?
2. Tu veux aller dans les boutiques avec moi?
3. Est-ce que tu as envie d'aller au cinéma?
4. Et après *(afterwards)* qu'est-ce qu'on fait?

a. Eh bien, allons au restaurant!
b. Bonne idée! Il y a un nouveau film au «Majestic».
c. Écoute! Je n'ai pas besoin de vêtements.
d. Non, je reste ici.

Jean-François

2 Créa-dialogue

When we are with our friends, it is not always easy to agree on what to do. With your classmates, discuss the following possibilities.

Quand?	Première suggestion	Deuxième suggestion
▶ samedi	aller au cinéma	rendre visite à nos amis
1. ce soir *(tonight)*	étudier	regarder la télé
2. dimanche	aller au café	dîner au restaurant
3. après *(after)* les classes	jouer au basket	faire une promenade
4. cet été	trouver un job	voyager
5. ce weekend	faire un pique-nique	??
6. demain	aller à la bibliothèque	??

3 Conseils

Your friends tell you what they would like to do. Give them appropriate advice, either positive or negative. Use your imagination.

▶ Je voudrais maigrir. **Alors, mange moins.**
(Alors, ne mange pas de pizza.)

1. Je voudrais avoir un «A» en français.
2. Je voudrais gagner beaucoup d'argent.
3. Je voudrais organiser une boum.
4. Je voudrais préparer un pique-nique.

4 Que faire?

Give a classmate advice about what to do or not to do in the following circumstances.

Pendant *(During)* **la classe**	**Après** *(After)* **la classe**	**Ce weekend**	**Pendant les vacances**
écouter le prof parler à tes copains regarder les bandes dessinées *(comics)* manger un sandwich répondre en français ??	étudier aller au cinéma préparer tes leçons rentrer chez toi regarder la télé ??	rester à la maison aller en ville dépenser ton argent organiser une boum faire une promenade à pied ??	voyager travailler grossir oublier *(forget)* ton français ??

▶ **Pendant la classe, écoute le prof. Ne parle pas à tes copains.**

5 Bon voyage!

Your French friend Ariane is going to visit the United States next summer with her cousin. They are traveling on a low budget and are asking you for advice as to how to save money. Make a list of suggestions, including five things they could do and five things they should not do. You may want to use some of the following ideas:

- voyager (comment?)
- rester (dans quels hôtels?)
- dîner (dans quels restaurants?)
- visiter (quelles villes?)
- aller (où?)
- acheter (quelles choses?)
- apporter (quelles choses?)

▶ *Voyagez en bus.*
Ne voyagez pas en train.

ENTRACTE 7

Petit test culturel

La mode et les vêtements

Aujourd'hui la mode° est internationale. Les jeunes Français adoptent le «look» américain ou anglais. Les Américains achètent des vêtements de style français ou italien.

Imaginez que vous habitez en France. Est-ce que vous pouvez° répondre aux questions suivantes?° Vérifiez° vos réponses au bas° de la page.

1 Vincent va en ville pour acheter des «tennis». Qu'est-ce qu'il va acheter?
a. une raquette
b. un short
c. des chaussures
d. des chemises

2 Monique habite à Paris. Elle a envie d'acheter un blouson. Où va-t-elle?
a. à la Villette
b. aux Galeries Lafayette
c. au Zénith
d. au Centre Pompidou

3 Dans ce magasin on vend des vêtements de marques° différentes. Voici quatre marques. Quelle est la marque qui n'est *pas* française?
a. Benetton
b. Christian Dior
c. Pierre Cardin
d. Yves Saint-Laurent

4 René Lacoste est un champion français de tennis. Aujourd'hui son nom° est associé° avec une marque de . . .
a. vêtements de sport
b. chaussures de ski
c. chocolats
d. vitamines

5 Jean Vuarnet est un champion olympique de ski. À quels produits° est-ce que son nom est associé?
a. des skis
b. des chaussures
c. des vêtements de sport
d. des lunettes de soleil

6 Coco Chanel est le nom d'une couturière° française très célèbre.° Son nom est aussi associé avec . . .
a. un parfum
b. un festival de cinéma
c. une compétition sportive
d. une eau minérale°

7 Les jeans sont faits° avec un coton spécial appelé° «denim». Ce mot vient du français «de Nîmes». Nîmes est le nom . . .
a. d'un textile
b. d'un vêtement
c. d'un couturier° français
d. d'une ville française

RÉPONSES:
1. c; 2. b; 3. a; 4. a; 5. d; 6. a; 7. d

mode *fashion* **pouvez** *can* **suivantes** *following* **Vérifiez** *Check* **au bas** *at the bottom* **marques** *designer labels* **nom** *name* **associé** *associated* **produits** *products* **couturière** *fashion designer* **célèbre** *famous* **eau minérale** *mineral water* **faits** *made* **appelé** *called* **couturier** *fashion designer*

EN FRANCE

Les Trois Suisses

La compagnie Les Trois Suisses vend des vêtements par corresponance. Voici une page de son catalogue.

- Sur cette page, trois articles sont en «promo».° Quels sont ces trois articles?
- Combien coûte le pantalon jogging?
- Combien coûtent les tennis en francs? et en dollars? (un dollar = 6 francs) Est-ce que c'est cher? Quelles couleurs est-ce qu'on peut choisir? Quelle couleur préférez-vous?
- Combien coûte le sweat? Quelles couleurs est-ce qu'on peut° choisir? Quelle couleur préférez-vous?

promo = promotion *special sale*
peut *can*

Entre amis: Les jeunes Français et la mode

Est-ce que vous aimez être à la mode?° Où est-ce que vous achetez vos vêtements? Et qu'est-ce qui compte° le plus° pour vous? le style? la qualité? le prix? Nous avons posé° ces questions à cinq jeunes Français. Voilà leurs réponses.

Florence (16 ans)
J'aime être à la mode. Malheureusement,° mon budget est limité. La solution? Le samedi après-midi je travaille dans une boutique de mode. Là, je peux acheter mes jupes et mes pulls à des prix très avantageux.° Pour le reste, je compte sur la générosité de mes parents.

Jean-Marc (15 ans)
Aujourd'hui la présentation extérieure° est très importante. Mais il n'est pas nécessaire d'être à la mode pour être bien habillé.° Pour moi, la qualité des vêtements est aussi importante que leur style. En général, j'attends les soldes.° J'achète peu de° vêtements mais je fais attention à la qualité.

Chloé (15 ans)
Pour moi, le style, c'est tout.° Hélas, la mode n'est pas bon marché. Heureusement° j'ai une cousine qui a une machine à coudre° et qui est très très adroite.° Alors, nous faisons nos propres° robes! Nous choisissons le tissu,° la couleur, le style . . . Ainsi, nous sommes toujours à la mode. C'est chouette, non?

Antoine (12 ans)
Moi, je n'ai pas le choix!° C'est ma mère qui choisit mes vêtements. En ce qui concerne° la mode, elle n'est pas dans le coup.° Elle achète tout dans les grandes surfaces. C'est pas° drôle!

Julien (14 ans)
Vous connaissez° le proverbe: «L'habit ne fait pas le moine».° Eh bien, pour moi les vêtements n'ont aucune° importance. Avec mon argent je préfère acheter des compacts. Quand j'ai besoin de jeans ou de tee-shirts, je vais aux Puces.* C'est pas cher et c'est marrant!°

***Marché aux puces** *flea market*

à la mode *in style* **compte** *counts* **le plus** *the most*
avons posé *asked* **Malheureusement** *Unfortunately*
avantageux *reasonable*
présentation extérieure *outward appearance* **habillé** *dressed*
soldes *sales* **peu de** *few* **tout** *everything*
Heureusement *Fortunately* ***machine à coudre*** *sewing machine*
adroite *skillful* **propres** *own* **tissu** *fabric* **choix** *choice*
En ce qui concerne *As for* **dans le coup** *"with it"*
C'est pas = Ce n'est pas **connaissez** *know* **moine** *monk*
aucune *no* **marrant** *fun*

NOTES CULTURELLES

1 Les grandes surfaces

Les grandes surfaces sont des magasins en libre-service° où on peut acheter toutes° les marchandises nécessaires à la vie quotidienne.° En général les prix ne sont pas très élevés,° mais la qualité est moyenne.°

Comment lire

DIFFERENCES IN SPOKEN AND WRITTEN LANGUAGE

The interviews you read were conducted orally. Notice how casual speech is different from standard written language.

- Spoken language often contains slang expressions.

  Elle n'est pas dans le coup! **C'est marrant!** **C'est chouette!**

- Spoken French sometimes drops the **ne** in **ne . . . pas.**

  C'est pas cher. = Ce n'est pas cher.

Enrichissez votre vocabulaire

MORE COGNATE PATTERNS

Here are a few common cognate patterns to help you recognize new words more easily.

FRENCH	ENGLISH	FRENCH	ENGLISH
-x	*-ce*	**le prix**	*price*
-eux	*-ous*	**avantageux**	*advantageous, reasonable*
-eur	*-or*	**la couleur**	*color*
-aire	*-ary*	**nécessaire**	*necessary*

Activité

Can you identify the English equivalents of the following French words?

- **le choix** **la voix** • **courageux** **sérieux** **dangereux** **curieux**
- **un acteur** **une odeur** **un docteur** **supérieur** **une erreur**
- **un salaire** **le vocabulaire** **un commentaire** **un anniversaire**

Activité: Et toi?

Voici ce que disent° les jeunes Français. Est-ce que c'est vrai pour vous aussi?

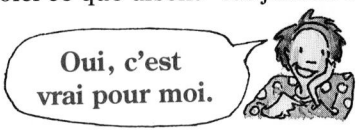

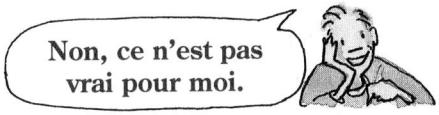

OUI OU NON?

▶ 1. J'aime être à la mode.
2. Mon budget est limité.
3. J'attends les soldes.
4. Je fais attention à la qualité.

OUI OU NON?

5. J'achète le tissu et je fais mes vêtements.
6. Ma mère choisit mes vêtements.
7. Je préfère acheter des compacts.
8. J'achète mes vêtements aux Puces.

2 Les soldes

En général, les boutiques de vêtements ont des soldes° deux ou trois fois° par an. On peut alors acheter des vêtements de bonne qualité à des prix avantageux. Certaines boutiques ont des soldes toute l'année.°

libre-service *self-service* **toutes** *all* **quotidienne** *daily* **élevés** *high*
moyenne *average* **soldes** *sales* **fois** *times* **toute l'année** *all year long*

Variétés

L'argent et vous

Nous avons tous° besoin d'argent. L'argent est nécessaire, mais l'argent crée° aussi des problèmes. Quelle est votre attitude envers° l'argent? Répondez aux questions suivantes.°

1 Que représente l'argent pour vous?

a. l'indépendance
b. la possibilité d'acheter beaucoup de choses
c. la possibilité d'aider vos amis

2 Selon vous, quel est le rapport° entre l'argent et le bonheur?°

a. L'argent est nécessaire.
b. L'argent est utile.°
c. Il n'y a pas de rapport.

3 Vous avez trois possibilités de job ce weekend. Qu'est-ce que vous choisissez?

a. faire du baby-sitting (3 dollars par l'heure pour 4 heures)
b. laver° la voiture des voisins (5 dollars au total)
c. vendre des hot dogs à un match de football (un pourcentage de 10% sur les ventes°)

4 C'est votre anniversaire. Vos grands-parents vous donnent° cinquante dollars. Qu'est-ce que vous faites?

a. J'invite mes copains à un concert.
b. J'achète des vêtements.
c. Je mets mon argent à la banque.°

5 Pendant les vacances vous avez le choix entre les trois possibilités suivantes. Qu'est-ce que vous choisissez?

a. faire un grand voyage avec la famille
b. travailler comme volontaire° dans un hôpital
c. travailler dans un supermarché

6 Selon vous, quel est l'aspect le plus° important quand on cherche un travail?°

a. avoir un bon salaire
b. avoir un travail intéressant
c. avoir la possibilité de travailler avec des gens sympathiques

tous *all* **crée** *creates* **envers** *toward* **suivantes** *following*
rapport *relationship* **bonheur** *happiness* **utile** *useful*
laver *wash* **ventes** *sales* **vous donnent** *give you* **banque** *bank*
comme volontaire *as a volunteer* **le plus** *the most* **travail** *job*

INTERPRÉTATION

Comptez° vos points en utilisant° la grille° suivante.

Questions		1	2	3	4	5	6
Options	a	3	3	2	1	1	3
	b	2	2	1	2	2	1
	c	1	1	3	3	3	2

Combien de points avez-vous?

15 points ou plus:

Vous avez beaucoup d'énergie. Pour vous, l'argent est important et vous êtes prêt(e)° à travailler dur° pour gagner votre argent.

entre 9 et 14 points:

Vous êtes réaliste. Pour vous l'argent est un moyen° et pas un but.°

8 points ou moins:

Vous êtes idéaliste et généreux (généreuse). Entre l'amitié° et l'argent, vous préférez l'amitié.

Comptez *Count* **en utilisant** *by using*
grille *grid* **prêt(e)** *ready* **dur** *hard* **moyen** *means*
but *end* **amitié** *friendship*

NIVEAU C

Le monde

Salut et félicitations!

Greetings again and congratulations! Now you are able to carry on a real conversation in French: greeting people, talking about yourself and your family, and discussing things you plan to do. You can go shopping for clothes and discuss fashion. Now in this last part of your program, you will learn more about getting around in **Le monde des jeunes** — the world of French young people.

In this part of your French program, you will learn . . .

- how to talk about weekend and holiday plans
- how to discuss summer and winter sports
- how to order in a restaurant
- how and where to buy food in France
- how to plan leisure activities such as picnics and parties

You will also be able . . .

- to talk about things you did yesterday, last week, or last month
- to make suggestions
- to ask people to do things for you

Along the way, you will learn a little more about how the French language works.

Et maintenant, continuons!

Jean-Paul Valette Rebecca M. Valette

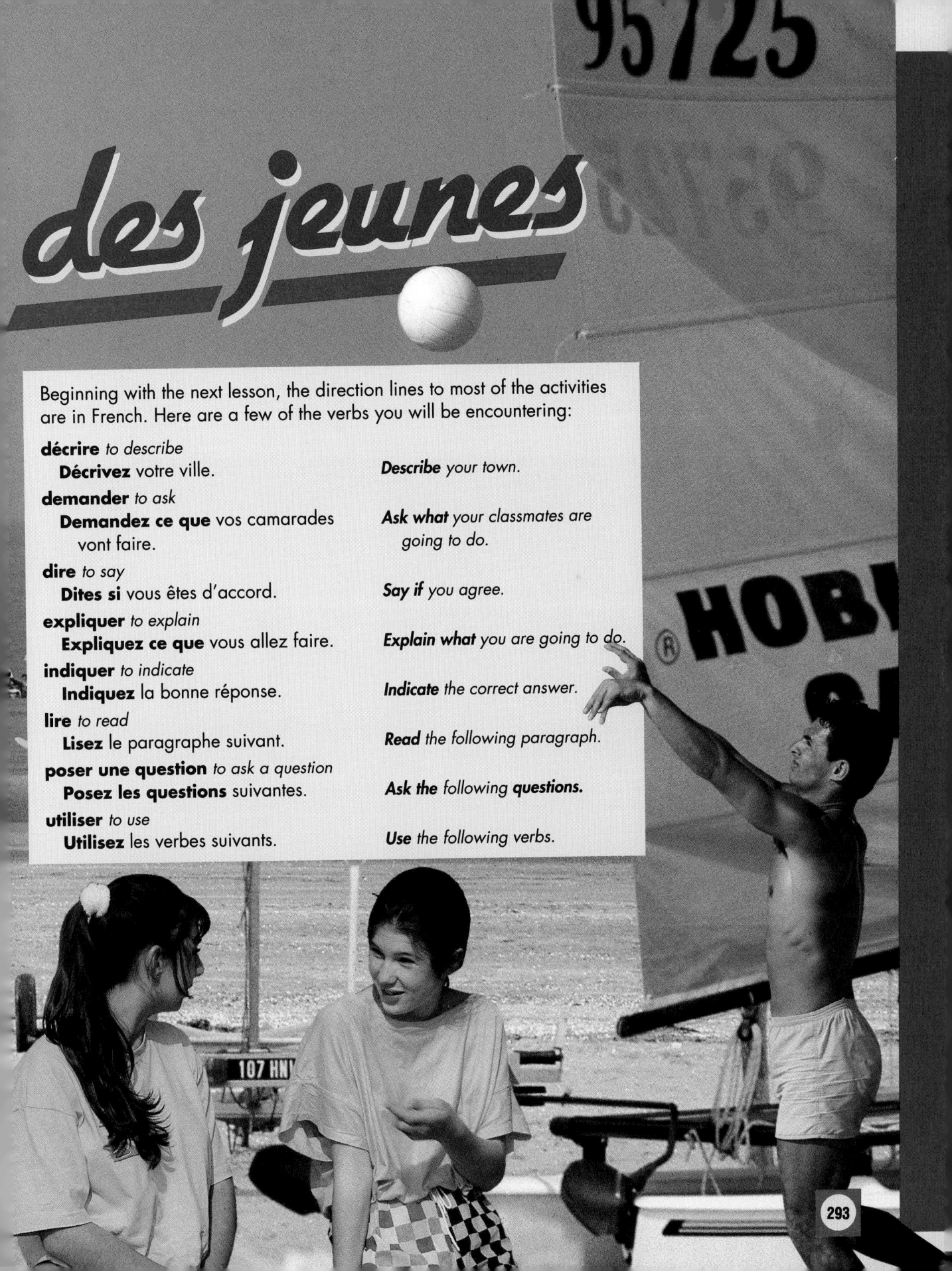

des jeunes

Beginning with the next lesson, the direction lines to most of the activities are in French. Here are a few of the verbs you will be encountering:

décrire *to describe*
Décrivez votre ville. — ***Describe*** *your town.*

demander *to ask*
Demandez ce que vos camarades vont faire. — ***Ask what*** *your classmates are going to do.*

dire *to say*
Dites si vous êtes d'accord. — ***Say if*** *you agree.*

expliquer *to explain*
Expliquez ce que vous allez faire. — ***Explain what*** *you are going to do.*

indiquer *to indicate*
Indiquez la bonne réponse. — ***Indicate*** *the correct answer.*

lire *to read*
Lisez le paragraphe suivant. — ***Read*** *the following paragraph.*

poser une question *to ask a question*
Posez les questions suivantes. — ***Ask the*** *following* ***questions.***

utiliser *to use*
Utilisez les verbes suivants. — ***Use*** *the following verbs.*

UNITÉ

8 Le temps libre

LEÇON 29 Le français pratique: Le weekend et les vacances

LEÇON 30 Vive le weekend!

LEÇON 31 L'alibi

LEÇON 32 Qui a de la chance?

THÈME ET OBJECTIFS

Leisure-time activities

As students, you probably study very hard in school. You also help at home and you may have an outside job to earn spending money. But life is not all work. It also includes leisure time for pursuing one's favorite activities.

In this unit, you will learn . . .

- to discuss your weekend activities
- to talk about individual summer and winter sports
- to describe what you do to help around the house
- to describe your vacation and travel plans

You will also be able . . .

- to talk about what you do and what you never do
- to describe what you did and where you went yesterday, last week, or last summer
- more generally, to narrate what happened at any time in the past

LEÇON 29

LE FRANÇAIS PRATIQUE

Le weekend et les vacances

Accent sur . . . Les loisirs

If you had to decide between earning more money or having more free time, what would you choose? When asked this question on a survey, French people indicated their overwhelming preference for more leisure time.

For the French, leisure plays an important role in what they call **la qualité de la vie** *(quality of life)*. In fact, they consider leisure time to be not only a necessity but a right. By law, French workers are entitled to five weeks of paid vacation, as compared to two weeks for the average American.

French teenagers also place great value on their leisure time. Because they have so much homework and need to study so hard for their exams, they have no real time — and also little opportunity — to take an outside job. Instead, they try to make the most of their leisure hours. What are their favorite activities? Here is how French young people answered the question "What do you do when you have a free evening?"

Qu'est-ce que tu aimes faire le soir?	GARÇONS	FILLES
Je regarde la télé.	24%	18%
Je sors° avec mes copains.	20%	18%
Je vais au cinéma.	16%	14%
Je lis.°	14%	20%
Je vais au concert ou au théâtre.	10%	12%
Je vais danser.	8%	12%
Je fais un sport.	6%	4%
Je bricole.°	2%	2%

sors *go out* **lis** *read*
bricole *do things around the house*

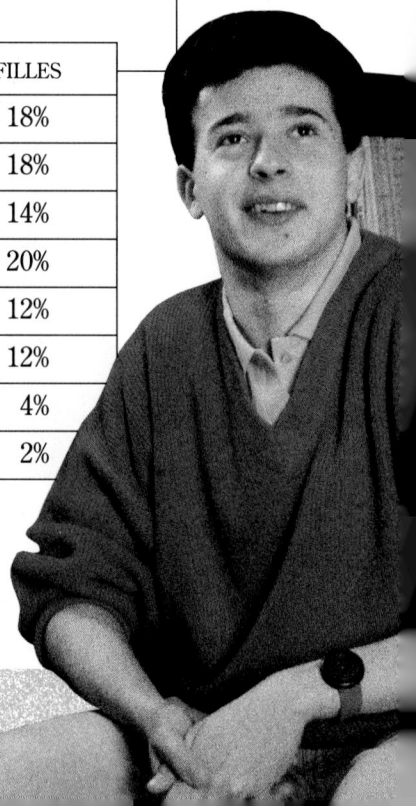

Je regarde la télé.

Je sors avec mes copains.

Je vais au cinéma.

Je lis.

Je fais du sport.

A. Le weekend

How to plan your weekend activities:

Qu'est-ce que tu vas faire
- samedi?
- samedi **matin**
- dimanche **après-midi**
- demain **soir**
- ce **weekend**
- le weekend **prochain** *(next)*

le matin *morning*
l'après-midi *afternoon*
le soir *evening*

Je vais rester chez moi **pour** *(in order to)*
- faire mes **devoirs** *(homework)*.
- **réparer** *(to fix)* mon vélo
- **préparer** le dîner
- **aider** *(to help)* mes parents
- **laver** *(to wash)* ma mobylette
- **nettoyer** *(to clean)* ma chambre

Je vais aller ...
- en ville
- dans les magasins
- au **centre commercial** *(mall)*

pour ...
- **faire des achats** *(go shopping)*.

Moi, je vais aller en ville pour faire des achats.

- au cinéma
- au café
- au stade
- **à la campagne** *(countryside)*

- **voir** *(to see)* **un film**
- **rencontrer** *(to meet)* mes copains
- **assister à** *(to go to, attend)* un match de foot
- **faire un pique-nique** *(to have a picnic)*

Je vais aller à une boum.
Avant *(Before)* la boum, je vais faire des achats.
Pendant *(During)* la boum, je vais écouter des cassettes.
Après *(After)* la boum, je vais faire mes devoirs.

➡ The verb **nettoyer** is conjugated like **payer:**

je **nettoie** tu **nettoies** il / elle / on **nettoie** ils / elles **nettoient**

but: nous nettoyons vous nettoyez

1 Et toi?

Décris tes activités. Pour cela, complète les phrases suivantes.

1. En général, je vais au cinéma . . .	• le vendredi soir • le samedi soir	• le dimanche après-midi • . . . ?
2. En général, je rencontre mes copains . . .	• chez moi • chez eux	• dans un café • . . . ?
3. En général, je fais mes devoirs . . .	• avant le dîner • après le dîner	• pendant la classe • . . . ?
4. Je préfère assister à . . .	• un match de foot • un match de baseball	• un concert de rock • . . . ?
5. En général, je préfère faire mes achats . . .	• seul(e) *(by myself)* • avec mes copains	• avec mes frères et mes soeurs • . . . ?
6. En général, quand je rentre chez moi après les classes, . . .	• je fais mes devoirs • je regarde la télé	• j'aide ma mère ou mon père • . . . ?
7. En été, je préfère faire un pique-nique . . .	• dans mon jardin • à la campagne	• à la plage • . . . ?
8. Si *(If)* je dois aider mes parents à la maison et si j'ai le choix *(choice)*, je préfère . . .	• nettoyer le salon • laver la voiture	• faire la vaisselle *(dishes)* • . . . ?

2 Qu'est-ce qu'ils font?

Informez-vous sur les personnes suivantes. Décrivez ce qu'elles font ou ce qu'elles vont faire. Pour cela, complétez les phrases avec une expression du **vocabulaire** à la page 298.

▶ Sandrine est au garage.
Elle répare son vélo (sa mobylette).

1. Mme Jolivet est dans la cuisine. Elle . . .
2. Vincent Jolivet est aussi dans la cuisine. Il . . .
3. Anne et Sylvie sont au Bon Marché. Elles . . .
4. Je suis dans ma chambre et je regarde mon livre de français. Je . . .
5. Olivier et ses copains achètent des billets *(tickets)* de cinéma. Ils vont . . .
6. Mes amis vont à Yankee Stadium. Ils vont . . .
7. Tu vas au café. Tu vas . . .
8. Vous faites des sandwichs. Vous allez . . . à la campagne.

3 Mon calendrier personnel

Décrivez ce que vous allez faire.

B. Les vacances

How to plan your vacation activities:

Qu'est-ce que tu vas faire	à **Noël?** à **Pâques** **pendant les vacances** de printemps pendant **les grandes vacances** cet été	**Noël** *Christmas* **Pâques** *Easter* **les vacances** *vacation* **les grandes vacances** *summer vacation*

Je vais aller	à **la mer** *(ocean, shore).* à **la montagne** *(mountains)*

Je vais voyager	en avion.	**un avion** *plane*
	en train	**un train** *train*
	en autocar	**un autocar, un car** *touring bus*
	en bateau	**un bateau** *boat, ship*
	en voiture	

Je vais voyager	**seul(e)** *(alone).* avec ma famille

Je vais **passer** *(to spend)*	dix jours six semaines deux mois	là-bas.	**un jour** *day* **une semaine** *week* **un mois** *month*

J'aime	**le ski** *(skiing).* **le ski nautique** *(waterskiing)*	En hiver, je vais à la montagne pour **faire du ski** *(to ski).* En été, je vais à la mer pour **faire du ski nautique** *(to waterski).*

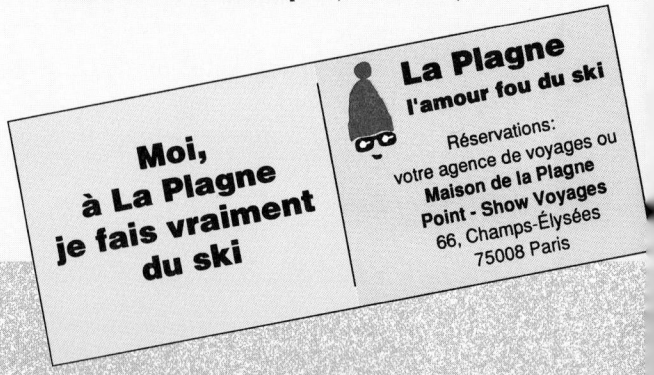

Activités sportives

le sport	*sport(s)*	Je **fais du sport.**	*I practice sports.*
le jogging	*jogging*	Nous **faisons du jogging.**	*We jog.*
le ski	*skiing*	Tu **fais du ski?**	*Do you ski?*
le ski nautique	*waterskiing*	Anne **fait du ski nautique.**	*Anne waterskis.*
la voile	*sailing*	Paul **fait de la voile.**	*Paul sails.*
la planche à voile	*windsurfing*	Vous **faites de la planche à voile?**	*Do you windsurf?*
la natation	*swimming*	Tu **fais de la natation** en été?	*Do you go swimming in (the) summer?*
l'alpinisme *(m.)*	*mountain climbing*	J'aime **faire de l'alpinisme.**	*I like to go mountain climbing.*

➡ To describe participation in individual sports or other activities, the French use the construction:

faire { **du** / **de la** / **de l'** } + SPORT or ACTIVITY

le camping → **faire du camping**
la voile → **faire de la voile**
l'alpinisme → **faire de l'alpinisme**

NOTE CULTURELLE

Le calendrier des fêtes françaises

Voici les principales fêtes *(holidays)* en France:

le jour de l'An	*New Year's Day*
Mardi Gras	*Shrove Tuesday*
Pâques	*Easter*
le premier mai	*Labor Day*
la Pentecôte	*Pentecost*
le 14 juillet	*Bastille Day* (French National Holiday)
la Toussaint	*All Saints' Day* (November 1)
le 11 novembre	*Armistice Day*
Noël	*Christmas* (December 25)

Mardi Gras

Le 14 juillet

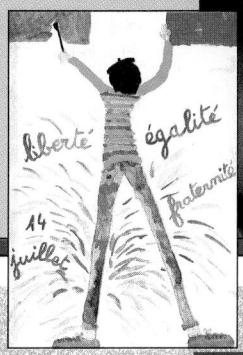

4 Et toi?

Indique tes préférences personnelles en complétant les phrases suivantes.

1. Mes vacances préférées sont . . .
   - les vacances de Noël
   - les vacances de printemps
   - les grandes vacances
   - . . . ?
2. Pendant les vacances de Noël, je préfère . . .
   - rester avec ma famille
   - rendre visite à mes grands-parents
   - faire du ski
   - . . . ?
3. Pendant les grandes vacances, je préfère . . .
   - aller à la mer
   - aller à la montagne
   - aller à la campagne
   - . . . ?
4. Quand je voyage pendant les vacances, je préfère voyager . . .
   - seul(e)
   - avec mes copains
   - avec ma famille
   - . . . ?
5. Quand je vais loin, je préfère voyager . . .
   - en train
   - en avion
   - en car
   - . . . ?

5 Leurs activités favorites

Les personnes suivantes ont certaines activités favorites. Lisez où elles sont et dites ce qu'elles font. Pour cela choisissez une activité appropriée de la liste à droite.

▶ Je suis à la plage.

1. Jean-Pierre est au stade.
2. Anne et Marie sont dans un studio de danse.
3. En juillet, nous allons dans le Colorado.
4. Tu passes les vacances de Noël en Suisse.
5. Mes copains passent les vacances à la campagne.
6. Pauline est à la salle *(room)* de gymnastique.
7. Vous êtes à la mer.
8. Nous sommes à Tahiti.
9. Avant le dîner, nous allons au parc municipal.
10. Je suis à la Martinique.

6. En été, je vais à la plage spécialement *(especially)* pour . . .	• nager • faire du ski nautique	• bronzer *(to get a tan)* • . . . ?
7. Je voudrais être un champion (une championne) de . . .	• ski • ski nautique	• planche à voile • . . . ?
8. Je voudrais aller à la Guadeloupe principalement *(mainly)* pour . . .	• nager • parler français	• faire de la planche à voile • . . . ?
9. Je voudrais aller dans le Colorado pour . . .	• faire du ski • faire des promenades à pied	• faire de l'alpinisme • . . . ?
10. Je voudrais aller à Paris et rester là-bas pendant . . .	• dix jours • trois semaines	• six mois • . . . ?

6 Questions personnelles

1. En général, qu'est-ce que tu fais pendant les vacances de Noël?
2. Est-ce que tu vas voyager pendant les grandes vacances? Où vas-tu aller? Combien de temps *(How long)* est-ce que tu vas rester là-bas?
3. Qu'est-ce que tu aimes faire quand tu es à la plage?
4. Est-ce que tu voyages souvent? Comment voyages-tu?

À votre tour!

1 Créa-dialogue

Des amis parlent de leurs projets. Avec un(e) camarade de classe, choisissez une scène et composez le dialogue correspondant.

▶ —Où vas-tu vendredi?
—Je vais en ville.
—Qu'est-ce que tu vas faire là-bas?
—Je vais faire des achats.

▶ vendredi | en ville

1. samedi matin			2. samedi après-midi			3. à Noël	à Aspen	
4. pendant les vacances de printemps	à la Floride		5. en juillet			6. en août		
7. demain matin			8. dimanche après-midi			9. cet été		

2 Conversation dirigée

Avec un(e) camarade, composez un dialogue basé sur les instructions suivantes. Jean-Pierre demande à Hélène si elle a des projets de vacances.

Jean-Pierre			Hélène
	asks Hélène where she is going this summer	→ ↙	says that she is going to the ocean with friends
	asks her if they are going to travel by car	→ ↙	answers that they are going to travel by train because they do not have a car
	asks her if she is going to go sailing	→ ↙	answers yes and says that she is also going to windsurf
	says good-bye to Hélène and wishes her a good vacation **(Bonnes vacances!)**	→	answers good-bye

3 Composition: Le weekend prochain

Make plans for next weekend. Prepare a list of activities describing …

- four things that you are going to do at home
- four things that you are going to do outside

4 Au club de vacances

Avec qui passez-vous vos vacances? On peut passer ses vacances avec sa famille ou avec des copains. On peut aussi aller dans un club de vacances. Là on peut faire du sport et rencontrer d'autres jeunes.

Lisez le document suivant.

Ce club de vacances offre la possibilité d'aller dans différents «villages de mer». Choisissez un des villages de mer proposés par le club.

- Dans quel pays est situé ce village?
- Quels sports est-ce qu'on peut pratiquer *(participate in)* dans ce village?
- Pourquoi est-ce que vous choisissez ce village?
- En général, quels sports pratiquez-vous?

VILLAGES DE MER	AGADIR MAROC	LES ALMADIES SÉNÉGAL	ASSINIE CÔTE D'IVOIRE	BORA-BORA TAHITI-POLYNÉSIE FR.SE	LES BOUCANIERS MARTINIQUE	CANCÚN MEXIQUE	CAP SKIRRING SÉNÉGAL	LA CARAVELLE GUADELOUPE	LES CORAUX EILAT-ISRAËL	DJERBA LA DOUCE TUNISIE
Village-hôtel, bungalow	✓	✓	✓	✓	✓	✓	✓	✓	✓	✓
Ski nautique, planche à voile		✓	✓	✓	✓	✓	✓	✓	✓	✓
Voile		✓		✓	✓	✓		✓	✓	✓
Plongée libre				✓	✓	✓				
Plongée scaphandre					✓	✓	✓		✓	✓
Piscine	✓	✓	✓							
Équitation	✓									
Tennis	✓	✓	✓		✓	✓	✓	✓	✓	✓
Tir à l'arc	✓	✓	✓				✓	✓	✓	✓
Promenades en mer			PIROGUE	✓	✓	✓		✓		✓
Pêche en haute mer		✓				✓	PÊCHE À LA TRAÎNE			
Arts appliqués	✓	✓				✓	✓	✓		✓

LEÇON 30 Vive le weekend!

Le weekend, nous avons nos occupations préférées. Certaines personnes aiment aller en ville et rencontrer leurs amis. D'autres préfèrent rester à la maison et bricoler. Qu'est-ce que les personnes suivantes ont fait le weekend dernier?

Others / do things around the house
did . . . do / last

Le weekend	Le weekend dernier	

J'aime acheter des vêtements.	J'ai acheté des vêtements.	*bought*

Tu aimes réparer ton vélo.	Tu as réparé ton vélo.	*fixed*

M. Lambert aime travailler dans le jardin.	Il a travaillé dans le jardin.	*worked*

Nous aimons organiser des boums.	Nous avons organisé une boum.	*organized*

Le weekend

Vous aimez jouer au foot.

Pluton et Philibert aiment rencontrer leurs amis.

Le weekend dernier

Vous <u>avez joué</u> au foot. *played*

Ils <u>ont rencontré</u> leurs amis. *met*

Et toi?

Indique si oui ou non tu as fait les choses suivantes le weekend dernier. Pour cela complète les phrases suivantes.

1. (J'ai / Je n'ai pas) ... acheté des vêtements.
2. (J'ai / Je n'ai pas) ... réparé mon vélo.
3. (J'ai / Je n'ai pas) ... travaillé dans le jardin.
4. (J'ai / Je n'ai pas) ... organisé une boum.
5. (J'ai / Je n'ai pas) ... joué au foot.
6. (J'ai / Je n'ai pas) ... rencontré mes amis.

NOTE CULTURELLE

Le weekend

Le weekend ne commence pas° le vendredi soir pour tout le monde.° Dans beaucoup d'écoles françaises, les élèves ont classe le samedi matin. Pour eux, le weekend commence seulement° le samedi à midi.

Que font les jeunes Français le samedi? Ça dépend. Beaucoup° vont en ville. Ils vont dans des magasins pour écouter les nouveaux disques ou pour regarder, essayer° et parfois° acheter des vêtements. Ils vont au café ou au cinéma avec leurs copains. Certains° préfèrent rester chez eux ou aller chez des copains. Parfois ils vont à une boum. Là on écoute de la musique, on mange des sandwichs et on danse ...

En général, le dimanche est réservé aux activités familiales.° Un weekend, on invite des cousins. Un autre° weekend, on rend visite aux grands-parents ... Le dimanche, on déjeune° et on dîne en famille.° Le soir, on regarde la télé et souvent on fait ses devoirs pour les classes du lundi matin.

ne commence pas *does not begin* **tout le monde** *everyone* **seulement** *only* **Beaucoup** *Many* **essayer** *try on* **parfois** *sometimes* **Certains** *Some of them* **activités familiales** *family activities* **Un autre** *Another* **déjeune** *has lunch* **en famille** *at home (with the family)*

A. Les expressions avec *avoir*

Note the use of **avoir** in the following sentences:

J'**ai faim.**	*I **am hungry**.*
Brigitte **a soif.**	*Brigitte **is thirsty**.*

French speakers use **avoir** in many expressions where English speakers use the verb *to be*.

Vocabulaire: Expressions avec *avoir*

avoir chaud	*to be (feel) warm*	Quand j'**ai chaud** en été, je vais à la plage.
avoir froid	*to be (feel) cold*	Est-ce que tu **as froid?** Voici ton pull.
avoir faim	*to be hungry*	Tu **as faim?** Est-ce que tu veux une pizza?
avoir soif	*to be thirsty*	J'**ai soif.** Je voudrais une limonade.
avoir raison	*to be right*	Est-ce que les profs **ont** toujours **raison?**
avoir tort	*to be wrong*	Marc n'étudie pas. Il **a tort!**
avoir de la chance	*to be lucky*	J'**ai de la chance.** J'ai des amis sympathiques.

1 Tort ou raison?

Informez-vous sur les personnes suivantes et dites si, à votre avis, elles ont tort ou raison.

▶ Les élèves n'étudient pas.
Ils ont tort!

▶ Tu écoutes le prof.
Tu as raison!

1. Catherine est généreuse avec ses copines.
2. Nous aidons nos parents.
3. Tu fais tes devoirs.
4. Vous êtes très impatients avec vos amis.
5. Mes copains étudient le français.
6. Jean-François dépense son argent inutilement *(uselessly)*.
7. M. Legros mange trop *(too much)*.
8. Alain et Nicolas sont impolis *(impolite)*.
9. Vous nettoyez votre chambre.

2 De bonnes questions

Étudiez ce que font les personnes suivantes. Ensuite, posez une question logique sur chaque personne. Pour cela, utilisez l'une des expressions suivantes:

avoir faim avoir soif avoir chaud
avoir froid avoir de la chance

▶ Philippe va au restaurant.
Est-ce que Philippe a faim?

1. Tu veux un soda.
2. Jean-Pierre mange une pizza.
3. Cécile porte un manteau.
4. Vous gagnez à la loterie.
5. Vous faites des sandwichs.
6. Tu mets ton blouson.
7. Mes copains vont aller à la piscine.
8. Ces élèves n'étudient pas beaucoup, mais ils réussissent toujours à leurs examens.
9. Tu as des grands-parents très généreux.

B. Le passé composé des verbes en *-er*

The sentences below describe past events. In the French sentences, the verbs are in the PASSÉ COMPOSÉ. Note the forms of the passé composé and its English equivalents.

Hier j'**ai réparé** mon vélo.	*Yesterday I **fixed** my bicycle.*
Le weekend dernier, Marc **a organisé** une boum.	*Last weekend, Marc **organized** a party.*
Pendant les vacances, nous **avons visité** Paris.	*During vacation, we **visited** Paris.*

FORMS

The PASSÉ COMPOSÉ is composed of two words. For most verbs, it is formed as follows:

PRESENT of **avoir** + PAST PARTICIPLE

Note the forms of the passé composé for **visiter.**

PASSÉ COMPOSÉ	PRESENT of **avoir** + PAST PARTICIPLE	
J'**ai visité** Québec.	j' **ai**	**visité**
Tu **as visité** Paris.	tu **as**	
Il/Elle/On **a visité** Montréal.	il/elle/on **a**	
Nous **avons visité** Genève.	nous **avons**	
Vous **avez visité** Strasbourg.	vous **avez**	
Ils/Elles **ont visité** Fort-de-France.	ils/elles **ont**	

➡ For all **-er** verbs, the past participle is formed by replacing the **-er** of the infinitive by **-é**.

jou er	→ **jou é**	Nous **avons joué** au tennis.
parl er	→ **parl é**	Éric **a parlé** à Nathalie.
téléphon er	→ **téléphon é**	Vous **avez téléphoné** à Cécile.

Learning about language

The PASSÉ COMPOSÉ, as its name indicates, is a "past" tense "composed" of two parts. It is formed like the present perfect tense in English.

AUXILIARY VERB + PAST PARTICIPLE of the main verb

Nous **avons** **travaillé.**
We have *worked.*

USES

The passé composé is used to describe past actions and events. It has several English equivalents.

J'**ai visité** Montréal. { *I **visited** Montreal.* / *I **have visited** Montreal.* / *I **did visit** Montreal.* }

3 Achats

Samedi dernier *(Last Saturday)*, les personnes suivantes ont fait des achats. Dites ce que chaque personne a acheté.

▶ Philippe (des compacts)
Philippe a acheté des compacts.

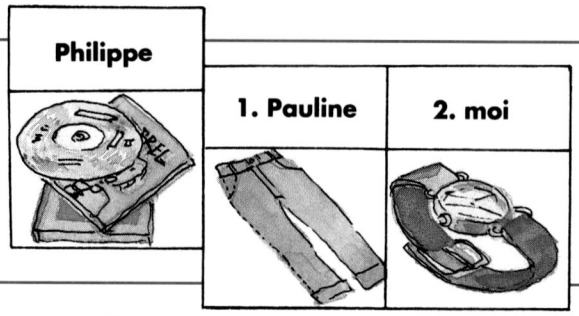

4 Vive la différence!

Caroline et Jean-Pierre sont des copains, mais ils aiment faire des choses différentes. Ils parlent de ce qu'ils ont fait ce weekend.

▶ jouer au volley (au tennis)

1. acheter des disques (des magazines)
2. dîner au restaurant (chez moi)
3. inviter mon cousin (un ami)
4. téléphoner à ma tante (à mon grand-père)
5. aider ma mère (mon père)
6. nettoyer ma chambre (le garage)
7. réparer ma mobylette (mon vélo)
8. assister à un match de foot (à un concert de rock)
9. laver mes tee-shirts (mes jeans)

5 La boum

Anne et Éric organisent une boum ce weekend. Florence demande à Philippe s'il a fait les choses suivantes. Il répond que oui.

▶ acheter des sodas?

1. acheter des jus de fruit
2. préparer les sandwichs
3. nettoyer le salon
4. réparer la chaîne stéréo
5. apporter des disques
6. inviter nos copains

6 Un jeu

Décrivez ce que certaines personnes ont fait samedi dernier. Pour cela, faites des phrases logiques en utilisant les éléments des Colonnes A, B et C. Combien de phrases est-ce que vous pouvez *(can)* faire en cinq minutes?

▶ **Vous avez assisté à un concert de jazz.**

A	B	C
nous	acheter	une boum
vous	assister	un musée
Marc	dîner	des vêtements
Hélène et Juliette	jouer	un film à la télé
Éric et Stéphanie	organiser	au Monopoly
mes copains	regarder	dans le jardin
les voisins	travailler	dans un restaurant vietnamien
	visiter	à un concert de jazz

3. toi	4. vous	5. nous	6. Stéphanie et Isabelle	7. Patrick et Jean-Paul	8. M. et Mme Dupont

Expressions pour la conversation

How to indicate the order in which actions take place:

d'abord	*first*	**D'abord,** nous avons invité nos copains à la boum.
après	*after, afterwards*	**Après,** tu as préparé des sandwichs.
ensuite	*then, after that*	**Ensuite,** Jacques a acheté des jus de fruit.
enfin	*at last*	**Enfin,** vous avez décoré le salon.
finalement	*finally*	**Finalement,** j'ai apporté mes cassettes.

7 Dans quel ordre?

Décrivez ce que les personnes suivantes ont fait dans l'ordre logique.

▶ nous (manger/préparer la salade/acheter des pizzas)
D'abord, nous avons acheté des pizzas.
Après, nous avons préparé la salade.
Ensuite, nous avons mangé.

1. Alice (travailler/trouver un job/acheter une moto)
2. les touristes canadiens (voyager en avion/visiter Paris/réserver les billets [*tickets*])
3. tu (assister au concert/acheter un billet/acheter le programme)
4. vous (danser/apporter des disques/inviter des copains)
5. nous (payer l'addition [*check*]/dîner/trouver un restaurant)

C. Le passé composé: forme négative

Compare the affirmative and negative forms of the passé composé in the sentences below.

AFFIRMATIVE	NEGATIVE	
Alice **a travaillé**.	Éric **n'a pas travaillé.**	*Éric **has not worked.*** *Éric **did not work.***
Nous **avons visité** Paris.	Nous **n'avons pas visité** Lyon.	*We **have not visited** Lyon.* *We **did not visit** Lyon.*

In the negative, the passé composé follows the pattern:

negative form of **avoir** + PAST PARTICIPLE

Note the negative forms of the passé composé of **travailler.**

PASSÉ COMPOSÉ (NEGATIVE)	PRESENT of **avoir** (NEGATIVE) + PAST PARTICIPLE	
Je **n'ai pas travaillé.** Tu **n'as pas travaillé.** Il/Elle/On **n'a pas travaillé.** Nous **n'avons pas travaillé.** Vous **n'avez pas travaillé.** Ils/Elles **n'ont pas travaillé.**	je **n'ai pas** tu **n'as pas** il/elle/on **n'a pas** nous **n'avons pas** vous **n'avez pas** ils/elles **n'ont pas**	**travaillé**

8 Oublis *(Things forgotten)*

Éric a décidé de faire certaines choses, mais il a oublié *(forgot)*. Sabine demande s'il a fait les choses suivantes.

▶ nettoyer ta chambre?

1. réparer ta chaîne stéréo?
2. apporter tes livres?
3. étudier?
4. téléphoner à ta tante?
5. inviter tes copains?
6. acheter *Paris-Match*?
7. laver tes chemises?

9 Quel mauvais temps!

Le weekend, il a fait mauvais et les personnes suivantes sont restées *(stayed)* chez elles. Dites qu'elles n'ont pas fait les choses suivantes.

▶ nous / nager
Nous n'avons pas nagé.

1. vous / jouer au tennis
2. Philippe / rencontrer ses copains à la plage
3. Nathalie / dîner en ville
4. les voisins / travailler dans le jardin
5. Mlle Lacaze / laver sa voiture
6. mes copains / organiser un pique-nique
7. nous / assister au match de foot
8. toi / visiter le musée

10 Une question d'argent

Les personnes suivantes n'ont pas beaucoup d'argent. Décrivez leur choix. Pour cela, dites ce qu'elles ont fait et ce qu'elles n'ont pas fait.

▶ nous / dîner au restaurant ou chez nous?
Nous avons dîné chez nous. Nous n'avons pas dîné au restaurant.

1. Philippe / acheter un tee-shirt ou une chemise?
2. vous / manger un steak ou un sandwich?
3. nous / assister au concert ou au match de foot?
4. les touristes / voyager en car ou en avion?
5. mes voisins / acheter une Mercedes ou une Ford?
6. Marc / passer dix jours ou trois semaines à Paris?

11 Impossibilités

Sans *(Without)* certaines choses il n'est pas possible de faire certaines activités. Expliquez cela logiquement en choisissant une personne de la Colonne A, un objet de la Colonne B et une activité de la Colonne C.

▶ **Je n'ai pas d'aspirateur. Je n'ai pas nettoyé le salon.**

A	B	C
je	une raquette	écouter les disques
vous	un billet *(ticket)*	voyager en Europe
nous	un passeport	nettoyer le salon
Frédéric	une chaîne stéréo	regarder la comédie
Éric et Olivier	une télé	assister au concert
Claire et Caroline	un aspirateur *(vacuum cleaner)*	jouer au tennis

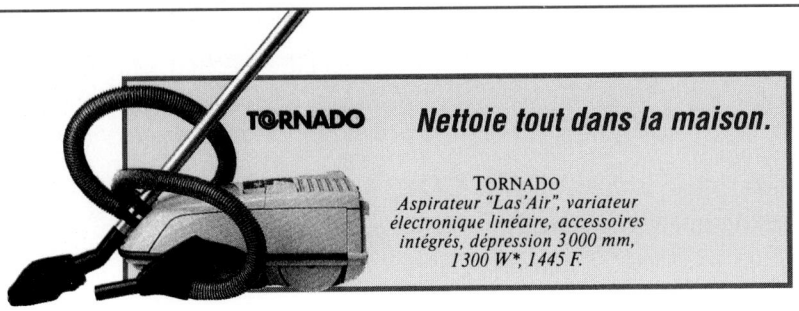

D. Les questions au passé composé

Compare the statements and questions in the passé composé.

STATEMENT	QUESTION	
Tu as travaillé.	Tu as travaillé? **Est-ce que** tu as travaillé?	*Did you work?*
Philippe a voyagé cet été.	**Quand est-ce que** Philippe a voyagé? **Où est-ce qu'**il a voyagé?	*When did Philippe travel?* *Where did he travel?*

For most verbs, questions in the passé composé are formed as follows:

PRESENT of **avoir** (interrogative form) + PAST PARTICIPLE

	YES/NO QUESTIONS	INFORMATION QUESTIONS
WITH INTONATION	Tu as voyagé? Paul a téléphoné?	— —
WITH **est-ce que**	**Est-ce que** tu as voyagé? **Est-ce qu'**Alice a téléphoné?	**Avec qui est-ce que** tu as voyagé? **À qui est-ce qu'**Alice a téléphoné?

➡ When the subject is a pronoun, questions in the passé composé can also be formed by inversion.

As-tu assisté au match de foot? *Did you go to the soccer game?*
Avec qui **avez-vous joué** au foot? *With whom did you play soccer?*
Who(m) did you play soccer with?

12 Expériences personnelles

Demandez à vos camarades s'ils ont déjà *(already)* fait les choses suivantes.

▶ visiter Paris?

1. visiter le Tibet? (Non, je n'ai pas visité Paris.)
2. voyager en Alaska?
3. piloter un avion?
4. dîner dans un restaurant vietnamien?
5. manger des escargots *(snails)*?
6. gagner à la loterie?
7. assister à un match de catch *(wrestling)*?
8. rencontrer un fantôme *(ghost)*?

13 Curiosité

Lisez ce que les personnes suivantes ont fait et posez des questions sur leurs activités.

▶ Paul a joué au tennis. (avec qui?)
Avec qui est-ce qu'il a joué au tennis?

1. Thomas a visité Québec. (quand?)
2. Corinne a téléphoné. (à quelle heure?)
3. Nathalie a voyagé en Italie. (comment?)
4. Marthe a acheté une robe. (où?)
5. Michèle a visité Genève. (avec qui?)
6. Philippe a trouvé un job. (où?)
7. Éric et Véronique ont dîné en ville. (dans quel restaurant?)
8. Les voisins ont téléphoné. (quand?)

14 Jérôme et Valérie

Jérôme est très curieux. Il veut toujours savoir ce que Valérie a fait. Valérie répond à ses questions.

▶ où/ dîner? (dans un restaurant italien)
JÉRÔME: **Où est-ce que tu as dîné?**
VALÉRIE: **J'ai dîné dans un restaurant italien.**

1. avec qui/ jouer au tennis? (avec Marc)
2. quand/ assister au concert? (samedi après-midi)
3. qui/ inviter au café? (ma copine Nathalie)
4. où/ rencontrer Pierre? (dans la rue)
5. où/ acheter ta veste? (au Bon Marché)
6. combien/ payer ce disque? (50 francs)
7. à qui/ téléphoner? (à ma grand-mère)
8. chez qui/ passer le weekend? (chez une amie)

15 Conversation

Demandez à vos camarades ce qu'ils ont fait hier.

▶ à quelle heure/ dîner?

1. avec qui/ dîner?
2. à qui/ téléphoner?
3. quel programme/ regarder à la télé?
4. quel programme/ écouter à la radio?
5. qui/ rencontrer après les classes?
6. quand/ étudier?

Prononciation

Les lettres «ain» et «in»

ain /ɛ̃/

sa main

aine /ɛn/

semaine

in /ɛ̃/

magasin

ine /in/

magazine

When the letters "**ain**", "**aim**", "**in**", "**im**" are at the end of a word or are followed by a *consonant*, they represent the nasal vowel /ɛ̃/.

REMEMBER: Do not pronounce an /n/ after the nasal vowel /ɛ̃/.

Répétez: /ɛ̃/ **demain faim train main voisin cousin jardin magasin maintenant intelligent intéressant important**

When the letters "**ain**", "**aim**", "**in(n)**", "**im**" are followed by a *vowel*, they do NOT represent a nasal sound.

Répétez: /ɛn/ **semaine américaine**
/ɛm/ **j'aime**

/in/ **voisine cousine cuisine magazine cinéma Corinne finir**
/im/ **timide dimanche Mimi centime**

Alain Minime a un rendez-vous important demain matin, avenue du Maine.

À votre tour!

1 Allô!

Reconstituez la conversation entre Alain et Christine. Pour cela, faites correspondre les réponses de Christine avec les questions d'Alain.

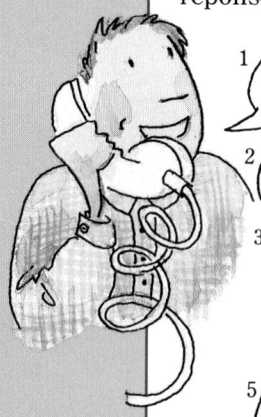

1. À quelle heure est-ce que tu as dîné hier soir?
2. Et après, tu as regardé la télé?
3. Qu'est-ce que tu as regardé après?
4. Qui a gagné?
5. Dis, tu as préparé la leçon pour demain?

a. Le match Marseille–Nice.
b. Nice. Par un score de trois à un.
c. Mais oui! J'ai étudié avant le dîner.
d. Oui, mais d'abord j'ai aidé ma mère.
e. À sept heures et demie.

2 Dis-moi . . .

I will tell you a few things that I did yesterday after school and a few things that I did not do, then you will tell me what you did and did not do.

- J'ai étudié.
- J'ai dîné avec mes parents.
- J'ai téléphoné à une copine.

- Je n'ai pas nettoyé ma chambre.
- Je n'ai pas rencontré mes copains.
- Je n'ai pas regardé la télé.

Et maintenant, dis-moi . . .

3 Créa-dialogue

Demandez à vos camarades s'ils ont fait les choses suivantes le weekend dernier. En cas de réponse affirmative, continuez la conversation.

▶ — Est-ce que tu as dîné au restaurant?
— Oui, j'ai dîné au restaurant.
— Avec qui?
— Avec mes cousins.
— Où est-ce que vous avez dîné?
— Nous avons dîné Chez Tante Lucie (à McDonald's, etc.).

avec qui?
où?

1: avec qui? / quand?
2: quand? / où?

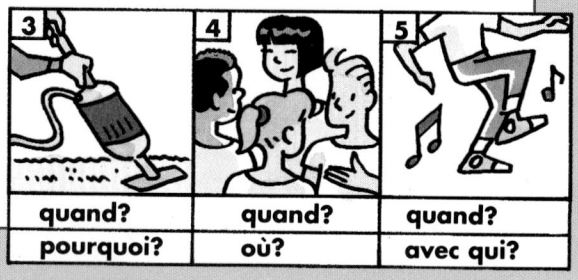

3: quand? / pourquoi?
4: quand? / où?
5: quand? / avec qui?

4 Situation

Avec un(e) camarade, composez un dialogue correspondant à la situation suivante. Jouez ce dialogue en classe.

You are spending a week in Paris with your best friend. Up to now you have been touring the city together, but today you both decided to go out on your own. At the end of the day, you both meet back at your hotel room. Discuss . . .

- what monuments you visited
- what things you bought
- whom you met
- what you ate at noon
- where you had dinner

5 Conversation libre *(free)*

Avec un(e) camarade analysez la situation suivante. Composez un dialogue original basé sur cette situation. Jouez le dialogue en classe.

Last weekend, you stayed home and your friend went into town. Now you are both trying to find out what the other one did. Ask each other questions, using the passé composé of **-er** verbs that you know. (Do not use **aller** or **rester,** since they have special passé composé forms that you have not learned yet.)

▶ — **Moi, j'ai nettoyé ma chambre. Et toi?**
— **J'ai assisté à un concert, mais d'abord j'ai dîné avec des copains.**

6 Composition: Vive les vacances!

Vacations are for fun, not for work. Write a brief composition in the passé composé about what you did on a recent vacation, describing . . .

- four things that you did
- four things that you did not do

You may want to use some of the verbs in the box. (Do not use **aller** or **rester.**)

jouer **inviter** **nager** **parler** **travailler** **voyager** **visiter**
téléphoner **rencontrer** **acheter** **trouver** **dépenser** **gagner**

Comment dit-on . . . ?

How to wish somebody a nice time:

Bon weekend! *(Have a nice weekend!)*

Bonnes vacances! *(Have a good vacation!)*

Bonne journée! *(Have a nice day!)*

Bon voyage! *(Have a good trip!)*

LEÇON 31

L'alibi

l'inspecteur Leflic

Êtes-vous bon (bonne) détective? Pouvez-vous trouver la solution du mystère suivant?

Samedi dernier à deux heures de l'après-midi, il y a eu une panne d'électricité dans la petite ville de Marcillac-le-Château. La panne a duré une heure. Pendant la panne, un cambrioleur a pénétré dans la Banque Populaire de Marcillac-le-Château. Bien sûr, l'alarme n'a pas fonctionné et c'est seulement lundi matin que le directeur de la banque a remarqué le cambriolage: un million de francs.

Lundi après-midi, l'inspecteur Leflic a interrogé quatre suspects, mais chacun a un alibi.

Can
following
there was / power failure
lasted / During / burglar / entered
only
noticed / burglary
police detective
each one

Sophie Filou

Euh, . . . excusez-moi, Monsieur l'Inspecteur.
Ma mémoire n'est pas très bonne.
Voyons, qu'est-ce que j'ai fait samedi après-midi?
Ah oui, j'ai fini un livre.
Le titre du livre? *Le crime ne paie pas!*

Let's see / did I do
I finished
title

Marc Laroulette

Qu'est-ce que j'ai fait samedi?
J'ai rendu visite à mes copains.
Nous avons joué aux cartes.
C'est moi qui ai gagné!

visited

Patrick Lescrot

Voyons, samedi dernier . . .
Ah oui . . . J'ai invité des amis chez moi.
Nous avons regardé la télé.
Nous avons vu le match de foot France-Allemagne.
Quel match! Malheureusement, c'est la France qui a perdu!
Dommage!

saw / Germany
Unfortunately / lost

Pauline Malin

Ce n'est pas moi, Monsieur l'Inspecteur!
Samedi j'ai fait un pique-nique à la campagne avec une copine.
Nous avons choisi un coin près d'une rivière.
Ensuite, nous avons fait une promenade à vélo.
Nous avons eu de la chance!
Il a fait un temps extraordinaire!

chose / spot
were lucky
The weather was great!

Lisez attentivement° les quatre déclarations. À votre avis, qui est le cambrioleur ou la cambrioleuse? Pourquoi? (Vous pouvez comparer votre réponse avec la réponse de l'inspecteur à la page 325.)

carefully

Compréhension

Certains événements ont eu lieu *(took place)* samedi dernier. Indiquez si oui ou non les événements suivants ont eu lieu.

1. Le directeur de la banque a vu *(saw)* le cambrioleur.
2. Un cambriolage a eu lieu *(took place)* à Marcillac-le-Château.
3. L'inspecteur Leflic a arrêté *(arrested)* le cambrioleur.
4. Sophie Filou a vu le film *Le crime ne paie pas* à la télé.
5. Marc Laroulette a perdu un million de francs.
6. L'Allemagne a gagné un match de foot.
7. Pauline Malin a fait une promenade à vélo à la campagne.
8. Il a fait beau.

Et toi?

Dis si oui ou non tu as fait les choses suivantes le weekend dernier.

1. (J'ai / Je n'ai pas) ... rendu visite à mes copains.
2. (J'ai / Je n'ai pas) ... vu un match de foot à la télé.
3. (J'ai / Je n'ai pas) ... fini un livre.
4. (J'ai / Je n'ai pas) ... fait une promenade à vélo.
5. (J'ai / Je n'ai pas) ... fait un pique-nique.

NOTE CULTURELLE

Les jeunes Français et la télé

Combien d'heures par° jour est-ce que tu regardes la télé? Une heure? deux heures? trois heures? plus? moins? En général, les jeunes Français regardent la télé moins souvent et moins longtemps° que les jeunes Américains: en moyenne° 1 heure 15 les jours d'école et 2 heures 15 les autres° jours (mercredi, samedi et dimanche). Dans beaucoup de familles, les parents contrôlent l'usage° de la télé. Souvent ils exigent° que leurs enfants finissent leurs devoirs avant de regarder la télé. Ainsi,° beaucoup de jeunes regardent la télé seulement° après le dîner.

Quels sont leurs programmes favoris? Les jeunes Français aiment surtout° les films, les programmes de sport, les variétés et les jeux télévisés,° comme «La roue° de la fortune» et «Le prix est juste».° Les séries américaines (comme «Deux flics° à Miami» et «Santa Barbara») sont aussi très populaires.

par *per* **moins longtemps** *for a shorter time* **en moyenne** *on an average of* **autres** *other* **usage** *use* **exigent** *insist* **Ainsi** *Thus* **seulement** *only* **surtout** *especially* **jeux télévisés** *TV games* **roue** *wheel* **juste** *right* **flics** *cops*

A. Le verbe *voir*

The verb **voir** *(to see)* is irregular. Note the forms of **voir** in the present tense.

INFINITIVE	**voir**	
PRESENT	Je **vois** Marc. Tu **vois** ton copain. Il/Elle/On **voit** un accident.	Nous **voyons** un film. Vous **voyez** un match de baseball. Ils/Elles **voient** le professeur.

1 Weekend à Paris

Les personnes suivantes passent le weekend à Paris. Décrivez ce que chacun voit.

▶ Olivier **Olivier voit Notre-Dame.**

▶ **Notre-Dame**

1. le musée d'Orsay

2. l'Arc de Triomphe

3. le Centre Pompidou

4. le Quartier latin

5. la pyramide du Louvre

6. le musée Picasso

1. nous
2. toi
3. moi
4. Sophie
5. vous
6. les touristes japonais

2 Questions personnelles

1. Est-ce que tu vois bien? Est-ce que tu portes des lunettes?
2. Est-ce que tu vois tes amis pendant les vacances? Est-ce que tu vois tes professeurs?
3. Est-ce que tu vois souvent tes cousins? Est-ce que tu vois tes cousins pendant les vacances? à Noël?
4. Qu'est-ce que tu préfères voir à la télé? un match de football ou un match de baseball?
5. Quand tu vas au cinéma, quels films aimes-tu voir? les comédies? les films d'aventures? les films policiers *(detective movies)*?

B. Le passé composé des verbes réguliers en *-ir* et *-re*

Note the passé composé of the verbs below, paying special attention to the ending of the past participle.

choisir	J'**ai choisi** ce disque.	Je **n'ai pas choisi** cette cassette.
finir	Nous **avons fini** le magazine.	Nous **n'avons pas fini** le livre.
vendre	Tu **as vendu** ton vélo.	Tu **n'as pas vendu** ta moto.
attendre	Jacques **a attendu** Paul.	Il **n'a pas attendu** François.
répondre	J'**ai répondu** au professeur.	Tu **n'as pas répondu** à la question.

The past participle of regular **-ir** and **-re** verbs is formed as follows:

-ir → -i	-re → -u
chois ir → chois i	vend re → vend u
fin ir → fin i	attend re → attend u

3 Besoins d'argent *(Money needs)*

Parce qu'elles ont besoin d'argent, les personnes suivantes ont vendu certains objets. Dites ce que chaque personne a vendu.

▶ Philippe/sa guitare
Philippe a vendu sa guitare.

1. M. Roche/sa voiture
2. mes copains/leur chaîne stéréo
3. moi/mon appareil-photo
4. toi/ton vélo
5. les voisins/leur piano
6. nous/nos livres
7. vous/votre ordinateur
8. François et Victor/leurs disques

4 Bravo!

Les personnes suivantes méritent *(deserve)* des félicitations *(congratulations)*. Expliquez pourquoi.

▶ les élèves/réussir à l'examen
Les élèves ont réussi à l'examen.

1. M. Bedon/maigrir
2. Mlle Legros/perdre dix kilos
3. Florence/gagner le match de tennis
4. ces enfants/finir leur soupe
5. nous/choisir une classe difficile
6. toi/finir les exercices
7. Marc/rendre visite à un copain à l'hôpital
8. vous/attendre vos copains
9. les élèves/répondre en français

5 Non!

Jean-Louis répond négativement aux questions de Béatrice. Jouez les deux rôles.

▶ gagner le match / perdre

1. étudier ce weekend / rendre visite à un copain
2. acheter une cassette / choisir un compact
3. finir ce livre / regarder la télé
4. vendre ta guitare / vendre mon appareil-photo
5. téléphoner à Marc / rendre visite à son cousin
6. maigrir / grossir
7. répondre à la lettre / téléphoner

6 Aujourd'hui et hier

Dites ce que les personnes suivantes font aujourd'hui et ce qu'elles ont fait hier.

▶ Paul / acheter un blouson / un pantalon
Aujourd'hui, Paul achète un blouson.
Hier, il a acheté un pantalon.

1. moi / téléphoner à mon cousin / à mes copains
2. toi / finir ce livre / ce magazine
3. nous / manger des sandwichs / une pizza
4. Mélanie / choisir une jupe / un chemisier
5. les élèves / réussir à l'examen de français / à l'examen d'anglais
6. Philippe / vendre sa chaîne stéréo / ses disques
7. Philippe et Jean-Pierre / rendre visite à leurs cousins / à leur grand-mère
8. les touristes / attendre le train / le car

7 Excuses

Quand Olivier ne fait pas une chose, il a toujours une excuse. Jouez le dialogue entre Olivier et sa soeur Caroline.

▶ étudier / perdre mon livre

1. jouer au tennis / perdre ma raquette
2. acheter une veste / choisir un blouson
3. finir le livre / regarder la télé
4. rendre visite à Marc / étudier
5. réussir à l'examen / perdre mes notes
6. écouter tes disques / vendre ma chaîne stéréo

C. Le passé composé des verbes *être, avoir, faire, mettre* et *voir*

The verbs **être, avoir, faire, mettre,** and **voir** have irregular past participles.

être	→ **été**	Nous **avons été** à Paris.
avoir	→ **eu**	M. Lambert **a eu** un accident.
faire	→ **fait**	Qu'est-ce que tu **as fait** hier?
mettre	→ **mis**	Nous **avons mis** des jeans.
voir	→ **vu**	J'**ai vu** un bon film.

➡ In the passé composé, the verb **être** has two different meanings:

Mme Lebrun **a été** malade. — *Mme Lebrun **has been** sick.*
Elle **a été** à l'hôpital. — *She **was** in the hospital.*

8 Dialogue

Demandez à vos camarades s'ils ont fait les choses suivantes récemment *(recently)*.

▶ faire une promenade.
—Est-ce que tu as fait une promenade récemment?
—Oui, j'ai fait une promenade. (Non, je n'ai pas fait de promenade.)

1. faire un pique-nique?
2. faire une promenade en voiture?
3. être malade *(sick)?*
4. avoir la grippe *(flu)?*
5. avoir une dispute *(fight)* avec ton copain?
6. avoir une bonne surprise?
7. avoir un «A» en français?
8. voir un film?
9. voir tes cousins?
10. mettre des posters dans ta chambre?

9 Pourquoi?

Avec vos camarades de classe, parlez des personnes suivantes.

▶ Éric est content.
(avoir un «A» à l'examen)

1. Mes copains sont furieux. (avoir un «F» à l'examen)
2. Pauline est très contente. (voir son copain)
3. Mon père n'est pas content. (avoir une dispute avec son chef [*boss*])
4. Philippe est pâle. (voir un accident)
5. Juliette est fatiguée *(tired)*. (faire du jogging)
6. Alice et Laure sont bronzées *(tanned)*. (être à la mer)
7. Mon frère est fatigué. (faire des exercices de gymnastique)
8. Patrick et Marc sont contents. (voir un bon film)
9. Isabelle est très élégante. (mettre une jolie robe)

10 Vive les vacances!

Dites où les personnes suivantes ont été pendant les vacances. Dites aussi si oui ou non elles ont fait les choses entre parenthèses. Soyez logique *(Be logical)*.

▶ Christophe: à la piscine (étudier / nager)
Christophe a été à la piscine. Il n'a pas étudié. Il a nagé.

1. Sylvie: à la montagne (nager / faire de l'alpinisme)
2. nous: à la campagne (visiter des monuments / faire du camping)
3. vous: à Paris (parler italien / voir la tour Eiffel)
4. moi: à la mer (faire de la planche à voile / travailler)
5. mes parents: en Égypte (voir les pyramides / visiter Paris)
6. vous: dans un club de sport (faire de la gymnastique / grossir)
7. Christine: à la plage (mettre des lunettes de soleil / jouer au tennis)

Vocabulaire: *Quand?*

	maintenant	avant	après
le jour	**aujourd'hui**	**hier**	**demain**
le matin	**ce matin**	**hier matin**	**demain matin**
l'après-midi	**cet après-midi**	**hier après-midi**	**demain après-midi**
le soir	**ce soir**	**hier soir**	**demain soir**
le jour	**samedi**	**samedi dernier** *(last)*	**samedi prochain** *(next)*
le weekend	**ce weekend**	**le weekend dernier**	**le weekend prochain**
la semaine	**cette semaine**	**la semaine dernière**	**la semaine prochaine**
le mois	**ce mois-ci**	**le mois dernier**	**le mois prochain**

11 Quand?

Demandez à vos camarades quand ils ont fait les choses suivantes. Ils vont répondre en utilisant une expression du **Vocabulaire.**

▶ faire tes devoirs?

1. faire des achats?
2. nettoyer ta chambre?
3. rencontrer tes voisins?
4. voir ton copain?
5. voir un film?
6. avoir un examen?
7. faire une promenade à pied?
8. être en ville?
9. mettre *(set)* la table?

(vendredi soir, le weekend dernier, . . .)

12 Le passé et le futur

Décrivez ce que vous avez fait (phrases 1 à 5) et ce que vous allez faire (phrases 6 à 10). Dites la vérité ... ou utilisez votre imagination!

1. Ce matin, j'ai . . . ✓
2. Hier matin, j'ai . . . ✓
3. Samedi après-midi, j'ai . . . ✓
4. La semaine dernière, j'ai . . . ✓
5. Le mois dernier, j'ai . . . ✓

6. Ce soir, je vais . . . ____
7. Demain soir, je vais . . . ____
8. Vendredi soir, je vais . . . ____
9. Le weekend prochain, je vais . . . ____
10. La semaine prochaine, je vais . . . ____

13 Questions personnelles

1. En général, est-ce que tu étudies avant ou après le dîner?
2. En général, est-ce que tu regardes la télé avant ou après le dîner?
3. À quelle heure est-ce que tu as dîné hier soir?
4. Quel programme de télé est-ce que tu as regardé hier après-midi?
5. Qu'est-ce que tu vas faire le weekend prochain?
6. Où vas-tu aller le weekend prochain?

Prononciation

Les lettres «gn» **gn** /ɲ/

The letters "**gn**" represent a sound similar to the "**ny**" in *canyon*. First, practice with words you know.

Répétez: **espagnol** **gagner** **mignon**
la montagne **la campagne**
un magnétophone

espagnol

Now try saying some new words. Make them sound French!

Répétez: **Champagne** **Espagne** *(Spain)* **un signe**
la vigne *(vineyard)* **la ligne** *(line)* **un signal**
la dignité **ignorer** **magnétique** **magnifique** **Agnès**

Agnès Mignard a gagné son match. C'est magnifique!

(L'alibi, p. 318)

La réponse de l'inspecteur:

C'est Patrick Lescrot le cambrioleur. Samedi après-midi, il y a eu une panne d'électricité. Patrick Lescrot n'a pas pu *(was not able to)* regarder la télé. Son alibi n'est pas valable *(valid)*.

À votre tour!

1 Allô!

Reconstituez la conversation entre Robert et Julien. Pour cela, faites correspondre les réponses de Julien avec les questions de Robert.

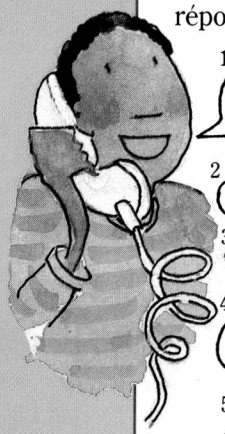

1. Tu as fini tes devoirs de français?
2. Qu'est-ce que tu as fait alors?
3. Tu as gagné?
4. Mais d'habitude *(usually)* tu joues bien?
5. Peut-être que Caroline a joué mieux *(better)* que toi?

a. Non, j'ai perdu!
b. Non, je n'ai pas étudié cet après-midi.
c. C'est vrai, mais aujourd'hui, je n'ai pas eu de chance . . .
d. J'ai joué au tennis avec Caroline.
e. Tu as raison. Elle a joué comme une championne.

2 Dis-moi . . .

I will tell you about some nice things that happened to me recently; then you will tell me about three nice things that happened to you.

- J'ai réussi à mon examen d'anglais. (J'ai eu un «A».)
- J'ai eu un rendez-vous avec une personne très intéressante.
- J'ai vu un très bon film.

Et maintenant, dis-moi . . .

3 Créa-dialogue

Avec vos camarades, discutez de ce que vous avez fait récemment *(recently)*. Vous pouvez utiliser les expressions et les activités suggérées. Continuez la conversation avec des questions supplémentaires.

Quand?

dimanche après-midi
hier soir
samedi soir
le weekend dernier
lundi dernier
la semaine dernière
le mois dernier

Quoi?

jouer au tennis
faire des achats
faire une promenade à la campagne
voir mes cousins
dîner au restaurant
voir un film
avoir un rendez-vous
rendre visite à un copain

▶ —Qu'est-ce que tu as fait dimanche après-midi?
—J'ai joué au tennis avec ma soeur.
—Est-ce que tu as gagné?
—Non, j'ai perdu.
—Dommage!

4 Situation

Avec un(e) camarade, composez un dialogue original correspondant à la situation suivante. Jouez ce dialogue en classe.

Your friend Michèle (played by a classmate) went to Canada for spring vacation.

Ask Michèle . . .

- how she traveled (by plane? by car?)
- if she visited Montreal
- whom she visited **(rendre visite à)**
- if she saw Quebec City **(Québec)**
- if she went skiing and with whom
- if she went shopping and what she bought

5 Conversation libre

Avec un(e) camarade, composez un dialogue basé sur la situation suivante. Jouez ce dialogue en classe.

Philippe spent spring vacation in Nice, on the French Riviera **(la Côte d'Azur).** Juliette spent her vacation in a small village high in the Alps **(les Alpes).** They meet and compare what they did. (In your dialogue, try to use several expressions with **faire.**)

▶ PHILIPPE: **J'ai été à Nice. J'ai fait de la voile.**
JULIETTE: **Moi, j'ai été dans les Alpes. J'ai fait du ski.**

6 Composition: Quand?

Describe two things that you or people you know have done at each of the times indicated below:

La semaine dernière, . . . | *Le mois dernier, . . .* | *L'an dernier (Last year), . . .*

▶ **La semaine dernière, mon père a vendu sa voiture.**
La semaine dernière, mes cousins ont acheté une moto.

Comment dit-on . . . ?

How to wish someone good luck or give encouragement:

Bonne chance!

Bon courage!

LEÇON 32 Qui a de la chance?

Vendredi après-midi

Anne et Valérie parlent de leurs projets pour le weekend.

ANNE: Qu'est-ce que tu vas faire samedi soir?
VALÉRIE: Je vais aller au cinéma avec Jean-Pierre.
ANNE: Tu as de la chance! Moi, je dois rester à la maison.
VALÉRIE: Mais pourquoi?
ANNE: Les amis de mes parents viennent chez nous ce weekend. Mon père insiste pour que je reste pour le dîner. Quelle barbe! *that / What a pain!*
VALÉRIE: C'est vrai! Tu n'as pas de chance!

Lundi matin

Anne et Valérie parlent de leur weekend.

ANNE: Alors, tu as passé un bon weekend?
VALÉRIE: Euh non, pas très bon.
ANNE: Mais tu es sortie avec Jean-Pierre! *went out*
VALÉRIE: C'est vrai. Je suis allée au cinéma avec lui . . . *went*

Nous avons vu un très, très mauvais film! Après le film, j'ai eu une dispute avec Jean-Pierre. Et, en plus, j'ai perdu mon porte-monnaie . . . et je suis rentrée chez moi à pied! Et toi, tu es restée chez toi?

quarrel
in addition
wallet / went back
stayed

ANNE: Non.
VALÉRIE: Comment? Les amis de tes parents ne sont pas venus? *didn't come*
ANNE: Si, si, ils sont venus . . . avec leur fils!
VALÉRIE: Et alors?
ANNE: Eh bien, c'est un garçon très sympa et très amusant . . . sympa = sympathique

Après le dîner, nous sommes allés au Zénith.* Nous avons assisté à un concert de rock absolument extraordinaire. Après, nous sommes allés dans un café et nous avons fait des projets pour le weekend prochain. *went*

VALÉRIE: Qu'est-ce que vous allez faire?
ANNE: Nous allons faire une promenade à la campagne dans la nouvelle voiture de sport de Thomas. (C'est le nom de mon nouveau copain!)
VALÉRIE: Toi, vraiment, tu as de la chance!

* Une salle *(hall)* de concert à Paris, parc de la Villette.

Compréhension

1. Qu'est-ce que Valérie va faire samedi soir?
2. Pourquoi est-ce qu'Anne doit *(must)* rester à la maison?
3. Est-ce que Valérie a aimé le film?
4. Qu'est-ce qu'elle a perdu?
5. Comment est-ce qu'elle est rentrée chez elle?
6. Où et avec qui est-ce qu'Anne a dîné?
7. Où est-ce qu'elle est allée après le dîner?
8. Qu'est-ce qu'elle va faire le weekend prochain?
9. Comment s'appelle son nouveau copain?

Et toi

Dis si oui ou non tu as fait les choses suivantes samedi dernier.

1. (Je suis/Je ne suis pas) ... allé(e) en ville.
2. (Je suis/Je ne suis pas) ... allé(e) au cinéma.
3. (Je suis/Je ne suis pas) ... allé(e) à un concert.
4. (Je suis/Je ne suis pas) ... rentré(e) chez moi pour le dîner.
5. (Je suis/Je ne suis pas) ... resté(e) chez moi le soir.

NOTE CULTURELLE

Les jeunes Français et la musique

«Pour moi, la musique c'est tout!»° déclare Anne, une jeune Française de quinze ans. Sa copine Hélène est d'accord:° «Aujourd'hui, on ne peut pas° vivre° sans° musique.»

Comme les jeunes Américains, les jeunes Français sont des «fanas»° de musique. Quel type de musique est-ce qu'ils préfèrent? D'abord le rock. Ils aiment aussi la chanson° française et la chanson étrangère,° la musique classique, la musique folk et le jazz.

Les jeunes Français ont l'équipement nécessaire pour écouter leur musique favorite: 70% ont une radio, 58% une chaîne stéréo, 42% une radiocassette et 39% un walkman. Dans les grandes villes, les jeunes vont au concert. À Paris, ils vont à Bercy ou au Zénith écouter les grandes vedettes° de la chanson française et de la musique anglaise et américaine.

Les jeunes Français ne se contentent pas° d'écouter la musique. Beaucoup jouent d'un instrument. Ils jouent du piano, de la flûte, de la guitare et du synthétiseur° . . . Et toi, est-ce que tu peux vivre sans musique? Est-ce que tu joues d'un instrument? De quel instrument joues-tu?

tout *everything* **est d'accord** *agrees* **ne peut pas** *cannot*
vivre *live* **sans** *without* **fanas = fanatiques**
chanson *song* **étrangère** *foreign* **vedettes** *stars*
ne se contentent pas *do not limit themselves*
synthétiseur *keyboard*

PARIS BERCY

A. Le passé composé avec *être*

Note the forms of the passé composé of **aller** in the sentences below, paying attention to the endings of the past participle **(allé).**

Jean-Paul **est allé** au cinéma.	*Jean-Paul **went** to the movies.*
Mélanie **est allée** à la plage.	*Mélanie **went** to the beach.*
Éric et Patrick **sont allés** en ville.	*Éric and Patrick **went** downtown.*
Mes copines **sont allées** à la campagne.	*My friends **went** to the country.*

The passé composé of **aller** and certain verbs of motion is formed with **être** according to the pattern:

PRESENT of **être** + PAST PARTICIPLE

➡ When the passé composé of a verb is conjugated with **être** (and not with **avoir**), the PAST PARTICIPLE *agrees* with the SUBJECT in gender and number.

INFINITIVE	**aller**	
PASSÉ COMPOSÉ	 je **suis allé** tu **es allé** il **est allé**	 je **suis allé**e tu **es allé**e elle **est allé**e
	 nous **sommes allé**s vous **êtes allé**s ils **sont allé**s	 nous **sommes allé**es vous **êtes allé**es elles **sont allé**es
NEGATIVE	je **ne suis pas allé**	je **ne suis pas allé**e
INTERROGATIVE	est-ce que tu **es allé?** tu **es allé?** **(es**-tu **allé?)**	est-ce que tu **es allé**e**?** tu **es allé**e**?** **(es**-tu **allé**e**?)**

➡ When **vous** refers to a single person, the past participle is in the singular:
Mme Mercier, est-ce que vous êtes **allée** au concert hier soir?

1 À Paris

Des amis sont allés à Paris samedi dernier. Chacun est allé à un endroit différent. Dites qui est allé aux endroits suivants. Complétez chaque phrase avec le sujet approprié et la forme correspondante du verbe **aller.**

Olivier | Claire | Éric et Jacques | Anne et Monique

▶ Anne et Monique **sont allées au Louvre.**

1. ... allée à la tour Eiffel.
2. ... allé au Centre Pompidou.
3. ... allés à l'Opéra.
4. ... allées aux Galeries Lafayette.
5. ... allé à la Villette.
6. ... allés au Zénith.
7. ... allé au musée d'Orsay.
8. ... allées au Quartier latin.

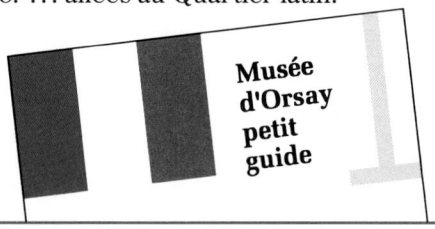

2 Conversation

Demandez à vos camarades s'ils sont allés aux endroits suivants.

▶ ce matin / à la bibliothèque?

(Non, je ne suis pas allé à la bibliothèque.)

1. hier matin/à l'école?
2. hier soir/au cinéma?
3. dimanche dernier/au restaurant?
4. samedi dernier/dans les magasins?
5. l'été dernier/chez tes cousins?
6. le weekend dernier/à la campagne?
7. le mois dernier/à un concert?
8. la semaine dernière/chez le coiffeur *(barber, hairdresser)*?
9. les vacances dernières/à la mer?

3 Le weekend dernier

Dites ce que les personnes de la Colonne A ont fait en choisissant une activité de la Colonne B. Puis dites où ces personnes sont allées en choisissant un endroit de la Colonne C. Soyez logiques!

A	B	C
je	voir des clowns	à la campagne
tu	nager	au zoo
nous	dîner en ville	dans un magasin de chaussures
Catherine	regarder les éléphants	à la bibliothèque
vous	choisir des livres	à la plage
mon petit frère	faire une promenade	au restaurant
André et Thomas	acheter des sandales	au cirque *(circus)*
les filles		

▶ **J'ai nagé. Je suis allé(e) à la plage.**

4 Weekend

Des amis parlent de leur weekend.
Jouez ces dialogues.

▶ en ville / acheter des vêtements

1. au stade / regarder un match de foot
2. à la plage / jouer au volley
3. à une boum / danser
4. à la campagne / faire une promenade à pied
5. au Bon Marché / acheter des cassettes
6. dans un restaurant italien / manger des spaghetti

Vocabulaire: Quelques verbes conjugués avec *être* au passé composé

INFINITIVE	PAST PARTICIPLE		
aller	**allé**	*to go*	Nous **sommes allés** en ville.
arriver	**arrivé**	*to arrive*	Vous **êtes arrivés** à midi.
rentrer	**rentré**	*to return, go back, come back*	Nous **sommes rentrés** à la maison à onze heures.
rester	**resté**	*to stay*	Les touristes **sont restés** à l'hôtel Ibis.
venir	**venu**	*to come*	Qui **est venu** hier?

5 Qui est resté à la maison?

Samedi après-midi, les personnes suivantes ont fait certaines choses. Dites si oui ou non elles sont restées à la maison.

▶ Paul a regardé la télé. **Il est resté à la maison.**
▶ Mélanie a fait des achats. **Elle n'est pas restée à la maison.**

1. Mlle Joly a lavé sa voiture.
2. Nous avons fait une promenade à vélo.
3. Tu as nettoyé le garage.
4. Éric et Olivier ont joué au volley.
5. Christine et Isabelle ont travaillé dans le jardin.
6. Vous avez fait une promenade en voiture.
7. Mes cousins ont fait de la voile.
8. J'ai fait du jogging.

6 La journée de Nathalie

Pendant les vacances, Nathalie travaille dans une agence de tourisme. Le soir, elle raconte *(tells about)* sa journée à son père.

▶ aller au bureau *(office)*

1. arriver à neuf heures
2. téléphoner à un client anglais
3. parler avec des touristes japonais
4. aller au restaurant à midi et demi
5. rentrer au bureau à deux heures
6. copier des documents
7. préparer des billets *(tickets)* d'avion
8. rester jusqu'à *(until)* six heures
9. dîner en ville
10. rentrer à la maison à neuf heures

7 Une question de circonstances *(A matter of circumstances)*

Nos activités dépendent souvent des circonstances. Dites si oui ou non les personnes suivantes ont fait les choses indiquées.

▶ On est mardi aujourd'hui.
- les élèves / rester à la maison?
  Les élèves ne sont pas restés à la maison.

1. On est dimanche.
   - M. Boulot / travailler?
   - nous / aller à l'école?
   - vous / dîner à la cantine *(school cafeteria)*?
2. Il fait très beau aujourd'hui.
   - moi / aller à la campagne?
   - mes copines / regarder la télé?
   - toi / venir à la piscine avec nous?
3. Il fait très mauvais!
   - Marc / faire un pique-nique?
   - Hélène et Juliette / rester à la maison?
   - ma mère / rentrer à la maison à pied?
4. Mes copains et moi, nous n'avons pas beaucoup d'argent.
   - toi / aller dans un restaurant cher?
   - mes copains / venir chez moi en taxi?
   - moi / acheter des vêtements?

B. La construction négative *ne . . . jamais*

Compare the following negative constructions.

Éric **ne** parle **pas** à Paul.	*Éric does **not** speak to Paul.*
Éric **ne** parle **jamais** à Paul.	*Éric **never** speaks to Paul.*
Nous **n'**étudions **pas** le dimanche.	*We do **not** study on Sundays.*
Nous **n'**étudions **jamais** le dimanche.	*We **never** study on Sundays.*

To say that one NEVER does something, French speakers use the construction **ne . . . jamais,** as follows:

SUBJECT	+	**ne**	+	VERB	+	**jamais** . . .
Nous		**ne**		regardons		**jamais** la télé.

➡ **Ne** becomes **n'** before a vowel sound.
Nous **n'**allons **jamais** à l'opéra.

➡ Note the use of **ne . . . jamais** in the passé composé:

Nous **n'**avons **jamais** visité Québec.	*We **never** visited Quebec.*
Je **ne** suis **jamais** allé à Genève.	*I **never** went to Geneva.*

8 Jamais le dimanche

Le dimanche les personnes suivantes ne font jamais ce qu'elles font pendant la semaine. Exprimez cette situation.

▶ François va à l'école.
Le dimanche, il ne va jamais à l'école.

1. Anne étudie.
2. Marc travaille.
3. Nous parlons français.
4. Vous allez à la bibliothèque.
5. M. Bernard va en ville.
6. Les élèves mangent à la cantine.
7. Tu rends visite à tes copains.
8. Vous dînez chez vous.
9. Je nettoie ma chambre.
10. Je lave la voiture.

9 Questions personnelles

Dans tes réponses, utilise les expressions **souvent, rarement** ou **ne . . . jamais.**

▶ Est-ce que tu vas souvent au zoo?
Oui, je vais souvent au zoo.
(Non, je vais rarement au zoo.)
(Non, je ne vais jamais au zoo.)

1. Est-ce que tu parles souvent français à la maison?
2. Est-ce que tu mets *(set)* la table?
3. Est-ce que tu fais souvent ton lit?
4. Est-ce que tu téléphones souvent au professeur?
5. Est-ce que tu nages souvent en hiver?
6. Est-ce que tu vas souvent à l'opéra?
7. Est-ce que tu vois souvent des matchs de boxe?
8. Est-ce que tu voyages souvent en limousine?

Do you like cars? Then you must know about Michelin radial tires. But did you know that Michelin employs over 16,000 people in its North American plants in South Carolina, Alabama, and Nova Scotia?

C. Les expressions *quelqu'un, quelque chose* et leurs contraires

Compare the affirmative and negative constructions in heavy print.

—Tu attends **quelqu'un?**	*Are you waiting for **someone (anyone)**?*
—Non, je **n'**attends **personne.**	*No, I'm **not** waiting for **anyone.***
—Vous faites **quelque chose** ce soir?	*Are you doing **something (anything)** tonight?*
—Non, nous **ne** faisons **rien.**	*No, we're **not** doing **anything.***
	*No, we're doing **nothing.***

To refer to unspecified people or things, French speakers use the following expressions:

quelqu'un	*someone, anyone* *somebody, anybody*	**ne . . . personne**	*no one, not anyone* *nobody, not anybody*
quelque chose	*something, anything*	**ne . . . rien**	*nothing, not anything*

➡ Like all negative expressions, **personne** and **rien** require **ne** before the verb. Remember that **ne** becomes **n'** before a vowel sound.

➡ In short answers, **personne** and **rien** may be used alone.

Qui est là? **Personne.**
Qu'est-ce que tu fais? **Rien.**

10 Florence est malade

Florence est malade *(sick)* aujourd'hui. Elle répond négativement aux questions de Paul.

▶ dîner avec quelqu'un?

1. inviter quelqu'un?
2. faire quelque chose ce soir?
3. manger quelque chose à midi?
4. regarder quelque chose à la télé?
5. attendre quelqu'un ce matin?
6. voir quelqu'un cet après-midi?
7. préparer quelque chose pour le dîner?
8. rencontrer quelqu'un après le dîner?

Prononciation

qu /k/

Les lettres «qu»

un bouquet

The letters "**qu**" represent the sound /k/. First, practice with words you know.

Répétez: **qui quand quelque chose quelqu'un quatre quatorze Québec Monique Véronique sympathique un pique-nique le ski nautique**

Now try reading some new words. Make them sound French!

Répétez: **un bouquet un banquet la qualité la quantité la conséquence une équipe** *(team)* **l'équipement fréquent la séquence**

Véronique pense que Monique aime la musique classique.

À votre tour!

1 Allô!

Reconstituez la conversation entre Sophie et Charlotte. Pour cela, faites correspondre les réponses de Charlotte avec les questions de Sophie.

1. Tu es restée chez toi samedi soir?
2. Qu'est-ce que vous avez vu?
3. Qu'est-ce que vous avez fait ensuite?
4. Vous avez mangé quelque chose?
5. À quelle heure es-tu rentrée chez toi?

a. Oui, des sandwichs.
b. À onze heures et demie.
c. Un vieux western avec Gary Cooper.
d. Nous sommes allées dans un café sur le boulevard Saint Michel.
e. Non! J'ai téléphoné à une copine et nous sommes allées au cinéma.

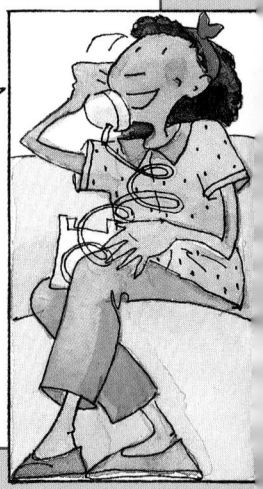

2 Dis-moi ...

I will tell you a few things that I did Saturday; then you will tell me where you went on Saturday and what you did.

- Le matin, je suis resté(e) à la maison. J'ai nettoyé ma chambre.
- L'après-midi, je suis allé(e) au cinéma avec mon copain Jean-Claude. Nous avons vu une comédie. Après, je suis rentré(e) chez moi.
- Le soir, j'ai dîné avec mes parents. Après, je suis resté(e) dans ma chambre et j'ai écouté mes cassettes.

Et maintenant, dis-moi ...

3 Créa-dialogue

Avec vos copains, discutez de ce que vous avez fait récemment *(recently)*. Utilisez les suggestions suivantes.

▶ —Tu es resté(e) chez toi hier matin?
—Oui, je suis resté(e) chez moi.
—Qu'est-ce que tu as fait?
—J'ai nettoyé ma chambre.

▶ —Tu es resté(e) chez toi hier matin?
—Non, je ne suis pas resté(e) chez moi.
—Qu'est-ce que tu as fait?
—Je suis allé(e) à l'école.

▶

hier matin
rester chez toi
??

1. samedi après-midi	2. vendredi soir	3. samedi matin
aller en ville	rentrer chez toi	rester à la maison
??	??	??

4 Situation

Avec un(e) camarade, composez un dialogue correspondant à la situation suivante. Jouez ce dialogue en classe.

Your French friend Marie-Hélène (played by your classmate) has just come back from a vacation with a great suntan. Try to find out . . .

- where she went
- how long **(combien de temps)** she stayed there
- what she did
- when she came back

5 Conversation libre

Avec un(e) camarade, composez un dialogue original basé sur la situation suivante.

You and your cousin Valérie have not seen each other for a while. Talk about what you did either . . .

- last night **(hier soir)**, or
- during spring vacation **(pendant les vacances de printemps)**, or
- during summer vacation **(pendant les vacances d'été)**

You will each ask the other at least three different questions to find out where your cousin went and what she saw or did, etc.

6 Composition: Un voyage

Write a short paragraph describing a trip you took — real or imaginary! You may want to use some of the following suggestions.

aller (où?)
voyager (comment?)
arriver (quel jour?)
rester (où? combien de temps?)
visiter (quoi?)
voir (quoi?)
rencontrer (qui?)
acheter (quoi?)
faire (quoi?)
rentrer (quel jour?)

▶ **L'été dernier, je suis allé(e) à Montréal . . .**

dimanche dernier	5. le weekend dernier	6. la semaine dernière	7. le mois dernier	8. l'été dernier
aller à la plage	aller à la campagne	aller à une boum	faire un voyage	travailler
??	??	??	??	??

Comment dit-on . . . ?

How to celebrate a happy occasion:

Bon anniversaire!

Bonne année!

Petit test culturel

Sports, vacances et tourisme

Quand on est en vacances, on aime voyager. Est-ce que vous pouvez répondre aux questions suivantes? Vérifiez vos réponses au bas° de la page.

1 Christèle habite à Paris. Elle va passer les vacances à Nice chez des cousins. Où est-ce qu'elle va passer les vacances?
a. à la mer
b. à la montagne
c. à la campagne
d. chez elle

2 Les Dupont adorent passer les vacances à la montagne. Cette année ils ont réservé une chambre d'hôtel. Dans quelle ville?
a. à Bordeaux
b. à Marseille
c. à Grenoble
d. à Tours

3 En hiver, beaucoup de touristes vont à la Martinique. Quel sport est-ce qu'on ne peut° pas pratiquer là-bas?
a. le ski
b. le ski nautique
c. la voile
d. la planche à voile

4 Nous sommes en février. Un copain revient de vacances bien bronzé.° Il dit:° «J'ai passé d'excellentes vacances dans une île° où on parle français.» Où est-il allé?
a. aux Bermudes
b. à Tahiti
c. à Puerto Rico
d. à la Jamaïque

5 Madame Gilbert travaille pour une agence de tourisme. Samedi dernier, elle est allée de Paris à New York. Elle dit: «J'ai fait la traversée° de l'Atlantique en trois heures!» Quel avion est-ce qu'elle a pris?°
a. un Boeing 747
b. un DC-10
c. un Airbus
d. un Concorde

6 Quand il est rentré de vacances, Jean-François a dit:° «J'ai passé un mois magnifique chez mon oncle en Bretagne.» Dans quelle partie de la France est-ce qu'il est allé?
a. à l'ouest°
b. à l'est
c. au sud
d. au nord

RÉPONSES:
1a. Nice est une ville située sur la mer Méditerranée. 2c. Grenoble est une ville située dans les Alpes. 3a. La Martinique est une île tropicale. On ne peut pas faire de ski à la Martinique. 4b. Tahiti est une île française située dans l'océan Pacifique sud. 5d. Le Concorde est un avion supersonique. 6a. La Bretagne est une région située dans l'ouest de la France.

au bas *at the bottom* **peut** *can* **bronzé** *tanned* **dit** *says* **île** *island* **traversée** *crossing* **a pris** *did . . . take* **a dit** *said* **ouest** *west*

EN FRANCE

Vive le sport!

Quels sports pratiquez-vous pendant les vacances? Où allez-vous pour pratiquer votre sport favori? Voici plusieurs possibilités:

- Quels sports est-ce qu'on peut pratiquer dans ce club?
- En quelle saison?
- Quel est le numéro de téléphone du club?

- Comment s'appelle ce club?
- Quels sports est-ce qu'on peut pratiquer dans ce club?

- Comment s'appelle ce centre de loisirs?°
- Quels sports est-ce qu'on peut pratiquer?
- Quelles autres° activités sont offertes?

Vous avez la possibilité d'aller dans un des endroits mentionnés plus haut.° Quel endroit est-ce que vous allez choisir? Pourquoi?

loisirs *leisure activities* **autres** *other* **plus haut** *above*

Entre amis: Le weekend

Qu'est-ce que vous faites le weekend? Qu'est ce que vous avez fait le weekend dernier? Voici les réponses de cinq jeunes du monde° francophone.°

Carole, 15 ans, France
Le weekend dernier, j'ai fait une promenade en mobylette avec une copine. Nous sommes allées à la campagne. À midi, on a fait un pique-nique. Après, on a visité un vieux château en ruines. Malheureusement,° j'ai eu une crevaison.° Je suis rentrée chez moi seulement° pour le dîner. Après le dîner, j'ai regardé la télé et j'ai fait mes devoirs pour lundi.

Pierre, 16 ans, la Martinique
Le samedi, je joue généralement au foot. Je fais partie de° l'équipe° junior de mon village. Le week-end dernier, nous avons fait un match. Nous avons bien joué, mais nous avons perdu! Après le match, je suis allé à la plage. Le soir, je suis allé chez des copains. Nous avons mis de la musique et nous avons dansé.

Yvan, 14 ans, Québec
Le matin, je suis allé à la patinoire° avec des copains, mais je ne suis pas resté très longtemps.° À midi, je suis rentré chez moi. L'après-midi, j'ai aidé mes parents à repeindre° la cuisine. Pour le dîner, nous sommes allés au restaurant.

monde *world* **francophone** *French-speaking* **Malheureusement** *Unfortunately* **crevaison** *flat tire* **seulement** *just* **cadeau** *present* **soie** *silk* **d'autres** *other* **soirée** *evening* **fais partie de** *am a member of* **équipe** *team* **Une centaine** *About a hundred* **repas** *meal* **rôtit** *roasts* **mouton** *sheep* **à la broche** *on the spit* **occasion** *chance* **tous** *all* **On s'est bien amusé!** *We had a good time!* **patinoire** *skating rink* **très longtemps** *for a very long time* **repeindre** *to repaint*

Élisabeth, 15 ans, Belgique
Samedi matin, j'ai fait des achats. J'ai choisi un cadeau° pour l'anniversaire de mon père. (J'ai acheté une cravate en soie.°) L'après-midi, je suis allée au ciné-club avec un copain. Nous avons vu *Les Temps modernes*, un vieux film de Charlie Chaplin. Après, nous sommes allés dans un café et nous avons rencontré d'autres° copains. J'ai passé la soirée° en famille.

Djemila, 16 ans, Algérie
Samedi dernier, nous avons eu une grande réunion de famille chez mon oncle Karim. Une centaine° de personnes sont venues. Nous avons fait un «méchoui». (C'est un repas° où on rôtit° un mouton° entier à la broche.°) J'ai eu l'occasion° de voir tous° mes cousins et cousines. On s'est bien amusé!°

NOTES CULTURELLES

1 L'Algérie

L'Algérie est un pays° d'Afrique du Nord. C'est une ancienne° colonie française. Aujourd'hui beaucoup de familles d'origine algérienne habitent en France. Dans ces familles, on parle généralement français et arabe.

Comment lire

WORDS WITH SEVERAL MEANINGS

Sometimes a word may have several meanings. For example, the French word **temps** can mean:

weather	Quel beau **temps!**
time	Je n'ai pas le **temps** d'aller au cinéma.

Enrichissez votre vocabulaire

MORE COGNATE PATTERNS

Here are two important cognate patterns that will help you read French more easily.

- French verbs in **-er** sometimes correspond to English verbs in *-ate.*
  situer *situate*
  Note also how this pattern works in past participles:
  situé *situated*
- The circumflex accent on a vowel often indicates that the English cognate contains an *"s"*.
  rôtir *to roast*
  coûter *to cost*

Activité

Can you identify the English equivalents of the following French words?

- **séparer indiquer associer apprécier opérer décoré créé libéré illustré agité animé**
- **un hôpital une forêt honnête en hâte une hôtesse une île**

2 La Belgique

La Belgique est un petit pays situé au nord-est° de la France. Sa capitale, Bruxelles, est un centre européen important. La Belgique est un pays bilingue. Les langues officielles sont le français et le flamand.°

pays *country* **ancienne** *former*
nord-est *northeast* **flamand** *Flemish*

Activité: Une lettre

Imaginez que vous avez passé le weekend avec l'une des cinq personnes. Choisissez cette personne (Carole, Élisabeth, Pierre, Djemila ou Yvan). Dans une lettre, décrivez ce weekend de votre point de vue personnel.

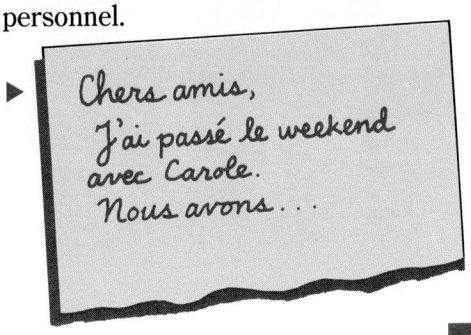

Variétés

Les quatre erreurs d'Hélène

Pendant les vacances, Hélène Ladoucette, une jeune étudiante québécoise, est allée en France. Là, elle a voyagé et elle a visité beaucoup d'endroits différents. Pendant son voyage, elle a écrit des cartes postales à ses copains. Dans chaque° carte postale, Hélène a fait une erreur.° (Les erreurs d'Hélène concernent l'histoire ou la géographie.) Pouvez-vous° trouver ces erreurs? Lisez° attentivement chaque carte et découvrez° l'erreur qui s'y trouve.°

Paris, le 2 juillet

Cher Alain,

Je suis arrivée à Paris samedi dernier. Avant hier,° j'ai visité Notre-Dame et le musée d'Orsay. Hier, j'ai rendu visite à une copine parisienne. Nous avons fait une promenade sur la Saône en bateau-mouche.° Après, nous sommes allées dans un restaurant qui s'appelle la "Petite Marmite". J'ai mangé des escargots!°

Amitiés, Hélène

PARIS

Deauville, le 8 juillet

Ma chère Pauline,

Je suis maintenant en Normandie. Je suis venue ici avec Véronique, ma copine parisienne. Il y a beaucoup de choses à faire ici. Hier, nous avons visité le Havre, un grand port sur l'Atlantique. Aujourd'hui, nous sommes allées sur les plages où les soldats° canadiens et américains ont débarqué° en 1944. C'est très impressionnant!°

Amicalement, Hélène

NORMANDIE

chaque *each* **erreur** *mistake*
Pouvez-vous *Can you* **Lisez** *Read* **découvrez** *discover*
qui s'y trouve *that is there* **Avant hier** *The day before yesterday*
bateau-mouche *sight-seeing boat* **escargots** *snails*
soldats *soldiers* **ont débarqué** *landed* **impressionnant** *impressive*

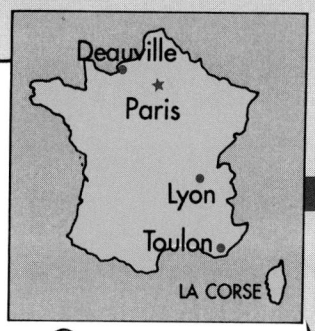

Lyon, le 10 juillet

Mes chers cousins,

Un grand bonjour de Lyon! Je suis arrivée ici hier matin. J'ai voyagé en TGV. Le TGV est un train très confortable et très rapide. (Je suis allée de Paris à Lyon en moins de° deux heures!) Lyon est une ville très moderne et très ancienne aussi. Elle a été fondée en 43 avant Jésus-Christ°. Ce matin, j'ai visité le musée du Louvre. Là, j'ai admiré les antiquités romaines.°

Affectueusement,
Hélène

LYON

TOULON

Toulon, le 15 juillet

Ma chère Michèle,

Je suis arrivée ici hier, 14 juillet, pour la fête nationale française. Le matin, j'ai vu un défilé° militaire. Le soir, j'ai assisté aux feux d'artifices° et j'ai dansé dans les rues. Toulon est situé sur la Méditerranée. Demain, je vais aller en Corse° en bateau. La Corse est une île italienne très célèbre° parce que c'est là que Napoléon est né.°

Je t'embrasse,
Hélène

LES QUATRE ERREURS D'HÉLÈNE:

1. Paris est situé sur la Seine, et non sur la Saône. 2. Les soldats canadiens et américains ont débarqué en Normandie en 1944, et non en 1844. 3. Le musée du Louvre est à Paris, pas à Lyon. 4. La Corse est une île française, et non italienne.

moins de *less than* **43 avant Jésus-Christ** *43 B.C.* **romaines** *Roman* **défilé** *parade* **feux d'artifices** *fireworks* **Corse** *Corsica* **célèbre** *famous* **est né** *was born*

UNITÉ

9 Les repas

LEÇON 33 Le français pratique: Les repas et la nourriture

LEÇON 34 À la cantine

LEÇON 35 Un client difficile

LEÇON 36 Pique-nique

THÈME ET OBJECTIFS

Food and meals

Eating well is essential if we want to stay fit and healthy. Moreover, it can also be an enjoyable experience.

In the lessons of this unit, you will learn . . .

- to talk about your favorite foods
- to describe the different meals of the day
- to prepare a shopping list and do the grocery shopping
- to order a meal in a restaurant
- to set the table

You will also be able . . .

- to ask for a certain amount or a certain quantity of something
- to ask people to do things for you

Finally, you will learn how to express yourself more fluently by using object pronouns.

LEÇON 33

LE FRANÇAIS PRATIQUE

Les repas et la nourriture

Accent sur . . . Les repas français

For French people, a meal is more than just food served on a plate. It is a social occasion in which family and friends sit down together to enjoy one another's company. French meals are different from American meals not only in terms of the foods and beverages that are served, but also in the way these foods are presented and in the order in which they are served.

- **Le petit déjeuner** (*Breakfast*)
  The French **petit déjeuner** is simpler and not as abundant as the American breakfast. Usually it consists of bread, warm toast **(du pain grillé)** or dry toast **(des biscottes),** eaten with butter and jam. Children drink hot milk with coffee **(du café au lait)** or hot chocolate served in deep bowls. On Sundays or special occasions, the first person up may go out to buy fresh croissants.

- **Le déjeuner** (*Lunch*)
  The French **déjeuner** is traditionally the main meal of the day. It begins with one or several appetizers **(les hors d'oeuvre),** such as salami, cucumber salad, radishes, and grated carrots. Next, comes the main course **(le plat principal),** which may be a meat or fish dish accompanied by vegetables. This is followed by a green salad, a cheese course, and a dessert. Children drink water, mineral water, apple cider, or carbonated fruit juices. Adults drink mineral water and sometimes may enjoy a glass of wine. When coffee is served, it always comes at the very end of the meal.

- **Le goûter** (*Afternoon snack*)
  When children come back from school, they often have a light snack which traditionally consists of bread and a piece of chocolate. Some days they may stop at the pastry shop **(la pâtisserie)** for a **pain au chocolat** (a croissant-like pastry with chocolate inside).

- **Le dîner** (*Supper*)
  In France, supper is served between seven and eight o'clock. It is traditionally a simpler meal than lunch, consisting of soup, a light main course (such as a slice of ham, an omelet, pasta, or a light meat dish), and then a green salad and a simple dessert (yogurt or fruit).

  Supper is a sit-down meal, served once everyone is home. This is the occasion for parents and children to spend time together and talk about the events of the day. (In France, children are not allowed to go to the refrigerator and fix their own meals. They are expected to sit down at the table and are not excused until everyone is finished.)

A. Les repas et la table

How to talk about meals:

—En général, à quelle heure est-ce que tu **prends le petit déjeuner** *(have breakfast)*?
—Je prends le petit déjeuner à sept heures et demie.
—Où est-ce que tu vas **déjeuner** *(to have lunch)* aujourd'hui?
—Je vais déjeuner à **la cantine de l'école** *(school cafeteria)*.

Les repas et la nourriture

NOMS		VERBES	
un repas	*meal*		
le petit déjeuner	*breakfast*	**prendre le petit déjeuner**	*to have breakfast*
le déjeuner	*lunch*	**déjeuner**	*to have lunch*
le dîner	*dinner*	**dîner**	*to have dinner*
la nourriture	*food*		
la cuisine	*cooking, cuisine*		

—Tu peux **mettre** *(set)* la table?
—D'accord. Je vais mettre la table.

1 Et toi?

Exprime tes préférences. Pour cela complète les phrases suivantes.

1. Mon repas préféré est …	• le petit déjeuner • le dîner	• le déjeuner
2. Je préfère déjeuner …	• chez moi • à la cantine de l'école	• dans un fast food • … ?
3. En général, la nourriture de la cantine de l'école est …	• excellente • bonne	• mauvaise • … ?
4. Je préfère dîner …	• chez moi • chez mes copains	• au restaurant • … ?
5. Je préfère la nourriture …	• mexicaine • italienne	• chinoise • … ?
6. Quand je dois aider avec le dîner, je préfère …	• préparer la salade • mettre la table	• laver les assiettes • … ?

2 Questions personnelles

1. À quelle heure est-ce que tu prends ton petit déjeuner le lundi? Et le dimanche?
2. En général, à quelle heure est-ce que tu dînes?
3. Où est-ce que tu déjeunes pendant la semaine? le samedi? le dimanche?
4. Où est-ce que tu as déjeuné hier? Avec qui?
5. Où est-ce que tu vas dîner ce soir? Avec qui?
6. Est-ce que tu vas souvent au restaurant? Quand? Avec qui? Quel est ton restaurant préféré?
7. Est-ce que tu as jamais *(ever)* déjeuné dans un restaurant français? (dans un restaurant mexicain? dans un restaurant italien? dans un restaurant chinois? dans un restaurant vietnamien?) Quand et avec qui?
8. Est-ce que tu mets la table chez toi? Qui a mis la table pour le petit déjeuner? Et pour le dîner?

3 Au restaurant

Vous êtes dans un restaurant français. Vous avez commandé *(ordered)* les choses suivantes. Le serveur a oublié *(forgot)* d'apporter le nécessaire (les ustensiles, etc.).

▶ pour le jus d'orange

1. pour l'eau minérale *(mineral water)*
2. pour le thé
3. pour la soupe
4. pour les frites
5. pour le steak
6. pour le gâteau *(cake)*

B. La nourriture et les boissons

How to express food preferences:

— Est-ce que tu aimes **le poisson** *(fish)*?
— Oui, j'aime le poisson mais je préfère **la viande** *(meat)*.
— Quelle viande est-ce que tu aimes?
— J'aime **le rosbif** *(roast beef)* et **le poulet** *(chicken)*.

Les plats *(m.)*
(Dishes)

Les Plats

Pour le déjeuner et le dîner

Les hors d'oeuvre *(m.)*
(appetizers)

la soupe

le jambon
(ham)

le saucisson
(salami)

Le poisson
(fish)

la sole

le thon
(tuna)

La viande
(meat)

le veau
(veal)

le rosbif

le poulet

Pour le petit déjeuner

le pain

la confiture

le beurre

un oeuf

les céréales *(f.)*

Les autres plats
(other dishes)

les spaghetti *(m.)*

les frites *(f.)*
(French fries)

le riz
(rice)

aimer	*to like*	Alice **aime** le poulet.
préférer	*to prefer*	Philippe **préfère** le rosbif.
détester	*to hate*	Paul **déteste** le poisson.

Les Plats

Les ingrédients *(m.)*

la mayonnaise

le ketchup

le sucre *(sugar)*

le sel *(salt)*

La salade et le fromage

le fromage *(cheese)*

la salade *(lettuce)*

le yaourt

Le dessert

le gâteau *(cake)*

la glace *(ice cream)*

la tarte *(pie)*

Les boissons (une boisson) *(drink, beverage)*

le jus d'orange

le thé glacé *(iced tea)*

le lait *(milk)*

l'eau *(f.)* *(water)*

l'eau minérale

le jus de pomme *(apple juice)*

4 Vous aimez ça?

Dites si oui ou non vous aimez les choses suivantes.

- J'aime ...
- J'aime beaucoup ...
- Je n'aime pas ...
- Je déteste ...

5 Dîner avec André

Vous dînez avec André, un ami canadien. Demandez à André de passer les choses suivantes.

▶ —S'il te plaît, André, passe-moi le pain.
—Tiens. Voilà le pain.
—Merci.

6 La Petite Marmite

Vous dînez au restaurant français La Petite Marmite. Le garçon demande ce que vous préférez. Répondez-lui.

La Petite Marmite
menu

- soupe / saucisson
- viande / poisson
- poulet / veau
- sole / thon
- frites / spaghetti
- fromage / salade
- yaourt / glace
- tarte / gâteau
- thé / café

7 Dans le réfrigérateur ou sur la table?

Choisissez un produit et demandez à vos camarades où est le produit. Ils vont dire si le produit est dans le réfrigérateur ou sur la table.

8 Les préférences

Indiquez les préférences culinaires des personnes suivantes en complétant les phrases.

1. J'aime . . .
2. Je déteste . . .
3. Ma mère aime . . .
4. Mon petit frère (ma petite soeur) déteste . . .
5. Mon copain aime . . .
6. Ma copine déteste . . .
7. Les enfants aiment . . .
8. En général, les Italiens aiment . . .
9. En général, les Japonais aiment . . .

9 Les courses *(Food shopping)*

Vous passez les vacances en France avec votre famille. Faites la liste des courses pour les repas suivants.

▶ un repas végétarien

LISTE

▶ Un repas végétarien:
- oeufs
- salade
- fromage
- pain
- yaourt
- eau minérale

1. un pique-nique à la campagne
2. un bon petit déjeuner
3. un repas d'anniversaire
4. le dîner de ce soir
5. le déjeuner de demain
6. un repas de régime *(diet)*

C. Les fruits et les légumes *(Fruits and vegetables)*

How to shop for food:

À la maison

— Où vas-tu?
— Je vais au **marché.**
Je vais **faire les courses** *(to do the food shopping).*
— Qu'est-ce que tu vas acheter?
— Je vais acheter des **tomates** et des **oranges.**

Au marché

— Pardon, madame. Combien coûtent les **pommes?**
— Elles coûtent dix francs le kilo.
— Donnez-moi deux **kilos de** pommes, s'il vous plaît.
— Voilà. Ça fait vingt francs.

10 Qu'est-ce que vous préférez?

Indiquez vos préférences.

▶ pour le petit déjeuner: un oeuf ou des céréales? **Je préfère des céréales.**

1. pour le petit déjeuner: un pamplemousse ou une banane?
2. après le déjeuner: une pomme ou une poire?
3. avec le poulet: des haricots verts ou des petits pois?
4. avec le steak: des pommes de terre ou des carottes?
5. comme *(as)* salade: une salade de tomates ou une salade de concombres *(cucumbers)?*
6. pour le dessert: une tarte aux cerises ou une tarte aux poires?
7. comme glace: une glace à la vanille ou une glace à la fraise?

11 Les achats

Vos copains reviennent du marché. Demandez ce qu'ils ont acheté.

▶ **—Qu'est-ce que tu as acheté au marché?**
— J'ai acheté des carottes et des tomates.

Les fruits (un fruit)

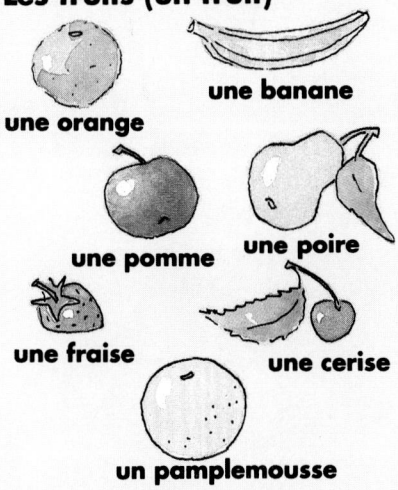

Les légumes (un légume *vegetable*)

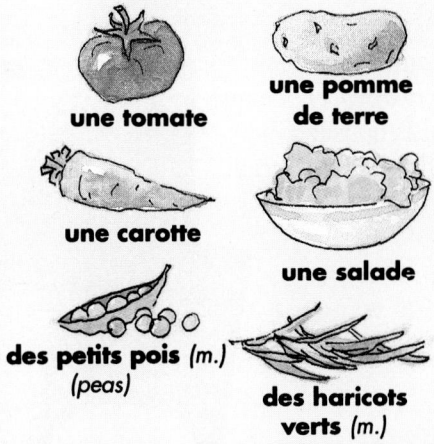

NOTE CULTURELLE

Le marché

In France, as in the United States, most people do their food shopping at the supermarket **(le supermarché).** However, to have fresher fruits and vegetables, many people still go to the local open-air market **(le marché)** where farmers come to sell their produce.

LES QUANTITÉS

une livre (de)	*pound*	**Donnez-moi**	**une livre de** tomates.
un kilo (de)	*kilo (2.2 pounds)*		**un kilo de** pommes.
une douzaine (de)	*dozen*		**une douzaine *d'***oeufs.

12 Au marché

Vous êtes au marché. Demandez au vendeur combien coûtent certaines choses. Dites aussi quelle quantité vous voulez acheter.

À votre tour!

1 Créa-dialogue

Vous êtes à Deauville avec un(e) ami(e). Essayez de découvrir *(try to discover)* ce que votre ami(e) aime manger. Proposez à votre ami(e) de déjeuner dans le restaurant correspondant à ses préférences.

▶ —Tu aimes la viande?
—Non, je n'aime pas la viande.
—Tu aimes les légumes?
—Non, je n'aime pas les légumes.
—Tu aimes le poisson?
—Oui, j'aime beaucoup le poisson.
—On déjeune à La Marine?
—D'accord. ▶

1 CHEZ RIGOLETTO
spécialités italiennes

2 AU PALAIS DES GLACES
spécialités de glaces

3 À la Normandie
spécialités de fromages

4 À LA CAMPAGNE
Restaurant végétarien

5 L'Auvergnat
spécialités de jambon

6 CHEZ OBÉLIX
spécialités de bonnes viandes

7 Au petit gourmand
ses glaces et ses gâteaux

2 Conversation dirigée

Avec un(e) camarade, composez un dialogue basé sur les instructions suivantes. C'est samedi aujourd'hui. Ce matin Marc et Juliette ont fait des achats en ville. Il est midi et demi maintenant.

Marc		Juliette
asks Juliette if she is hungry	→ ←	says she is very hungry
asks her if she wants to have lunch	→ ↙	answers yes
asks if she likes Italian cooking (**la cuisine italienne**)	→ ↙	says that she prefers French cooking
asks her if she likes meat	→ ↙	says she does, but that she also likes vegetables
suggests they go to La Campagne	→	accepts

3 Composition: À la pension

This summer you are going to spend two weeks in France with your family. There are five people in your family and you are going to stay in a **pension** *(an inn offering a room and all meals)*. Write a letter to the owner saying what each family member likes or does not like to eat. Use your imagination.

le 18 mai

Chère Madame,

J'aime . . .
Je n'aime pas . . .
Mon père aime . . .
Il n'aime pas . . .
Ma mère . . .
Mon frère . . .
Ma soeur . . .

4 Au «Départ»

Vous êtes à Paris avec des copains. Il est une heure et vous avez faim. Vous allez déjeuner dans le café suivant.

Regardez bien les illustrations.

- Comment s'appelle le café?
- Où est-il situé?

Regardez le menu et choisissez un sandwich ou une salade et un dessert (crêpe ou pâtisserie).

- Qu'est-ce que vous avez choisi?
- Combien coûte le sandwich ou la salade? le dessert?
- Quel est le prix total de votre repas?

Salades Composées

SALADE NIÇOISE 38,00
Salade, thon, olives, tomates, oeuf dur, anchois, poivron
Lettuce, tuna, olives, tomatoes, hard-boiled egg, anchovies, sweet pepper

SALADE 4 SAISON 30,00
Crudités de saison
Vegetables in season

SALADE SAINT-MICHEL 35,00
Salade, jambon épaule, comté, pomme fruit
Lettuce, ham, Comté cheese, apples

SALADE MIXTE..... 28,00
Salade, tomates, oeuf dur
Lettuce, tomatoes, hard-boiled egg

SALADE DE POULET..... 38,00
Salade, poulet, comté, mayonnaise
Lettuce, chicken, Comté cheese, mayonnaise

SALADE CAMPAGNARDE 38,00
Salade, pommes de terre à l'huile, cantal, jambon cru
Lettuce, potato salad, Cantal cheese, country ham

SALADE VERTE.....17,00
Green salad

Sandwichs

Rillettes paysannes 14,00
Country minced potted pork

Paté du Quercy 14,00
Quercy style meat pie

Jambon de Paris 14,00
Paris ham

Saucisson d'Auvergne ...14,00
Dry sausage from Auvergne

Le Végétarien 26,00
Salade, tomate, oeuf dur
Lettuce, tomato, hard-boiled egg

Fromage 14,00
Cheese

Mixte (jambon et gruyère) 26,00
Combination (ham and Gruyère cheese)

Club Sandwich 35,00
Poulet, tomate, oeuf dur, salade, mayonnaise
Chicken, tomato, hard-boiled egg, lettuce, mayonnaise

Saucisses chaudes 21,00
Hot sausages

Crêpes Maison

Crêpe au sucre.....14,00
Pancake sprinkled with sugar

Crêpe à la confiture.....18,00
Groseille, abricot, fraise
Pancake with red currant, apricot, or strawberry jam

Crêpe aux noix et crème de cassis 27,00
Pancake with nuts and black currant cream

Crêpe aux marrons et Chantilly 27,00
Pancake with chestnuts and whipped cream

Crêpe au miel 23,00
Pancake with honey

Crêpe au Grand-Marnier 27,00
Pancake with Grand-Marnier

Crêpe Belle-Époque 37,00
Banane fruit, glace vanille, noisettes, Chantilly
Pancake with bananas, vanilla ice cream, chestnuts, whipped cream

Crêpe au chocolat 23,00
Pancake with chocolate sauce

Pâtisseries

Tarte du jour 25,00
Tart of the day

Tarte aux pommes 22,00
Apple tart

Tarte aux fraises (selon saison) 29,00
Strawberry tart (in season)

Salade de fruits rafraîchis.....21,00
Cold fruit salad

Gâteau du jour 25,00
Cake of the day

Tarte Tatin chaude....29,00
Hot Tatin tart

Tarte Tatin chaude, crème fraîche.....33,00
Hot Tatin tart with cream

PRIX SERVIS COMPRIS (15%)

LEÇON 34

À la cantine

Il est midi et demi. Sophie va à la cantine. Elle rencontre Jean-Paul.

SOPHIE: Est-ce que tu veux déjeuner avec moi?
JEAN-PAUL: Ça dépend. Qu'est-ce qu'il y a aujourd'hui?
SOPHIE: Il y a du poisson!
JEAN-PAUL: Du poisson?
SOPHIE: Oui, du poisson.
JEAN-PAUL: Quelle horreur! Bon, aujourd'hui, je ne veux pas déjeuner. *How disgusting!*
SOPHIE: Il y a aussi du gâteau.
JEAN-PAUL: Du gâteau! Hm . . .
SOPHIE: Et de la glace!
JEAN-PAUL: Une minute . . . je vais prendre un plateau. *to take/tray*

Compréhension

1. À quelle heure est-ce que Sophie va déjeuner?
2. Qui est-ce qu'elle rencontre?
3. Est-ce que Jean-Paul aime le poisson?
4. Qu'est-ce qu'il aime?
5. Est-ce qu'il va déjeuner avec Sophie? Pourquoi?

Et toi?

1. En général, où est-ce que tu déjeunes?
2. À quelle heure est-ce que tu déjeunes?
3. En général, est-ce que tu aimes la nourriture de la cantine?
4. Qu'est-ce que tu fais quand tu n'aimes pas la nourriture de la cantine?

NOTE CULTURELLE

À la cantine

Où est-ce que tu déjeunes pendant la semaine? Quand on habite près de l'école, on peut° rentrer à la maison. Quand on habite loin, on déjeune à la cantine. À midi, beaucoup de jeunes Français déjeunent à la cantine de leur école.

À la cantine, chacun° prend° un plateau et va chercher° sa nourriture. Cette nourriture est généralement bonne, abondante° et variée. Le menu change chaque° jour de la semaine. Un repas typique inclut° les plats suivants:

- **un hors d'oeuvre**
  salade de concombres,
  salade de pommes de terre,
  carottes râpées,° jambon . . .
- **un plat principal° chaud**
  poulet, steak, côtelette de porc°
- **une garniture°**
  spaghetti, frites, petits pois,
  purée de pommes de terre°
- **une salade verte**
- **du fromage**
- **un dessert**
  glace ou fruit
- **une boisson**
  eau minérale, limonade, jus de fruit

Où est-ce que tu préférerais° déjeuner? À ton école ou dans une école française?

peut *can* **chacun** *each one* **prend** *takes* **chercher** *to get* **abondante** *plentiful* **chaque** *each* **inclut** *includes* **râpées** *grated* **principal** *main* **côtelette de porc** *pork chop* **garniture** *side dish* **purée de pommes de terre** *mashed potatoes* **est-ce que tu préférerais** *would you prefer*

A. Le verbe *vouloir*

Note the forms of the irregular verb **vouloir** *(to want)*.

INFINITIVE	**vouloir**	
PRESENT	Je **veux** aller au café. Tu **veux** déjeuner. Il / Elle / On **veut** dîner.	Nous **voulons** une glace. Vous **voulez** des spaghetti. Ils / Elles **veulent** des frites.
PASSÉ COMPOSÉ	J'**ai** **voulu** dîner chez Maxim's.	

➡ When making a request, French people often use **je voudrais** *(I would like)*, which is more polite than **je veux** *(I want)*.

Je voudrais un café. — ***I would like*** *a cup of coffee.*
Je voudrais dîner. — ***I would like*** *to have dinner.*

➡ When accepting an offer, the French often use the expression **je veux bien.**

— Est-ce que tu veux déjeuner avec moi? — *Do you want to have lunch with me?*
— Oui, **je veux bien.** — *Yes,* ***I do.*** *(Yes, I want to.)*

1 Vive la différence!

Nous sommes samedi. Des amis vont en ville. Pour le déjeuner, chacun veut faire des choses différentes.

▶ Cécile / aller dans un café
Cécile veut aller dans un café.

1. nous / manger des frites
2. toi / manger une pizza
3. vous / aller dans un restaurant italien
4. moi / aller dans un restaurant chinois
5. Patrick et Alain / déjeuner à midi
6. Isabelle / déjeuner à une heure

2 Oui ou non?

Dites si oui ou non les personnes entre parenthèses veulent faire les choses indiquées.

▶ Il est midi. (nous / déjeuner?)
Oui, nous voulons déjeuner.

▶ C'est samedi. (les élèves / étudier?)
Non, les élèves ne veulent pas étudier.

1. Il fait froid. (Éric / jouer au foot?)
2. Il fait beau. (mes copains / aller à la plage?)
3. La nourriture est mauvaise. (vous / déjeuner à la cantine?)
4. Il y a des spaghetti. (moi / dîner?)
5. Il y a une excellente comédie. (toi / regarder la télé?)
6. C'est dimanche. (nous / travailler)

3 Expression personnelle

Complétez les phrases suivantes avec une expression personnelle.

1. Ce weekend, je voudrais ...
   Je ne veux pas ...
2. Cet été, je voudrais ...
   Je ne veux pas ...
3. Après l'école, je voudrais ...
   Je ne veux pas ...
4. Dans la vie *(life)*, je voudrais ...
   Je ne veux pas ...

B. Le verbe *prendre*

Note the forms of the irregular verb **prendre** *(to take)*.

INFINITIVE	**prendre**	
PRESENT	Je **prends** une pizza. Tu **prends** un sandwich. Il / Elle/On **prend** une salade.	Nous **prenons** le train. Vous **prenez** l'avion. Ils / Elles **prennent** des photos.
PASSÉ COMPOSÉ	J'**ai** **pris** un steak.	

➡ The singular forms of **prendre** follow the pattern of regular **-re** verbs. The plural forms are irregular.

Vocabulaire: Verbes comme *prendre*

prendre	*to take*	Nous **prenons** le métro.
	to have (food)	Est-ce que tu **prends** un café?
apprendre	*to learn*	Nous **apprenons** le français.
apprendre à + *inf.*	*to learn how to*	Sophie **apprend à** jouer de la guitare.
comprendre	*to understand*	Est-ce que vous **comprenez** quand le professeur parle français?

4 Qu'est-ce qu'ils prennent?

Dites ce que les personnes suivantes prennent. Pour cela, choisissez une expression logique de la liste.

▶ Philippe a faim.
Il prend un steak et des frites.

1. J'ai très soif.
2. Vous n'avez pas très faim.
3. Hélène a un nouvel appareil-photo.
4. Tu vas à l'aéroport.
5. Nous allons à l'école.
6. Les touristes vont à la Statue de la Liberté.

un bateau
un taxi
le bus
des photos
une salade
une limonade
un steak et des frites

5 Questions personnelles

1. À quelle heure est-ce que tu prends le petit déjeuner le lundi? Et le dimanche?
2. Est-ce que tu prends le bus pour aller à l'école? Et tes copains?
3. Est-ce que tu prends des photos? Avec quel appareil?
4. Quand tu fais un grand voyage, est-ce que tu prends l'autocar? le train? l'avion?
5. Est-ce que tu apprends le français? l'italien? l'espagnol? Et ton copain?
6. Est-ce que tu apprends à jouer du piano? à jouer de la guitare? à faire du ski? à faire de la planche à voile?
7. Où est-ce que tu as appris à nager? À quel âge?
8. Est-ce que tu comprends bien quand le professeur parle français? Et les autres *(other)* élèves?
9. À ton avis, est-ce que les adultes comprennent les jeunes? Est-ce que les jeunes comprennent les adultes?

C. L'article partitif: *du, de la*

Learning about language

The pictures on the left represent *whole* items: a whole chicken, a whole cake, a whole head of lettuce, a whole fish. The nouns are introduced by INDEFINITE ARTICLES: **un, une.**

The pictures on the right represent a *part* or *some quantity* of these items: a serving of chicken, a slice of cake, some leaves of lettuce, a piece of fish. The nouns are introduced by PARTITIVE ARTICLES: **du, de la.**

Voici . . .

un poulet

un gâteau

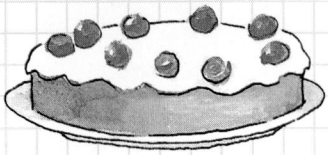

une salade

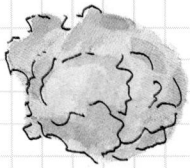

une sole

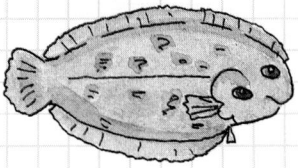

Voilà . . .

du poulet

du gâteau

de la salade

de la sole

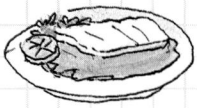

FORMS

The PARTITIVE ARTICLE is used to refer to A CERTAIN QUANTITY or A CERTAIN AMOUNT OF SOMETHING and corresponds to the English *some* or *any.* It has the following forms:

MASCULINE	**du** *some*	**du** fromage, **du** pain
FEMININE	**de la** *some*	**de la** salade, **de la** limonade

➡ Note that **du** and **de la** become **de l'** before a vowel sound.

de l'eau minérale

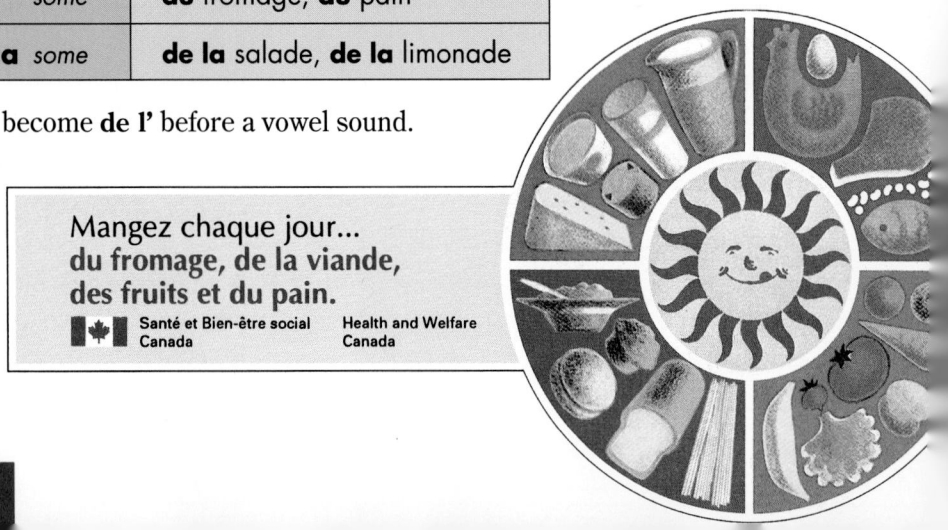

USES

Note how the partitive article is used in the sentences below.

Philippe mange **du** fromage.	*Philippe is eating (some) cheese.*
Nous prenons **de la** salade.	*We are having (some) salad.*
—Est-ce que tu veux **du** lait?	*Do you want (any, some) milk?*
—Non, mais je voudrais **de l'**eau.	*No, but I would like some water.*

- While the words *some* or *any* are often omitted in English, the articles **du** and **de la** must be used in French.
- Partitive articles may also be used with nouns designating things other than foods and beverages. For example:

Tu as **de l'argent?**	*Do you have (any) money?*

Partitive articles are often, but not always, used after the following expressions and verbs.

voici	**Voici du** pain.	*Here is (some) bread.*
voilà	**Voilà de la** mayonnaise.	*Here is (some) mayonnaise.*
il y a	Est-ce qu'**il y a de la** salade?	*Is there (any) salad?*
acheter	Nous **achetons du** fromage.	*We are buying (some) cheese.*
avoir	Est-ce que tu **as de la** limonade?	*Do you have (any) lemon soda?*
manger	Marc **mange du** rosbif.	*Marc is eating (some) roast beef.*
prendre	Est-ce que vous **prenez du** café?	*Are you having (any) coffee?*
vouloir	Est-ce que tu **veux de la** glace?	*Do you want (any) ice cream?*

Voici un gâteau.

Voici du gâteau.

6 Le menu

Vous avez préparé un dîner pour le Club Français. Dites à un(e) camarade ce qu'il y a au menu.

▶ la viande **Il y a de la viande.**

1. le rosbif
2. le poulet
3. la salade
4. le fromage
5. la glace
6. la tarte
7. l'eau minérale
8. le jus d'orange

7 Au choix

Vous déjeunez avec votre famille. Offrez aux membres de votre famille le choix entre les choses suivantes. Ils vont indiquer leurs préférences.

▶ le lait ou l'eau minérale?

1. la soupe ou la salade?
2. le poisson ou la viande?
3. le rosbif ou le poulet?
4. le ketchup ou le mayonnaise?
5. le fromage ou la yaourt?
6. le beurre ou la margarine?
7. le gâteau ou la tarte?
8. le jus d'orange ou le jus de pomme?

8 Qu'est-ce qu'on met?

Dites quels produits de la liste on met dans ou sur les choses suivantes.

▶ **On met du beurre (de la confiture) sur le pain.**

1. On met … dans le café.
2. On met … dans le thé.
3. On met … dans la soupe.
4. On met … dans un sandwich.
5. On met … sur un hamburger.
6. On met … sur un hot dog.
7. On met … dans les céréales.
8. On met … sur un toast.

le fromage
le jambon
le beurre
la confiture
le ketchup
la mayonnaise
le sel
la crème
le sucre
la moutarde (mustard)
le lait

9 Les courses

M. Simon a fait les courses. Dites ce qu'il a acheté.

▶ **Il a acheté de la viande.**

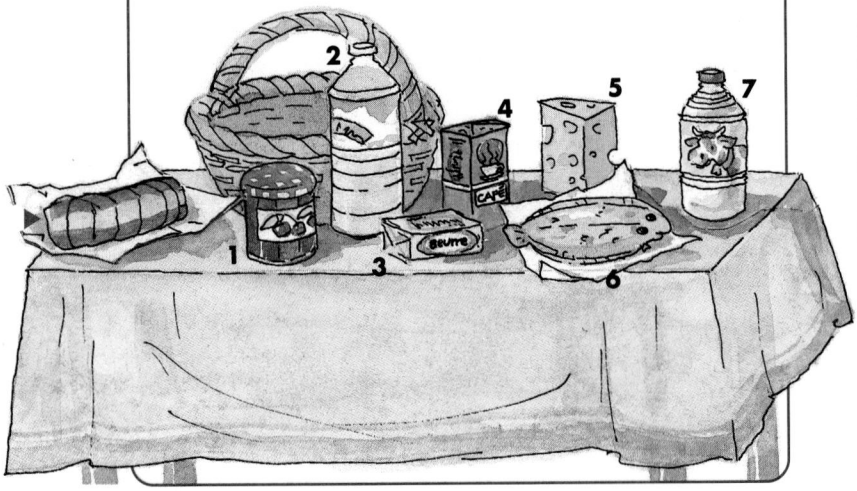

10 Le cochon d'or

Jacqueline est allée au restaurant. Voici l'addition. Dites ce qu'elle a pris.

▶ **Jacqueline a pris de la salade de tomates.**

RESTAURANT
Le Cochon d'Or

salade de tomates	10F
jambon	12F
poulet	20F
salade	10F
fromage	12F
glace	15F
eau minérale	10F
café	8F
	97F

11 Au café

Au café, une cliente demande les choses suivantes. Le serveur apporte ces choses.

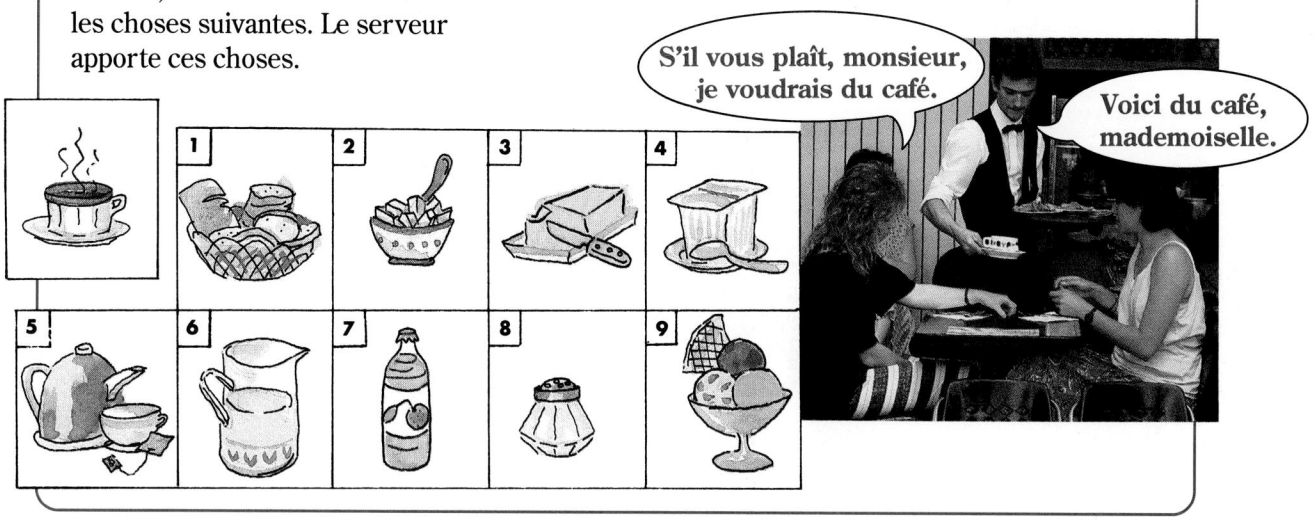

12 Menus

Préparez des menus pour les personnes suivantes. Dites ce que vous allez acheter pour chaque personne.

▶ une personne qui aime manger
Je vais acheter du rosbif, du fromage, de la glace . . .

1. une personne malade *(sick)*
2. un(e) athlète
3. un petit enfant
4. un végétarien (une végétarienne)
5. une personne qui veut maigrir
6. un invité *(guest)* japonais
7. une invitée française

D. L'article partitif dans les phrases négatives

Note the forms of the partitive articles in the negative sentences below.

AFFIRMATIVE	NEGATIVE	
Tu manges **du jambon?**	Non, je **ne** mange **pas de jambon.**	*No, I don't eat ham.*
Tu veux **de la salade?**	Merci, je **ne** veux **pas de salade.**	*Thanks, I don't want any salad.*
Est-ce qu'il y a **de l'eau minérale?**	Non, il **n'**y a **pas d'eau minérale.**	*No, there is no mineral water.*

In negative sentences, the PARTITIVE ARTICLE follows the pattern:

du, de la (de l') →	**ne . . . pas de (d')**
Marc prend **du** café.	Éric **ne** prend **pas de** café.
Sophie prend **de la** limonade.	Alain **ne** prend **pas de** limonade.
Anne prend **de l'**eau.	Nicole ne prend **pas d'**eau.

13 Un mauvais restaurant

Une cliente demande au serveur s'il y a certaines choses au menu. Le serveur répond négativement.

▶ le rosbif

1. le jambon
2. le melon
3. le thon
4. la sole
5. le veau
6. le yaourt
7. le jus de pamplemousse
8. l'eau minérale
9. le champagne

14 Au régime *(On a diet)*

Les personnes suivantes sont au régime parce qu'elles veulent maigrir. Répondez négativement aux questions suivantes.

▶ — Est-ce qu'Anne mange du pain?
— Non, elle ne mange pas de pain.

1. Est-ce que Marc prend de la mayonnaise?
2. Est-ce que Pauline veut du gâteau?
3. Est-ce que Jean-Pierre mange de la glace?
4. Est-ce qu'Alice prend du beurre?
5. Est-ce que Monsieur Ledodu veut de la tarte?
6. Est-ce que Mademoiselle Poix met de la crème dans son café?

15 Conversation

Demandez à vos camarades s'ils mangent souvent les choses suivantes.

▶ du poisson

1. de la glace
2. du veau
3. du pain français
4. du fromage français
5. de la tarte aux fraises
6. de la soupe
7. du rosbif
8. du poulet
9. du thon

16 Dans le réfrigérateur

Vous préparez le dîner. Demandez à un(e) camarade s'il y a les choses suivantes dans le réfrigérateur.

▶ le lait — **Est-ce qu'il y a du lait?**
— Non, il n'y a pas de lait.

1. le jus d'orange?
2. le pain?
3. la glace?
4. le beurre?
5. le jambon?
6. l'eau minérale?
7. le jus de pomme?
8. le fromage?
9. la mayonnaise?
10. le ketchup?

E. Le verbe *boire*

Note the forms of the irregular verb **boire** *(to drink)*.

INFINITIVE	**boire**	
PRESENT	Je **bois** du lait. Tu **bois** de l'eau. Il / Elle / On **boit** du soda.	Nous **buvons** du café. Vous **buvez** du thé glacé. Ils / Elles **boivent** du jus d'orange.
PASSÉ COMPOSÉ	J'**ai bu** du jus de tomate.	

17 Pique-nique

Philippe a organisé un pique-nique avec ses amis. Chacun *(Each person)* boit quelque chose de différent.

▶ **Philippe boit de l'eau.**

▶ Philippe	1. nous	2. toi	3. vous	4. Cécile	5. mes copains	6. moi

18 Expression personnelle

Complétez les phrases suivantes avec la forme appropriée du verbe **boire** et une expression de votre choix. Attention: utilisez le passé composé dans les phrases 6 à 8.

1. Au petit déjeuner, je ...
2. Au petit déjeuner, mes parents ...
3. À la cantine de l'école, nous ...
4. Quand il fait chaud, on ...
5. Quand il fait froid, on ...
6. Hier soir au dîner, j' ...
7. Hier matin, au petit déjeuner, ma mère ...
8. À la dernière boum, nous ...

Prononciation — **ou** /u/ — **u** /y/

Les lettres «ou» et «u»

la poule — **le pull**

The letters "**ou**" always represent the sound /u/.

Répétez: /u/ **vous nous poulet soupe fourchette couteau douzaine**

The letter "**u**" always represents the sound /y/.

Répétez: /y/ **tu du une légume jus sucre bien sûr avenue musée**

Now distinguish between the two vowel sounds:

Répétez: /u/ – /y/ **poule** *(hen)* – **pull**
roue *(wheel)* – **rue** **vous** – **vue** *(view)*
je joue – **le jus**

Vous buvez du jus de pamplemousse.
Je voudrais de la soupe, du poulet et du jus de raisin.

À votre tour!

1 Allô!

Reconstituez la conversation entre Frédéric et Sandrine. Pour cela, faites correspondre les réponses de Sandrine avec les questions de Frédéric.

1. Tu dînes au restaurant ce soir?
2. Tu as fait les courses?
3. Qu'est-ce que tu as acheté?
4. Tu n'as pas acheté de viande?
5. C'est vrai. Et pour le dessert, tu as acheté de la glace?

a. Oui, je suis allée au supermarché ce matin.
b. Du riz, des oeufs, de la salade et du fromage.
c. Non, j'ai pris un gâteau au chocolat.
d. Non, j'ai invité mon copain Fabien à dîner chez moi.
e. Mais non, tu sais *(know)* bien que Fabien est végétarien.

2 Dis-moi ...

I will tell you about my breakfast this morning.

- J'ai pris le petit déjeuner à sept heures.
- J'ai mangé du pain avec du beurre et de la confiture.
- J'ai bu du café noir.

Now choose one of the meals you had yesterday and tell me ...

- *at what time you had that meal*
- *what you ate*
- *what you drank*

3 Créa-dialogue

Avec vos camarades, décrivez où vous êtes allés et ce que vous avez fait aux endroits suivants.

au supermarché
acheter

4 Situation

Avec un(e) camarade, composez un dialogue correspondant à la situation suivante et jouez ce dialogue en classe.

You are talking to Florence, a French friend (played by your classmate). You have just invited her for dinner, but you understand she is on a special diet. Try to find out:

- what she eats
- what she does not eat
- what she drinks
- what she does not drink

5 Conversation libre

Avec un(e) camarade, composez un dialogue original basé sur la situation suivante.

You and your friend Caroline are in charge of the French Club picnic. Now you are walking up and down the aisles of a supermarket, discussing what things to buy or not to buy. For example:

▶ **—Est-ce qu'on achète du pain?**
—Oui, achetons du pain.
(Non, n'achetons pas de pain. J'ai du pain à la maison.)

6 Composition: Un bon repas

Think of a nice meal you had not too long ago — perhaps for a birthday or special holiday. Using the passé composé, write a short paragraph in which you describe . . .

- when, where, and with whom you had that meal
- what you ate and drank

Comment dit-on . . . ?

How to show your appreciation for good food:

Hm. . . C'est délicieux! **C'est exquis!** **C'est fameux!**

1. à la cantine manger	2. au restaurant manger	3. au marché acheter	4. à la boum boire

5. à la cuisine prendre	6. au café boire	7. dans un restaurant chinois ??

LEÇON 35 Un client difficile

M. Ronchon a beaucoup d'appétit . . . mais pas beaucoup de patience. En fait, M. Ronchon est rarement de bonne humeur. Et quand il est de mauvaise humeur, c'est un client difficile. Aujourd'hui, par exemple, au restaurant . . .

As a matter of fact/in a good mood
for instance

— Garçon!
— J'arrive!
— Qu'est-ce que vous avez comme hors d'oeuvre?
— Nous avons du jambon et du saucisson.
— Apportez-moi tout ça . . . avec du pain et du beurre!
— Bien, monsieur.

Waiter!
I'm coming!
as, for
all of that

— Et comme boisson, qu'est-ce que je vous apporte?
— Donnez-moi de l'eau minérale . . . Dépêchez-vous! J'ai soif!

Hurry up!

— Apportez-moi du poulet et des frites. . . Vite! J'ai très faim!
— Je vous apporte ça tout de suite.

Fast!
right away

— Et apportez-moi aussi du fromage, de la glace, de la tarte aux pommes et de la tarte aux abricots. . . Mais, qu'est-ce que vous attendez?
— Tout de suite, monsieur, tout de suite.

apricots

— Mais qu'est-ce que vous m'apportez?
— Je vous apporte l'addition!

check

Compréhension

1. En général, est-ce que M. Ronchon est de bonne humeur ou de mauvaise humeur?
2. Qu'est-ce qu'il va prendre comme hors d'oeuvre?
3. Qu'est-ce qu'il va prendre comme plat principal *(main course)?*
4. Qu'est-ce qu'il va boire?
5. Qu'est-ce qu'il va manger comme dessert?
6. Qu'est-ce que le garçon apporte après le dessert?
7. Quelle est la réaction de M. Ronchon? Est-ce qu'il est de bonne humeur ou de mauvaise humeur?

Et toi?

1. En général, est-ce que tu es de bonne humeur?
2. Et aujourd'hui, est-ce que tu es de bonne humeur ou de mauvaise humeur?
3. En général, est-ce que tu as beaucoup d'appétit?
4. Est-ce que tu es une personne patiente?
5. Quand tu vas au restaurant avec un copain (une copine), qui paie l'addition?

NOTE CULTURELLE

Les restaurants français et la cuisine française

Les Français aiment manger chez eux, mais ils aiment aussi aller au restaurant. Pour les gens pressés,° il y a les «self-service», les «fast foods» et les pizzerias.

Pour les gens qui veulent faire un bon repas, il y a toutes° sortes de restaurants spécialisés: auberges,° restaurants régionaux, restaurants de poisson, . . . Il y a aussi les «grands restaurants» où la cuisine est extraordinaire . . . et très chère!

La cuisine française a une réputation internationale. Pour beaucoup de personnes, c'est la meilleure° cuisine du monde.°

Les Américains ont emprunté° un grand nombre de mots° au vocabulaire de la cuisine française. Est-ce que tu connais les mots suivants: **soupe, sauce, mayonnaise, omelette, filet mignon, tarte, purée, soufflé?** Est-ce que tu aimes **les croissants? les crêpes? la mousse au chocolat?**

pressés *in a hurry* **toutes** *all* **auberges** *country inns*
meilleure *best* **du monde** *in the world*
ont emprunté *have borrowed* **mots** *words*

A. Les pronoms compléments *me, te, nous, vous*

In the sentences below, the pronouns in heavy print are called OBJECT PRONOUNS. Note the form and the position of these pronouns in the sentences below.

Anne **me** parle.	Elle **m'**invite.	*Anne talks **to me.***	*She invites **me.***
Mes amis **te** parlent.	Ils **t'**invitent.	*My friends talk **to you.***	*They invite **you.***
Tu **nous** parles.	Tu **nous** invites.	*You talk **to us.***	*You invite **us.***
Je **vous** parle.	Je **vous** invite.	*I am talking **to you.***	*I invite **you.***

FORMS

The OBJECT PRONOUNS that correspond to the subject pronouns **je, tu, nous, vous** are:

me ↓ **m'** (+ VOWEL SOUND)	*me, to me*	**nous**	*us, to us*
te ↓ **t'** (+ VOWEL SOUND)	*you, to you*	**vous**	*you, to you*

POSITION

In French, object pronouns usually come *before* the verb, according to the following patterns:

AFFIRMATIVE	NEGATIVE
SUBJECT + OBJECT PRONOUN + VERB ...	SUBJECT + **ne** + OBJECT PRONOUN + VERB + **pas** ...
Paul **nous** invite.	Éric **ne** **nous** invite **pas.**

1 D'accord!

Demandez à vos camarades de faire les choses suivantes pour vous.
Ils sont d'accord pour faire ces choses.

▶ téléphoner ce soir?

1. téléphoner demain?
2. attendre après la classe?
3. inviter à ta boum?
4. inviter à dîner?
5. rendre visite ce weekend?
6. rendre visite cet été?
7. acheter une glace?
8. apporter un sandwich?
9. vendre ta raquette?
10. écouter?

2 Pauvre Nathalie!

Stéphanie a de la chance. Sa copine Nathalie n'a pas de chance. Jouez les deux rôles.

▶ mon copain/inviter

1. ma tante / inviter au restaurant
2. mes cousins / téléphoner souvent
3. mon frère / écouter
4. mes parents / comprendre
5. mes voisins / inviter à dîner
6. ma copine / aider avec mes devoirs
7. mon grand-père / acheter des cadeaux *(gifts)*
8. mes amis / attendre après la classe

Vocabulaire: Les services personnels

aider quelqu'un	*to help*	J'**aide** mes copains avec les devoirs.
amener quelqu'un	*to bring*	Le taxi **amène** les touristes à la gare *(train station)*.
apporter quelque chose **à** quelqu'un	*to bring*	Le serveur **apporte** le menu **aux** clients.
donner quelque chose **à** quelqu'un	*to give*	Mme Marin **donne** 10 francs **à** sa fille.
montrer quelque chose **à** quelqu'un	*to show*	Est-ce que tu **montres** tes photos **à** ton copain?
prêter quelque chose **à** quelqu'un	*to lend, loan*	Est-ce que tu **prêtes** tes disques **à** tes amis?

3 Questions personnelles

Réponds affirmativement ou négativement aux questions suivantes.

1. Est-ce que tes copains t'aident avec tes devoirs?
2. Est-ce que ta mère ou ton père t'aide avec les devoirs de français?
3. Est-ce que ton père ou ta mère te prête sa voiture?
4. Est-ce que ton frère ou ta soeur te prête ses disques?
5. Est-ce que tes profs te donnent des conseils *(advice)*?
6. Est-ce que ton copain te montre ses photos?
7. Est-ce que tes cousins t'apportent des cadeaux *(gifts)* quand ils viennent chez toi?
8. Est-ce que tes parents t'amènent au restaurant pour ton anniversaire?

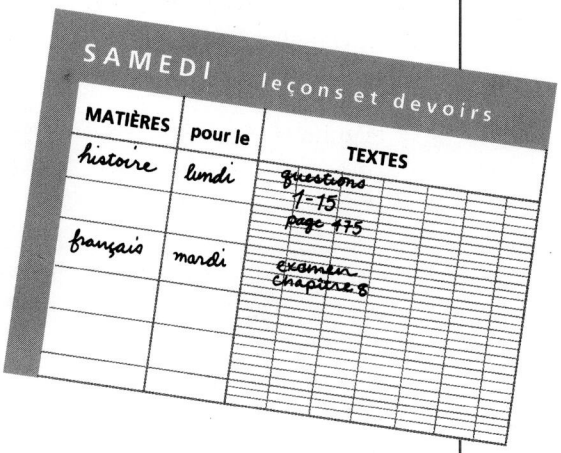

4 Bons services

Informez-vous sur les personnes suivantes. Dites ce que leurs amis ou leurs parents font pour eux. Pour cela, complétez les phrases avec les pronoms **me (m'), te (t'), nous** ou **vous.**

▶ J'organise une boum. **Ma soeur me prête ses cassettes.**
▶ Nous avons faim. **Cécile nous apporte des sandwichs.**

1. Nous organisons un pique-nique. Nos copains ... aident.
2. Tu as soif. Je ... apporte un soda.
3. Vous préparez l'examen. Le prof ... donne des conseils *(advice)*.
4. J'ai besoin d'argent. Mon cousin ... prête cent francs.
5. Tu es chez les voisins. Ils ... montrent leur appartement.
6. Nous sommes à l'hôpital. Nos amis ... rendent visite.
7. Vous êtes sympathiques. Je ... invite chez moi.
8. Nous allons prendre l'avion. Le taxi ... amène à l'aéroport.
9. Je nettoie le garage. Mon frère ... aide.

B. Les pronoms compléments à l'impératif

Compare the position and the form of the object pronouns when the verb is in the imperative.

AFFIRMATIVE	NEGATIVE
Téléphone-**moi** ce soir!	Ne **me** téléphone pas demain!
Invite-**moi** samedi!	Ne **m'**invite pas dimanche!
Apporte-**nous** du thé!	Ne **nous** apporte pas de café!

When the IMPERATIVE verb is AFFIRMATIVE, the object pronouns come *after* the verb.
➡ **me** becomes **moi**

When the imperative verb is negative, the object pronouns come *before* the verb.

5 Prêts *(Loans)*

Demandez à vos copains de vous prêter les choses suivantes. Ils vont accepter.

6 À Paris

Vous visitez Paris. Demandez certains services aux personnes suivantes.

▶ au garçon de café *(waiter)*
- apporter un sandwich

S'il vous plaît, apportez-moi un sandwich.

1. au garçon de café
   - apporter de l'eau
   - apporter une limonade
   - donner un croissant
2. à la serveuse *(waitress)* du restaurant
   - montrer le menu
   - donner du pain
   - apporter l'addition *(check)*
3. au chauffeur de taxi *(cab driver)*
   - amener au musée d'Orsay
   - montrer Notre-Dame
   - aider avec les bagages
4. à un copain parisien
   - téléphoner ce soir
   - donner ton adresse
   - prêter ton plan *(map)* de Paris

7 Quel service?

Demandez à vos camarades certains services. Pour cela complétez les phrases en utilisant ces verbes.

aider	amener	apporter
donner	montrer	prêter

▶ J'ai soif. ... de la limonade.
S'il te plaît, apporte-moi (donne-moi) de la limonade.

▶ J'ai faim. ... un sandwich
S'il te plaît, apporte-moi (donne-moi) un sandwich.

1. Je ne comprends pas les devoirs de maths. ... avec le problème.
2. Je voudrais téléphoner à ta cousine. ... son numéro de téléphone.
3. Je n'ai pas d'argent pour aller au cinéma. ... six dollars.
4. Je voudrais voir tes photos. ... tes photos.
5. J'ai soif. ... de l'eau minérale.
6. J'organise une boum. ... tes disques.
7. Je vais peindre *(to paint)* ma chambre. ... avec ce projet.
8. Je vais à l'aéroport. ... là-bas avec ta voiture.
9. Je ne sais pas où tu habites. ... ton adresse.

8 Non!

Proposez à vos camarades de faire les choses suivantes pour eux. Ils vont refuser et donner une explication.

▶ téléphoner ce soir (Je ne suis pas chez moi.)

1. téléphoner demain soir (Je dois faire mes devoirs.)
2. inviter ce weekend (Je vais à la campagne.)
3. inviter dimanche (Je dîne chez mes cousins.)
4. attendre après la classe (Je dois rentrer chez moi.)
5. prêter mes disques (Je n'ai pas de chaîne stéréo.)
6. acheter un sandwich (Je n'ai pas faim.)
7. rendre visite ce soir (Je vais au cinéma.)

C. Les verbes *pouvoir* et *devoir*

FORMS

Note the forms of the irregular verbs **pouvoir** *(can, may, be able)* and **devoir** *(must, have to)*.

INFINITIVE	pouvoir	devoir
PRESENT	Je **peux** venir. Tu **peux** travailler. Il / Elle / On **peut** voyager. Nous **pouvons** dîner ici. Vous **pouvez** rester. Ils / Elles **peuvent** aider.	Je **dois** rentrer avant midi. Tu **dois** gagner de l'argent. Il / Elle / On **doit** visiter Paris. Nous **devons** regarder le menu. Vous **devez** finir vos devoirs. Ils / Elles **doivent** mettre la table.
PASSÉ COMPOSÉ	J'**ai pu** étudier.	J'**ai dû** faire mes devoirs.

USES

- **Pouvoir** has several English equivalents.

can	Est-ce que tu **peux** venir au pique-nique?	***Can** you come to the picnic?*
may	Est-ce que je **peux** prendre la voiture?	***May** I take the car?*
to be able	Jacques ne **peut** pas réparer sa mobylette.	*Jacques **is** not **able** to fix his moped.*

- **Devoir** is used to express an OBLIGATION.

must	Vous **devez** faire vos devoirs.	*You **must** do your homework.*
to have to	Est-ce que je **dois** nettoyer ma chambre?	***Do** I **have to** clean my room?*

➡ **Devoir** is usually followed by an infinitive. It cannot stand alone.

Est-ce que tu **dois étudier** ce soir?	*Do you **have to study** tonight?*
Oui, je **dois étudier.**	*Yes, I **have to (study).***
Non, je **ne dois pas étudier.**	*No, I **don't have to (study).***

9 Le coût de la vie *(The cost of living)*

Décrivez ce que les personnes suivantes peuvent acheter avec leur argent.

▶ Philippe a quatre-vingts francs.
Il peut acheter des lunettes de soleil.

1. Alice et Françoise ont cinquante francs.
2. J'ai cinq cents francs.
3. Tu as trois cent cinquante francs.
4. Vous avez trois cents francs.
5. Ma copine a deux cent cinquante francs.
6. Nous avons deux cents francs.
7. Mon petit frère a trente francs.

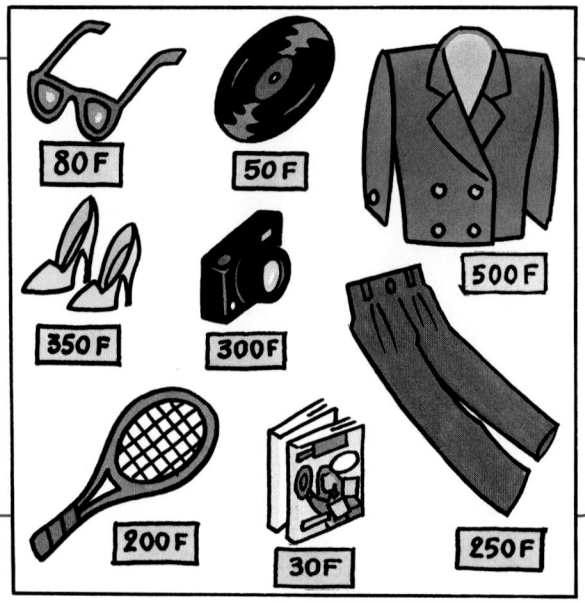

10 Obligations?

Demandez à vos camarades s'ils doivent faire les choses suivantes.

▶ étudier?

1. étudier ce soir?
2. nettoyer ta chambre?
3. mettre la table?
4. réussir à l'examen?
5. aller chez le dentiste cette semaine?
6. parler au professeur après la classe?
7. être poli(e) *(polite)* avec tes voisins?
8. rentrer chez toi après la classe?

(Non, je ne dois pas étudier.)

11 Excuses

Thomas demande à ses amis de repeindre *(to repaint)* sa chambre avec lui, mais chacun a une excuse. Dites que les personnes suivantes ne peuvent pas aider Thomas. Dites aussi ce qu'elles doivent faire.

▶ Hélène (étudier)
Hélène ne peut pas aider Thomas. Elle doit étudier.

1. nous (faire les courses)
2. Lise et Rose (acheter des vêtements)
3. moi (aider ma mère)
4. toi (nettoyer le garage)
5. Alice (rendre visite à sa grand-mère)
6. vous (déjeuner avec vos cousins)
7. mon frère et moi (laver la voiture)
8. Nathalie et toi (préparer l'examen)

12 Expression personnelle

Complétez les phrases suivantes avec vos idées personnelles.

1. Chez moi, je peux ...
   Je ne peux pas ...
2. À l'école, nous devons ...
   Nous ne devons pas ...
3. À la maison, je dois ...
   Mes frères (Mes soeurs) doivent ...
4. Quand on est riche, on peut ...
   On doit ...
5. Quand on est malade *(sick)*, on doit ...
   On ne doit pas ...
6. Quand on veut maigrir, on doit ...
   On ne peut pas ...

Prononciation

s /z/ **ss** /s/

Les lettres «s» et «ss»

Be sure to distinguish between "**s**" and "**ss**" in the middle of a word.

Répétez: /z/ **mauvaise cuisine fraise mayonnaise quelque chose magasin**

/s/ **poisson saucisson dessert boisson assiette pamplemousse**

/z/ – /s/ **poison – poisson désert** *(desert)* **– dessert**

Comme dessert nous choisissons une tarte aux fraises.

À votre tour!

1 Allô!

Reconstituez la conversation entre Corinne et Philippe. Pour cela, faites correspondre les réponses de Philippe avec ce que dit Corinne.

Corinne

1. Dis, Philippe, j'ai besoin d'un petit service.
2. Prête-moi ta mobylette, s'il te plaît.
3. Dans ce cas, apporte-moi *Paris-Match.*
4. Alors, achète-moi aussi le nouvel album d'Astérix.
5. Je t'ai prêté cent francs hier!

Philippe

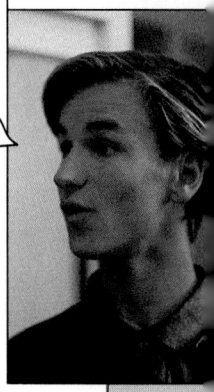

a. C'est vrai . . . Bon, je t'achète tout ça *(all that).*
b. D'accord! Je vais aller à la librairie *(bookstore)* Duchemin.
c. Écoute, je n'ai pas assez d'argent.
d. Ah, je ne peux pas. Je dois aller en ville cet après-midi.
e. Qu'est-ce que je peux faire pour toi?

2 Dis-moi . . .

I am going to spend a month living in your city and studying at your school. Since you are my friend, I will ask you a few favors, for instance:

- Prête-moi ton livre d'anglais.
- Montre-moi où est la cantine.
- Amène-moi à la bibliothèque.
- Invite-moi à ton club.
- Donne-moi le plan *(map)* de la ville.
- Téléphone-moi ce weekend.

Now imagine that you are visiting me in France. I am ready to help you. Ask me three or four favors.

3 Créa-dialogue

Demandez certains services à vos camarades. Ils vont vous demander pourquoi. Répondez à leurs questions. Ils vont accepter le service.

▶ —S'il te plaît, prête-moi ton vélo!
—Pourquoi?
—Parce que je voudrais faire une promenade à la campagne.
—D'accord, je te prête mon vélo.

▶	prêter	1. prêter	2. prêter	3. apporter	4. prêter	5. donner	6. donner
QUEL SERVICE?					$1.00	$5.00	??
POURQUOI?	faire une promenade à la campagne	jouer au tennis	organiser une boum	prendre des photos	acheter une glace	??	??

4 Situation

Avec un(e) camarade, préparez un dialogue original correspondant à la situation suivante.

You are having dinner at a French restaurant called Sans-Souci. You have a friendly but inexperienced waiter/waitress (played by your classmate) who forgets to bring you what you need. Whenever you mention something however, he/she agrees to bring it right away **(tout de suite).** Tell your waiter/waitress . . .

- to please show you the menu **(le menu)**
- to please give you some water
- to bring you a napkin
- to give you a beverage (of your choice)
- to bring you a dessert (of your choice)
- to bring you the silverware that you need for eating the dessert

5 Conversation libre

Avec un(e) camarade, composez une conversation basée sur la situation suivante.

Imagine you are looking for someone to help you out. Ask a classmate to do you five favors. He/she will accept or refuse. In case of refusal, he/she will give you a reason. You may want to use some of the following verbs:

aider, amener, apporter, inviter, donner, montrer, prêter, vendre, acheter

For example, your conversation might begin like this:

▶ **—S'il te plaît, invite-moi chez toi samedi après-midi.**
—Je regrette, mais je ne peux pas.
—Pourquoi?
—Je dois faire les courses.

6 Composition: Bonnes relations

Select a person you like (a friend, a neighbor, a relative, a teacher) and write a short paragraph mentioning at least four things this person does for you. You may want to use some of the following verbs:

acheter amener aider donner inviter montrer prêter rendre visite téléphoner

J'ai une bonne copine. Elle s'appelle Stéphanie. Elle est très sympathique. Elle me téléphone souvent et le weekend, elle m'invite chez elle. Elle est très intelligente et quand je ne comprends pas, elle m'aide avec mes devoirs de français. Elle me donne toujours des conseils (advice) excellents.

Now tell me about a friend of yours and let me know some of the things this friend does for you.

Comment dit-on . . . ?

How to show your reaction to bad food:

Pouah! . . . C'est infect! C'est dégoûtant! C'est infâme!

LEÇON 36

Pique-nique

Florence et Jérôme organisent un pique-nique ce weekend. Ils préparent la liste des invités. *guests*
Qui vont-ils inviter?

FLORENCE: Tu connais Stéphanie?
JÉRÔME: Oui, je la connais. C'est une copine.
FLORENCE: Je l'invite au pique-nique?
JÉRÔME: Bien sûr. Invite-la.
FLORENCE: Et son cousin Frédéric, tu le connais?
JÉRÔME: Oui, je le connais un peu.
FLORENCE: Je l'invite aussi?
JÉRÔME: Non, ne l'invite pas. Il est trop snob.

NOTE CULTURELLE

Un pique-nique français

Quand ils vont à la campagne, les Français adorent faire des pique-niques. Un pique-nique est un repas froid assez simple. Il y a généralement du poulet froid et des oeufs durs° et aussi du jambon, du saucisson ou du pâté* pour les sandwichs. Quand on a l'équipement nécessaire, on peut aussi faire des grillades° sur un barbecue. Comme dessert, il y a des fruits (bananes, oranges, pommes, poires, raisin°). Comme boisson, il y a de l'eau minérale ou du cidre.

* The French have created dozens of varieties of **pâté,** ranging from the expensive and refined **pâté de foie gras** (made from the livers of fattened geese) to the everyday **pâté de campagne** (a type of cold meat loaf served in thin slices with bread).

durs *hard-boiled* **grillades** *grilled meat* **raisin** *grapes*

FLORENCE: Comment? Tu le trouves snob? Moi, je le trouve intelligent et sympathique. Et puis, il a une voiture et nous avons besoin d'une voiture pour transporter tout le monde...

JÉRÔME: Florence, tu es géniale ... C'est vrai, Frédéric n'est pas aussi snob que ça ... Téléphonons-lui tout de suite et invitons-le au pique-nique!

What?
also
everyone
brilliant
that snobbish / right away

Compréhension

1. Qui est Stéphanie?
2. Qui est Frédéric?
3. Est-ce que Jérôme a une bonne ou une mauvaise opinion de Frédéric? Pourquoi?
4. Et Florence, comment est-ce qu'elle trouve Frédéric?
5. Finalement, est-ce que Jérôme va inviter Frédéric au pique-nique? Pourquoi?

Et toi?

1. Est-ce que tu aimes faire des pique-niques?
2. Quand tu fais un pique-nique avec des copains, où allez-vous?
3. Qui invites-tu?
4. En général, qu'est-ce qu'on mange à un pique-nique américain?
5. Qu'est-ce qu'on boit?
6. Dans ta famille, est-ce qu'on fait des barbecues? Où? Qui est le «chef»? Qu'est-ce qu'on mange et qu'est-ce qu'on boit?

A. Le verbe *connaître*

Note the forms of the irregular verb **connaître** *(to know)*.

INFINITIVE	**connaître**	
PRESENT	Je **connais** Stéphanie. Tu **connais** son cousin? Il / Elle / On **connaît** ces garçons.	Nous **connaissons** Paris. Vous **connaissez** Montréal? Ils / Elles **connaissent** ce café.
PASSÉ COMPOSÉ	J'**ai connu** ton frère pendant les vacances.	

➡ In the passé composé, **connaître** means *to meet for the first time.*

➡ The French use **connaître** to say that they *know* or *are acquainted with people or places.* To say that they *know information,* they use **je sais, tu sais.** Compare:

PEOPLE/PLACES	INFORMATION
Je **connais** Éric.	Je **sais** où il habite.
Tu **connais** Frédéric.	Tu **sais** à quelle heure il vient?
Je **connais** un bon restaurant.	Je **sais** qu'il est près du théâtre.

Je connais Éric.

Je sais où il habite.

1 On ne peut pas connaître tout

Les personnes suivantes connaissent la première personne ou la première chose entre parenthèses. Elles ne connaissent pas la deuxième.

▶ Philippe (Isabelle/sa soeur)
Philippe connaît Isabelle.
Il ne connaît pas sa soeur.

1. nous (Paul/ ses copains)
2. vous (le prof d'anglais/ le prof de maths)
3. moi (les voisins/ leurs amis)
4. toi (Paris/ Bordeaux)
5. les touristes (le Louvre/ le musée d'Orsay)
6. mon copain (ce café/ ce restaurant)

2 Questions personnelles

1. Est-ce que tu connais New York? Chicago? San Francisco? Montréal? Quelles villes est-ce que tu connais bien?
2. Dans ta ville est-ce que tu connais un bon restaurant? Comment est-ce qu'il s'appelle? Est-ce que tu connais un supermarché? un centre commercial? un magasin de disques? Comment est-ce qu'ils s'appellent?
3. Est-ce que tu connais des monuments à Paris? Quels monuments?
4. Est-ce que tu connais bien tes voisins? Est-ce qu'ils sont sympathiques? Est-ce que tu connais personnellement le directeur (la directrice) de ton école? Est-ce qu'il (elle) est strict(e)?
5. Quels acteurs de cinéma est-ce que tu connais? Quelles actrices? Quels musiciens? Quels athlètes professionnels?

B. Les pronoms compléments: *le, la, les*

In the questions below, the nouns in heavy type follow the verb directly. They are the DIRECT OBJECTS of the verb. Note the forms and position of the DIRECT OBJECT PRONOUNS which are used to replace those nouns in the answers.

Tu connais **Éric?**	Oui, je **le** connais.	*Yes, I know **him.***
	Je **l'**invite souvent.	*I invite **him** often.*
Tu connais **Stéphanie?**	Oui, je **la** connais.	*Yes, I know **her.***
	Je **l'**invite aussi.	*I invite **her** also.*
Tu connais **mes copains?**	Je **les** connais bien.	*I know **them** well.*
	Je **les** invite.	*I invite **them.***
Tu connais **mes amies?**	Je **les** connais aussi.	*I know **them** too.*
	Je **les** invite souvent.	*I invite **them** often.*

FORMS AND USES

Direct object pronouns have the following forms:

	SINGULAR	PLURAL
MASCULINE	**le** ↓ **l'** (+ VOWEL SOUND) *him, it*	**les** *them*
FEMININE	**la** ↓ **l'** (+ VOWEL SOUND) *her, it*	

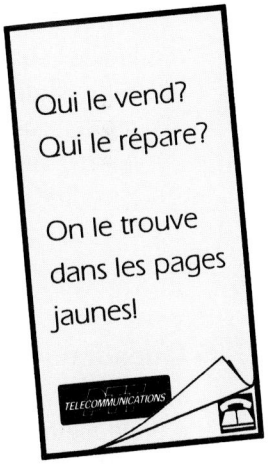

➡ The direct object pronouns **le, la, l', les** can refer to either people or things.

Tu vois **Nicole?**	Oui, je **la** vois.	*Yes, I see **her.***
Tu vois **ma voiture?**	Oui, je **la** vois.	*Yes, I see **it.***
Tu comprends **le professeur?**	Oui, je **le** comprends.	*Yes, I understand **him.***
Tu comprends **ce mot** *(word)?*	Oui, je **le** comprends.	*Yes, I understand **it.***

POSITION

Direct object pronouns generally come *before* the verb according to the following patterns:

	AFFIRMATIVE	NEGATIVE
	SUBJECT + **le/la/les** + VERB ...	SUBJECT + **ne** + **le/la/les** + VERB + **pas** ...
Éric?	Je **le** connais bien.	Tu **ne** **le** connais **pas.**
Ces filles?	Nous **les** invitons.	Vous **ne** **les** invitez **pas.**

3 À la boum de Delphine

Pierre connaît tous les invités *(all the guests)* à la boum de Delphine, mais Lise ne les connaît pas. Jouez les trois rôles.

▶ ces garçons?

1. Christophe
2. Jacqueline?
3. Anne et Valérie?
4. Jérôme et Jean-François?
5. la fille là-bas?
6. cette étudiante?
7. ma cousine?
8. les cousins de Véronique?
9. la copine de Jacques?
10. ses frères?

4 Un choix difficile

Vous allez passer le mois de juillet en France. Vous êtes limité(e) à 20 kilos de bagages. Un(e) camarade demande si vous allez prendre les choses suivantes. Répondez affirmativement ou négativement.

▶ ta raquette?
—Tu prends ta raquette?
— Oui, je la prends.
(Non, je ne la prends pas.)

1. tes cassettes?
2. ton livre de français?
3. ta guitare?
4. ton walkman?
5. ta chaîne stéréo?
6. ton maillot de bain?
7. ton vélo?
8. tes tee-shirts?
9. tes sandales?

5 Questions et réponses

Michèle pose des questions à Jérôme en utilisant les éléments des Colonnes A et B. Jérôme répond logiquement en utilisant les éléments des Colonnes B et C et un pronom complément. Avec un(e) camarade, jouez les deux rôles.

A	B	C
où	rencontrer tes copains	le samedi matin
quand	voir ta cousine	à 8 heures du matin
à quelle heure	regarder la télé	à 9 heures du soir
	nettoyer ta chambre	à la Boîte à Musique
	faire les courses	à Mod' Shop
	acheter tes disques	au café Le Pont Neuf
	acheter tes vêtements	dans un supermarché
	prendre le petit déjeuner	le weekend
		pendant les vacances
		dans la cuisine
		dans le salon

C. La place des pronoms à l'impératif

Note the position of the object pronoun when the verb is in the imperative.

	AFFIRMATIVE COMMAND	NEGATIVE COMMAND
J'invite **Frédéric?**	Oui, invite-**le!**	Non, ne **l'**invite pas!
Je prends **la guitare?**	Oui, prends-**la!**	Non, ne **la** prends pas!
J'achète **les cassettes?**	Oui, achète-**les!**	Non, ne **les** achète pas!

In AFFIRMATIVE COMMANDS, the object pronoun comes *after* the verb and is joined to it by a hyphen.

In NEGATIVE COMMANDS, the object pronoun comes *before* the verb.

6 Invitations

Vous préparez une liste de personnes à inviter à une boum. Vous êtes limité(e)s à quatre *(4)* des personnes suivantes. Faites vos suggestions d'après les modèles.

▶ Caroline est sympathique.
Invitons-la!

▶ Jean-Louis est pénible.
Ne l'invitons pas!

1. Sylvie est très sympathique.
2. Cécile et Anne aiment danser.
3. Jacques est stupide.
4. Robert joue bien de la guitare.
5. Ces filles sont intelligentes.
6. Martin et Thomas sont snobs.
7. Nicolas n'est pas mon ami.
8. Ces garçons sont pénibles.
9. Cette fille est gentille.
10. Tes copains sont méchants.

7 Le pique-nique

Olivier demande à Claire s'il doit prendre certaines choses pour le pique-nique.

▶ ma guitare (oui)

1. la limonade (oui)
2. les sandwichs (non)
3. la salade (oui)
4. le lait (non)
5. le gâteau (non)
6. mon appareil-photo (oui)
7. mes lunettes de soleil (oui)
8. les impers (non)

8 Oui ou non?

Votre petit cousin de Québec passe deux semaines chez vous. Il vous demande s'il doit ou peut faire les choses suivantes. Répondez affirmativement ou négativement.

1. Je fais les courses?
2. Je regarde tes photos?
3. Je nettoie ma chambre?
4. J'achète le journal *(newspaper)?*
5. J'invite les voisins à déjeuner?
6. Je prépare le dîner?
7. Je prends ton vélo?
8. J'écoute tes disques?
9. J'aide ta mère?
10. Je mets la télé?

D. Les pronoms compléments *lui, leur*

In the questions below, the nouns in heavy type are INDIRECT OBJECTS. These nouns represent PEOPLE and are introduced by **à.**

Note the forms and position of the corresponding INDIRECT OBJECT PRONOUNS in the answers on the right.

Tu téléphones **à Philippe?**	Oui, je **lui** téléphone.
Tu parles **à Juliette?**	Non, je ne **lui** parle pas.
Tu téléphones **à tes amis?**	Oui, je **leur** téléphone.
Tu prêtes ton vélo **à tes cousines?**	Non, je ne **leur** prête pas mon vélo.

FORMS

INDIRECT OBJECT PRONOUNS replace **à** + noun representing people. They have the following forms:

	SINGULAR	PLURAL
MASCULINE/FEMININE	**lui** *to him, to her*	**leur** *to them*

POSITION

Like other object pronouns, **lui** and **leur** come *before* the verb, *except* in affirmative commands.

Voici Henri. Parle-**lui!** Prête-**lui** ton vélo!

➡ In negative sentences, **lui** and **leur,** like other object pronouns, come *between* **ne** and the verb.

Voici Éric. Je ne **lui** téléphone pas.
Voici mes voisins. Je ne **leur** parle pas.

9 Au téléphone

Demandez à vos camarades s'ils téléphonent aux personnes suivantes.

▶ ta copine

(Non, je ne lui téléphone pas.)

1. ton copain
2. tes cousins
3. ta grand-mère
4. ton prof de français
5. tes voisins
6. ta tante favorite

Vocabulaire: Verbes suivis *(followed)* d'un complément indirect

parler à	*to speak, talk (to)*	Je **parle à** mon copain.
rendre visite à	*to visit*	Nous **rendons visite à** nos voisins.
répondre à	*to answer*	Tu **réponds au** professeur.
téléphoner à	*to phone, call*	Jérôme **téléphone à** Juliette.
demander à	*to ask*	Je ne **demande** pas d'argent **à** mes frères.
donner à	*to give (to)*	Tu **donnes** ton adresse **à** ta copine.
montrer à	*to show (to)*	Nous **montrons** nos photos **à** nos amis.
prêter à	*to lend, loan (to)*	Je ne **prête** pas mon walkman **à** ma soeur.

➡ **Répondre** is a regular **-re** verb.
Je réponds à François. **J'ai répondu** à Catherine.

➡ The verbs **téléphoner, répondre,** and **demander** take indirect objects in French, but not in English. Compare:

téléphoner

Nous **téléphonons**	**à**	Paul.	Nous **lui téléphonons.**
*We **are calling***	. . .	*Paul.*	*We **are calling him.***

répondre

Tu **réponds**	**à**	tes parents.	Tu **leur réponds.**
*You **answer***	. . .	*your parents.*	*You **answer them.***

demander

Je **demande**	**à**	Sylvie	. . .	ses disques.	Je **lui demande** ses disques.
*I **am asking***	. . .	*Sylvie*	*for*	*her records.*	*I **am asking her** for her records.*

10 Les copains de Dominique

Dominique a beaucoup de copains. Décrivez ce que chacun fait pour elle. Complétez les phrases avec **Dominique** ou **à Dominique.**

▶ **Françoise invite Dominique.**
Patrick rend visite à Dominique.

1. Marc téléphone . . .
2. Jean-Paul voit . . . samedi prochain.
3. Sophie prête son vélo . . .
4. Corinne écoute . . .
5. François donne son adresse . . .
6. Philippe regarde . . . pendant la classe.
7. Delphine attend . . . après la classe.
8. Nathalie parle . . .
9. Pauline invite . . . au concert.
10. Pierre répond . . .
11. Isabelle montre ses photos . . .
12. Thomas demande . . . son numéro de téléphone.

11 Joyeux anniversaire!

Choisissez un cadeau d'anniversaire pour les personnes suivantes. Un(e) camarade va vous demander ce que vous donnez à chaque personne.

▶ à ton copain

Qu'est-ce que tu donnes à ton copain?

Cadeaux

un pull
des compacts
une cravate
un livre
des billets (tickets) de théâtre
un magazine
ma photo
une boîte (box) de chocolats
un gâteau
??

1. à ton petit frère
2. à ta mère
3. à ta grand-mère
4. à ta copine
5. à tes cousins
6. à ton (ta) prof
7. à tes copains

12 Questions personnelles

Réponds aux questions suivantes. Utilise **lui** ou **leur** dans tes réponses.

1. Le weekend, est-ce que tu rends visite à tes copains? à ton oncle?
2. Est-ce que tu prêtes tes disques à ta soeur? à ton frère? à tes copains?
3. Est-ce que tu demandes de l'argent à ton père? à ta mère?
4. Est-ce que tu demandes des conseils *(advice)* à tes parents? à tes professeurs?
5. Est-ce que tu donnes de bons conseils à tes copains?
6. Est-ce que tu montres tes photos à ton frère? à ta soeur? à ta copine? à ton copain? à tes cousins?
7. En classe, est-ce que tu réponds en français à ton professeur?
8. Quand tu as un problème, est-ce que tu parles à tes copains? à ton professeur? à tes grands-parents? à tes parents?

E. Les verbes *dire* et *écrire*

Note the forms of the irregular verbs **dire** *(to say, tell)* and **écrire** *(to write)*.

INFINITIVE	**dire**	**écrire**
PRESENT	je **dis** tu **dis** il/elle/on **dit** nous **disons** vous **dites** ils/elles **disent**	j' **écris** tu **écris** il/elle/on **écrit** nous **écrivons** vous **écrivez** ils/elles **écrivent**
PASSÉ COMPOSÉ	j'**ai dit**	j'**ai écrit**

➡ Note the use of **que/qu'** *(that)* after **dire** and **écrire.**

Florence **dit que** Frédéric est sympathique. — *Florence **says (that)** Frédéric is nice.*
Alain **écrit qu'**il est allé à un pique-nique. — *Alain **writes (that)** he went on a picnic.*

➡ **Décrire** *(to describe)* follows the same pattern as **écrire.**

Did you know that French is an official language in many countries? Learning French can help you correspond with French-speaking pen pals throughout the world.

13 Correspondance

Pendant les vacances, on écrit beaucoup de lettres. Dites à qui les personnes suivantes écrivent.

▶ Juliette / à Marc
Juliette écrit à Marc.

1. nous / à nos copains
2. toi / à ta cousine
3. moi / à ma grand-mère
4. Nicolas / à ses voisins
5. vous / à vos parents
6. les élèves / au professeur

14 La boum

Des amis sont à une boum. Décrivez ce que chacun dit.

▶ toi / la musique est super
Tu dis que la musique est super.

1. Nicole / les sandwichs sont délicieux
2. nous / les invités *(guests)* sont sympathiques
3. Pauline / Jérôme danse bien
4. moi / ces garçons dansent mal
5. vous / vous n'aimez pas cette cassette
6. mes copains / ils vont organiser une boum le weekend prochain

15 Questions personnelles

1. Est-ce que tu aimes écrire?
2. Pendant les vacances, est-ce que tu écris à tes copains? à tes voisins? à ton(ta) meilleur(e) *(best)* ami(e)?
3. À Noël, est-ce que tu écris des cartes *(cards)?* À qui?
4. À qui as-tu écrit récemment *(recently)?*
5. Est-ce que tu dis toujours la vérité *(truth)?*
6. À ton avis, est-ce que les journalistes disent toujours la vérité? Et les politiciens?

Prononciation

Les lettres «on» et «om»

Be sure to distinguish between the nasal and non-nasal vowel sounds.

REMEMBER: Do not pronounce an /n/ or /m/ after the nasal vowel /ɔ̃/.

on /ɔ̃/

lion

on(n)e /ɔ/

lionne

Répétez: /ɔ̃/ **mon ton son bon avion montrer répondre invitons blouson**

/ɔn/ **téléphone Simone donner connais mayonnaise personne bonne**

/ɔm/ **fromage promenade tomate pomme dommage comment**

/ɔ̃/–/ɔn/ **lion–lionne bon–bonne Simon–Simone Yvon–Yvonne**

Monique donne une pomme à Raymond.
Simone connaît mon oncle Léon.

À votre tour!

1 Allô!

Reconstituez la conversation entre Jacques et Florence. Pour cela, faites correspondre les réponses de Florence avec les questions de Jacques.

1 Qu'est-ce que tu fais ce weekend?

2 Tu m'invites?

3 Et Catherine? Tu l'invites aussi?

4 C'est ma nouvelle copine.

5 Tu veux son numéro de téléphone?

6 C'est le 44.32.28.50.

a. Je lui téléphone tout de suite *(right away)*.
b. Oui, je ne l'ai pas.
c. Bien sur, je t'invite.
d. J'organise une boum.
e. Catherine? Je ne la connais pas. Qui est-ce?
f. Ah oui, je vois qui c'est maintenant. Eh bien, d'accord! Je l'invite.

2 Dis-moi ...

I met your cousin at a party last weekend. She is a very bright and pleasant person. I would like to see her again. Tell me ...

- Comment est-ce qu'elle s'appelle?
- Où est-ce qu'elle habite?
- Est-ce que tu la vois souvent?
- Est-ce que je lui téléphone? Quand?
- Est-ce que je l'invite au restaurant? À quel restaurant?

3 Créa-dialogue

Avec vos camarades, discutez de certaines choses que vous faites. Posez plusieurs questions sur chaque activité.

regarder la télé?	
à quelle heure?	

1. inviter tes amis?	2. voir tes cousins?
quand? à quelle occasion?	quand? où?
5. faire tes devoirs?	**6. téléphoner à tes copains?**
quand? où?	quand? pourquoi?

Tu regardes la télé?

Oui je la regarde.

À quelle heure est-ce que tu la regardes?

À huit heures.

4 Situation

Avec un(e) camarade, composez un dialogue original correspondant à la situation suivante. Jouez ce dialogue en classe.

You and another classmate know a very nice Canadian girl by the name of Catherine. Next weekend is her birthday and you want to do something special. With your friend discuss . . .

- whether to invite her to your house or to a restaurant
- what small gift *(petit cadeau)* you may buy for her
- what else you may do for her

5 Conversation libre

Avec un(e) camarade, composez un dialogue basé sur la situation suivante. Jouez ce dialogue en classe.

A group of French students are going to visit your town next week. As members of the Foreign Students Club, you and a classmate discuss what kinds of activities you will organize for them. You may want to use the following verbs:

inviter (où?), montrer (quels endroits?), amener (où?), donner (quels petits cadeaux *[gifts]***?)**

6 Composition: Les personnes dans ma vie *(life)*

Make a list of two or three people you know well. Give the name of each person and describe one thing you do for this person and one thing you don't do.
You may want to select:

- un cousin/une cousine
- un frère/une soeur
- un copain/une copine
- un voisin/une voisine
- un ami/une amie
- un professeur de français (d'anglais, de maths, d'histoire)

Ma cousine s'appelle Denise. Je la vois pendant les vacances de Noël. Je ne lui rends pas souvent visite.

3. faire les courses?	4. aider ta mère?
quand? où?	quand? comment?

7. rendre visite à ta grand-mère?	8. écrire à ton cousin?
quand? pourquoi?	pourquoi?

Comment dit-on . . . ?

How to tell someone to leave you alone:

Laisse-moi tranquille!

Fiche-moi la paix!

Petit test culturel

Bon appétit!

Répondez aux questions suivantes. Vérifiez vos réponses au bas° de la page.

1 Dans un repas français, quand est-ce qu'on mange la salade en général?
a. comme° premier plat
b. avec la viande
c. après le plat principal
d. après le dessert

2 En général, avec quel repas est-ce qu'on mange des croissants en France?
a. avec le petit déjeuner
b. avec le déjeuner
c. avec le dîner
d. avec les trois repas

3 Dans un restaurant français typique, qu'est-ce qu'on mange généralement avec un steak?
a. du riz
b. des spaghetti
c. des frites
d. des épinards°

Réponses:
1. c; 2. a; 3. c; 4. d; 5. b; 6. b; 7. b

au bas *at the bottom* **comme** *as*
épinards *spinach* **fin** *end*
vin *wine* **célèbre** *famous*

4 Quand est-ce que les Français boivent le café?
a. avant le repas
b. pendant le repas
c. avec le fromage
d. à la fin° du repas

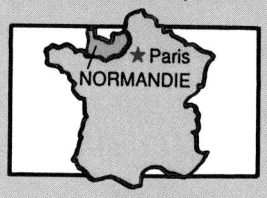

5 Le «camembert» est une spécialité qui vient originairement de Normandie. Qu'est-ce que c'est?
a. un gâteau
b. un fromage
c. une glace
d. un jus de fruit

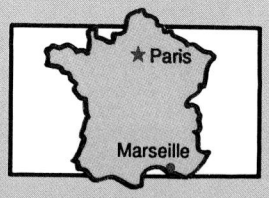

6 La «bouillabaisse» est le plat traditionnel de Marseille, un grand port français sur la Méditerranée. Qu'est-ce que c'est?
a. une salade de fruits
b. une soupe de poisson
c. une tarte aux bananes
d. une omelette au jambon

7 Quelle province française a donné son nom à un vin° célèbre?°
a. la Savoie
b. la Champagne
c. la Bretagne
d. la Picardie

AU CANADA

Petit déjeuner au Château Frontenac

Vous voyagez au Canada avec votre famille. Cette semaine vous êtes à Québec. Vous restez au Château Frontenac, un célèbre hôtel de la ville. Regardez bien le menu.

- À quelle heure est servi° le petit déjeuner?
- Vous avez le choix entre deux menus. Quel menu allez-vous choisir? Combien coûte-t-il?
- Vous avez décidé de choisir le menu «Le Comte de Frontenac».
- Quel jus de fruit allez-vous choisir?
- Quelle boisson allez-vous choisir?
- Quels oeufs allez-vous prendre?
- Est-ce que vous allez prendre du jambon, du bacon ou des saucisses?
- Est-ce que vous allez choisir des rôties, un croissant ou une danoise? Et qu'est-ce que vous allez prendre comme° confiture?

servi *served* **comme** *as, for*

Le Château Frontenac

PETIT DÉJEUNER CONTINENTAL (De 6h30 à midi) — **CONTINENTAL BREAKFAST** (From 6:30 to noon)

$7.75

- ☐ Jus d'orange ou / ☐ Orange juice or
- ☐ Jus de tomate ou / ☐ Tomato juice or
- ☐ Jus de pamplemousse / ☐ Grapefruit juice
- ☐ Café ou / ☐ Coffee or
- ☐ Thé ou / ☐ Tea or
- ☐ Lait / ☐ Milk

avec ☐ rôties, ou ☐ croissant, ou ☐ danoise, beurre et confitures

served with ☐ toast, or ☐ croissant, or ☐ sweet roll, butter and preserves

LE COMTE DE FRONTENAC

$11.25

- ☐ Jus d'orange ou / ☐ Orange juice or
- ☐ Jus de tomate ou / ☐ Tomato juice or
- ☐ Jus de pamplemousse ou / ☐ Grapefruit juice or
- ☐ 1/2 pamplemousse ou / ☐ 1/2 grapefruit or
- ☐ Pruneaux / ☐ Stewed prunes
- ☐ Café ou / ☐ Coffee or
- ☐ Thé ou / ☐ Tea or
- ☐ Lait / ☐ Milk
- ☐ Deux oeufs frits ou / ☐ Two fried eggs or
- ☐ Oeufs brouillés ou / ☐ Scrambled eggs or
- ☐ Deux oeufs à la coque ou / ☐ Two boiled eggs or
- ☐ Crêpes canadiennes ou / ☐ Canadian pancakes or
- ☐ Crêpes françaises / ☐ French pancakes
- ☐ Jambon ou / ☐ Ham or
- ☐ Bacon ou / ☐ Bacon or
- ☐ Saucisses / ☐ Sausages

avec
- ☐ rôties ou
- ☐ croissant ou
- ☐ danoise

beurre et confitures
- ☐ Fraises
- ☐ Framboises
- ☐ Orange
- ☐ Miel

served with
- ☐ toast or
- ☐ croissant or
- ☐ sweet roll

butter and preserves
- ☐ Strawberry
- ☐ Raspberry
- ☐ Orange
- ☐ Honey

LE CAFÉ CANADIEN
Pour un petit déjeuner léger ou complet service à la carte ou buffet de 07h00 à 11h00.

LE CAFÉ CANADIEN
Light and full course breakfast à la carte or buffet from 7 to 11:00 a.m.

Entre amis: Le petit déjeuner

«Qu'est-ce que vous prenez au petit déjeuner?» Aux États-Unis, le petit déjeuner est généralement un repas abondant.° En France, c'est un repas simple.

Fabrice (13 ans)

Chez nous, nous sommes très traditionnels. Je mange du pain avec du beurre et de la confiture. Je bois un grand bol° de café au lait.

Sylvie (14 ans)

Je mange des tartines de pain grillé° et je bois du lait chaud ou du chocolat avec beaucoup de sucre. Le dimanche, il y a parfois° des croissants. (Ça dépend si quelqu'un veut faire les courses!)

Daniel (12 ans)

Chez nous, nous prenons le petit déjeuner «à l'américaine». Je mange des céréales et je bois du jus d'orange.

Marie-Hélène (16 ans)

Je ne veux pas grossir. Alors, je mange une ou deux biscottes.° Sans° beurre, bien sûr. Et je bois du thé.

Chantal (13 ans)

Je suis martiniquaise. En général, je mange du pain et de la confiture comme° tout le monde.° Parfois ma mère prépare un petit déjeuner martiniquais typique. On mange du blaff de poisson° et des bananes vertes cuites.° On mange aussi des ananas,° des papayes et de la gelée de goyave.° C'est délicieux!

abondant *copious, large* **bol** *deep bowl* **pain grillé** *buttered toast* **parfois** *sometimes* **biscottes** *dried toast* **Sans** *Without* **comme** *like* **tout le monde** *everybody* **blaff de poisson** *fish stew* **cuites** *cooked* **ananas** *pineapples* **gelée de goyave** *guava jelly*

NOTE CULTURELLE

La cuisine créole

La cuisine créole est une cuisine régionale typique de la Martinique et de la Guadeloupe. C'est une cuisine assez épicée° qui utilise les produits locaux,° principalement les produits de la mer et les fruits exotiques.

épicée *hot (spiced)* **locaux** *local*

Comment lire
MORE GUESSING FROM CONTEXT

When you are reading, the context is not only the printed word. Sometimes there are illustrations to help you understand the text. As you read the recipe for **crêpes** on the next page, try guessing what the new words mean by studying the pictures. (You can check how well you are doing by looking at the English equivalents at the bottom of the page.)

Enrichissez votre vocabulaire
INCREASING YOUR ENGLISH VOCABULARY

Learning French will also help you increase your English vocabulary. Sometimes a French word you know will help you guess the meaning of an unfamiliar English word. For example:

a repast looks like **un repas** and is an old word for *meal*

Activité
Match these English words with their corresponding definitions.

1. to blanch
2. facile
3. travail
4. famished

a. painfully difficult work
b. easily done
c. very hungry
d. to whiten, to bleach

Activité: Mon petit déjeuner
Décrivez le petit déjeuner chez vous.
- pendant la semaine
- le dimanche matin

Voici certaines spécialités:

boudin créole	*hot sausage, creole style*	**bifteck de tortue**	*turtle steak*
blaff de poisson	*fish stew*	**matoutou crabes**	*stewed crabs served with rice*
crabes farcis	*stuffed crabs*		
langoustes grillées	*(small) lobsters, grilled*		

Variétés

Les crêpes

Les crêpes sont d'origine bretonne.° Aujourd'hui, on vend les crêpes dans les «crêperies». On peut aussi faire des crêpes à la maison. Voici une recette° très simple.

LES INGRÉDIENTS

3 oeufs
3 cuillères à soupe de sucre
une pincée° de sel
2 tasses de lait
1 tasse de farine°
1 cuillère à soupe d'huile°
du beurre

LES USTENSILES

un petit bol

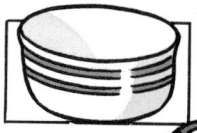
un grand bol

un fouet

une poêle

D'abord: Pour faire la pâte°

Mettez les oeufs dans le petit bol. Battez-les° bien avec le fouet.

Ajoutez° le sucre, le sel et un peu de lait.

Mettez la farine dans le grand bol. Versez° le contenu° du petit bol dans le grand bol.

Ajoutez l'huile et le reste du lait. Mélangez° bien la pâte. Attendez deux heures.

La Crêperie Québécoise
1775 St-Hubert, Montréal H2L 3Z1 (Métro Berri-de-Montigny)
Tél: 521-8362

bretonne *from Brittany* **recette** *recipe* **pincée** *pinch* **farine** *flour* **huile** *oil* **pâte** *batter*
Battez-les *Beat them* **Ajoutez** *Add* **Versez** *Pour* **contenu** *contents* **Mélangez** *Mix, Stir*

Ensuite: Pour faire les crêpes

Chauffez° la poêle. Mettez du beurre dans la poêle.

Mettez une cuillère de pâte dans la poêle.

Agitez° la poêle pour étendre° la pâte.

Retournez° la crêpe quand elle est dorée.°

Si vous êtes adroit(e), faites sauter° la crêpe en l'air. Si vous n'êtes pas adroit(e), abstenez-vous!°

Enfin: Pour servir les crêpes

Mettez la crêpe sur une assiette chaude. Faites les autres° crêpes.

Mettez du sucre ou de la confiture sur chaque° crêpe.

Au choix, roulez-la° ou pliez-la° en quatre.

Chauffez *Heat* **Agitez** *Shake* **étendre** *spread*
Retournez *Turn over* **dorée** *golden brown* **faites sauter** *flip*
abstenez-vous *don't try* **autres** *other* **chaque** *each*
roulez-la *roll it* **pliez-la** *fold it*

Bon appétit!

REFERENCE SECTION

CONTENTS

Appendix 1	**Maps**	**R2**
Appendix 2	**Sound/Spelling Correspondences**	**R5**
Appendix 3	**Numbers**	**R7**
Appendix 4	**Verbs**	**R8**
French-English Vocabulary		**R13**
English-French Vocabulary		**R35**
Index		**R49**
Photo Credits		**R51**

APPENDIX 1

Maps

The French-Speaking World

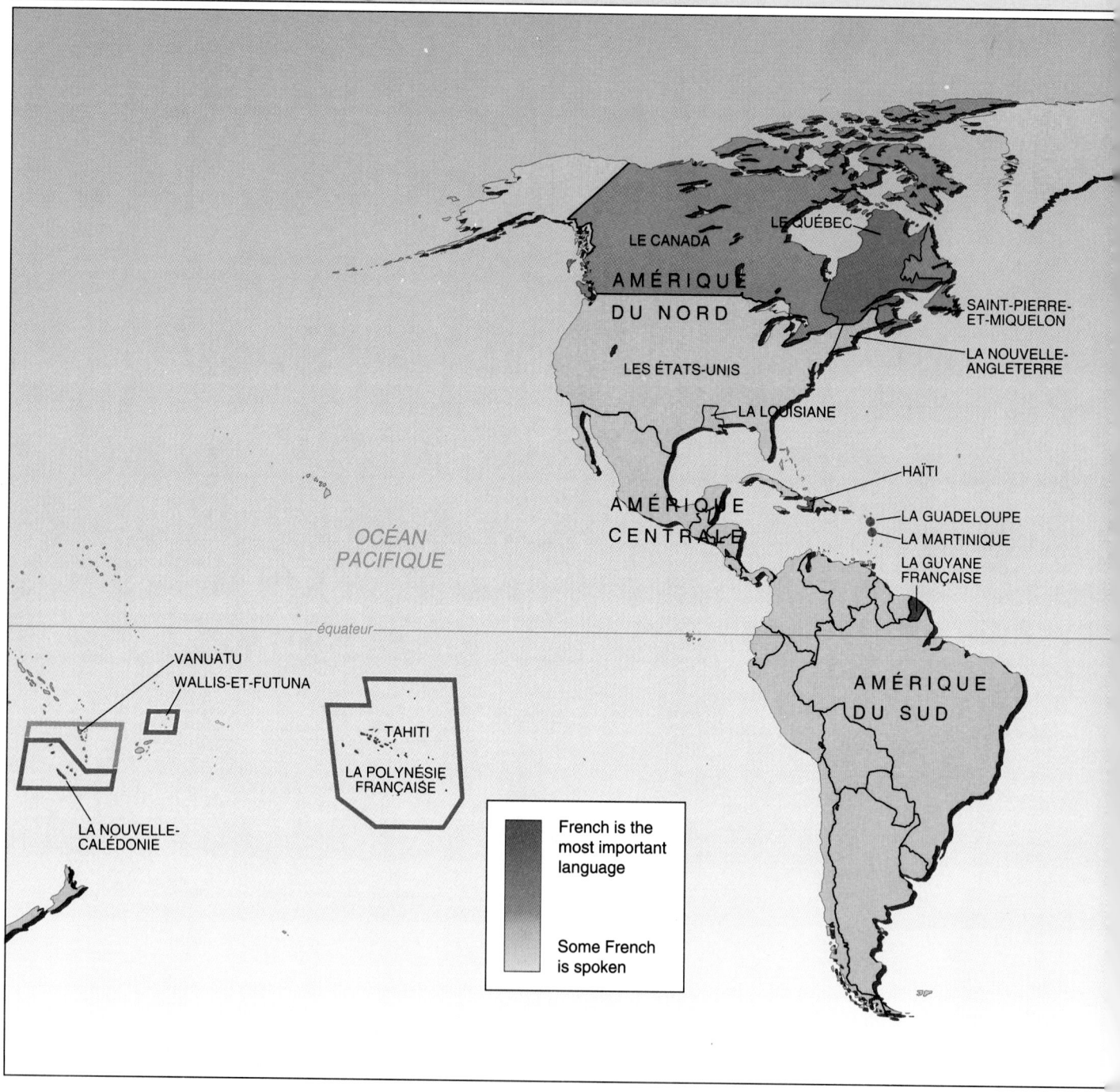

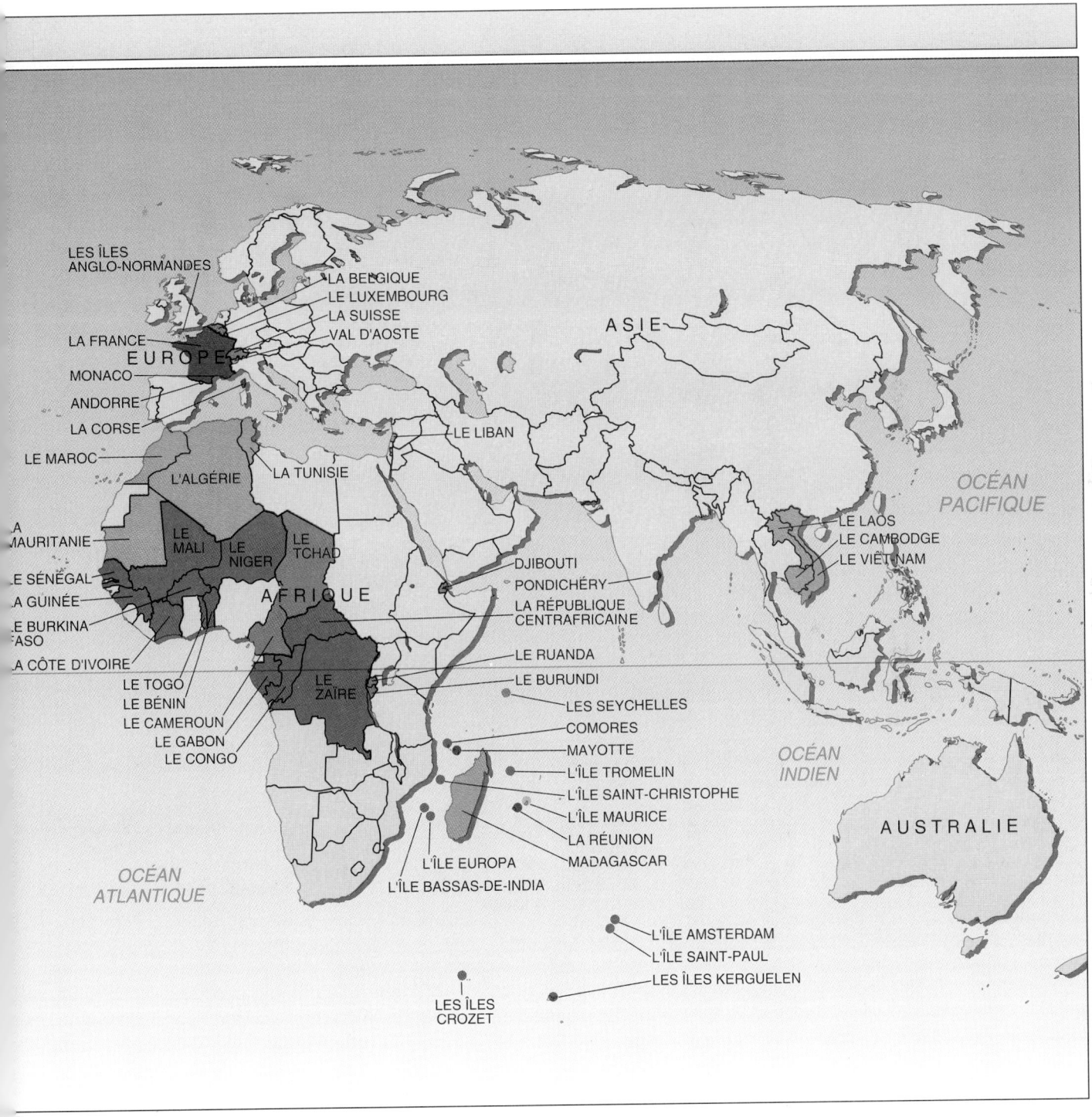
LES ÎLES ANGLO-NORMANDES
LA BELGIQUE
LE LUXEMBOURG
LA SUISSE
VAL D'AOSTE
LA FRANCE
EUROPE
MONACO
ANDORRE
LA CORSE
ASIE
LE LIBAN
LE MAROC
L'ALGÉRIE
LA TUNISIE
OCÉAN PACIFIQUE
LE LAOS
LE CAMBODGE
LE VIÊT-NAM
LE MALI
LE NIGER
LE TCHAD
DJIBOUTI
PONDICHÉRY
AFRIQUE
LA RÉPUBLIQUE CENTRAFRICAINE
LE RUANDA
LE BURUNDI
LE ZAÏRE
LES SEYCHELLES
COMORES
MAYOTTE
L'ÎLE TROMELIN
L'ÎLE SAINT-CHRISTOPHE
L'ÎLE MAURICE
LA RÉUNION
MADAGASCAR
L'ÎLE EUROPA
L'ÎLE BASSAS-DE-INDIA
LE TOGO
LE BÉNIN
LE CAMEROUN
LE GABON
LE CONGO
OCÉAN INDIEN
AUSTRALIE
OCÉAN ATLANTIQUE
L'ÎLE AMSTERDAM
L'ÎLE SAINT-PAUL
LES ÎLES KERGUELEN
LES ÎLES CROZET

France

[1]Also known as Île-de-France
[2]Also known as Nord-Pas-de-Calais
[3]Also known as Provence-Alpes-Côte d'Azur *(Bottin 1989)*

APPENDIX 2

Sound-Spelling Correspondences

Vowels

Sound	*Spelling*	*Examples*
/a/	**a, à, â**	Madame, là-bas, théâtre
/i/	**i, î**	visite, Nice, dîne
	y (initial, final, or between consonants)	Yves, Guy, style
/u/	**ou, où, oû**	Toulouse, où, août
/y/	**u, û**	tu, Luc, sûr
/o/	**o** (final or before silent consonant)	piano, idiot, Margot
	au, eau	jaune, Claude, beau
	ô	hôtel, drôle, Côte-d'Ivoire
/ɔ/	**o**	Monique, Noël, jolie
	au	Paul, restaurant, Laure
/e/	**é**	Dédé, Québec, télé
	e (before silent final **z, t, r**)	chez, et, Roger
	ai (final or before final silent consonant)	j'ai, mai, japonais
/ɛ/	**è**	Michèle, Ève, père
	ei	seize, neige, tour Eiffel
	ê	tête, être, Viêt-nam
	e (before two consonants)	elle, Pierre, Annette
	e (before pronounced final consonant)	Michel, avec, cher
	ai (before pronounced final consonant)	française, aime, Maine
/ə/	**e** (final or before single consonant)	je, Denise, venir
/ø/	**eu, oeu**	deux, Mathieu, oeufs
	eu (before final **se**)	nerveuse, généreuse, sérieuse
/œ/	**eu** (before final pronounced consonant except /z/)	heure, neuf, Lesieur
	oeu	soeur, coeur, oeuf
	oe	oeil

Nasal vowels

Sound	*Spelling*	*Examples*
/ɑ̃/	**an, am**	France, quand, lampe
	en, em	Henri, pendant, décembre
/ɔ̃/	**on, om**	non, Simon, bombe
/ɛ̃/	**in, im**	Martin, invite, impossible
	yn, ym	syndicat, sympathique, Olympique
	ain, aim	Alain, americain, faim
	(o) + in	loin, moins, point
	(i) + en	bien, Julien, viens
/œ̃/	**un, um**	un, Lebrun, parfum

Semi-vowels

Sound	*Spelling*	*Examples*
/j/	**i, y** (before vowel sound)	bien, piano, Lyon
	-il, -ill (after vowel sound), **-ll**	oeil, travaille, Marseille, fille
/ɥ/	**u** (before vowel sound)	lui, Suisse, juillet
/w/	**ou** (before vowel sound)	oui, Louis, jouer
/wa/	**oi, oî**	voici, Benoît
	oy (before vowel)	voyage

Consonants

Sound	*Spelling*	*Examples*
/b/	**b**	Barbara, banane, Belgique
/k/	**c** (before **a, o, u,** or consonant)	Coca-Cola, cuisine, classe
	ch(r)	Christine, Christian, Christophe
	qu, q (final)	Québec, qu'est-ce que, cinq
	k	kilo, Kiki, ketchup
/ʃ/	**ch**	Charles, blanche, chez
/a/	**d**	Didier, dans, médecin
/f/	**f**	Félix, franc, neuf
	ph	Philippe, téléphone, photo
/g/	**g** (before **a, o, u,** or consonant)	Gabriel, gorge, légumes, gris
	gu (before **e, i, y**)	vague, Guillaume, Guy
/ɲ/	**gn**	mignon, champagne, Allemagne
/ʒ/	**j**	je, Jérôme, jaune
	g (before **e, i, y**)	rouge, Gigi, gymnastique
	ge (before **a, o, u**)	orangeade, Georges, nageur
/l/	**l**	Lise, elle, cheval
/m/	**m**	Maman, moi, tomate
/n/	**n**	banane, Nancy, nous
/p/	**p**	peu, Papa, Pierre
/r/	**r**	arrive, rentre, Paris
/s/	**c** (before **e, i, y**)	ce, Cécile, Nancy
	ç (before **a, o, u**)	ça, garçon, déçu
	s (initial or before consonant)	sac, Sophie, reste
	ss (between vowels)	boisson, dessert, Suisse
	t (before **i** + vowel)	attention, Nations Unies, natation
	x	dix, six, soixante
/t/	**t**	trop, télé, Tours
	th	Thérèse, thé, Marthe
/v/	**v**	Viviane, vous, nouveau
/gz/	**x**	examen, exemple, exact
/ks/	**x**	Max, Mexique, excellent
/z/	**s** (between vowels)	désert, Louise, télévision
	z	Suzanne, zut, zéro

APPENDIX 3

Numbers

A. Cardinal numbers

0	zéro	18	dix-huit	82	quatre-vingt-deux
1	un (une)	19	dix-neuf	90	quatre-vingt-dix
2	deux	20	vingt	91	quatre-vingt-onze
3	trois	21	vingt et un (une)	100	cent
4	quatre	22	vingt-deux	101	cent un (une)
5	cinq	23	vingt-trois	102	cent deux
6	six	30	trente	200	deux cents
7	sept	31	trente et un (une)	201	deux cent un
8	huit	32	trente-deux	300	trois cents
9	neuf	40	quarante	400	quatre cents
10	dix	41	quarante et un (une)	500	cinq cents
11	onze	50	cinquante	600	six cents
12	douze	60	soixante	700	sept cents
13	treize	70	soixante-dix	800	huit cents
14	quatorze	71	soixante et onze	900	neuf cents
15	quinze	72	soixante-douze	1.000	mille
16	seize	80	quatre-vingts	2.000	deux mille
17	dix-sept	81	quatre-vingt-un (une)	1.000.000	un million

Notes:

1. The word **et** occurs only in the numbers 21, 31, 41, 51, 61, and 71: **vingt et un**, **soixante et onze**
2. **Un** becomes **une** before a feminine noun: **trente et une filles**
3. **Quatre-vingts** becomes **quatre-vingt** before another number: **quatre-vingt-cinq**
4. **Cents** becomes **cent** before another number: **trois cent vingt**
5. **Mille** never adds an **-s:** **quatre mille**

B. Ordinal numbers

1er (ère)	**premier (première)**	5e	**cinquième**	9e	**neuvième**
2e	**deuxième**	6e	**sixième**	10e	**dixième**
3e	**troisième**	7e	**septième**	11e	**onzième**
4e	**quatrième**	8e	**huitième**	12e	**douzième**

Note: Premier becomes **première** before a feminine noun: **la première histoire**

C. Metric equivalents

1 gramme	=	0.035 ounces	1 ounce	=	**28,349 grammes**
1 kilogramme	=	2.205 pounds	1 pound	=	**0,453 kilogrammes**
1 litre	=	1.057 quarts	1 quart	=	**0,946 litres**
1 mètre	=	39.37 inches	1 foot	=	**30,480 centimètres**
1 kilomètre	=	0.62 miles	1 mile	=	**1,609 kilomètres**

APPENDIX 4

Verbs

A. Regular verbs

Infinitive	*Present*		*Passé composé*	
parler *(to talk, speak)*	je **parle** tu **parles** il **parle**	nous **parlons** vous **parlez** ils **parlent**	j'**ai parlé** tu **as parlé** il **a parlé**	nous **avons parlé** vous **avez parlé** ils **ont parlé**
	IMPERATIVE: **parle, parlons, parlez**			
finir *(to finish)*	je **finis** tu **finis** il **finit**	nous **finissons** vous **finissez** ils **finissent**	j'**ai fini** tu **as fini** il **a fini**	nous **avons fini** vous **avez fini** ils **ont fini**
	IMPERATIVE: **finis, finissons, finissez**			
vendre *(to sell)*	je **vends** tu **vends** il **vend**	nous **vendons** vous **vendez** ils **vendent**	j'**ai vendu** tu **as vendu** il **a vendu**	nous **avons vendu** vous **avez vendu** ils **ont vendu**
	IMPERATIVE: **vends, vendons, vendez**			

B. *-er* verbs with spelling changes

Infinitive	*Present*		*Passé composé*
acheter *(to buy)*	j'**achète** tu **achètes** il **achète**	nous **achetons** vous **achetez** ils **achètent**	j'**ai acheté**
	Verb like **acheter**: amener *(to bring, take along)*		
espérer *(to hope)*	j'**espère** tu **espères** il **espère**	nous **espérons** vous **espérez** ils **espèrent**	j'**ai espéré**
	Verbs like **espérer**: célébrer *(to celebrate)*, préférer *(to prefer)*		
commencer *(to begin, start)*	je **commence** tu **commences** il **commence**	nous **commençons** vous **commencez** ils **commencent**	j'**ai commencé**
manger *(to eat)*	je **mange** tu **manges** il **mange**	nous **mangeons** vous **mangez** ils **mangent**	j'**ai mangé**
	Verbs like **manger**: nager *(to swim)*, voyager *(to travel)*		
payer *(to pay, pay for)*	je **paie** tu **paies** il **paie**	nous **payons** vous **payez** ils **paient**	j'**ai payé**

C. Irregular verbs

Infinitive	*Present*		*Passé composé*
avoir *(to have, own)*	j'**ai** tu **as** il **a**	nous **avons** vous **avez** ils **ont**	j'**ai eu**
	IMPERATIVE: **aie, ayons, ayez**		
être *(to be)*	je **suis** tu **es** il **est**	nous **sommes** vous **êtes** ils **sont**	j'**ai été**
	IMPERATIVE: **sois, soyons, soyez**		
aller *(to go)*	je **vais** tu **vas** il **va**	nous **allons** vous **allez** ils **vont**	je **suis allé(e)**
boire *(to drink)*	je **bois** tu **bois** il **boit**	nous **buvons** vous **buvez** ils **boivent**	j'**ai bu**
connaître *(to know)*	je **connais** tu **connais** il **connaît**	nous **connaissons** vous **connaissez** ils **connaissent**	j'**ai connu**
devoir *(to have to, should, must)*	je **dois** tu **dois** il **doit**	nous **devons** vous **devez** ils **doivent**	j'**ai dû**
dire *(to say, tell)*	je **dis** tu **dis** il **dit**	nous **disons** vous **dites** ils **disent**	j'**ai dit**
dormir *(to sleep)*	je **dors** tu **dors** il **dort**	nous **dormons** vous **dormez** ils **dorment**	j'**ai dormi**
écrire *(to write)*	j'**écris** tu **écris** il **écrit**	nous **écrivons** vous **écrivez** ils **écrivent**	j'**ai écrit**
	Verb like **écrire:** décrire *(to describe)*		
faire *(to make, do)*	je **fais** tu **fais** il **fait**	nous **faisons** vous **faites** ils **font**	j'**ai fait**
lire *(to read)*	je **lis** tu **lis** il **lit**	nous **lisons** vous **lisez** ils **lisent**	j'**ai lu**
mettre *(to put, place)*	je **mets** tu **mets** il **met**	nous **mettons** vous **mettez** ils **mettent**	j'**ai mis**
	Verb like **mettre:** promettre *(to promise)*		

C. Irregular verbs, continued

Infinitive	*Present*		*Passé composé*
ouvrir *(to open)*	j'**ouvre** tu **ouvres** il **ouvre**	nous **ouvrons** vous **ouvrez** ils **ouvrent**	**j'ai ouvert**
Verbs like **ouvrir**: découvrir *(to discover)*, offrir *(to offer)*			
partir *(to leave)*	je **pars** tu **pars** il **part**	nous **partons** vous **partez** ils **partent**	je **suis parti(e)**
pouvoir *(to be able, can)*	je **peux** tu **peux** il **peut**	nous **pouvons** vous **pouvez** ils **peuvent**	**j'ai pu**
prendre *(to take)*	je **prends** tu **prends** il **prend**	nous **prenons** vous **prenez** ils **prennent**	**j'ai pris**
Verbs like **prendre**: apprendre *(to learn)*, comprendre *(to understand)*			
savoir *(to know)*	je **sais** tu **sais** il **sait**	nous **savons** vous **savez** ils **savent**	**j'ai su**
sortir *(to go out, get out)*	je **sors** tu **sors** il **sort**	nous **sortons** vous **sortez** ils **sortent**	je **suis sorti(e)**
venir *(to come)*	je **viens** tu **viens** il **vient**	nous **venons** vous **venez** ils **viennent**	je **suis venu(e)**
Verb like **venir**: revenir *(to come back)*			
voir *(to see)*	je **vois** tu **vois** il **voit**	nous **voyons** vous **voyez** ils **voient**	**j'ai vu**
vouloir *(to want)*	je **veux** tu **veux** il **veut**	nous **voulons** vous **voulez** ils **veulent**	**j'ai voulu**

D. Verbs with *être* in the *passé composé*

aller *(to go)*	je **suis allé(e)**	**passer** *(to go by, through)*	je **suis passé(e)**
arriver *(to arrive, come)*	je **suis arrivé(e)**	**rentrer** *(to go home)*	je **suis rentré(e)**
descendre *(to go down)*	je **suis descendu(e)**	**rester** *(to stay)*	je **suis resté(e)**
entrer *(to enter, go in)*	je **suis entré(e)**	**revenir** *(to come back)*	je **suis revenu(e)**
monter *(to go up)*	je **suis monté(e)**	**sortir** *(to go out, get out)*	je **suis sorti(e)**
mourir *(to die)*	Il/elle **est mort(e)**	**tomber** *(to fall)*	je **suis tombé(e)**
naître *(to be born)*	je **suis né(e)**	**venir** *(to come)*	je **suis venu(e)**
partir *(to leave)*	je **suis parti(e)**		

FRENCH-ENGLISH VOCABULARY

R13

VOCABULARY

French-English

The French-English vocabulary contains active and passive words from the text, as well as the important words of the illustrations used within the units. Obvious passive cognates have not been listed.

The numbers following an entry indicate the lesson in which the word or phrase is activated. (**B** stands for the photo essay that precedes **Niveau B; C** stands for the list of phrases and expressions that precedes **Niveau C;** and **E** stands for **Entracte.**)

Nouns: If the article of a noun does not indicate gender, the noun is followed by *m.* (*masculine*) or *f.* (*feminine*). If the plural (*pl.*) is irregular, it is given in parentheses.

Adjectives: Adjectives are listed in the masculine form. If the feminine form is irregular, it is given in parentheses. Irregular plural forms (*pl.*) are also given in parentheses.

Verbs: Verbs are listed in the infinitive form. An asterisk (*) in front of an active verb means that it is irregular. (For forms, see the verb charts in Appendix 4C.) Irregular present tense forms are listed when they are used before the verb has been activated. Irregular past participle (*p.p.*) forms are listed separately.

Words beginning with an **h** are preceded by a bullet (•) if the **h** is aspirate; that is, if the word is treated as if it begins with a consonant sound.

A

a: il y a there is, there are **17**
à at, in, to **14, 22**
à côté next door
à demain see you tomorrow **8**
à droite on (to) the right **21**
à gauche on (to) the left **21**
à la mode popular; in fashion; fashionable **25**
à mon avis in my opinion **27**
à partir de as of, beginning
à pied on foot **22**
à samedi! see you Saturday! **8**
à vélo by bicycle **22**
abolir to abolish
abondant plentiful, copious, large
abord: d'abord (at) first **30**
un **abricot** apricot
absolument absolutely
un **accent** accent mark, stress
accepter to accept
des **accessoires** *m.* accessories **25**
un **accord** agreement
d'accord okay, all right **13**
être d'accord to agree **14**
un **achat** purchase
faire des achats to go shopping **29**
acheter to buy **25, 26**
acheter + du, de la *(partitive)* to buy (some) **34**
un **acteur, une actrice** actor, actress
une **activité** activity
l' **addition** *f.* check
adorer to love
une **adresse** address **21**
quelle est ton adresse? what's your address? **21**
adroit skilled, skillful
un **adulte** adult
aéronautique aeronautic, aeronautical
un **aéroport** airport
affectueusement affectionately *(at the end of a letter)*
une **affiche** poster **17**
affirmativement affirmatively
l' **Afrique** *f.* Africa
l' **âge** *m.* age
quel âge a-t-il/elle? how old is he/she? **17**
quel âge as-tu? how old are you? **7**
quel âge a ton père/ta mère? how old is your father/your mother? **7**
âgé old
une **agence** agency
une agence de tourisme tourist office
une agence de voyages travel agency
agiter to shake
agité agitated
ah! ah!, oh!
ah bon? oh? really? **16**
ah non! ah, no!
ai (*see* **avoir**): **j'ai** I have **17**
j'ai... ans I'm . . . (years old) **7**
aider to help **29, 35**
une **aile** wing
aimer to like **15, 33**
est-ce que tu aimes...? do you like . . .? **13**
j'aime... I like . . . **13**
j'aimerais I would like
je n'aime pas... I don't like . . . **13**

ainsi thus
aîné older
un frère aîné older brother
une soeur aînée older sister
ajouter to add
l' **Algérie** *f.* Algeria *(country in North Africa)*
algérien (algérienne) Algerian
l' **Allemagne** *f.* Germany
allemand German
* **aller** to go **22**
aller + *inf.* to be going to + *inf.* **22**
allez (*see* **aller**): **allez-vous-en** go away!
allez-y come on!, go ahead!, do it!
comment allez-vous? how are you? **3**
allô! hello! *(on the telephone)*
allons (*see* **aller**): **allons-y** let's go! **22**
alors so, then **19**
une **alouette** lark
les **Alpes** *f.* (the) Alps
l' **alphabet** *m.* alphabet
l' **alpinisme** *m.* mountain climbing **29**
faire de l'alpinisme to go mountain climbing **29**
l' **Alsace** *f.* Alsace *(province in eastern France)*
amener to bring *(a person)* **26, 35**
américain American **2, 19**
à l'américaine American-style
un **Américain, une Américaine** American person
l' **Amérique** *f.* America
un **ami, une amie** (close) friend **5**
amicalement love *(at the end of a letter)*
l' **amitié** *f.* friendship
amitiés best regards *(at the end of a letter)*
amusant funny, amusing **19**
amuser to amuse
s'amuser to have fun
on s'est bien amusé! we had a good time!
un **an** year
avoir... ans to be . . . (years old) **18**
il/elle a... ans he/she is . . . (years old) **7**
j'ai... ans I'm . . . (years old) **7**
l'an dernier last year
par an per year
un **ananas** pineapple
ancien (ancienne) former, old, ancient
un **âne** donkey
un **ange** angel
anglais English **2, 19**
un **Anglais, une Anglaise** English person
un **animal** (*pl.* **animaux**) animal
une **animation** live entertainment
animé animated, lively
une **année** year **8**
bonne année! Happy New Year! **32**
toute l'année all year long
un **anniversaire** birthday **8**
bon anniversaire! happy birthday! **32**
c'est quand, ton anniversaire? when is your birthday? **8**
mon anniversaire est le (2 mars) my birthday is (March 2nd) **8**
un **annuaire** telephone directory
un **anorak** ski jacket
les **antiquités** *f.* antiquities, antiques
août *m.* August **8**
un **appareil-photo** (*pl.* **appareils-photo**) (still) camera **17**
un **appartement** apartment **21**
s' **appeller** to be named, called
comment s'appelle...? what's . . .'s name? **6**
comment s'appelle-t-il/elle? what's his/her name? **17**
comment t'appelles-tu? what's your name? **1**
il/elle s'appelle... his/her name is . . . **6**
je m'appelle... my name is . . . **1**
apporter to bring *(things)* **26**
apporter quelque chose à quelqu'un to bring something to someone **35**
apporte-moi (apportez-moi) bring me **B**
* **apprendre (à)** + *inf.* to learn (to) **34**
apprécier to appreciate
approprié appropriate
après after **29;** after, afterwards **30, 31**
d'après according to
l' **après-midi** *m.* afternoon **29**
cet après-midi this afternoon **31**
de l'après-midi in the afternoon, P.M. **4**
demain après-midi tomorrow afternoon **31**
hier après-midi yesterday afternoon **31**
l' **arabe** *m.* Arabic *(language)*
un **arbre** tree
un arbre généalogique family tree
l' **arche** *f.* **de Noé** Noah's Ark
l' **argent** *m.* money **28**
l'argent de poche allowance, pocket money
arrêter to arrest
arriver to arrive, come **22**
j'arrive! I'm coming!
une **arrivée** arrival
un **arrondissement** district
un **artifice: le feu d'artifice** fireworks
un **artiste, une artiste** artist
as (*see* **avoir**): **est-ce que tu as...?** do you have . . . ? **17**
un **ascenseur** elevator
un **aspirateur** vacuum cleaner
asseyez-vous! sit down! **B**
assez rather **19;** enough
assieds-toi! sit down! **B**
une **assiette** plate **33**
assister à to go to, attend **29**
associer to associate
l' **Atlantique** *m.* Atlantic Ocean
attendre to wait, wait for **28**
attention *f.:* **faire attention** to be careful, pay attention **16**
attentivement carefully

au (à + le) to (the), at (the), in (the) **14, 22**
au revoir! good-bye! **3**
une **auberge** inn
une auberge de campagne country inn **30**
aucun: ne... aucun none, not any
aujourd'hui today **8, 31**
aujourd'hui, c'est... today is . . . **8**
aussi also, too **2, 15**
aussi... que as . . . as **27**
une **auto (automobile)** car, automobile **17**
une auto-école driving school
un **autobus** bus
un **autocar** touring bus **29**
l' **automne** *m.* autumn, fall
en automne in (the) autumn, fall **12**
autre other **33**
d'autres others
un(e) autre another
aux (à + les) to (the), at (the), in (the) **22**
avant before **29, 31**
avant hier the day before yesterday
en avant let's begin
avantageux (avantageuse) reasonable, advantageous
avec with **14**
avec moi, avec toi with me, with you **13**
avec qui? with who(m)? **16**
une **avenue** avenue **21**
un **avion** airplane, plane **29**
en avion by airplane **29**
un **avis** opinion
avis de recherche missing person's bulletin
à mon avis in my opinion **27**
à votre avis in your opinion
* **avoir** to have **18**
avoir... ans to be . . . (years old) **18**
avoir besoin de to need **28**
avoir chaud to be warm, hot **30**
avoir de la chance to be lucky **30**
avoir envie de to feel like, want **28**
avoir faim to be hungry **18**
avoir froid to be cold **30**
avoir lieu to take place
avoir raison to be right **30**
avoir soif to be thirsty **18, 30**
avoir tort to be wrong **30**
avril *m.* April **8**

B

le **babyfoot** tabletop soccer game
le **babysitting: faire du babysitting** to baby-sit
les **bagages** *m.* bags, baggage
bain: un maillot de bain bathing suit **25**
une **banane** banana **33**
une **bande** reel-to-reel tape **B**
une **bande dessinée** comic strip
des bandes dessinées comics
la **Bannière étoilée** Star-Spangled Banner
une **banque** bank
une **barbe: quelle barbe!** what a pain! *(colloq.)*
bas: en bas downstairs **21**
au bas at the bottom
le **baseball** baseball **23**
basé based
le **basket (basketball)** basketball **23**
jouer au basket to play basketball **13**
des **baskets** *m.* hightops (sneakers) **25**
bateau boat, ship **29**
un bateau-mouche sightseeing boat
la **batterie** drums **23**
battre to beat
bavard talkative
beau (bel, belle; *m.pl.* **beaux)** handsome, good-looking, beautiful **17, 20, 27**
il est beau he is good-looking, handsome **17**
il fait beau it's beautiful (nice) out **12**
un **beau-frère** stepbrother, brother-in-law
un **beau-père** stepfather, father-in-law
beaucoup (de) much, very much, many, a lot **15**
la **beauté** beauty
un **bec** beak
bel (*see* **beau**) beautiful, handsome **27**
la **Belgique** Belgium
belle (*see* **beau**) beautiful **17, 20, 27**
elle est belle she is beautiful **17**
une **belle-mère** stepmother, mother-in-law
une **belle-soeur** stepsister, sister-in-law
les **Bermudes** *f.* Bermuda
le **besoin** need
avoir besoin de to need, to have to **28**
des besoins d'argent money needs
bête dumb, silly **19**
le **beurre** butter **33**
une **bibliothèque** library **21**
une **bicyclette** bicycle **17**
bien well, very well, carefully **15**
bien sûr of course **13**
ça va bien everything's fine (going well) **3**
ça va très bien I'm (everything's) very well **3**
c'est bien that's good (fine) **20**
eh bien! well! **26**
je veux bien (...) I'd love to (. . .), I do, I want to **13, 34**
oui, bien sûr... yes, of course . . . **14**
très bien very well **15**
bientôt: à bientôt! see you soon!
bienvenue welcome
le **bifteck** steak
un biftek de tortue turtle steak

bilingue bilingual
un **billet** bill, paper money **28;** ticket
la **biologie** biology
une **biscotte** dry toast
blaff de poisson *(m.)* fish stew
blanc (blanche) white **20**
Blanche-Neige *f.* Snow White
blanchir to blanch, turn white
bleu blue **20**
blond blonde **17**
il/elle est blond(e) he/she is blond **17**
un **blouson** jacket **25**
* **boire** to drink **34**
une **boisson** drink, beverage **10, 33**
une **boîte** box
un **bol** deep bowl
bon (bonne) good **20**
bon marché *(inv.)* inexpensive **25**
ah bon? oh, really? **16**
de bonne humeur in a good mood
il fait bon the weather's good (pleasant) **12**
le **bonheur** happiness
bonjour hello **1, 3**
une **botte** boot **25**
une **bouche** mouth **E3**
une **boucherie** butcher shop
le **boudin** sausage
une **boulangerie** bakery
un **boulevard** boulevard **21**
une **boum** party *(colloq.)* **22**
une **boutique** boutique, shop **25**
boxe: un match de boxe boxing match
un **bras** arm **E3**
brésilien (brésilienne) Brazilian
la **Bretagne** Brittany *(province in northwestern France)*
bricoler to do things around the house
broche: à la broche on the spit
bronzé tan
un **bruit** noise
brun brown, dark-haired **17**
il/elle est brun(e) he/she has dark hair **17**
brunir to turn brown
Bruxelles *f.* Brussels
le **bulletin des notes** report card
un **bureau** desk **B, 17;** office
un **bus** bus
en bus by bus **22**
un **but** goal; end

C

ça that, it
ça fait combien? ça fait... how much is that (it)? that (it) is . . . **11**
ça, là-bas that (one), over there **17**
ça va? how's everything? how are you? **3**
ça va everything's fine, I'm OK **3**
ça va (très) bien, ça va bien everything's going very well, everything's fine (going well) **3**
ça va comme ci, comme ça everything's (going) so-so **3**
ça va (très) mal things are going (very) badly **3**
regarde ça look at that **17**
une **cabine d'essayage** fitting room
les **cabinets** *m.* toilet
un **cadeau** (*pl.* **cadeaux**) gift, present
cadet (cadette) younger
un frère cadet (a) younger brother
une soeur cadette (a) younger sister
le **café** coffee **10, 21**
un café au lait coffee with hot milk
un **café** café *(French coffee shop)* **14**
au café to (at) the café **14**
un **cahier** notebook **B**
une **calculatrice** calculator **17**
un **calendrier** calendar
un **camarade, une camarade** classmate **17**
le **Cambodge** Cambodia *(country in Asia)*
un **cambriolage** burglary
un **cambrioleur** burglar
une **caméra** movie camera
la **campagne** countryside **29**
à la campagne to (in) the countryside **29**
une auberge de campagne country inn
camping: faire du camping to go camping **29**
le **Canada** Canada
canadien (canadienne) Canadian **2, 19**
un **Canadien, une Canadienne** Canadian person
un **canard** duck
une **cantine de l'école** school cafeteria **33**
un **car** touring bus **29**
un car scolaire school bus
une **carotte** carrot **33**
des carottes rapées grated carrots
un **carré** square
le Vieux Carré *the French Quarter in New Orleans*
une **carte** map **B;** card
une carte postale postcard
les cartes *f.* (playing) cards **23**
jouer aux cartes to play cards **23**
un **cas** case
en cas de in case of
une **cassette** cassette tape **B, 17**
le **catch** wrestling
une **cathédrale** cathedral
une **cave** cellar
ce (c') this, that, it
ce n'est pas that's/it's not **20**
ce que what **C**
ce sont these are, those are, they are **20**
c'est it's, that's **5, 17, 20**
c'est + *day of the week* it's . . . **8**
c'est + *name or noun* it's . . . **5**
c'est bien/mal that's good/bad **20**
c'est combien? how much is that/it? **11**
c'est le (12 octobre) it's (October 12) **8**

qu'est-ce que c'est? what is it? what's that? **17**
qui est-ce? who's that/this? **17**
ce (cet, cette; ces) this, that, these, those **26**
ce... -ci this . . . (over here) **26**
ce mois-ci this month **31**
ce n'est pas it's (that's) not **20**
ce soir this evening, tonight **31**
une **cédille** cedilla
une **ceinture** belt **25**
cela that
célèbre famous
cent one hundred **6, 25**
cent un, cent deux 101, 102 **25**
deux cents, trois cents, ... neuf cents 200, 300, . . . 900 **25**
une **centaine** about a hundred
un **centime** centime *(1/100 of a franc)*
un **centre** center
un centre commercial shopping center **21**
les **céréales** *f.* cereal **33**
une **cerise** cherry **33**
certain certain
certains some of them
ces (*see* **ce**) these, those **26**
c'est (*see* **ce**)
cet (*see* **ce**) this, that **26**
cette (*see* **ce**) this, that **26**
chacun each one, each person
une **chaise** chair **B, 17**
une **chaîne** (TV) channel
une **chaîne stéréo** stereo set **17**
une mini-chaîne compact stereo
la **chaleur** heat, warmth
une **chambre** bedroom **17, 21**
un **champion, une championne** champion
la **chance** luck
avoir de la chance to be lucky **30**
bonne chance! good luck! **31**
une **chanson** song
chanter to sing **13, 15**
un **chanteur, une chanteuse** singer
un **chapeau** (*pl.* **chapeaux**) hat **25**
chaque each, every
charmant charming
un **chat** cat **7, E5**
un **château** (*pl.* **châteaux**) castle
chaud warm, hot
avoir chaud to be warm (hot) *(people)* **30**
il fait chaud it's warm (hot) *(weather)* **12**
chauffer to warm, heat up
un **chauffeur, une chauffeuse** driver
une **chaussette** sock **25**
une **chaussure** shoe **25**
un **chef** boss; chef
une **chemise** shirt **25**
un **chemisier** blouse **25**
cher (chère) expensive; dear **25**
chercher to look for, to get, to find **25**
je cherche... I'm looking for . . . **25**
un **cheval** (*pl.* **chevaux**) horse **E5**
les **cheveux** *m.* hair **E3**
chez + *person* at (to) someone's house **22;** at (to) the office of
chez moi (toi, lui...) (at) home **23**
chic *(inv.)* nice; elegant, in style
une chic fille a great girl
un **chien** dog **7**
la **chimie** chemistry
chinois Chinese **19**
le **chinois** Chinese (*language*)
le **chocolat** hot chocolate, cocoa **10**
une glace au chocolat chocolate ice cream
choisir to choose **27**
un **choix** choice
au choix choose one, your choice
une **chorale** choir
une **chose** thing **17**
quelque chose something **32**
chouette great, terrific **20, 25**
le **cidre** cider
un **cinéaste, une cinéaste** film maker
un **cinéma** movie theater **21**
le cinéma the movies
au cinéma to (at) the movies, movie theater **14**
cinq five **1**
cinquante fifty **3**
cinquième fifth **24**
une **circonstance** circumstance
cité: la Cité Interdite Forbidden City
une **clarinette** clarinet **23**
une **classe** class
en classe in class **14**
classique classical
un **clavier** keyboard **23**
un **client, une cliente** customer
un **clip** music video
un **cochon** pig
un **coiffeur, une coiffeuse** hairdresser
un **coin** spot
une **coïncidence** coincidence
le **Colisée** the Coliseum (*a large stadium built by the Romans*)
des **collants** *m.* (pair of) tights, pantyhose **25**
un **collège** junior high school
une **colonie** colony
une **colonne** column
combien how much **28**
combien coûte...? how much does . . . cost? **11, 25**
combien de how much, how many **28**
combien de temps? how long?
combien d'heures? how many hours?
ça fait combien? how much is this (it)? **11**
c'est combien? how much is this (it)? **11**
commander to order
comme like, as, for
comme ci, comme ça so-so
ça va comme ci, comme ça everything's so-so **3**
commencer to begin, start

comment? how? **16;** what?
comment allez-vous? how are you? **3**
comment est-il/elle? what's he/she like? what does he/she look like? **17**
comment dit-on... en français? how do you say . . . in French? **B**
comment lire reading hints
comment s'appelle...? what's . . .'s name? **6**
comment s'appelle-t-il/elle? what's his/her name? **17**
comment t'appelles-tu? what's your name? **1**
comment trouves-tu...? what do you think of . . .? **25**
comment vas-tu? how are you? **3**
un **commentaire** comment, commentary
commercial: un centre commercial shopping center **21**
le **commérage** gossip
communiquer to communicate
un **compact disque** compact disc **17**
complément object
compléter to complete
* **comprendre** to understand **34**
je (ne) comprends (pas) I (don't) understand **B**
compter to count (on); to expect, intend
concerne: en ce qui concerne as for
un **concert** concert **22**
un **concombre** cucumber
la **confiture** jam **33**
confortable comfortable **21**
une **connaissance** acquaintance
faire connaissance (avec) to become acquainted (with)
* **connaître** to know, be acquainted with; *(in passé composé)* to meet for the first time **36**
tu connais...? do you know . . .? are you acquainted with . . .? **6**
connu (*p.p. of* **connaître**) knew, met **36**
un **conseil** piece of advice, counsel
des conseils *m.* advice
un **conservatoire** conservatory
une **consonne** consonant
se **contenter** to limit oneself
le **contenu** contents
continuer to continue **21**
une **contradiction** disagreement
une **contravention** (traffic) ticket
cool cool, neat
un **copain, une copine** friend, pal **5**
un petit copain, une petite copine boyfriend, girlfriend
copier to copy
une **copine** friend **5**
coréen (coréenne) Korean
un **corps** body
correspondant corresponding
correspondre to correspond, agree
la **Corse** Corsica *(French island off the Italian coast)*
un **costume** man's suit
la **Côte d'Azur** Riviera *(southern coast of France on the Mediterranean)*
la **Côte d'Ivoire** Ivory Coast *(French-speaking country in West Africa)*
côté: à côté (de) next door; next to
une **côtelette de porc** pork chop
le **cou** neck **E3**
une **couleur** color **20**
de quelle couleur ...? what color . . .? **20**
un **couloir** hall, corridor
coup: dans le coup with it
courage: bon courage! good luck! **31**
courageux (courageuse) courageous
une **course** race
faire les courses to go shopping *(for food)* **33**
court short **25**
un **cousin, une cousine** cousin **7, 24**
le **coût: le coût de la vie** cost of living
un **couteau** (*pl.* **couteaux**) knife **33**
coûter to cost
combien coûte...? how much does . . . cost? **11, 25**
il (elle) coûte... it costs . . . **11**
un **couturier, une couturière** fashion designer
un **couvert** place setting **33**
un **crabe** crab
des matoutou crabes stewed crabs with rice
la **craie** chalk
un morceau de craie piece of chalk **B**
une **cravate** tie **25**
un **crayon** pencil **B, 17**
créer to create
un **crétin** idiot
une **crêpe** crepe (pancake) **9**
une **crêperie** crepe restaurant
une **crevaison** flat tire
une **croisade** crusade
un **croissant** crescent (roll) **9**
une **cuillère** spoon **33**
une cuillère à soupe soup spoon
la **cuisine** cooking **33**
une **cuisine** kitchen **21**
cuit cooked
culturel (culturelle) cultural
curieux (curieuse) curious, strange
la **curiosité** curiosity
un **cyclomoteur** moped

D

d'abord (at) first **30**
d'accord okay, all right
être d'accord to agree **14**
oui, d'accord yes, okay **13**
une **dame** lady, woman *(polite term)* **5**
les **dames** *f.* checkers *(game)* **23**
dangereux (dangereuse) dangerous

dans in **17**
danser to dance **13, 15**
la **date** date **8**
quelle est la date? what's the date? **8**
de (d') of, from, about **14, 23**
de l'après-midi in the afternoon **4**
de quelle couleur... ? what color . . .? **20**
de qui? of whom? **16**
de quoi? about what?
de temps en temps from time to time
pas de not any, no **18, 34**
débarquer to land
décembre *m.* December **8**
décider (de) to decide (to)
une **déclaration** statement
décoré decorated
* **découvrir** to discover
* **décrire** to describe **C**
décrivez... describe. . . **C**
un **défaut** shortcoming
un **défilé** parade
dégoûtant: c'est dégoûtant! it's (that's) disgusting **35**
dehors outside
en dehors de outside of
déjà already; ever
déjeuner to eat (have) lunch **33**
le **déjeuner** lunch **33**
le petit déjeuner breakfast **33**
délicieux (délicieuse) delicious **34**
demain tomorrow **8**
à demain! see you tomorrow! **8**
demain, c'est... (jeudi) tomorrow is . . . (Thursday) **8**
demander (à) to ask **C, 36**
demandez ... ask . . . **C**
un **demi-frère** half-brother
une **demi-soeur** half-sister
demi: ... heures et demie half past . . . **4**
midi et demi half past noon **4**
minuit et demi half past midnight **4**
démodé out of style, unfashionable **25**
un **démon** devil
une **dent** tooth
un **départ** departure
se **dépêcher: dépêchez-vous!** hurry up!
dépend: ça dépend that depends
une **dépense** expense
dépenser to spend (money) **28**
dernier (dernière) last **31**
derrière behind, in back of **17**
des some, any **18;** of (the), from (the), about (the) **23**
le **désert** desert
désirer to wish, want
vous désirez? what would you like? may I help you? **10, 25**
désolé sorry
le **dessert** dessert **33**
le **dessin** art, drawing
un dessin animé cartoon
détester to hate, detest **3**
deux two **1**
deuxième second **24**
le deuxième étage third floor
devant in front of **17**
développer to develop
deviner to guess
* **devoir** to have to, should, must **35**
un **devoir** homework assignment **B**
les **devoirs** *m.* homework
faire mes devoirs to do my homework **29**
d'habitude usually
différemment differently
différent different
difficile hard, difficult **20**
la **dignité** dignity
dimanche *m.* Sunday **8**
dîner to have dinner **15, 33**
dîner au restaurant to have dinner at a restaurant **13**
le **dîner** dinner, supper **33**
* **dire** to say, tell **C, 36**
que veut dire...? what does . . . mean? **B**
directement straight
un **directeur, une directrice** director, principal
dirigé directed, guided
dis! (*see* **dire**) say!, hey! **20**
dis donc! say there!, hey there! **20**
discuter to discuss
une **dispute** quarrel, dispute
un **disque** record **17**
un compact disque compact disc **17**
dit (*p.p. of* **dire**) said
dit (*see* **dire**)**: comment dit-on... en français?** how do you say . . . in French? **B**
dites... (*see* **dire**) say . . ., tell . . . **C**
dix ten **1, 2**
dix-huit eighteen **2**
dixième tenth **24**
dix-neuf nineteen **2**
dix-sept seventeen **2**
un **docteur** doctor
dois (*see* **devoir**)**: je dois** I have to (must) **13**
domestique domestic
les animaux *m.* **domestiques** pets **7**
dommage! too bad! **15**
donner (à) to give (to) **35, 36**
donne-moi... give me . . . **9, B**
donnez-moi... give me **10, B**
s'il te plaît, donne-moi... please, give me . . . **10**
doré golden brown
* **dormir** to sleep
le **dos** back **E3**
une **douzaine** dozen **33**
douze twelve **2**
douzième twelfth **24**
droit: tout droit straight **21**
droite right
à droite to (on) the right **21**
drôle funny **20**
du (de + le) of (the), from (the) **23;** some, any **34**
du matin in the morning, A.M. **4**

du soir in the evening, P.M. **4**
dû (*p.p. of* **devoir**) had to **35**
dur hard
des oeufs durs hard-boiled eggs
durer to last
dynamique dynamic

E

l' **eau** *f.* (*pl.* **eaux**) water **33**
l'eau minérale mineral water **33**
un **échange** exchange
des **échecs** *m.* chess **23**
une **éclosion** hatching
une **école** school **21**
économiser to save money
écouter to listen to **B, 15**
écouter la radio to listen to the radio **13**
écouter des cassettes to listen to cassettes **29**
* **écrire** to write **36**
l' **éducation** *f.* education
l'éducation civique civics
l'éducation physique physical education
une **église** church **21**
égyptien (égyptienne) Egyptian
eh bien! well! **26**
électronique: une guitare électronique electric guitar
élégant elegant **25**
un **éléphant** elephant **E5**
un **élève, une élève** pupil, student **17**
élevé high
elle she, it **11, 14, 18;** her **23**
elle coûte... it costs . . . **11**
elle est (canadienne) she's (Canadian) **6**
elle s'appelle... her name is . . . **6**
embrasser: je t'embrasse love and kisses *(at the end of a letter)*
un **emploi du temps** time-table *(of work)*
emprunter à to borrow from
en in, on, to, by
en avion by airplane, plane **29**
en bas (haut) downstairs (upstairs) **21**
en bus (métro, taxi, train, voiture) by bus (subway, taxi, train, car) **22**
en ce qui concerne as for
en face opposite, across (the street)
en fait in fact
en famille at home
en plus in addition
en scène on stage
en solde on sale
va-t'en! go away! **22**
un **endroit** place **22**
un **enfant, une enfant** child **24**
enfin at last **30**
ensuite then, after that **30**
entendre to hear **28**
entier (entière) entire
l' **entracte** *m.* interlude
entre between
une **entrée** entry *(of a house)*
un **entretien** discussion
envers toward
l' **envie** *f.* envy; feeling
avoir envie de to want; to feel like, want to **28**
épicé hot (spicy)
une **épicerie** grocery store
les **épinards** *m.* spinach
une **équipe** team
une **erreur** error, mistake
es (*see* **être**)
tu es + *nationality* you are . . . **2**
tu es + *nationality?* are you . . .? **2**
tu es de...? are you from . . .? **2**
un **escalier** staircase
un **escargot** snail
l' **Espagne** *f.* Spain
espagnol Spanish **19**
parler espagnol to speak Spanish **13**
espérer to hope **26**
un **esprit** spirit
essayer to try on, to try
l' **essentiel** *m.* the important thing
est (*see* **être**)
est-ce que (qu')...? *phrase used to introduce a question* **14**
c'est... it's . . ., that's . . . **5, 7, 20**
c'est le + *date* it's . . . **8**
il/elle est + *nationality* he/she is . . . **6**
n'est-ce pas...? isn't it? **14**
où est...? where is . . . ? **14**
quel jour est-ce? what day is it? **8**
qui est-ce? who's that (this)? **5, 17**
l' **est** *m.* east
et and **2, 14**
et demi(e), et quart half past, quarter past **4**
et toi? and you? **1**
établir to establish
un **étage** floor of a building, story
les **États-Unis** *m.* United States
été *(p.p. of* **être***)* been, was **31**
l' **été** *m.* summer
en été in (the) summer **12**
l'heure d'été daylight savings time
étendre to spread
une **étoile** star
étrange strange
étranger (étrangère) foreign
* **être** to be **14**
être à to belong to
être d'accord to agree **14**
une **étude** study
un **étudiant, une étudiant** (college) student **17**
étudier to study **13, 15**
eu (*p.p. of* **avoir**) had **31**
il y a eu there was
euh... er . . ., uh . . .
euh non... well, no
européen (européenne) European
eux they, them **23**
eux-mêmes themselves
un **événement** event
un **examen** exam, test
réussir à un examen to pass an exam, a test

excusez-moi excuse me **21**
un **exemple** example
par exemple for instance
un **exercice** exercise
faire des exercices to exercise
exiger to insist
expliquer to explain **C**
expliquez... explain . . . **C**
exprimer to express
exquis: c'est exquis! it's exquisite! **34**
extérieur: à l'extérieur outside
extra terrific **20**
extraordinaire extraordinary
il a fait un temps extraordinaire! the weather was great!

F

face: en face (de) opposite, across (the street) from
facile easy **20**
faible weak
la **faim** hunger
avoir faim to be hungry **30**
j'ai faim I'm hungry **9**
tu as faim? you're hungry **9**
faire to do, make **16**
faire attention to pay attention, be careful **16**
faire de + *activity* to do, play, study, participate in **29**
faire des achats to go shopping **29**
faire les courses to go shopping **33**
faire mes devoirs to do my homework **29**
faire partie de to be a member of
faire sauter to flip
faire un match to play a game (match) **16**
faire un pique-nique to have a picnic **29**
faire un voyage to take a trip **16**
faire une promenade to take a walk **16**
faire une promenade à pied (à vélo, en voiture) to take a walk (a bicycle ride, a drive) **22**
fait *(p.p. of* **faire***)* did, done, made **31**
fait: en fait in fact
fait (*see* **faire**)**: ça fait combien?** how much is that (it)? **11**
ça fait... francs that's (it's) . . . francs **11**
il fait (beau, etc.) it's (beautiful, etc.) *(weather)* **12**
quel temps fait-il? what (how) is the weather? **12**
fameux: c'est fameux! it's superb! **34**
familial with the family
une **famille** family **7, 24**
en famille at home
un **fana, une fana** fan
un **fantôme** ghost
la **farine** flour
fatigué tired
faux (fausse) false **20**
favori (favorite) favorite
une **femme** woman **17;** wife **24**
une **fenêtre** window **B, 17**
fermer to close **B**
une **feuille** sheet, leaf **B**
une feuille de papier sheet of paper **B**
un **feuilleton** series, serial story (*in newspaper*)
le **feu d'artifice** fireworks
les **félicitations** *f.* congratulations
février *m.* February **8**
une **fête** holiday
fîche-moi la paix! leave me alone! *(colloq.)* **36**
la **fièvre** fever
une **fille** girl **5;** daughter **24**
un **film** movie **22, 29**
un film policier detective movie
un **fils** son **24**
la **fin** end
finalement finally **30**
fini *(p.p. of* **finir***)* over, finished **31**
finir to finish **27**
flamand Flemish
un **flamant** flamingo
une **fleur** flower
un **fleuve** river
un **flic** cop *(colloq.)*
une **flûte** flute **23**
une **fois** time
à la fois at the same time
la **folie: à la folie** madly
folklorique: une chanson folklorique folksong
fonctionner to work, function
fondé founded
le **foot (football)** soccer **23**
le football américain football
jouer au foot to play soccer **13**
une **forêt** forest
formidable great!
fort strong
plus fort louder **B**
un **fouet** whisk
une **fourchette** fork **33**
la **fourrure** fur
un manteau de fourrure fur coat
frais: il fait frais it's cool *(weather)* **12**
une **fraise** strawberry **33**
un **franc** franc *(monetary unit of France, Belgium, and Switzerland)* **11**
ça fait... francs that's (it's) . . . francs **11**
la **France** France **14**
en France in France **14**
francophone French-speaking
français French **2, 19**
comment dit-on... en français? how do you say . . . in French? **B**
parler français to speak French **13**
le **français** French *(language)*
un **Français, une Française** French person
un **frère** brother **7, 24**
des **frites** *f.* French fries **33**
un steak-frites steak and French fries **9**
froid cold
avoir froid to be (feel) cold *(people)* **30**
il fait froid it's cold out *(weather)* **12**

le **fromage** cheese **33**
un sandwich au fromage cheese sandwich
un **fruit** fruit **33**
furieux (furieuse) furious
une **fusée** rocket

G

gagner to earn, to win **28**
un **garage** garage **21**
un **garçon** boy **5;** waiter
une **gare** train station
une **garniture** side dish
un **gâteau** (*pl.* **gâteaux**) cake **33**
gauche left
à gauche to (on) the left **21**
une **gelée** jelly
généralement generally
généreux (généreuse) generous
la **générosité** generosity
génial brilliant
des **gens** *m.* people **18**
gentil (gentille) nice, kind **19;** sweet
la **géographie** geography
une **girafe** giraffe **E5**
une **glace** ice cream **9, 33;** mirror, ice
glacé iced
un thé glacé iced tea **33**
un **goûter** afternoon snack
une **goyave** guava
grand tall **17;** big, large **20;** big *(size of clothing)* **25**
un grand magasin department store **25**
une grande surface big store, self-service store
grandir to get tall
une **grand-mère** grandmother **7, 24**
un **grand-père** grandfather **7, 24**
les **grands-parents** *m.* grandparents **24**
grec (greque) Greek
un **grenier** attic
une **grillade** grilled meat
une **grille** grid
grillé: le pain grillé toast
une tartine de pain grillé buttered toast
la **grippe** flu
gris gray **20**
gros (grosse) fat, big
grossir to gain weight, get fat **27**
la **Guadeloupe** Guadeloupe *(French island in the West Indies)*
une **guerre** war
une **guitare** guitar **17, 23**
un **gymnase** gym

H

habillé dressed
habiter to live **15**
Haïti Haiti *(French island in the West Indies)*
un **hamburger** hamburger **9**
les• **haricots** *m.* **verts** green beans **33**
la• **hâte** haste
en hâte quickly
• **haut** high
en haut upstairs **21**
plus haut above
• **hélas!** too bad!
hésiter to hesitate
l' **heure** *f.* time, hour; o'clock **4**
... heure(s) (dix) (ten) past . . . **4**
... heure(s) et demie half past . . . **4**
... heure(s) et quart quarter past . . . **4**
... heure(s) moins (dix) (ten) of . . . **4**
... heure(s) moins le quart quarter to . . . **4**
à... heures at . . . o'clock **14**
à quelle heure...? at what time . . . ? **16**
à quelle heure est...? at what time is . . .? **4**
il est... heure(s) it's . . . o'clock **4**
par heure per hour, an hour
quelle heure est-il? what time is it? **4**
heureux (heureuse) happy
hier yesterday **31**
avant hier the day before yesterday
un **hippopotame** hippopotamus **E5**
une **histoire** story, history
l' **hiver** *m.* winter **12**
en hiver in (the) winter **12**
• **hollandais** Dutch
un **homme** man **17**
honnête honest
un **hôpital** (*pl.* **hôpitaux**) hospital **21**
une **horreur** horror
quelle horreur! what a scandal! how awful!
un• **hors-d'oeuvre** appetizer **33**
un• **hot dog** hot dog **9**
un **hôte, une hôtesse host,** hostess
un **hôtel** hotel **21**
un hôtel de police police department
l' **huile** *f.* oil
• **huit** eight **1**
• **huitième** eighth **24**
l' **humeur** *f.* mood
de bonne humeur in a good mood
un **hypermarché** shopping center

I

ici here **14**
une **idée** idea
c'est une bonne idée! it's (that's) a good idea! **28**
ignorer to be unaware of
il he, it **11, 14, 18**
il est it is **20**
il/elle est + *nationality* he/she is . . . **6**
il y a there is, there are **17**
il y a + **du, de la** *(partitive)* there is (some) **34**
il y a eu there was
il n'y a pas de... there is/are no . . . **18**
est-ce qu'il y a...? is there, are there . . .? **17**
qu'est-ce qu'il y a...? what is there . . .? **17**
une **île** island

illustré illustrated
un **immeuble** apartment building **21**
un **imper (imperméable)** raincoat **25**
l' **impératif** *m.* imperative (command) mood
impoli impolite
l' **importance** *f.* importance
ça n'a pas d'importance it doesn't matter
importé imported
impressionnant impressive
inactif (inactive) inactive
inclure to include
l' **indicatif** *m.* area code
indiquer to indicate, show **C**
indiquez... indicate . . . **C**
infâme: c'est infâme! that's (it's) awful! **35**
infecte: c'est infecte! that's revolting! *(colloq.)* **35**
les **informations** *f.* news
l' **informatique** *f.* computer science
s' **informer** to find out about
un **ingénieur** engineer
un **ingrédient** ingredient **33**
un **inspecteur, une inspectrice** police detective
un **instrument** instrument **23**
intelligent intelligent **19**
intéressant interesting **19**
l' **intérieur** *m.* interior, inside
interroger to question
interviewer to interview
inutilement uselessly
un **inventaire** inventory
un **invité, une invitée** guest
inviter to invite **15**
israélien (israélienne) Israeli
italien (italienne) Italian **19**
un **Italien, une Italienne** Italian person

J

j' (*see* **je**)
jamais ever; never
jamais le dimanche! never on Sunday!
ne... jamais never **32**
la **Jamaïque** Jamaica
une **jambe** leg **E3**
un **jambon** ham **33**
janvier *m.* January **8**
japonais Japanese **19**
un **jardin** garden **21**
jaune yellow **20**
jaunir to turn yellow
je I **14**
un **jean** pair of jeans **23**
un **jeu** (*pl.* **jeux**) game **25**
les jeux télévisés TV game shows
jeudi *m.* Thursday **8**
jeune young **17**
les **jeunes** *m.* young people
un **job** (part-time) job
le **jogging** jogging **29**
faire du jogging to jog **29**
un **jogging** jogging suit **25**
joli pretty *(for girls, women)* **17;** *(for clothing)* **25**
plus joli(e) que prettier than
jouer to play **15**
jouer à + *game, sport* to play a game, sport **23**
jouer au tennis (volley, basket, foot) to play tennis (volleyball, basketball, soccer) **13**
jouer de + *instrument* to play a musical instrument **23**
un **jour** day **8, 29**
le Jour de l'An New Year's Day
par jour per week, a week
quel jour est-ce? what day is it? **8**
un **journal** (*pl.* **journaux**) newspaper
une **journée** day, whole day
bonne journée! have a nice day!
joyeux (joyeuse) happy
juillet *m.* July **8**
le quatorze juillet Bastille Day *(French national holiday)*
juin *m.* June **8**
un **jumeau** (*pl.* **jumeaux**), une **jumelle** twin
une **jupe** skirt **25**
le **jus** juice
le jus d'orange orange juice **10, 33**
le jus de pomme apple juice **10, 33**
le jus de raisin grape juice **10**
le jus de tomate tomato juice **10**
jusqu'à until
juste right, fair
le mot juste the right word

K

un **kangourou** kangaroo **E5**
le **ketchup** ketchup **33**
un **kilo** kilogram
un kilo (de) a kilogram (of) **33**

L

l' (*see* **le, la**)
la the **6, 18;** her, it **36**
là here, there **14**
là-bas over there **14**
ça, là-bas that (one), over there **17**
ce... -là that . . . (over there) **26**
oh là là! uh, oh!; oh, dear!; wow!; oh, yes!
laid ugly
laisser: laisse-moi tranquille! leave me alone! **36**
le **lait** milk **33**
une **langue** language
large wide
laver to wash **29**
se laver to wash (oneself), wash up
le the **6, 18;** him, it **36**
le + *number* + *month* the . . . **8**
le (lundi) on (Mondays) **18**
une **leçon** lesson
un **légume** vegetable **33**
lent slow
les the **18;** them **36**
une **lettre** letter
leur(s) their **24**
leur (to) them **36**
se **lever: lève-toi!** stand up! **B**
levez-vous! stand up! **B**
un **lézard** lizard **E5**

le **Liban** Lebanon *(country in the Middle East)*
libanais Lebanese
libéré liberated
une **librairie** bookstore
libre free
un **lieu** place, area
avoir lieu to take place
une **ligne** line
limité limited
la **limonade** lemon soda **10**
un **lion** lion **E5**
* **lire** to read **C**
comment lire reading hints
lisez... (*see* **lire**) read . . . **B, C**
une **liste** list
une liste des courses shopping list
un **lit** bed **17**
un **living** living room *(informal)*
un **livre** book **B, 17**
une **livre** metric pound **33**
local (*m.pl.* **locaux**) local
une **location** rental
logique logical
logiquement logically
loin far **21**
loin d'ici far (from here)
le **loisir** leisure, free time
un **loisir** leisure-time activity
Londres London
long (longue) long **25**
longtemps (for) a long time
moins longtemps que for a shorter time
le **loto** lotto, lottery, bingo
un **loup** wolf **E5**
lui him **23;** (to) him/her **36**
lui-même: en lui-même to himself
lundi *m.* Monday **8**
des **lunettes** *f.* glasses **25**
des lunettes de soleil sunglasses **25**
le **Luxembourg** Luxembourg
un **lycée** high school

M

m' (*see* **me**)
M. (monsieur) Mr. (Mister) **3**
ma my **7, 24**
et voici ma mère and this is my mother **7**
ma chambre my bedroom **17**
une **machine** machine
une machine à coudre sewing machine
le **Madagascar** Madagascar *(French-speaking island off of East Africa)*
Madame (Mme) Mrs., ma'am **3**
Mademoiselle (Mlle) Miss **3**
un **magasin** store, shop **21, 25**
faire les magasins to go shopping (browsing from store to store)
un grand magasin department store **25**
magnétique magnetic
un **magnétophone** tape recorder **17**
un **magnétoscope** VCR (videocassette recorder) **B**
magnifique magnificent
mai *m.* May **8**
maigre thin, skinny
maigrir to lose weight, get thin **27**
un **maillot de bain** bathing suit **25**
une **main** hand **E3**
maintenant now **15, 31**
mais but **14**
j'aime..., mais je préfère... I like . . ., but I prefer . . . **13**
je regrette, mais je ne peux pas... I'm sorry, but I can't . . . **13**
mais oui! sure! **14**
mais non! of course not! **14**
une **maison** house **21**
à la maison at home **14**
mal badly, poorly **3, 15**
ça va mal things are going badly **3**
ça va très mal things are going very badly **3**
c'est mal that's bad **20**
malade sick
malheureusement unfortunately
malin clever
manger to eat **15**
j'aime manger I like to eat **13**
manger + du, de la *(partitive)* to eat (some) **34**
une salle à manger dining room **21**
un **manteau** (*pl.* **manteaux**) overcoat **25**
un manteau de fourrure fur coat
un **marchand, une marchande** merchant, shopkeeper, dealer
marcher to work, to run *(for objects)* **17;** to walk *(for people)* **17**
il/elle (ne) marche (pas) bien it (doesn't) work(s) well **17**
est-ce que la radio marche? does the radio work? **17**
un **marché** open-air market **33**
un marché aux puces flea market
bon marché *(inv.)* inexpensive **25**
mardi *m.* Tuesday **8**
le Mardi gras Shrove Tuesday
un **mari** husband **24**
le **mariage** wedding, marriage
marié married
une **marmite** covered stew pot
le **Maroc** Morocco *(country in North Africa)*
une **marque** brand (name)
une **marraine** godmother
marrant fun
marron (*inv.*) brown **20**
mars *m.* March **8**
martiniquais from Martinique
la **Martinique** Martinique *(French island in the West Indies)*
un **match** game, (sports) match
faire un match to play a game, (sports) match **16**
les **maths** *f.* math
le **matin** morning **29**

ce matin this morning **31**
demain matin tomorrow morning **31**
du matin in the morning, A.M. **4**
hier matin yesterday morning **31**
le matin in the morning
des matoutou crabes *m.* stewed crabs with rice
mauvais bad **20**
c'est une mauvaise idée that's a bad idea
il fait mauvais it's bad *(weather)* **12**
la mayonnaise mayonnaise **33**
me (to) me **35**
méchant mean, nasty **19**
un médecin doctor
un médecin de nuit doctor on night duty
la Méditerranée Mediterranean Sea
meilleur better, best **27**
mélanger to mix, stir
même same; even
une mémoire memory
mentionner to mention
la mer ocean, shore **29**
à la mer to (at) the sea **29**
merci thank you **3**
oui, merci yes, thank you **13**
mercredi *m.* Wednesday **8**
une mère mother **7, 24**
mériter to deserve
mes my **24**
le métro subway
en métro by subway **22**
* **mettre** to put on, to wear **25;** to put, to place, to turn on **26**
mettre la table to set the table **33**
mexicain Mexican **19**
midi noon **4**
mieux better
mignon (mignonne) cute **19**
militaire military
mille one thousand **25**
une mini-chaîne compact stereo
minuit midnight **4**
minérale: l'eau *f.* **minérale** mineral water **33**
mis *(p.p. of* **mettre***)* put, placed **31**
mixte mixed
Mlle Miss **3**
Mme Mrs. **3**
une mob (mobylette) motorbike, moped **17**
moche plain, ugly **25**
la mode fashion
à la mode popular; in fashion; fashionable **25**
moderne modern **21**
moi me **1, 23;** (to) me **35**
moi, je m'appelle (Marc) me, my name is (Marc) **1**
avec moi with me **13**
donne-moi give me **9**
donnez-moi give me **10**
excusez-moi... excuse me . . . **21**
prête-moi... lend me . . . **11**
s'il te plaît, donne-moi... please give me . . . **10**
un moine monk
moins less
moins de less than
moins... que less . . . than **27**
... heure(s) moins (dix) (ten) of . . . **4**
... heure(s) moins le quart quarter of . . . **4**
un mois month **8, 29**
ce mois-ci this month **31**
le mois dernier last month **31**
le mois prochain next month **31**
par mois a month
mon (ma; mes) my **7, 24**
mon anniversaire est le... my birthday is the . . . **8**
voici mon père this is my father **7**
le monde world
du monde in the world
tout le monde everyone
la monnaie money; change
le Monopoly Monopoly **23**
Monsieur (M.) Mr., sir **3**
un monsieur (*pl.* **messieurs**) gentleman, man *(polite term)* **5**
une montagne mountain **29**
à la montagne to (at) the montains **29**
une montre watch **17**
montrer à to show . . . to **35, 36**
montre-moi (montrez-moi) show me **B**
un morceau piece
un morceau de craie piece of chalk **B**
un mot word
une moto motorcycle **17**
la moutarde mustard
un mouton sheep
moyen (moyenne) average, medium
en moyenne on the average
un moyen means
muet (muette) silent
un musée museum **21**
la musique music **23**

N

n' (*see* **ne**)
nager to swim **15**
j'aime nager I like to swim **13**
une nationalité nationality **2**
nautique: le ski nautique water-skiing **29**
ne (n')
ne... aucun none, not any
ne... jamais never **32**
ne... pas not **14**
ne... personne nobody **32**
ne... plus no longer
ne... rien nothing **32**
n'est-ce pas? right?, no?, isn't it (so)?, don't you?, aren't you? **14**
né born
nécessaire necessary
négatif (négative) negative
négativement negatively
la neige snow
neiger to snow
il neige it's snowing **12**
nettoyer to clean **29**
neuf nine **1**
neuvième ninth **24**

(10)
12

ROGERS™
WIRELESS

AND

Call your friends

The way better Deal than anywhere else!

Rogers deals for students are so good we can't even advertise them. So come check for yourself @ www.spclive.com/onlinedeals

→R2 O R1 L2 ↓L1, R1

47701

www.spclive.com/onlinedeals

R1 R2 L1 L1 ← ↓ → ↑...

un **neveu** (*pl.* **neveux**) nephew
un **nez** nose **E3**
une **nièce** niece
un **niveau** (*pl.* **niveaux**) level
Noël *m.* Christmas
à Noël at Christmas **29**
noir black **20**
un **nom** name; noun
un **nombre** number
nombreux (nombreuses) numerous
nommé named
non no **2, 14**
non! no! **14**
non plus neither
mais non! of course not! **14**
le **nord** north
le nord-est northeast
normalement normally
nos our **24**
une **note** grade
notre (*pl.* **nos**) our **24**
la **nourriture** food **33**
nous we **14;** us **23;** (to) us **35**
nouveau (nouvel, nouvelle; *m.pl.* **nouveaux)** new **27**
la **Nouvelle-Angleterre** New England
la **Nouvelle-Calédonie** New Caledonia *(French island in the South Pacific)*
novembre *m.* November **8**
le onze novembre Armistice Day
la **nuit** night
un **numéro** number

O

objectif (objective) objective
un **objet** object **17**
une **occasion** occasion; opportunity
occupé occupied
un **océan** ocean
octobre *m.* October **8**
une **odeur** odor
un **oeil** (*pl.* **yeux**) eye **E3**
un **oeuf** egg **33**
officiel (officielle) official
offert (*p.p. of* **offrir**) offered
* **offrir** to offer, to give
oh là là! uh,oh!, oh, dear!, wow!, oh, yes!
un **oiseau** (*pl.* **oiseaux**) bird
une **omelette** omelet **9**
on one, they, you, people **28**
on est... today is . . .
on va dans un café? shall we go to a café?
on y va let's go
comment dit-on... en français? how do you say . . . in French? **B**
un **oncle** uncle **7, 24**
onze eleven **2**
opérer to operate
l' **or** *m.* gold
orange *(inv.)* orange *(color)* **20**
une **orange** orange *(fruit)*
le jus d'orange orange juice **10, 33**
un **ordinateur** computer **B, 17**
une **oreille** ear **E3**
organiser to organize **15**
originairement originally
l' **origine** *f.* origin, beginning
d'origine bretonne from Brittany
orthographiques: les signes *m.* **orthographiques** spelling marks
ou or **2, 14**
où where **14, 16**
où est...? where is . . .? **14**
où est-ce? where is it? **21**
d'où? from where? **23**
oublier to forget
l' **ouest** *m.* west
oui yes **2, 14**
oui, bien sûr... yes, of course . . . **13**
oui, d'accord... yes, okay . . . **13**
oui, j'ai... yes, I have . . . **17**
oui, merci... yes, thank you . . . **13**
mais oui! sure! **14**
un **ouragan** hurricane
un **ours** bear **E5**
ouvert open
* **ouvrir** to open
ouvre... (ouvrez...) open . . . **B**

P

le **pain** bread **33**
pâle pale
un **pamplemousse** grapefruit **33**
une **panne** breakdown
une panne d'électricité power failure
un **pantalon** pants, trousers **25**
une **panthère** panther
une **papaye** papaya
le **papier** paper
une feuille de papier a sheet (piece) of paper **B**
Pâques *m.* Easter **29**
à Pâques at Easter **29**
par per
par exemple for example
par jour per day
un **parc** park **21**
un parc public city park
parce que (parce qu') because **16**
pardon excuse me **21, 25**
les **parents** *m.* parents, relatives **24**
paresseux (paresseuse) lazy
parfait perfect
rien n'est parfait nothing is perfect
parfois sometimes
parisien (parisienne) Parisian
parler to speak, talk **B, 15**
parler à to speak (talk) to **36**
parler (français, anglais, espagnol) to speak (French, English, Spanish) **13**
un **parrain** godfather
une **partie** part
* **partir** to leave
à partir de as of, beginning
partitif (partitive) partitive
pas not
ne... pas not **14**
pas de not a, no, not any **18, 34**
pas du tout not at all, definitely not **23**
pas possible not possible

pas toujours not always **13**
pas très bien not very well
le **passé composé** compound past tense
passer to spend (time) **29;** to pass by
passionnément passionately
une **pâte** dough
patient patient
le **patinage** ice skating, roller skating
une **patinoire** skating rink
une **pâtisserie** pastry, pastry shop
une **patte** foot, paw *(of bird or animal)*
pauvre poor **28**
payer to pay, pay for **28**
un **pays** country
la **peau** skin, hide
* **peindre** to paint
peint painted
une **pellicule** film (camera)
pendant during **29**
pénétrer to enter
pénible bothersome, a pain **20**
penser to think **25**
penser de to think of **25**
penser que to think that **25**
qu'est-ce que tu penses de...? what do you think of . . .? **25**
une **pension** inn, boarding house
Pentecôte *f.* Pentecost
perdre to lose, to waste **28**
perdu (*p.p. of* **perdre**) lost
un **père** father **7, 24**
* **permettre** to permit
un **perroquet** parrot
personne (de) nobody **32**
ne... personne nobody, not anybody, not anyone **32**
une **personne** person **5**
personnel (personnelle) personal
personnellement personally
péruvien (péruvienne) Peruvian
petit small, short **17, 20, 25**
il/elle est petit(e) he/she is short **17**
un petit copain, une petite copine boyfriend, girlfriend
plus petite smaller
le **petit déjeuner** breakfast **33**
prendre le petit déjeuner to have breakfast **33**
le **petit-fils, la petite-fille** grandson, granddaughter
les **petits pois** *m.* peas **33**
peu little, not much
un peu a little, a little bit **15**
un peu de a few
peut (*see* **pouvoir**)
peut-être perhaps, maybe **14**
peux (*see* **pouvoir**)
est-ce que tu peux...? can you . . .? **13**
je regrette, mais je ne peux pas... I'm sorry, but I can't . . . **13**
la **photo** photography
une **phrase** sentence **B**
la **physique** physics
un **piano** piano **23**
une **pie** magpie **E5**
une **pièce** coin **28;** room
un **pied** foot **E3**
à pied on foot **22**
faire une promenade à pied to take a walk **22**
piloter to pilot (a plane)
une **pincée** pinch
le **ping-pong** Ping-Pong **23**
un **pique-nique** picnic **22**
faire un pique-nique to have a picnic **29**
une **piscine** swimming pool **21**
une **pizza** pizza **9**
un **placard** closet
une **plage** beach **21**
plaît: s'il te plaît please *(informal)* **9;** excuse me (please)
s'il te plaît, donne-moi... please, give me . . .**10**
s'il vous plaît please *(formal)* **10;** excuse me (please)
un **plan** map
la **planche à voile** windsurfing **29**
faire de la planche à voile to windsurf **29**
une **plante** plant
un **plat** dish, course *(of a meal)* **33**
le plat principal main course
un **plateau** tray
pleut: il pleut it's raining **12**
plier to fold
plumer to pluck
plus more
plus de more than
plus joli que prettier than
plus... que more . . . than, . . .-er than **27**
en plus in addition
le plus the most
ne... plus no longer, no more
non plus neither
plusieurs several
une **poche** pocket
l'argent *m.* **de poche** allowance, pocket money
une **poêle** frying pan
un **point de vue** point of view
une **poire** pear **33**
pois: les petits pois *m.* peas **33**
un **poisson** fish **E5, 33**
un poisson rouge goldfish
blaff de poisson fish stew
poli polite
un **politicien, une politicienne** politician
un **polo** polo shirt **25**
une **pomme** apple
le jus de pomme apple juice **10, 33**
une **pomme de terre** potato **33**
une purée de pommes de terre mashed potatoes
le **porc: une côtelette de porc** pork chop
une **porte** door **B, 17**
un **porte-monnaie** change purse, wallet
porter to wear **25**
portugais Portuguese
poser: poser une question to ask a question **C**
une **possibilité** possibility
la **poste** post office

pouah! yuck! yech!
une **poule** hen **E5**
le **poulet** chicken **33**
pour for **14;** in order to **29**
pour que so that
pour qui? for whom? **16**
le **pourcentage** percentage
pourquoi why **16**
* **pouvoir** to be able, can, may **35**
pratique practical
pratiquer to participate in
des **précisions** *f.* details
préféré favorite
préférer to prefer **26;** to like (in general)
je préfère I prefer **13**
tu préférerais? would you prefer?
premier (première) first **24**
le premier de l'an New Year's Day
le premier étage second floor
le premier mai Labor Day *(in France)*
c'est le premier juin it's June first **8**
* **prendre** to take, to have *(food)* **B, 34**
prendre + du, de la *(partitive)* to have (some) **34**
prendre le petit déjeuner to have breakfast **33**
un **prénom** first name
préparer to prepare; to prepare for **29**
près nearby **21**
près d'ici nearby, near here
tout près very close
une **présentation** appearance
la présentation extérieure outward appearance
des **présentations** *f.* introductions
pressé in a hurry
prêt ready
un **prêt** loan
prêter à to lend to, to loan **35, 36**
prête-moi... lend me . . . **11**
principalement mainly
le **printemps** spring **12**
au printemps in the spring **12**
pris (*p.p. of* **prendre**) took **34**
un **prix** price
quel est le prix ...? what's the price . . .? **25**
un **problème** problem
prochain next **29, 31**
le weekend prochain next weekend **29**
un **produit** product
un **prof, une prof** teacher *(informal)* **5, 17**
un **professeur** teacher **17**
professionnel (professionnelle) professional
un **programme** program
un **projet** plan
une **promenade** walk
faire une promenade à pied to go for a walk **16, 22**
faire une promenade à vélo to go for a ride (by bike) **22**
faire une promenade en voiture to go for a drive (by car) **22**
* **promettre** promise
une **promo** special sale
proposer to suggest
propre own
un **propriétaire, une propriétaire** landlord/landlady, owner
la **Provence** Provence *(province in southern France)*
pu (*p.p. of* **pouvoir**) could, was able to **35**
n'a pas pu was not able to
public: un parc public city park
un jardin public public garden
la **publicité** commercials, advertising, publicity
une **puce** flea
un marché aux puces flea market
puis then, also
puisque since
un **pull** sweater, pullover **25**
les **Pyrénées** (the) Pyrenees *(mountains between France and Spain)*

Q

qu' (*see* **que**)
une **qualité** quality
quand when **16**
c'est quand, ton anniversaire? when is your birthday? **8**
une **quantité** quantity **33**
quarante forty **3**
un **quart** one quarter
... heure(s) et quart quarter past . . . **4**
... heure(s) moins le quart quarter of . . . **4**
un **quartier** district, neighborhood **21**
un joli quartier a nice neighborhood **21**
quatorze fourteen **2**
quatre four **1**
quatre-vingt-dix ninety **6**
quatre-vingts eighty **6**
quatrième fourth **24**
que that, which
que veut dire...? what does . . . mean? **B**
qu'est-ce que (qu') what *(phrase used to introduce a question)* **16**
qu'est-ce que c'est? what is it? what's that? **17**
qu'est-ce que tu penses de...? what do you think of . . .? **25**
qu'est-ce que tu veux? what do you want? **9**
qu'est-ce qu'il y a? what is there? **17;** what's the matter?
qu'est-ce qui ne va pas? what's wrong?
quel (quelle) what, which, what a **26**
quel (quelle)...! what a . . .!
quel âge a ta mère/ton père? how old is your mother/your father? **7**
quel âge a-t-il/elle? how old is he/she? **17**

quel âge as-tu? how old are you? **7**
quel est le prix...? what is the price . . .? **25**
quel jour est-ce? what day is it? **8**
quel temps fait-il? what's (how's) the weather? **12**
quelle est la date? what's the date? **8**
quelle est ton adresse? what's your address? **21**
quelle heure est-il? what time is it? **4**
à quelle heure? at what time? **4**
à quelle heure est...? at what time is . . .? **4**
de quelle couleur...? what color is . . .? **20**
quelqu'un someone **32**
quelque chose something **32**
quelques some, a few **17**
une **question** question
un **Québécois, une Québécoise** person from Quebec
québécois from Quebec
une **queue** tail
qui who, whom **16**
qui est-ce? who's that (this)? **5, 17**
qui se ressemble... birds of a feather . . .
à qui? to whom? **16**
avec qui? with who(m)? **16**
c'est qui? who's that? *(casual speech)*
de qui? about who(m)? **16**
pour qui? for who(m)? **16**
quinze fifteen **2**
quoi? what? **17**
quotidien (quotidienne) daily
la vie quotidienne daily life

R

raconter to tell about
une **radio** radio **17**
écouter la radio to listen to the radio **13**
une **radiocassette** boom box **17**
raisin: le jus de raisin grape juice **10**
une **raison** reason
avoir raison to be right **30**
rapidement rapidly
un **rapport** relationship
une **raquette** racket **17**
une raquette de tennis tennis racket **23**
rarement rarely, seldom **15**
un **rayon** department *(in a store)*
réalisé made
récemment recently
une **recette** recipe
recherche: un avis de recherche missing person's bulletin
un **récital** (*pl.* **récitals**) (musical) recital
reconstituer to reconstruct
un **réfrigérateur** refrigerator
refuser to refuse
regarder to look at, watch **B, 15**
regarde ça look at that **17**
regarder la télé to watch TV **13**
un **régime** diet
être au régime to be on a diet
régional (*m.pl.* **régionaux**) regional
regretter to be sorry
je regrette, mais... I'm sorry, but . . . **13**
régulier (régulière) regular
une **reine** queen
rencontrer to meet **29**
une **rencontre** meeting, encounter
un **rendez-vous** date, appointment **22**
j'ai un rendez-vous à... I have a date, appointment at . . . **4**
rendre visite à to visit, come to visit **28, 36**
la **rentrée** first day back at school in fall
rentrer to go back, come back **22;** to return, go back, come back **32**
réparer to fix, repair **29**
un **repas** meal **33**
* **repeindre** to repaint
répéter to repeat **B**
répondre (à) to answer, respond (to) **B, 36**
répondez-lui (moi) answer him (me)
répondre que oui to answer yes
une **réponse** answer
un **reportage** documentary
représenter to represent
réservé reserved
une **résolution** resolution
un **restaurant** restaurant **21**
au restaurant to (at) the restaurant **14**
dîner au restaurant to have dinner at a restaurant **13**
un restaurant trois étoiles three star restaurant
rester to stay **22, 32**
retard: un jour de retard one day behind
en retard late
retourner to return; to turn over
réussir to succeed **27**
réussir à un examen to pass an exam **27**
* **revenir** to come back **23**
revoir: au revoir! good-bye! **3**
le **rez-de-chaussée** ground floor
un **rhinocéros** rhinoceros **E5**
riche rich **28**
rien (de) nothing **32**
rien n'est parfait nothing is perfect
ne... rien nothing **32**
une **rive** (river)bank
une **rivière** river, stream
le **riz** rice **33**
une **robe** dress **25**
romain Roman
le **rosbif** roast beef **33**
rose pink **20**
rosse nasty *(colloq.)*

une rôtie toast *(Canadian)*
rôtir to roast
une roue wheel
rouge red **20**
rougir to turn red
rouler to roll
roux (rousse) red-head
une rue street **21**
dans la rue (Victor Hugo) on (Victor Hugo) street **21**
russe Russian

S

sa his, her **24**
un sac bag, handbag **17**
sais (*see* **savoir**)
je sais I know **B, 17, 36**
je ne sais pas I don't know **B, 17**
tu sais you know **36**
une saison season **12**
toute saison all year round (any season)
une salade salad **9, 33;** lettuce **33**
un salaire salary
une salle hall, large room
une salle à manger dining room **21**
une salle de bains bathroom **21**
une salle de séjour informal living room
un salon formal living room **21**
salut hi!, good-bye! **3**
une salutation greeting
samedi Saturday **8, 31**
samedi soir Saturday night
à samedi! see you Saturday! **8**
le samedi on Saturdays **18**
une sandale sandal **25**
un sandwich sandwich **9**
sans without
des saucisses *f.* sausages
le saucisson salami **33**
* **savoir** to know *(information)*
je sais I know **B, 17, 36**
je ne sais pas I don't know **B, 17**
tu sais you know **36**
un saxo (saxophone) saxophone **23**
une scène scene, stage
les sciences *f.* **économiques** economics
les sciences *f.* **naturelles** natural science
un scooter motorscooter **17**
second second
seize sixteen **2**
un séjour stay; informal living room
le sel salt **33**
selon according to
selon toi in your opinion
une semaine week **8, 29**
cette semaine this week **31**
la semaine dernière last week **31**
la semaine prochaine next week **31**
par semaine per week, a week
semblable similar
le Sénégal Senegal *(French-speaking country in Africa)*
sensationnel (sensationnelle) sensational
séparer to separate
sept seven **1**
septembre *m.* September **8**
septième seventh **24**
une série series
sérieux (sérieuse) serious
un serveur, une serveuse waiter, waitress
servi served
une serviette napkin **33**
ses his, her **24**
seul alone, only; by oneself **29**
seulement only, just
un short shorts **25**
si if, whether **C**
si! so, yes! *(to a negative question)* **18**
un signal (*pl.* **signaux**) signal
un signe sign
un signe orthographique spelling mark
un singe monkey **E5**
situé situated
six six **1**
sixième sixth **24**
un skate skateboard
le ski skiing
le ski nautique waterskiing **29**
faire du ski to ski **29**
faire du ski nautique to go water-skiing **29**
skier to ski
snob snobbish
la Société Nationale des Chemins de Fer (SNCF) *French railroad system*
une société society
un soda soda **10**
une soeur sister **7, 24**
la soie silk
la soif thirst
avoir soif to be thirsty **30**
j'ai soif I'm thirsty **10**
tu as soif? are you thirsty? **10**
un soir evening **29**
ce soir this evening, tonight **31**
demain soir tomorrow night (evening) **29, 31**
du soir in the evening, P.M. **4**
hier soir last night **31**
le soir in the evening
une soirée (whole) evening, evening party
soixante sixty **3, 5**
soixante-dix seventy **5**
un soldat soldier
un solde (clearance) sale
en solde on sale
la sole sole (fish) **33**
le soleil sun
les lunettes *f.* **de soleil** sunglasses **25**
sommes (*see* **être**)
nous sommes... it is, today is . . . *(date)*
son (sa; ses) his, her **24**
un sondage poll
une sorte sort, type, kind
* **sortir** to leave, come out
un souhait wish
la soupe soup **33**
une souris mouse
sous under **17**
le sous-sol basement

souvent often **15**
soyez (*see* **être**): **soyez logique** be logical
les **spaghetti** *m.* spaghetti **33**
spécialement especially
spécialisé specialized
une **spécialité** specialty
le **sport** sports **23, 29**
faire du sport to play sports **29**
des vêtements *m.* **de sport** sports clothing **25**
une voiture de sport sports car **23**
sportif (sportive) athletic **19**
un **stade** stadium **21**
un **stage** sports training camp; internship
une **station-service** gas station
un **steak** steak **9**
un **steak-frites** steak and French fries **9**
un **stylo** pen **B, 17**
le **sucre** sugar **33**
le **sud** south
suggérer to suggest
suis (*see* **être**)
je suis + *nationality* I'm . . . **2**
je suis de... I'm from . . . **2**
suisse Swiss **19**
la **Suisse** Switzerland
suivant following
suivi followed
un **sujet** subject, topic
super terrific **15;** great **20, 25**
un **supermarché** supermarket **21**
supersonique supersonic
supérieur superior
supplémentaire supplementary, extra
sur on **17;** about
sûr sure, certain
bien sûr! of course! **14**
oui, bien sûr... yes, of course . . .! **13**
tu es sûr(e)? are you sure? **24**
sûrement surely
la **surface: une grande surface** big store, self-service store
surtout especially
un **survêtement** jogging or track suit **25**
un **sweat** sweatshirt **25**
une **sweaterie** shop specializing in sweatshirts and sportswear
sympa nice, pleasant *(colloq.)*
sympathique nice, pleasant **19**
une **synagogue** Jewish temple or synagogue
un **synthétiseur** electronic keyboard, synthesizer

T

t' (*see* **te**)
ta your **7, 24**
une **table** table **B, 17**
mettre la table to set the table **33**
un **tableau** (*pl.* **tableaux**) chalkboard **B**
Tahiti Tahiti *(French island in the South Pacific)*
une **taille** size
de taille moyenne of medium height or size
un **tailleur** woman's suit
se **taire: tais-toi!** be quiet!
une **tante** aunt **7, 24**
la **tarte** pie **33**
une **tasse** cup **33**
un **taxi** taxi
en taxi by taxi **22**
te (to) you **35**
un **tee-shirt** T-shirt **25**
un **temple** Protestant church
le **temps** time; weather
combien de temps? how long?
de temps en temps from time to time
quel temps fait-il? what's (how's) the weather? **12**
tout le temps all the time
le **tennis** tennis **23**
jouer au tennis to play tennis **13**
des **tennis** *m.* tennis shoes, sneakers **25**
un **terrain de sport** (playing) field
une **terrasse** outdoor section of a café, terrace
la **terre** earth
une pomme de terre potato **33**
terrifiant terrifying
tes your **24**
la **télé** TV **B, 17**
à la télé on TV
regarder la télé to watch TV **13**
un **téléphone** telephone **17**
téléphoner (à) to call, phone **13, 15, 36**
télévisé: des jeux *m.* **télévisés** TV game shows
la **tête** head **E3**
le **thé** tea **10**
un thé glacé iced tea **33**
un **théâtre** theater **21**
le **thon** tuna **33**
tiens! look!, hey! **5, 18**
un **tigre** tiger **E5**
timide timid, shy **19**
le **tissu** fabric
un **titre** title
toi you **23**
avec toi with you **13**
et toi? and you? **1**
la **toilette** bathroom, toilet **21**
un **toit** roof
une **tomate** tomato **33**
le jus de tomate tomato juice **10**
un **tombeau** tomb
ton (ta; tes) your **7, 24**
c'est quand, ton anniversaire? when's your birthday? **8**
tort: avoir tort to be wrong **30**
une **tortue** turtle **E5**
un bifteck de tortue turtle steak
toujours always **15**
je n'aime pas toujours... I don't always like . . . **13**
un **tour** turn
à votre tour it's your turn
la **Touraine** Touraine *(province in central France)*
tourner to turn **21**
la **Toussaint** All Saint's Day *(November 1)*

tout (toute; tous, toutes) all, every, the whole
tous les jours every day
tout ça all that
tout le monde everyone
tout le temps all the time
toutes sortes all sorts, kinds
tout completely, very
tout droit straight **21**
tout de suite right away
tout près very close
tout all, everything
pas du tout not at all **23**
un **train** train **29**
tranquille quiet
laisse-moi tranquille! leave me alone! **36**
un **transistor** transistor radio
un **travail** (*pl.* **travaux**) job
travailler to work **13, 15**
une **traversée** crossing
treize thirteen **2**
trente thirty **3**
un **tréma** diaeresis
très very **19**
très bien very well **15**
ça va très bien things are going very well **3**
ça va très mal things are going very badly **3**
trois three **1**
troisième third **24;** *9th grade in France*
trop too, too much **25**
trouver to find, to think of **25**
comment trouves-tu...? what do you think of . . .? how do you find . . .? **25**
s'y trouve is there
tu you **14**
la **Tunisie** Tunisia *(country in North Africa)*

U

un, une one **1;** a, an **5, 18**
unique only
uniquement only
une **université** university, college
l' **usage** *m.* use
un **ustensile** utensil
utile useful
utiliser to use **C**
en utilisant (by) using
utilisez... use . . . **C**

V

va (*see* **aller**)
va-t'en! go away! **22**
ça va? how are you? how's everything? **3**
ça va! everything's fine (going well); fine, I'm OK **3**
on va dans un café? shall we go to a café?
on y va let's go
les **vacances** *f.* vacation
bonnes vacances! have a nice vacation!
en vacances on vacation **14**
les grandes vacances summer vacation **29**
une **vache** cow
vais (*see* **aller**): **je vais** I'm going **22**
la **vaisselle** dishes
faire la vaisselle to do the dishes
valable valid
une **valise** suitcase
vanille: une glace à vanille vanilla ice cream
varié varied
les **variétés** *f.* variety show
vas (*see* **aller**)
comment vas-tu? how are you? **3**
vas-y! come on!, go ahead!, do it! **22**
le **veau** veal **33**
une **vedette** star
un **vélo** bicycle **17**
à vélo by bicycle **22**
faire une promenade à vélo to go for a bicycle ride **22**
un **vendeur, une vendeuse** salesperson
vendre to sell **28**
vendredi *m.* Friday **8**
vendu *(p.p. of* **vendre***)* sold **31**
* **venir** to come **23**
le **vent** wind
une **vente** sale
le **ventre** stomach **E3**
venu *(p.p. of* **venir***)* came, come **32**
vérifier to check
la **vérité** truth
un **verre** glass **33**
verser to pour
vert green **20**
les • haricots *m.* **verts** green beans **33**
une **veste** jacket **25**
des **vêtements** *m.* clothing **25**
des vêtements de sport sports clothing **25**
veut (*see* **vouloir**): **que veut dire...?** what does . . . mean? **B**
veux (*see* **vouloir**)
est-ce que tu veux...? do you want . . .? **13**
je ne veux pas... I don't want . . . **13**
je veux... I want . . . **13, 34**
je veux bien... I'd love to, I do, I want to . . . **13, 34**
qu'est-ce que tu veux? what do you want? **9**
tu veux...? do you want . . .? **9**
la **viande** meat **33**
une **vidéocassette** videocassette **B**
la **vie** life
la vie quotidienne daily life
viens (*see* **venir**)
viens... come . . . **B**
oui, je viens yes, I'm coming along with you
vieux (vieil, vieille; *m.pl.* **vieux)** old **27**
le Vieux Carré *the French Quarter in New Orleans*
le **Viêt-nam** Vietnam *(country in Southeast Asia)*
vietnamien (vietnamienne) Vietnamese
une **vigne** vineyard
un **village** town, village **21**
un petit village small town **21**
une **ville** city
en ville downtown, in town, in the city **14**

une grande ville big city, town **21**
le **vin** wine
vingt twenty **2, 3**
un **violon** violin **23**
une **visite** visit
rendre visite à to visit *(a person)* **28, 36**
visiter to visit *(places)* **15, 28**
vite! fast!, quick!
vive: vive les vacances!
* **vivre** to live
le **vocabulaire** vocabulary
voici... here is, this is..., here come(s) . . . **5**
voici + du, de la *(partitive)* here's some **34**
voici mon père/ma mère here's my father/my mother **7**
voilà... there is . . ., there come(s) . . . **5**
voilà + du, de la *(partitive)* there's some **34**
la **voile** sailing **29**
faire de la voile to sail **29**
la planche à voile windsurfing **29**
* **voir** to see **29, 31**
voir un film to see a movie **29**
un **voisin, une voisine** neighbor **17**
une **voiture** car **17**
une voiture de sport sports car **23**
en voiture by car **22**
faire une promenade en voiture to go for a drive by car **22**
une **voix** voice
le **volley (volleyball)** volleyball **23**
jouer au volley to play volleyball **13**
un **volontaire, une volontaire** volunteer
comme volontaire as a volunteer
vos your **24**
votre (*pl.* **vos**) your **24**
voudrais (*see* **vouloir**): **je voudrais** I'd like **9, 10, 13, 34**
* **vouloir** to want **34**
vouloir + du, de la *(partitive)* to want some (of something) **34**
vouloir dire to mean **34**
voulu *(p.p. of* **vouloir**) wanted **34**
vous you **14;** (to) you **35**
vous désirez? what would you like? may I help you? **10, 25**
s'il vous plaît please **10**
un **voyage** trip
bon voyage! have a nice trip!
faire un voyage to take a trip **16**
voyager to travel **13, 15**
vrai true, right, real **20**
vraiment really **23**
vu *(p.p. of* **voir**) saw, seen **31**
une **vue** view
un point de vue point of view

W

un **walkman** walkman **17**
les **WC** *m.* toilet
un **weekend** weekend **29, 31**
bon weekend! have a nice weekend!
ce weekend this weekend **29, 31**
le weekend on weekends
le weekend dernier last weekend **31**
le weekend prochain next weekend **29, 31**

Y

y there
il y a there is, there are **17**
est-ce qu'il y a...? is there . . .?, are there . . .? **17**
qu'est-ce qu'il y a? what is there? **17**
allons-y! let's go! **22**
vas-y! come on!, go ahead!, do it! **22**
le **yaourt** yogurt **33**
des **yeux** *m.* (*sg.* **oeil**) eyes **E3**

Z

le **Zaïre** Zaire *(French-speaking country in Central Africa)*
un **zèbre** zebra
zéro zero **1**
zut! darn! **3**

ENGLISH-FRENCH VOCABULARY

R35

VOCABULARY

English-French

The English-French vocabulary contains only active vocabulary.

The numbers following an entry indicate the lesson in which the word or phrase is activated. (**B** stands for the photo essay that precedes **Niveau B; C** stands for the list of phrases and expressions that precedes **Niveau C;** and **E** stands for **Entracte.**)

Nouns: If the article of a noun does not indicate gender, the noun is followed by *m.* (*masculine*) or *f.* (*feminine*). If the plural (*pl.*) is irregular, it is given in parentheses.

Verbs: Verbs are listed in the infinitive form. An asterisk (*) in front of an active verb means that it is irregular. (For forms, see the verb charts in Appendix 4C.)

Words beginning with an **h** are preceded by a bullet (•) if the **h** is aspirate; that is, if the word is treated as if it begins with a consonant sound.

A

a, an un, une **5, 18**
a few quelques **17**
a little (bit) un peu **15**
a lot beaucoup **15**
able: to be able (to) *pouvoir **35**
about de **23**
about whom? de qui? **16**
accessories des accessoires *m.* **25**
acquainted: to be acquainted with *connaître **36**
are you acquainted with . . . ? tu connais...? **6**
address une adresse **21**
what's your address? quelle est ton adresse? **21**
after après **29, 30**
after that ensuite **30**
afternoon l'après-midi *m.* **29**
in the afternoon de l'après-midi **4**
this afternoon cet après-midi **31**
tomorrow afternoon demain après-midi **31**
yesterday afternoon hier après-midi **31**
afterwards après **30**
to **agree** *être d'accord **14**
airplane un avion **29**
by airplane en avion **29**
all tout
all right d'accord **13**
not at all pas du tout **23**
alone seul **29**
leave me alone! laisse-moi tranquille! **36**
also aussi **2, 15**
always toujours **15**
not always pas toujours **13**
A.M. du matin **4**
am (*see* **to be**)
I am . . . je suis + *nationality* **2**
American américain **2, 19**
I'm American je suis américain(e) **2**
amusing amusant **19**
an un, une **5, 18**
and et **2, 14**
and you? et toi? **1**
annoying pénible **20**
another un(e) autre
to **answer** répondre (à) **36**
any des **18;** du, de la, de l', de **34**
not any pas de **18, 34**
anybody: not anybody ne... personne **32**
anyone quelqu'un **32**
anything quelque chose **32**
not anything ne... rien **32**
apartment un appartement **21**
apartment building un immeuble **21**
appetizer un •hors-d'oeuvre **33**
apple une pomme
apple juice le jus de pomme **10, 33**
appointment un rendez-vous **22**
I have an appointment at . . . j'ai un rendez-vous à... **4**
April avril *m.* **8**
are (*see* **to be**)
are there? est-ce qu'il y a? **17**
are you . . .? tu es + *nationality?* **2**
there are il y a **17**
these/those/they are ce sont **20**
arm un bras **E3**
to **arrive** arriver **22**
as . . . as aussi... que **27**
to **ask** demander (à) **36**
at à **14;** chez **22**
at (the) au, à la, à l', aux **22**
at . . .'s house chez... **22**
at . . . o'clock à... heure(s) **14**
at home à la maison **14**
at last enfin **30**
at the restaurant au restaurant **14**
at what time? à quelle heure? **4, 16**
at what time is . . .? à quelle heure est...? **4**
athletic sportif (sportive) **19**
to **attend** assister à **29**
attention: to pay attention *faire attention **16**
August août *m.* **8**
aunt une tante **7, 24**
automobile une auto, une voiture **17**
autumn l'automne *m.*

in (the) autumn en automne **12**
avenue une avenue **21**
away: go away! va-t'en! **22**

B

back le dos **E3**
back: to come back rentrer **22, 32;** *revenir **23**
to go back rentrer **22, 32**
in back of derrière **17**
bad mauvais **20**
I'm/everything's (very) bad ça va (très) mal **3**
it's bad (weather) il fait mauvais **12**
that's bad c'est mal **20**
too bad! dommage! **15**
badly mal **3**
things are going (very) badly ça va (très) mal **3**
bag un sac **17**
banana une banane **33**
banknote un billet **28**
baseball le baseball **23**
basketball le basket (basketball) **23**
bathing suit un maillot de bain **25**
bathroom une salle de bains **21**
to be *être **14**
to be . . . (years old) *avoir... ans **18**
to be able (to) *pouvoir **35**
to be acquainted with *connaître **36**
to be active in *faire de + *activity* **29**
to be careful *faire attention **16**
to be cold *(people)* *avoir froid **30;** *(weather)* il fait froid **12**
to be going to *(do something)* *aller + *inf.* **22**
to be hot *(people)* *avoir chaud **30**
to be hungry *avoir faim **18, 30**
to be lucky *avoir de la chance **30**
to be present at assister à **29**
to be right *avoir raison **30**
to be supposed to *devoir **35**
to be thirsty *avoir soif **18, 30**
to be warm *(people)* *avoir chaud **30, 31**
to be wrong *avoir tort **30**
beach une plage **21**
beans: green beans les •haricots *m.* verts **33**
beautiful beau (bel, belle; *m.pl.* beaux) **17**
it's beautiful (nice) weather il fait beau **12**
because parce que (qu') **16**
bed un lit **17**
bedroom une chambre **17, 21**
been été (*p.p. of* *être) **31**
before avant **29, 31**
behind derrière **17**
below en bas **21**
belt une ceinture **25**
best meilleur **27**
better meilleur **27**
beverage une boisson **10, 33**
bicycle un vélo, une bicyclette **17**
by bicycle à vélo **22**
take a bicycle ride *faire une promenade à velo **22**
big grand **17, 20**
bill *(money)* un billet **28**
birthday un anniversaire **8**
my birthday is (March 2) mon anniversaire est le (2 mars) **8**
when is your birthday? c'est quand, ton anniversaire? **8**
bit: a little bit un peu **15**
black noir **20**
blond blond **17**
blouse un chemisier **25**
blue bleu **20**
boat un bateau (*pl.* bateaux) **29**
book un livre **B, 17**
boom box une radiocassette **17**
boots des bottes *f.* **25**
bothersome pénible **20**
boulevard un boulevard **21**
boutique une boutique **25**
boy le garçon **5, 6**
boyfriend un petit copain
bread le pain **33**
breakfast le petit déjeuner **33**
to have breakfast prendre le petit déjeuner **33**
to bring *(a person)* amener **26;** *(things)* apporter **35**
to bring something to someone apporter quelque chose à quelqu'un **35**
brother un frère **7, 24**
brown brun **17;** marron *(inv.)* **20**
building: apartment building un immeuble **21**
bus un bus
by bus en bus **22**
touring bus un autocar, un car **29**
but mais **13**
butter le beurre **33**
to buy acheter **25, 26**
to buy (some) acheter + du, de la *(partitive)* **34**
by: by airplane, plane en avion **29**
by bicycle à vélo **22**
by bus en bus **22**
by car en voiture **22**
by oneself seul(e) **29**
by subway en métro **22**
by taxi en taxi **22**
by train en train **22**

C

café un café **14**
at (to) the café au café **14**
cafeteria: school cafeteria une cantine de l'école **33**
cake un gâteau (*pl.* gâteaux) **33**
calculator une calculatrice **17**
to call téléphoner **15**
came venu (*p.p. of* *venir) **31**
camera un appareil-photo (*pl.* appareils-photo) **17**
camping le camping **29**
to go camping *faire du camping **29**
can *pouvoir **35**
can you . . .? est-ce que tu peux...? **13**
I can't je ne peux pas **13**
Canada le Canada
Canadian canadien (canadienne) **2, 19**
he's/she's (Canadian) il/elle est (canadien/canadienne) **6**
cannot: I cannot je ne peux pas **13**

I'm sorry, but I cannot je regrette, mais je ne peux pas **13**
car une auto, une voiture **17**
by car en voiture **22**
card une carte
(playing) cards des cartes *f.* **23**
careful: to be careful *faire attention **16**
carrot une carotte **33**
cassette tape une cassette **B, 17**
cassette recorder une magnétophone **17**
cat un chat **7**
cereal les céréales *f.* **33**
chair une chaise **B, 17**
chalk la craie **B**
piece of chalk un morceau de craie **B**
chalkboard un tableau (*pl.* tableaux) **B**
checkers les dames *f.* **23**
cheese le fromage **33**
cherry une cerise **33**
chess les échecs *m.* **23**
chicken le poulet **33**
child un (une) enfant **24**
children des enfants *m.* **24**
Chinese chinois **19**
chocolate: hot chocolate un chocolat **10**
to **choose** choisir **27**
chose, chosen choisi (*p.p. of* choisir) **31**
Christmas le Noël **29**
at Christmas à Noël **29**
church une église **21**
cinema le cinéma **14**
to the cinema au cinéma **14**
city une ville **21**
in the city en ville **14**
clarinet une clarinette **23**
class une classe **14**
in class en classe **14**
classmate un (une) camarade **17**
to **clean** nettoyer **29**
clothing des vêtements *m.* **25**
sports clothing des vêtements *m.* de sport **25**
coffee le café **10, 21**
coin une pièce **28**
cold le froid
to be (feel) cold *avoir froid **30**
it's cold *(weather)* il fait froid **12**
college student un étudiant, une étudiante **17**
color une couleur **20**
what color? de quelle couleur? **20**
to **come** arriver **22;** *venir **23**
come on! vas-y! **22**
here comes . . . voici... **5**
to come back rentrer **22, 32;** *revenir **23**
to come to visit rendre visite à **28, 36**
comfortable confortable **21**
compact disc un compact disque (un CD) **17**
computer un ordinateur **B, 17**
concert un concert **22**
to **continue** continuer **21**
cooking la cuisine **33**
cool: it's cool *(weather)* il fait frais **12**
cost le coût **25**
to **cost** coûter
how much does . . . cost? combien coûte...? **11, 25**
it costs . . . il/elle coûte... **11**
country(side) la campagne **29**
to (in) the country(side) à la campagne **29**
course: of course! bien sûr! **13;** mais oui! **14**
of course not! mais non! **14**
cousin un cousin, une cousine **7, 24**
crepe une crêpe **9**
croissant un croissant **9**
cuisine la cuisine **33**
cup une tasse **33**
cute mignon (mignonne) **19**

D

to **dance** danser **13, 15**
dark-haired brun **17**
darn! zut! **3**
date la date **8;** un rendez-vous **22**
I have a date at . . . j'ai un rendez-vous à... **4**
what's the date? quelle est la date? **8**
daughter une fille **24**
day un jour **8, 29**
what day is it? quel jour est-ce? **8**
whole day une journée
December décembre *m.* **8**
dear cher (chère) **25**
department store un grand magasin **25**
to **describe** *décrire **C**
describe . . . décrivez... **C**
desk un bureau **B, 17**
dessert le dessert **33**
to **detest** détester **33**
did fait (*p.p. of* *faire) **31**
difficult difficile **20**
dining room une salle à manger **21**
dinner le dîner **33**
to have (eat) dinner dîner **15, 33**
to have dinner at a restaurant dîner au restaurant **13**
dish *(course of a meal)* un plat **33**
to **do** *faire **16**
do it! vas-y! **22**
I do je veux bien **34**
to do + *activity* *faire de + *activity* **29**
to do my homework *faire mes devoirs **29**
dog un chien **7**
door une porte **B, 17**
done fait (*p.p. of* *faire) **31**
downstairs en bas **21**
downtown en ville **14**
dozen une douzaine **33**
dress une robe **25**
drink une boisson **10, 33**
to **drink** *boire **34**
drive: to take a drive *faire une promenade en voiture **22**
drums une batterie **23**
dumb bête **19**
during pendant **29**

E

ear une oreille **E3**
to **earn** gagner **28**
Easter Pâques *m.* **29**

at Easter à Pâques **29**
easy facile **20**
to **eat** manger **15**
I like to eat j'aime manger **13**
to eat breakfast *prendre le petit déjeuner **33**
to eat dinner dîner **15, 33**
to eat lunch déjeuner **33**
to eat (some) manger + du, de la *(partitive)* **34**
egg un oeuf **33**
eight •huit **1**
eighteen dix-huit **2**
eighth •huitième **24**
eighty quatre-vingts **6**
elegant élégant **25**
elephant un éléphant **E5**
eleven onze **2, 11**
eleventh onzième **24**
England l'Angleterre *m.*
English anglais(e) **2, 19**
errand: to run errands *faire les courses **33**
evening un soir **29**
in the evening du soir **4**
this evening ce soir **31**
tomorrow evening demain soir **29, 31**
everything tout
everything's going (very) well ça va (très) bien **3**
everything's (going) so-so ça va comme ci, comme ça **3**
how's everything? ça va? **3**
exam un examen
to pass an exam réussir à un examen **27**
excuse me excusez-moi **21**
expensive cher (chère) **25**
to **explain** expliquer **C**
eye un oeil (*pl.* yeux) **E3**

F

fall l'automne **12**
in (the) fall en automne **12**
false faux (fausse) **20**
family une famille **7, 24**
far (from) loin (de) **21**
fashion la mode
in fashion (fashionable) à la mode **25**
fat: to get fat grossir **27**
father un père **24**
this is my father voici mon père **7**
February février *m.* **8**
to **feel like** *avoir envie de + *inf.* **28**
few: a few quelques **17**
fifteen quinze **2**
fifth cinquième **24**
fifty cinquante **3**
film un film **22, 29**
finally finalement **30**
to **find** trouver **25**
fine ça va **3**
fine! d'accord **13**
everything's fine ça va bien **3**
that's fine c'est bien **20**
to **finish** finir **27**
finished fini (*p.p. of* finir) **31**
first d'abord **30;** premier (première) **24**
it's (June) first c'est le premier (juin) **8**
fish un poisson **33**
five cinq **1**
to **fix** réparer **29**
flute une flûte **23**
food la nourriture **33**
foot un pied **E3**
on foot à pied **22**
for pour **14**
for whom? pour qui? **16**
fork une fourchette **33**
forty quarante **3**
four quatre **1**
fourteen quatorze **2**
fourth quatrième **24**
franc un franc **11**
that's (it's) . . . francs ça fait... francs **11**
France la France **14**
in France en France **14**
French français(e) **2, 19**
how do you say . . . in French? comment dit-on... en français? **B**
French fries des frites *f.* **33**
steak and French fries un steak-frites **9**
Friday vendredi *m.* **8**
friend un ami, une amie **5;** un copain, une copine **5**
boyfriend, girlfriend un petit copain, une petite copine
school friend un (une) camarade **17**
from de **14**
from (the) du, de la, de l', des **23**
from where? d'où? **23**
are you from . . .? tu es de...? **2**
I'm from . . . je suis de... **2**
front: in front of devant **17**
fruit(s) des fruits *m.* **33**
funny amusant **19;** drôle **20**

G

to **gain weight** grossir **27**
game un jeu (*pl.* jeux) **23;** un match **16**
to play a game (match) *faire un match **16**
to play a game jouer à + *game* **23**
garage un garage **21**
garden un jardin **21**
gentleman un monsieur (*pl.* messieurs) **5**
to **get: to get fat** grossir **27**
to get thin maigrir **27**
girl une fille **15**
girlfriend une petite copine
to **give (to)** donner (à) **35, 36**
give me donne-moi, donnez-moi **9, 10**
please give me s'il te plâit, donne-moi **10**
glass un verre **33**
glasses des lunettes *f.* **25**
sunglasses des lunettes *f.* de soleil **25**
to **go** *aller **22**
go ahead! vas-y! **22**
go away! va-t'en! **22**
to go (come) back rentrer **22, 32;** *revenir **23**
to go by bicycle *aller en vélo **22**
to go by car, by train . . . *aller en auto, en train... **22**
to go camping *faire du camping **29**
to go food shopping *faire les courses **33**
to go mountain climbing *faire de l'alpinisme **29**
to go shopping *faire des achats **29**

to go to assister à **29**
gone allé (*p.p. of* *aller) **32**
good bon (bonne) **20**
good morning (afternoon) bonjour **1**
that's good c'est bien **20**
the weather's good (pleasant) il fait bon **12**
good-bye! au revoir!, salut! **3**
good-looking beau (bel, belle; *m.pl.* beaux) **17, 20, 27**
grandfather un grand-père **7, 24**
grandmother une grand-mère **7, 24**
grandparents les grands-parents *m.* **24**
grape juice le jus de raisin **10**
grapefruit un pamplemousse **33**
gray gris **20**
great chouette, super **20, 25**
green vert **20**
green beans les •haricots *m.* verts **33**
guitar une guitare **17, 23**

H

had eu (*p.p. of* *avoir) **31**
hair les cheveux *m.* **E3, 23**
he/she has dark hair il/elle est brun(e) **17**
half: half past . . . ... heure(s) et demie **4**
half past midnight minuit et demi **4**
half past noon midi et demi **4**
ham le jambon **33**
hamburger un hamburger **9**
hand une main **E3**
handbag un sac **17**
handsome beau (bel, belle; *m.pl.* beaux) **17, 20, 27**
hard difficile **20**
hat un chapeau (*pl.* chapeaux) **25**
to hate détester **33**
to have *avoir **18;** *(food)* *prendre **34**
do you have . . .? est-ce que tu as...? **17**
I have j'ai **17**
I have to (must) je dois **13**
to have (some) *avoir + du, de la *(partitive)*; *prendre + du, de la *(partitive)* **34**
to have a picnic *faire un pique-nique **29**
to have breakfast *prendre le petit déjeuner **33**
to have dinner dîner **33**
to have dinner at a restaurant dîner au restaurant **13**
to have to *avoir besoin de + *inf.* **28;** *devoir **35**
he il **11, 14, 18;** lui **23**
he/she is . . . il/elle est + *nationality* **6**
head la tête **E3**
to hear entendre **28**
hello bonjour **1, 3**
to help aider **29, 35**
may I help you? vous désirez? **10, 25**
her elle **23;** son, sa; ses **24;** la **36**
(to) her lui **36**
her name is . . . elle s'appelle... **6**
what's her name? comment s'appelle-t-elle? **17**
here ici **14**
here comes, here is voici **5**
here's my mother/father voici ma mère/mon père **7**
here's some voici + du, de la *(partitive)* **34**
this . . . (over here) ce...-ci **26**
hey! dis! **20;** tiens! **5, 18**
hey there! dis donc! **20**
hi! salut! **3**
high school student un (une) élève **17**
him lui **23;** le **36**
(to) him lui **36**
his son, sa; ses **24**
his name is . . . il s'appelle... **6**
what's his name? comment s'appelle-t-il? **17**
home, at home à la maison **14;** chez (moi, toi...) **23**
to go home rentrer **22, 32**
homework les devoirs *m.* **29**
homework assignment un devoir **B**
to do my homework *faire mes devoirs **29**
to hope espérer **26**
horse un cheval (*pl.* chevaux) **E5**
hospital un hôpital **21**
hot chaud **12, 31**
hot chocolate un chocolat **10**
hot dog un •hot dog **9**
to be hot *(people)* *avoir chaud **30**
it's hot *(weather)* il fait chaud **12**
hotel un hôtel **21**
house une maison **21**
at someone's house chez + *person* **22**
how? comment? **16**
how are you? comment allez-vous?, comment vas-tu?, ça va? **3**
how do you find . . .? comment trouves-tu...? **25**
how do you say . . . in French? comment dit-on... en français? **B**
how much? combien (de)? **28**
how much does . . . cost? combien coûte...? **11, 25**
how much is that/this/it? c'est combien?, ça fait combien? **11**
how old are you? quel âge as-tu? **7**
how old is he/she? quel âge a-t-il/elle? **17**
how old is your father/mother? quel âge a ton père/ta mère? **7**
how's everything? ça va? **3**
how's the weather? quel temps fait-il? **12**
to learn how to *apprendre à **34**
hundred cent **6, 25**
hungry faim **9**
are you hungry? tu as faim? **9**
I'm hungry j'ai faim **9**
to be hungry avoir faim **18, 30**
husband un mari **24**

I

I je **14,** moi **23**
I don't know je ne sais pas **B, 17**
I have a date/appointment at . . . j'ai un rendez-vous à... **4**
I know je sais **B, 17, 36**
I'm fine/okay ça va **3**
I'm (very) well/so-so/(very) bad ça va (très) bien/comme ci, comme ça/(très) mal **3**
ice la glace **9, 33**
ice cream une glace **9, 33**
iced tea un thé glacé **33**
idea une idée **28**
it's (that's) a good idea c'est une bonne idée **28**
if si **C**
in à **14, 22;** dans **17**
in (Boston) à (Boston) **14**
in class en classe **14**
in front of devant **17**
in order to pour **29**
in the afternoon de l'après-midi **4**
in the morning/evening du matin/soir **4**
in town en ville **14**
in (the) au, à la, à l', aux **22**
to **indicate** indiquer **C**
inexpensive bon marché *(inv.)* **25**
ingredient un ingrédient **33**
instrument un instrument **23**
to play a musical instrument jouer de + *instrument* **23**
intelligent intelligent **33**
interesting intéressant **19**
to **invite** inviter **15**
is (*see* **to be**)
is there? est-ce qu'il y a? **17**
isn't it (so)? n'est-ce pas? **14**
there is il y a **17**
there is (some) il y a + du, de la *(partitive)* **34**
it il, elle **14, 18;** le, la **36**
it's . . . c'est... **5**
it's . . . (o'clock) il est... heure(s) **4**
it's . . . francs ça fait... francs **11**
it's fine/nice/hot/cool/cold/bad *(weather)* il fait beau/bon/chaud/frais/froid/mauvais **12**
it's (June) first c'est le premier (juin) **8**
it's not ce n'est pas **20**
it's raining il pleut **12**
it's snowing il neige **12**
what time is it? quelle heure est-il? **4**
who is it? qui est-ce? **5, 17**
its son, sa; ses **24**
Italian italien, italienne **19**

J

jacket un blouson, une veste **25**
jam la confiture **33**
January janvier *m.* **8**
Japanese japonais(e) **19**
jeans: pair of jeans un jean **25**
to **jog** *faire du jogging **29**
jogging le jogging **29**
jogging suit un jogging, un survêtement **25**
juice le jus
apple juice le jus de pomme **10, 33**
grape juice le jus de raisin **10**
orange juice le jus d'orange **10, 33**
tomato juice le jus de tomate **10**
July juillet *m.* **8**
June juin *m.* **8**

K

ketchup le ketchup **33**
keyboard un clavier **23**
kilogram un kilo (de) **33**
kind gentil (gentille) **19**
kitchen une cuisine **21**
knife un couteau **33**
to **know** *connaître **36**
do you know . . .? tu connais...? **6**
I (don't) know je (ne) sais (pas) **B, 17, 36**
you know tu sais **36**

L

lady une dame **5**
large grand **17, 20**
last dernier (dernière) **31**
last month le mois dernier **31**
last night hier soir **31**
last Saturday samedi dernier **31**
at last enfin **30**
to **learn (how to)** *apprendre (à) + *inf.* **34**
left gauche
on (to) the left à gauche **21**
leg une jambe **E3**
lemon soda la limonade **10**
to **lend** prêter (à) **35, 36**
lend me prête-moi **11**
less . . . than moins... que **27**
let's go! allons-y! **22**
lettuce la salade **33**
library une bibliothèque **21**
like: what does he/she look like? comment est-il/elle? **17**
what's he/she like? comment est-il/elle? **17**
to **like** aimer **15**
do you like? est-ce que tu aimes? **13**
I also like j'aime aussi **13**
I don't always like je n'aime pas toujours **13**
I don't like je n'aime pas **13**
I like j'aime **13**
I like . . ., but I prefer . . . j'aime..., mais je préfère... **13**
I'd like je voudrais **9, 10, 13**
what would you like? vous désirez? **10, 25**
to **listen** écouter **15**
to listen to cassettes écouter des cassettes **29**
to listen to the radio écouter la radio **13**
little petit **17, 20, 25**
a little (bit) un peu **15**
to **live** habiter **15**
living room *(formal)* un salon **21**
to **loan** prêter (à) **35, 36**
long long (longue) **25**
to **look (at)** regarder **15**

look! tiens! **5, 18**
look at that regarde ça **17**
I'm looking for . . . je cherche... **25**
to look for chercher **25**
what does he/she look like? comment est-il/elle? **17**
to lose perdre **28**
to lose weight maigrir **27**
lot: a lot beaucoup **15**
to love: I'd love to je veux bien **13**
luck la chance **30**
to be lucky *avoir de la chance **30**
lunch le déjeuner **33**
to have (eat) lunch déjeuner **33**

M

made fait (*p.p. of* *faire) **31**
to make *faire **16**
man un homme **17;** un monsieur *(polite term)* **5**
many beaucoup (de) **15**
how many combien de **28**
map une carte **B**
March mars *m.* **8**
match un match **16**
to play a match *faire un match **16**
May mai *m.* **8**
may *pouvoir **35**
maybe peut-être **14**
mayonnaise la mayonnaise **33**
me moi **1, 35**
excuse me pardon **21, 25**
(to) me me, moi **35**
meal un repas **33**
mean méchant **19**
to mean *vouloir dire **34**
what does . . . mean? que veut dire...? **B**
meat la viande **33**
to meet rencontrer **29**
to meet for the first time *connaître *(in passé composé)* **36**
Mexican mexicain(e) **19**
midnight minuit **4**
milk le lait **33**
mineral water l'eau *f.* minérale **33**
Miss Mademoiselle (Mlle) **3**
modern moderne **21**
Monday lundi *m.* **8**
money l'argent *m.* **29**
Monopoly le Monopoly **23**
month un mois **8, 27**
last month le mois dernier **31**
next month le mois prochain **31**
this month ce mois-ci **31**
moped une mob (mobylette) **17**
more . . . than plus... que **27**
morning le matin **29**
good morning bonjour **1**
in the morning du matin **4**
this morning ce matin **29**
tomorrow morning demain matin **31**
yesterday morning hier matin **31**
mother une mère **7, 24**
this is my mother voici ma mère **7**
motorbike une mob (mobylette) **17**
motorcycle une moto **17**
motorscooter un scooter **17**
mountain une montagne **29**
mountain climbing l'alpinisme *f.* **29**
to (at/in) the mountain(s) à la montagne **29**
to do mountain climbing *faire de l'alpinisme **29**
mouth une bouche **E3**
movie un film **22, 29**
movie theater un cinéma **14**
movies le cinéma **21**
at (to) the movies au cinéma **14**
Mr. Monsieur (M.) **3**
Mrs. Madame (Mme) **3**
much, very much beaucoup **15**
how much? combien? **28**
how much does . . . cost? combien coûte...? **11, 25**
how much is it? ça fait combien?, c'est combien? **11**
too much trop **25**
museum un musée **21**
music la musique **23**
must *devoir **35**
I must je dois **13**
my mon, ma; mes **7, 24**
my birthday is (March 2) mon anniversaire est le (2 mars) **8**
my name is . . . je m'appelle... **1**

N

name: his/her name is . . . il/elle s'appelle... **6**
my name is . . . je m'appelle... **1**
what's . . .'s name? comment s'appelle...? **6**
what's his/her name? comment s'appelle-t-il/elle? **17**
what's your name? comment t'appelles-tu? **1**
napkin une serviette **33**
nasty méchant **19**
nationality la nationalité **2**
nearby près **21**
neck le cou **E3**
to need *avoir besoin de **28**
neighbor un voisin, une voisine **17**
neighborhood un quartier **21**
a nice neighborhood un joli quartier **21**
never ne... jamais **32**
new nouveau (nouvel, nouvelle; *m.pl.* nouveaux) **27**
next prochain **29, 31**
next week la semaine prochaine **31**
nice gentil (gentille), sympathique **19**
it's nice (beautiful) weather il fait beau **12**
night: tomorrow night demain soir **4**
last night hier soir **31**
nine neuf **1**
nineteen dix-neuf **2**
ninety quatre-vingt-dix **6**
ninth neuvième **24**
no non **2,14**
no . . . pas de **18, 34**
no? n'est-ce pas? **14**
nobody ne... personne, personne **32**
noon midi **4**

nose le nez **E3**
not ne... pas **14**
not a, not any pas de **18, 34**
not always pas toujours **13**
not anybody ne... personne **32**
not anything ne... rien **32**
not at all pas du tout **23**
it's (that's) not ce n'est pas **20**
of course not! mais non! **14**
notebook un cahier **B**
nothing ne... rien, rien **32**
November novembre *m.* **8**
now maintenant **15, 31**

O

o'clock heure(s)
at . . . o'clock à... heures **4**
it's . . . o'clock il est... heure(s) **4**
object un objet **17**
ocean la mer **29;** l'océan *m.*
to (at) the oceanside à la mer **29**
October octobre *m.* **8**
of de **14**
of (the) du, de la, de l', des **23**
of course not! mais non! **14**
of course! bien sûr **13**
of whom de qui **16**
often souvent **15**
oh: oh, really? ah, bon? **16**
okay d'accord **13**
I'm okay ça va **3**
old vieux (vieil, vieille; *m.pl.* vieux) **27**
he/she is . . . (years old) il/elle a... ans **7**
how old are you? quel âge as-tu? **7**
how old is he/she? quel âge a-t-il/elle? **17**
how old is your father/mother? quel âge a ton père/ta mère? **7**
I'm . . . (years old) j'ai... ans **7**
to be . . . (years old) *avoir... ans **18**
omelet une omelette **9**
on sur **17**
on foot à pied **22**
on Monday lundi **18**
on Mondays le lundi **18**
on vacation en vacances **14**
one un, une **1;** *(we, they, people)* on **28**
oneself: by oneself seul **29**
only seul **29**
open *ouvrir
open . . . ouvre... (ouvrez...) **B**
opinion: in my opinion à mon avis **27**
or ou **2, 14**
orange *(color)* orange *(inv.)* **20**
orange une orange **33**
orange juice le jus d'orange **10, 33**
order: in order to pour **29**
to **organize** organiser **15**
other autre **33**
our notre; nos **24**
out of style démodé **25**
over: over (at) . . .'s house chez... **23**
over there là-bas **14**
that (one), over there ça, là-bas **17**
overcoat un manteau (*pl.* manteaux) **25**
to **own** *avoir **18**

P

P.M. du soir **4**
pain: a pain pénible **20**
pants un pantalon **25**
pantyhose des collants *m.* **25**
paper le papier **B**
sheet of paper une feuille de papier **B**
parents les parents *m.* **24**
park un parc **21**
party *(informal)* une boum **22**
to **pass a test (an exam)** réussir à un examen **27**
past: half past . . . ... heure(s) et demie **4**
quarter past . . . ... heure(s) et quart **4**
to **pay (for)** payer **28**
to pay attention *faire attention **16**
pear une poire **33**
peas les petits pois *m.* **33**
pen un stylo **B, 17**
pencil un crayon **B, 17**
people des gens *m.* **18;** on **28**
perhaps peut-être **14**
person une personne **5, 17**
pet un animal (*pl.* animaux) domestique **7**
to **phone** téléphoner **15**
piano un piano **23**
picnic un pique-nique **22**
to have a picnic *faire un pique-nique **29**
pie une tarte **33**
piece: piece of chalk un morceau de craie **B**
ping-pong le Ping-Pong **23**
pink rose **20**
pizza une pizza **9**
place un endroit **22**
place setting un couvert **33**
to **place** *mettre **26**
placed mis (*p.p. of* *mettre) **31**
plain moche **25**
plane un avion **29**
by plane en avion **29**
plate une assiette **33**
to **play** jouer **15**
to play a game jouer à + *game* **23**
to play a game (match) *faire un match **16**
to play a musical instrument jouer de + *instrument* **23**
to play basketball (soccer, tennis, volleyball) jouer au basket (au foot, au tennis, au volley) **13**
pleasant sympathique **19**
it's pleasant (good) weather il fait bon **12**
please s'il vous plaît *(formal)* **10;** s'il te plaît *(informal)* **9**
please give me . . . s'il te plâit, donne-moi... **10**
polo shirt un polo **25**
pool: swimming pool une piscine **21**
poor pauvre **28**
poorly mal **3**
popular à la mode **25**
poster une affiche **17**
potato une pomme de terre **33**
pound une livre (de) **33**

to prefer préférer **26, 33**
I prefer je préfère + *inf.* **13**
I like . . ., but I prefer . . . j'aime..., mais je préfère... **13**
to prepare préparer **29**
pretty joli **17, 25**
price un prix **25**
what's the price? quel est le prix? **25**
pullover un pull **25**
pupil un (une) éleve **17**
to purchase acheter **29**
to put *mettre **26**
to put on *mettre **26**

Q

quantity une quantité **33**
quarter un quart
quarter of . . . ... heure(s) moins le quart **4**
quarter past . . . ... heure(s) et quart **4**

R

racket une raquette **17**
radio une radio **17**
to listen to the radio écouter la radio **13**
rain: it's raining il pleut **12**
raincoat un imper (imperméable) **25**
rarely rarement **15**
rather assez **19**
really: oh, really? ah, bon? **16**
really?! vraiment?! **23**
record un disque **17**
red rouge **20**
reel-to-reel tape une bande **B**
relatives les parents *m.* **24**
to repair réparer **29**
to respond répondre **36**
restaurant un restaurant **21**
at (to) the restaurant au restaurant **14**
have dinner at a restaurant dîner au restaurant **13**
to return rentrer **32;** *revenir **23**
rice le riz **33**
rich riche **28**
ride: to take a bicycle ride *faire une promenade à velo **22**
right vrai **20;** droite
right? n'est-ce pas? **14**
all right d'accord **13**
to be right *avoir raison **30**
to (on) the right à droite **21**
roast beef le rosbif **33**
room une chambre **17;** une salle **21**
bathroom une salle de bains **21**
dining room une salle à manger **21**
formal living room un salon **21**
to run *(referring to objects)* marcher **17**

S

sailing la voile **29**
salad une salade **9, 33**
salami le saucisson **33**
salt le sel **33**
sandal une sandale **25**
sandwich un sandwich **9**
Saturday samedi *m.* **8, 31**
see you Saturday! à samedi! **8**
last Saturday samedi dernier **31**
next Saturday samedi prochain **31**
saw vu (*p.p. of* *voir) **31**
saxophone un sax (saxophone) **23**
say *dire **36**
say . . . dites... **C**
say! dis (donc)! **20**
how do you say . . . in French? comment dit-on... en français? **B**
school une école **21**
school cafeteria une cantine de l'école **33**
school friend un (une) camarade **17**
sea la mer **29**
to (at) the sea à la mer **29**
season une saison **12**
second deuxième **24**
to see *voir **29**
see you tomorrow! à demain! **8, 29**
seen vu (*p.p. of* *voir) **31**
seldom rarement **15**
to sell vendre **28**
September septembre *m.* **8**
to set the table *mettre la table **33**
seven sept **1**
seventeen dix-sept **2**
seventh septième **24**
seventy soixante-dix **5**
she elle **14, 18, 23**
sheet of paper une feuille de papier **B**
ship un bateau (*pl.* bateaux) **29**
shirt une chemise **25**
shoe une chaussure **5**
tennis shoes des tennis *m.* **25**
shop une boutique **25**
shopping: shopping center un centre commercial **21**
to go food shopping *faire les courses **33**
to go shopping *faire des achats **29**
shore la mer **29**
short court **25;** petit **17, 20, 25**
he/she is short il/elle est petit(e) **17**
shorts un short **25**
should *devoir **35**
to show indiquer **C;** montrer à **35, 36**
to shut fermer **B**
shy timide **19**
silly bête **19**
to sing chanter **13, 15**
sir Monsieur (M.) **3**
sister une soeur **7, 24**
six six **1**
sixteen seize **2**
sixth sixième **24**
sixty soixante **3, 5**
to ski *faire du ski **29**
skiing le ski **29**
skirt une jupe **25**
small petit **17, 20, 25**
sneakers des tennis *m.* **25**
hightop sneakers des baskets *m.* **25**
snow: it's snowing il neige **12**
so alors **19**
so-so comme ci, comme ça **3**
everything's (going) so-so ça va comme ci, comme ça **3**
soccer le foot (football) **23**
sock une chaussette **25**

soda un soda **10**
lemon soda une limonade **10**
sold vendu (*p.p. of* vendre) **31**
sole *(fish)* la sole **33**
some des **18;** du, de la, de l' **34;** quelques **17**
somebody quelqu'un **32**
someone quelqu'un **32**
something quelque chose **32**
son un fils **24**
sorry: to be sorry regretter
I'm sorry, but (I cannot) je regrette, mais (je ne peux pas) **13**
soup la soupe **33**
spaghetti les spaghetti *m.* **33**
Spanish espagnol(e) **19**
to **speak** parler **15**
to speak (French, English, Spanish) parler (français, anglais, espagnol) **13**
to speak to parler à **36**
to **spend** *(money)* dépenser **28;** *(time)* passer **29**
spoon une cuillère **33**
sports le sport **29**
to play a sport *faire du sport **29;** jouer à + *sport* **23**
sports clothing des vêtements *m.* de sport **25**
spring le printemps **12**
in the spring au printemps **12**
stadium un stade **21**
to **stay** rester **22**
steak un steak **9**
steak and French fries un steak-frites **9**
stereo set une chaîne stéréo **17**
stomach le ventre **E3**
store un magasin **21, 25**
department store un grand magasin **25**
straight tout droit **21**
strawberry une fraise **33**
street une rue **21**
student *(high school)* un (une) éleve **17;** *(college)* un étudiant, une étudiante **17**
to **study** étudier **13, 15**
stupid bête **19**
style: in style à la mode **25**
out of style démodé **25**
subway le métro **22**
by subway en métro **22**
to **succeed** réussir **27**
sugar le sucre **33**
summer l'été *m.* **12**
summer vacation les grandes vacances **29**
in the summer en été **12**
sun le soleil **25**
Sunday dimanche *m.* **8**
sunglasses des lunettes *f.* de soleil **25**
supermarket un supermarché **21**
supper le dîner **33**
to have (eat) supper dîner **15, 33**
sure bien sûr **13**
sure! mais oui! **14**
are you sure? tu es sûr(e)? **24**
sweater un pull **25**
sweatshirt un sweat **25**
to **swim** nager **15**
I like to swim j'aime nager **13**
swimming pool une piscine **21**
swimsuit un maillot de bain **25**
Swiss suisse **19**

T

table une table **B, 17**
to set the table *mettre la table **33**
to **take** *prendre **B, 34**
to take along amener **26, 35**
to take a bicycle ride *faire une promenade à velo **22**
to take a drive *faire une promenade en voiture **22**
to take a trip *faire un voyage **16**
to take a walk *faire une promenade à pied **22**
to **talk** parler **15**
to talk to parler à **36**
tall grand **17, 20**
tape: tape recorder un magnétophone **17**
cassette tape une cassette **B, 17**
reel-to-reel tape une bande **B**
taxi un taxi **22**
by taxi en taxi **22**
tea le thé **10**
iced tea un thé glacé **33**
teacher un (une) prof **5, 17;** un professeur **17**
telephone un téléphone **17**
to **telephone** téléphoner **15**
television la télé **B, 17**
to watch television regarder la télé **13**
to **tell** *dire **36**
ten dix **1, 2**
tennis le tennis **23**
tennis racket une raquette de tennis **23**
tennis shoes des tennis *m.* **25**
to play tennis jouer au tennis **13**
tenth dixième **24**
terrific chouette **20, 25;** extra **20;** super **20, 25**
test un examen
to pass a test réussir à un examen **27**
than que **27**
thank you merci **3**
that que **25;** ce, cet, cette **26**
that is . . . c'est... **17, 20**
that (one), over there ça, là-bas **17**
that's . . . c'est... **5, 17, 20;** voilà **5**
that's . . . francs ça fait... francs **11**
that's bad c'est mal **20**
that's a good idea! c'est une bonne idèe! **28**
that's good (fine) c'est bien **20**
that's not . . . ce n'est pas... **20**
what's that? qu'est-ce que c'est? **17**
the le, la, l' **6, 18;** les **18**
theater un théâtre **21**
movie theater un cinéma **21**
their leur, leurs **24**
them eux, elles **23;** les **36**
(to) them leur **36**
then alors **19;** ensuite **30**
there là **14**
there is (are) il y a **17**
there is (here comes someone) voilà **5**

there is (some) il y a + du, de la *(partitive)* **34**
there's some voilà + du, de la *(partitive)* **34**
over there là-bas **14**
that (one), over there ça, là-bas **17;** ce...-là **26**
what is there? qu'est-ce qu'il y a? **17**
these ces **26**
these are ce sont **20**
they ils, elles **14;** eux **23;** on **28**
they are ce sont **20**
thin: to get thin maigrir **27**
thing une chose
things are going (very) badly ça va (très) mal **3**
to **think** penser **25**
to think of penser de, trouver **25**
to think that penser que **25**
what do you think of . . .? comment trouves-tu...?, qu'est-ce que tu penses de...? **25**
third troisième **24**
thirsty: to be thirsty *avoir soif **30**
are you thirsty? tu as soif? **10**
I'm thirsty j'ai soif **10**
thirteen treize **2**
thirty trente **3**
3:30 trois heures et demie **4**
this ce, cet, cette **26**
this is . . . voici... **5**
those ces **26**
those are ce sont **20**
thousand mille **25**
three trois **1**
Thursday jeudi *m.* **8**
tie une cravate **25**
tights des collants *m.* **25**
time: at what time is . . .? à quelle heure est...? **4**
at what time? à quelle heure? **4**
what time is it? quelle heure est-il? **4**
to à **14, 22;** chez **22, 23**
to (the) au, à la, à l', aux **22**
in order to pour **29**
to class en classe **14**
to someone's house chez + *person* **22**
to whom à qui **16**
today aujourd'hui **8, 31**
today is (Wednesday) aujourd'hui, c'est (mercredi) **8**
toilet les toilettes **21**
tomato une tomate
tomato juice le jus de tomate **10**
tomorrow demain **8**
tomorrow afternoon demain après-midi **31**
tomorrow is (Thursday) demain, c'est (jeudi) **8**
tomorrow morning demain matin **31**
tomorrow night (evening) demain soir **31**
see you tomorrow! à demain! **8, 29**
tonight ce soir **31**
too aussi **2, 15;** trop **25**
too bad! dommage! **15**
touring bus un autocar, un car **29**
town un village **21**
in town en ville **14**
track suit un survêtement **25**
train un train **29**
by train en train **22, 29**
to **travel** voyager **13, 15**
trip: to take a trip *faire un voyage **16**
trousers un pantalon **25**
true vrai **20**
T-shirt un tee-shirt **25**
Tuesday mardi *m.* **8**
tuna le thon **33**
to **turn** tourner **21**
to turn on *mettre **26**
TV la télé **B, 17**
to watch TV regarder la télé **13**
twelfth douzième **24**
twelve douze **2**
twenty vingt **2, 3**
two deux **1**

U

ugly moche **25**
uncle un oncle **7, 24**
under sous **17**
to **understand** *comprendre **34**
I (don't) understand je (ne) comprends (pas) **B**
unfashionable démodé **25**
United States les États-Unis *m.*
upstairs en •haut **21**
us nous **23**
(to) us nous **35**
to **use** utiliser **C**

V

vacation les vacances *f.* **29**
on vacation en vacances **14**
summer vacation les grandes vacances **29**
VCR (videocassette recorder) un magnétoscope **B**
veal le veau **33**
vegetable un légume **33**
very très **19**
very well très bien **15**
very much beaucoup **15**
videocassette une vidéocassette **B**
videocassette recorder un magnétoscope **B**
violin un violon **23**
to **visit** *(place)* visiter **15, 28;** *(people)* rendre visite à **28, 36**
volleyball le volley (volleyball) **23**

W

to **wait (for)** attendre **28**
walk une promenade **22**
to take (go for) a walk *faire une promenade à pied **16, 22**
to **walk** *aller à pied **22;** marcher **17**
walkman un walkman **17**
to **want** *avoir envie de **28;** *vouloir **34**
do you want . . .? tu veux...? **9**
do you want to . . .? est-ce que tu veux...? **13**
I don't want . . . je ne veux pas... **13**
I want . . . je veux... **13, 34**
I want to je veux bien **34**

what do you want? qu'est-ce que tu veux? **9;** vous désirez? **10, 25**
wanted voulu (*p.p. of* *vouloir) **34**
warm chaud **12, 31**
to be warm *(people)* *avoir chaud **30**
it's warm *(weather)* il fait chaud **12**
was été (*p.p. of* *être) **31**
to wash laver **29**
to waste perdre **28**
watch une montre **17**
to watch regarder **15**
to watch TV regarder la télé **13**
water l'eau *f.* **33**
mineral water l'eau minérale **33**
to waterski *faire du ski nautique **29**
waterskiing le ski nautique **29**
we nous **14, 23;** on **28**
to wear *mettre **26;** porter **25**
weather: how's (what's) the weather? quel temps fait-il? **12**
it's . . . weather il fait... **12**
Wednesday mercredi *m.* **8**
week une semaine **8, 29**
last week la semaine dernière **31**
next week la semaine prochaine **31**
this week cette semaine **31**
weekend un weekend **29**
last weekend le weekend dernier **31**
next weekend le weekend prochain **29, 31**
this weekend ce weekend **31**
weight: to gain weight grossir **27**
well bien **15**
well! eh bien! **26**
well then alors **19**
everything's going (very) well ça va (très) bien **3**
went allé (*p.p. of* *aller) **32**
what comment? quoi? **17;** qu'est-ce que **16**
what color? de quelle couleur? **20**
what day is it? quel jour est-ce? **8**
what do you think of . . .? comment trouves-tu...?, qu'est-ce que tu penses de...? **25**
what do you want? qu'est-ce que tu veux? **9;** vous désirez? **10, 25**
what does . . . mean? que veut dire...? **B**
what does he/she look like? comment est-il/elle? **17**
what is it? qu'est-ce que c'est? **17**
what is there? qu'est-ce qu'il y a? **17**
what time is it? quelle heure est-il? **4**
what would you like? vous désirez? **10, 25**
what's . . .'s name? comment s'appelle...? **6**
what's he/she like? comment est-il/elle? **17**
what's his/her name? comment s'appelle-t-il/elle? **17**
what's that? qu'est-ce que c'est? **17**
what's the date? quelle est la date? **8**
what's the price? quel est le prix? **25**
what's the weather? quel temps fait-il? **12**
what's your address? quelle est ton adresse? **21**
what's your name? comment t'appelles-tu? **1**
at what time is . . .? à quelle heure est...? **4**
at what time? à quelle heure? **4, 16**
when quand **16**
when is your birthday? c'est quand, ton anniversaire? **8**
where où **14, 16**
where is . . .? où est...? **14**
where is it? où est-ce? **21**
from where? d'où? **23**
whether si **C**
which quel (quelle) **26**
white blanc (blanche) **20**
who qui **16**
who's that/this? qui est-ce? **5, 17**
about whom? de qui? **16**
for whom? pour qui? **16**
of whom? de qui? **16**
to whom? à qui? **16**
with whom? avec qui? **16**
why pourquoi **16**
wife une femme **24**
to win gagner **28**
window une fenêtre **B, 17**
to windsurf *faire la planche à voile **29**
windsurfing la planche à voile **29**
winter l'hiver *m.* **12**
in the winter en hiver **12**
with avec **14**
with me avec moi **13**
with you avec toi **13**
with whom? avec qui? **16**
woman une dame *(polite term)* **5;** une femme **17**
to work travailler **13, 15;** *(referring to objects)* marcher **17**
does the radio work? est-ce que la radio marche? **17**
it (doesn't) work(s) well il/elle (ne) marche (pas) bien **17**
would: I'd like je voudrais **9, 10, 13**
to write *écrire **36**
wrong faux (fausse) **20**
to be wrong *avoir tort **30**

Y

year un an, une année **8**
he/she is . . . (years old) il/elle a... ans **7**
I'm . . . (years old) j'ai... ans **7**
to be . . . (years old) *avoir... ans **18**
yellow jaune **20**
yes oui **2, 14;** *(to a negative question)* si! **18**
yes, of course oui, bien sûr **13**

yes, okay (all right) oui, d'accord **13**
yes, thank you oui, merci **13**
yesterday hier **31**
yesterday afternoon hier après-midi **31**
yesterday morning hier matin **31**
yogurt le yaourt **33**
you tu, vous **14, 23;** on **28**
you are . . . tu es + *nationality* **2**
and you? et toi? **1**
(to) you te, vous **35**
your ton, ta; tes **7;** votre; vos **24**
what's your name? comment t'appelles-tu? **1**
young jeune **17**

Z

zero zéro **1**

INDEX

à 103, 202 + definite article 202 vs. **chez** 205 **à demain** 49 **à samedi** 49
acheter, and verbs like 258–259
activities, talking about daily 88
adjectives agreement and formation 20, 138–139, 162–163, 164 **beau, nouveau, vieux** 269 **bon/meilleur** 252, 270 comparison with 270 demonstrative 260 interrogative 261 invariable 172, 252 of nationality 19, 165 ordinal numbers as 227 position before and after the noun 166, 173 possessive 224, 226
adverbs ending in **-ment** 233 in impersonal expressions 176 of quantity 163 position of 114
age talking about your age and asking others 46, 47
agreement noun-adjective 164 subject-past participle 330 subject-verb 98, 108, 110, 112, 268, 278, 280, 330
aller in **passé composé** 330 present 24, 200 to express near future 206 expressions 200
alphabet 16
approval, expressing 114, 279
articles *see* definite article; indefinite article; partitive article
attention, how to get someone's 174
avoir expressions with 59, 150, 276, 308 **passé composé** formed with 309 past participle 323 present 150 to tell age 47

beau, belle 269
body, identifying head, neck, etc. 74
boire past participle 367 present 367

ça va (bien; comme çi, comme ça; mal) 24
celebrating, how to celebrate a happy occasion 337
ce, cet, cette, ces 260
c'est 37, 49, 50, 67, 140 in impersonal expressions 176 vs. **il est** 41, 175 with stress pronouns 215
chez 205, 215
classroom expressions 293
clothing, talking about 248, 250, 252
combien 67 **combien de** 276, 289
cognates 32, 131, 183, 233, 289
colors, talking about 172
commands *see* imperative
compliments, expressing 184
comparison with adjectives 270
conclusion, how to introduce 165
connaître 382 **tu connais** 41 vs. **savoir** 382
contractions **à** with **le, les** 202 **de** with **le, les** 213, 222
contradict, how to contradict negative statements or questions 155 how to contradict someone 216

danser 90
dates talking about the day and date 50, 51
days of week 49 with definite article 51
de 103 + definite article 213 in expressions of quantity 362 in negative sentences 154 in noun + **de** + noun 217 indicating possession 222
definite article 42, 60, 151, 153 contractions with **à** 202 contractions with **de** 213 in general sense 156 with days of week 51, 157
demonstrative adjectives 260
devoir 94, 376
dire 388
direct object pronouns **le, la, les** 383 **me, te, nous, vous** 372 position in present tense 383 with commands 374, 385
directions asking for information/directions 193

écrire 388
encourage, how to wish someone luck or encourage 327
elision 46, 103, 120
emphasize how to emphasize a question/remark 260
-er verbs imperative 281 past participle 309 present 109, 112
espérer, and verbs like 259
est-ce que in information questions 120 in **passé composé** 314 in "yes-no" questions 100–101
être **être de** 19 in descriptions 175 **passé composé** formed with 330, 332 past participle 323 present 98

faire expressions with 66, 71, 124, 301 past participle 323 present 124
familiar vs. formal 23
family members, talking about 45, 223
food and meals, talking about 59, 63, 348, 350, 354, 360, 361, 362, 367, 368, 379
future expressed with **aller** 206

games, talking about 214
gender 20, 37, 38, 60
geographical names prepositions with 19

holidays (French), talking about 301

il est 41 vs. **c'est** 175
il y a 144, 363
imperative 59, 67 forms and uses 281 position of object pronouns with 374 summary charts R8–R11
indefinite article 37, 38, 151, 153 in negative sentences 154
indirect object pronouns **lui, leur** 386 **me, te, nous, vous** 372 position in present tense 386 with commands 374, 386
infinitive 108 after certain verbs 90, 91, 115 in **aller** + infinitive 206
interrogative constructions **combien, combien de** 252 **est-ce que** 100 in **passé**

composé 314 information questions 120, 252 inversion 125 **quel, quelle** 261 **qu'est-ce que** 100, 123, 140, 252 **qui,** and expressions with 122 "yes-no" questions 100–101, 125 expressions 120
intonation 61, 65, 100–101, 120, 233
invitations accepting, extending, rejecting 94
inversion in the **passé composé** 314, 330 in the present 125
-ir verbs imperative 281 past participle 321 present 268

jouer à 90 **jouer de** 214

leisure time, talking about 296
liaison 27, 39, 42, 46, 51, 98, 103, 108, 110, 150, 151, 153, 154, 173, 200, 202, 213, 217, 222, 224, 226, 258, 260, 261, 269, 270, 372, 383
lire 293
live, describing where you live 190

maps 4, 6, R2
Martinique 19
mettre 240 past participle 323 present 240, 262, 348
Minitel 132
money (French) talking about how much things cost; borrowing money 66, 67, 275, 290 expressions 67
months of the year 50
music, talking about 214

nager 90
names giving your name; asking others 9, 15, 41
nationalities, talking about 19, 165
negation followed by **de** 365 how to answer yes/no questions 101 in the **passé composé** 312, 330 **ne...jamais** 334 **ne...pas** 90, 93, 94, 102, 112 **ne...personne** 335 **ne...rien** 335 position 206, 365 **si** 155
nouns abbreviations 23 gender: masculine/feminine 37, 38, 60, 138, 151 irregular plurals 248 noun + **de** + noun 217 number: singular/plural 152, 248 replaced by subject pronouns 67, 142 shortened forms 91
nouveau, nouvelle 269
numbers cardinal 17, 21, 25, 39, 43, 252 in dates 51 ordinal 50, 227 pronunciation of 43 summary chart R7

on 278
opinions, expressing 176 introducing personal opinions 271
ouvrir 82

parce que 120
partitive article 362–363 in negative phrases 365
parts of the body 75
passé composé 308 **-er** verbs 150 (TE) **-ir** verbs 268 (TE) **-re** verbs 280 (TE) **acheter (préférer)** 258–259 (TE) **aller** 200–201 (TE) **mettre** 262 (TE) **venir** 212 (TE) formed with **avoir** 309 formed with **être** 330, 332 in negative sentences 312 in questions 314 summary charts R8–R11
past events, talking about 309, 321, 323, 328
past participle agreement with subject 330 irregular verbs 323 regular verbs 309, 321
people, talking about and describing 37, 138
plural adjectives 164, 224, 226, 260–261 articles 152–153 nouns 152–153
possession possessive adjectives 46, 224 with **de** 222
possessions, talking about 142, 144
preferences expressing 258, 351 **j'aime, je n'aime pas, je préfère** 90 telling someone to leave you alone 391
pouvoir 94, 376
préférer 258
prendre past participle 361 present 348, 361, 363
prepositions 99 with cities, countries 19 with stress pronouns 215
present tense 108–109 of regular verbs: *see* **-er**, **-ir**, **-re** verbs; summary charts R8 of irregular verbs: *see* individual verb listings; summary charts R9
pronouns direct object 372, 374 indirect object 94 stress 15, 215 subject 67, 98–99, 142, 151, 278
pronunciation 17, 21, 25, 27, 39, 43, 47, 61, 65, 69, 98, 103, 108, 110, 115, 125, 151, 152, 153, 157, 162, 164, 167, 173, 177, 202, 207, 213, 217, 222, 226, 227, 233, 260, 261, 262, 263, 268, 269, 270, 271, 280, 283, 315, 325, 335, 362, 367, 377, 389 summary chart R5

quantity expressions of 354, 355 partitive article to express 362–363
quand 50, 324
Quebec 41
quel, quelle 261 **quel âge...** 47
quelqu'un, quelque chose 335
qu'est-ce que 123
questions information 314 inversion 125 "yes-no" 101, 314
qui 122 **qui est-ce** 37, 138 expressions with 122

regret, expressing 114
-re verbs imperative 281 past participle 321 present 280, 387

salutations, asking how someone is doing 23
salut vs. **bonjour** 23
savoir 140 vs. **connaître** 382
seasons 71
sequence, how to talk about the order in which things take place 311
Senegal 118
sound-spelling correspondence summary chart R5
spelling marks 17
sports, talking about 214
stress pronouns 15, 215
subject pronouns 67, 98–99, 142, 151, 278
surprise, mild doubt, expressing 121, 216, 225

time, how to tell 26–28 at what time? 28

tu vs. **vous** 63, 98

vacation, talking about 300
venir in **passé composé** 332
present 212
verbs regular **-er** singular 108
plural 108 negative 112: *see* **-er**, **-ir**, **-re** verbs; irregular: *see* individual verb listings; summary charts R8–R11
followed by indirect objects 387 followed by infinitive 90–91, 93, 115 stem-changing 212, 258, 276, 298
vieux, vieille 269
voici 37, 363
voilà 37, 363
voir past participle 323 present 320
vouloir 360 **je veux/ne veux pas, je voudrais** 93, 94, 360, 363 **tu veux** 59
vous vs. **tu** 63, 98

weekend, talking about 298
weather expressions, talking about the seasons and weather 71
wishes, expressing 93

Photo Credits

Cover: photo: Owen Franken; realia map: Galeries Lafayette, Paris. Owen Franken, (assignment/stock) except: 2: mr, Carol Palmer-Andrew Brilliant © D.C. Heath; 2: bl, Jack Elness/Miller-Comstock; 3: tl, P.W. Holzgraf/Monkmeyer Press; 3: tr, Kennon Cooke/Valan Photos; 3: ml, VPG/Woods; 3: mr, Susan Doheny; 3: bl, Jack Mitchell/Boston Ballet Co.; 3: br, Andrew Brilliant; 6: b David Ball/The Picture Cube; 7: m, Brian Robb; 7: b, G. Barone/Monkmeyer Press; 12, 13 Adine Sagalyn; 16: t, Yves Levy; 19: Ann Purcell; 20: l, Mark Antman/The Image Works; 23: bl 24 br, Patrick Pipard, Adine Sagalyn; 26: VPG/Woods; 30: br, Carol Palmer-Andrew Brilliant © D.C. Heath; 32: Peter Menzel/Stock Boston; 36: t, VPG/Woods; 37: t, Patrick Pipard; 38: tm, Nancy Sheehan; 38: bm, Patrick Pipard; 41: m, Ken Kaminsky/Nawrocki Stock Photo; 41: b, G. Zimbel/Monkmeyer Press; 45: t, Adine Sagalyn; 47: Patrick Pipard; 52: m, Palmer-Brilliant © D.C. Heath; 53: tl, tm, Patrick Pipard; 53: tr, Palmer-Brilliant © D.C. Heath; 53; bl, Adine Sagalyn; 53: bm, Henebry Photography © D.C. Heath; 54: tl, J. A. Wilkinson/Valan Photos; 54: tm, Kevin Galvin/Stock Boston; 54: tr, H. Mark Weidman; 54: ml, © Horii/-International Stock Photo; 54: mm, Ed Carlin/The Picture Cube; 54: mr, Mike Malyszko/Stock Boston; 54: b, Lynn McLaren/The Picture Cube; 57: t, J. Charlas; 57: b, Sophie Reiter; 58: J. Charlas; 61: Yves Levy; 63: t, 64b, 65 Adine Sagalyn; 66: b, 67 m, b Susan Doheny; 69/71, 72, 73, Adine Sagalyn; 76–77: Sophie Reiter; 77: t, mr, Patrick Pipard; 77: ml, Yves Levy; 78: tl, bl, br Patrick Pipard; 78: mr, Sophie Reiter; 78: tr, ml, ml, Yves Levy; 78: tm, VPG/Woods; 79: Yves Levy; 80: tl, "The Bridge at Mantes," Musée de Louvre; 80: tr, Art Resource; 80: b, Yves Levy; 84–85: Patrick Pipard; 86: Yves Levy; 86–87: Adine Sagalyn; 87: t, Patrick Pipard; 87, 89, 90: Yves Levy; 92: Adine Sagalyn; 83: Yves Levy; 94: Sophie Reiter; 96, 97 t, mr Patrick Pipard; 97: ml, Yves Levy; 101, 104: Patrick Pipard; 110: Yves Levy; 118: t, b, Carl Purcell; 118: m, J. Pavlovsky/Sygma; 119: t, Yves Levy; 119: b, UNESCO/Français-Hamell/Interphot; 130: b, Richard Lucas/The Image Works; 133: #4, Carl Purcell; 134: l, Yves Levy; 135: t, © D.C. Heath; 134–135: Yves Levy; 138: Adine Sagalyn; 139: t, D. Logan/H. Armstrong Roberts; 139: l-r Richard Pasley/Stock Boston, Jocelyn Boutin/The Picture Cube, Ann Purcell, Bob Daemmrich/Stock Boston, Carl Purcell, Fujihara-Ivamur/Monkmeyer Press; 140, 143: Patrick Pipard; 144: Adine Sagalyn; 146: Palmer-Brilliant © D.C. Heath; 147: Adine Sagalyn; 148: l, Mike Mazzaschi/Stock Boston; 148: r, Robert Fried/Stock Boston; 149: t, Dallas & John Heaton/Stock Boston; 149: b, © Tabuteau/The Image Works; 152: Patrick Pipard; 160: Yves Levy; 162: l, Adine Sagalyn; 162: r, Patrick Pipard; 163: l, Yves Levy; 163: r, Sophie Reiter; 167: Patrick Pipard; 169: tl, Sipa Press; 169: tr, Jim Colburn/Photoreporters; 169; bl, Claude Gassian; 169: br, Jim Colburn/Photoreporters; 170: Patrick Pipard; 171: t, Philippe Gontier/The Image Works; 171: b, Palmer-Brilliant © D.C. Heath; 175: Patrick Pipard; 176: Adine Sagalyn; 177: Andrew Brilliant; 181: Sophie Reiter; 182: b, Meauxsoone/Sygma; 186 (l), 187: Adine Sagalyn; 189: top to bottom, Palmer-Brilliant, Mike Mazzaschi/Stock Boston, Owen Franken, Andrew Brilliant, Guy Fleury/Tony Stone Worldwide; 190: t, Adine Sagalyn; 192: Yves Levy; 194: Adine Sagalyn; 196: Philippe Gontier/The Image Works; 198: t, J. Charlas; 199: tl, Raphael Koshas/Tony Stone Worldwide; 199: b, Suzanne & Nick Geary/Tony Stone Worldwide; 204: Patrick Pipard; 212: Yves Levy; 220: Mike Mazzaschi/Stock Boston; 221: t, Robert Fried; 229: l, Yves Levy; 229: tr Eva Demjen/Stock Boston; 230: Thomas Craig/The Picture Cube; 232: Yves Levy; 233: l-r Owen Franken, B. Rheims/Sygma, Luca Biamonte/Sipa Press, M. Rosenstiehl/Sygma; 236: Adine Sagalyn; 237: ml, Palmer-Brilliant © D.C. Heath; 237: br, Adine Sagalyn; 238: top to bottom, Lesley Desmond/Monkmeyer Press, Owen Franken, Superstock, Andrew Brilliant; 239: t, Jean Daniel Sudres © Scope; 239: b, Alain Nogues/Sygma; 242: Adine Sagalyn; 244: Patrick Pipard; 245: b, Patrick Pipard; 246: Charles Bowman © Scope; 247: top to bottom, Owen Franken, Patrick Pipard, Black Olive Studios/Doug Ayers, © Maria Valentino Chandoha/Photoreporters, Patrick Pipard; 248: Patrick Pipard; 250, 255: Adine Sagalyn; 256: t, Patrick Pipard; 257, 261: t, m, Patrick Pipard; 266: t, Adine Sagalyn; 267: b, Patrick Pipard; 266–67: Adine Sagalyn; 268: VPG/Woods; 271: Yves Levy; 272, 274: VPG/Woods; 276: Adine Sagalyn; 279, 284, 285: Yves Levy; 286: Adine Sagalyn; 288: tl, Patrick Pipard; 288: tr, Yves Levy; 290: t, J. Charlas; 292–93: Patrick Pipard; 294–95: Yves Levy; 295: b, Patrick Pipard; 296–97: Adine Sagalyn; 297: tr, Patrick Pipard; 297: bl, br, Yves Levy; 300: Sophie Reiter; 301: t, Carl Purcell; 301: m, © Hoa-Qui/Viesti Associates; 301: b, Daniel Aubry; 302: Patrick Pipard; 315: Adine Sagalyn; 320: t, Alex Bartel/The Picture Cube; 320: ml, Lesley Desmond/Monkmeyer Press; 320: mm, Mario Podesta/Monkmeyer Press; 320: bl, Beryl Goldberg; 320: bm, Owen Franken/Stock Boston; 320: br, Ken Ross/Viesti Associates; 322: Adine Sagalyn; 323, 324, 328: Patrick Pipard; 338: Richmond/The Image Works; 340: tl, Yves Levy; 340: b, Andrew Brilliant © D.C. Heath; 340: tr, Patrick Pipard; 340: mr, Robert Fried; 340–341: Douglas Waugh/Peter Arnold; 342: l, Jacques Guillard © Scope; 342: r, David Endersbee/Tony Stone Worldwide; 343: l, Jacques Guillard © Scope; 343: r, Daniel Aubry; 344–45: Yves Levy; 345: J. Charlas: 346: VPG/Woods; 352: Owen Franken/Stock Boston; 356: t, Patrick Pipard; 359: t, Yves Levy; 368: t, Yves Levy; 368: b, Patrick Pipard; 370: Patrick Pipard; 371: t, Joe Viesti/Viesti Associates; 371: ml, Philippe Gontier/The Image Works; 371: mr, Paul von Basch/The Image Works; 371: b, Four by Five/Superstock; 372: Yves Levy; 380–81: Mark Antman/The Image Works; 384: Henebry Photography © D.C. Heath; 386: VPG/Woods; 392: Hugh Rogers/Monkmeyer Press; 393: Fay Torresyap Stock Boston. Every effort will be made to correct any errors in later editions.